Project Maths

GW00633365

Text & Tests 6

Leaving Certificate Higher Level Maths

Strands 3 & 4 – Number & Algebra

Paul Cooke · O. D. Morris · Frances O'Regan

 The Celtic Press

Acknowledgements
I would like to express my deep gratitude to Aidan Raleigh for his invaluable advice at all stages of the production of this book.

First published in 2012 by
The Celtic Press
Ground Floor – Block B
Liffey Valley Office Campus
Dublin 22

This reprint May 2016

ISBN: 978-1-9077-0523-6

Design: Identikit Design
Layout and artwork: Tech-Set Limited, Gateshead

Contents

1. Algebra 1   **1**
1.1 Polynomial expressions   1
1.2 Polynomial functions, an introduction   8
1.3 Factorising algebraic expressions   11
1.4 Simplifying algebraic fractions   15
1.5 Algebraic identities   19
1.6 Manipulating formulae   24
1.7 Algebraic patterns, an introduction   28
1.8 Solving equations   32
1.9 Solving simultaneous linear equations   34
     Revision exercises   (a) Core   41
         (b) Advanced   42
         (c) Extended-Response   43

2. Algebra 2   **46**
2.1 Quadratic equations   46
2.2 Nature of quadratic roots   51
2.3 Solving quadratic and linear equations   56
2.4 Quadratic and linear equations in context   58
2.5 Forming quadratic equations from their roots   61
2.6 Max and min of quadratic graphs   63
2.7 Surds   68
2.8 Algebraic surd equations   71
2.9 The Factor Theorem   74
2.10 Graphs of cubic polynomials   78
     Revision exercises   (a) Core   86
         (b) Advanced   86
         (c) Extended-Response   88

3. Complex Numbers   **93**
3.1 Irrational numbers   93
3.2 Complex numbers   98
3.3 Division of complex numbers   101
3.4 Argand diagram – Modulus   105
3.5 Transformations of complex numbers   108
3.6 Conjugate Roots Theorem   114
3.7 Polar form of a complex number   117
3.8 Products and quotients of complex numbers in polar form   121
3.9 De Moivre's Theorem   123
3.10 Applications of de Moivre's Theorem   126
     Revision exercises   (a) Core   130
         (b) Advanced   131
         (c) Extended-Response   132

4. Sequences – Series – Patterns   **135**

     4.1   Sequences   135
     4.2   Arithmetic sequences   139
     4.3   Arithmetic series   144
     4.4   Geometric sequences   150
     4.5   Geometric series   156
     4.6   Number patterns revisited   161
     Revision exercises   (a) Core   165
                       (b) Advanced   166
                       (c) Extended-Response   168

5. Financial Maths   **170**

     5.1   Compound interest   170
     5.2   Depreciation   175
     5.3   Instalment savings (annuities)   179
     5.4   Loans – Mortgages   185
     Revision exercises   (a) Core   187
                       (b) Advanced   188
                       (c) Extended-Response   190

6. Length – Area – Volume   **192**

     6.1   Revision   192
     6.2   Sectors of circles   197
     6.3   3-Dimensional objects   202
     6.4   Trapezoidal rule for calculating area   209
     Revision exercises   (a) Core   214
                       (b) Advanced   216
                       (c) Extended-Response   219

7. Algebra 3   **222**

     7.1   Revision   222
     7.2   Quadratic and rational inequalities   226
     7.3   Modulus   231
     7.4   Mathematical proof   235
     7.5   Proofs of abstract inequalities   237
     7.6   Indices   240
     7.7   Exponential equations   244
     7.8   Exponential functions   246
     7.9   Logarithmic functions   251
     7.10   The graph of $y = \log_a(x)$ 257
     7.11   Problem-solving with exponential and
            logarithmic functions   259
     7.12   Proofs by induction   264
     Revision exercises   (a) Core   272
                       (b) Advanced   273
                       (c) Extended-Response   275

Answers   **278**

Preface

This book was compiled and written for **Project Maths – Strands 3 and 4** of the Leaving Certificate, Higher Level Course for examination in 2013 and onwards. The book reflects the overall approach to the teaching of maths as stated in the learning outcomes for *Project Maths*. It encourages the development of not only the students' mathematical knowledge and skills but also the understanding necessary to apply these skills.

There is an excellent range of imaginatively written and probing questions on each topic which will help students to understand what they are doing and to develop their problem-solving skills. A sufficient number of questions in varying degrees of difficulty have been provided to satisfy the needs of the vast majority of students at this level.

The motivating and stimulating full-colour design together with the large number of well constructed diagrams should help the student's understanding of the topic being studied. At the beginning of each chapter there is a list of *Key Words* that students are expected to know and understand when the chapter is completed. Each chapter concludes with a three-part revision exercise section consisting of (a) Core (b) Advanced and (c) Extended-response questions. These questions are graded in order of difficulty and thus enable the student to revise the basics of any topic before moving on to the more challenging exercises.

Paul Cooke
O.D. Morris
Frances O'Regan
July 2012

Algebra 1

Key words

polynomial   expression   equation   variable   linear   quadratic   cubic

expanding   degree   factors   identity   in terms of   simultaneous

Section 1.1 Polynomial expressions

Polynomial expressions are formed from the addition *ie many numbers*
of **many** algebraic terms with **positive integer powers.**

> A **monomial** expression contains one term.
>
> A **binomial** expression contains two terms.
>
> A **trinomial** expression contains three terms.

$5x^3 - 3x^2 + 4x - 6$ is a polynomial expression.

This expression consists of four **terms**;
$5x^3, -3x^2, 4x$ and -6.

The **degree** of a polynomial is given by the highest
power of x.

(a) $4x - 6$ is a **linear** polynomial since the highest power (degree) of x is 1.
(b) $-3x^2 + 4x - 6$ is a **quadratic** polynomial of degree 2.
(c) $5x^3 - 3x^2 + 4x - 6$ is a **cubic** polynomial of degree 3.

Each polynomial is written in order of   (i) decreasing powers of x, e.g. $5x^3 - 3x^2 + 4x - 6$,
  or (ii) increasing powers of x, e.g. $9 + 3x - 4x^2$.

The **coefficient** of x^3 is the number before x^3 in the expression.

In $4x^3 - 2x^2 + 5x - 6$, the coefficient of x^3 is 4, the coefficient of x^2 is -2, the coefficient of x
is 5, and -6 is the **constant term**.

1. Addition and subtraction of polynomial expressions

Each term in a polynomial represents a different quantity, e.g. $8, 6x, 4x^2$.

When simplifying an expression, all like terms should be combined into a single term.

Example 1

Expand and simplify each of the following expressions.

(i) $7(x^3 + 2x^2 - 5x) - 2(2 + 3x + 4x^2 - 2x^3)$
(ii) $3x^2(4x^2 - 5x + 6) + 4x(8x^3 - 2x - 3)$

(i) $7(x^3 + 2x^2 - 5x) - 2(2 + 3x + 4x^2 - 2x^3) = 7x^3 + 14x^2 - 35x - 4 - 6x - 8x^2 + 4x^3$
$$= 11x^3 + 6x^2 - 41x - 4$$

(ii) $3x^2(4x^2 - 5x + 6) + 4x(8x^3 - 2x - 3) = 12x^4 - 15x^3 + 18x^2 + 32x^4 - 8x^2 - 12x$
$$= 44x^4 - 15x^3 + 10x^2 - 12x$$

2. Multiplying polynomial expressions

To multiply algebraic expressions, we use the distributive law, i.e. $a(b + c) = ab + ac$.

Example 2

Simplify the following: $(x - 5)(2x^2 - 3x + 6)$

$$(x - 5)(2x^2 - 3x + 6) = x(2x^2 - 3x + 6) - 5(2x^2 - 3x + 6)$$
$$= 2x^3 - 3x^2 + 6x - 10x^2 + 15x - 30$$
$$= 2x^3 - 13x^2 + 21x - 30$$

Note: Multiplying polynomial expressions is often called **expanding**.

$$x^2 + 2ac + a^2$$

3. Perfect squares

Any polynomial of the form $(x + a)^2$ is called a perfect square.

$$(x + a)^2 = (x + a)(x + a)$$
$$= (x)(x + a) + (a)(x + a)$$
$$= x^2 + ax + ax + a^2$$
$$= x^2 + 2ax + a^2$$

$$(x + a)^2 = x^2 + 2ax + a^2$$
$$(x - a)^2 = x^2 - 2ax + a^2$$

Similarly, $(x - a)^2 = x^2 - 2ax + a^2$.

For example, $(2x - 3)^2 = (2x)^2 - 2(2x)(3) + (3)^2 = 4x^2 - 12x + 9$

Example 3

Given that $25x^2 + px + 16$ is a perfect square and $p > 0$, find the value of p.

Since $25x^2 = (5x)^2$ and $16 = (4)^2$, $\quad \therefore \quad 25x^2 + px + 16 = (5x + 4)^2$

$\qquad \therefore \quad 2(5x)(4) = px$

$\qquad \therefore \quad 40x = px \quad \Rightarrow p = 40.$

(**Note:** $16 = (-4)^2 \quad \therefore \quad 2(5x)(-4) = px \quad \Rightarrow p = -40$, which is not valid
because $p > 0$)

4. Expanding $(x - a)(x + a)$

The expansion of $(x - a)(x + a) = x^2 + ax - ax - a^2$
$$= x^2 - a^2$$

$$\boxed{(x - a)(x + a) = x^2 - a^2}$$

Similarly, $(a - 5b)(a + 5b) = a^2 - 5ab + 5ab - (5b)^2 = \mathbf{a^2 - (5b)^2}$
$$= a^2 - 25b^2$$

This expansion results in a binomial expression called the **difference of two squares.**

This result is important when we need to factorise an expression of the form $a^2 - b^2$ as we will see later on in the chapter.

5. Dividing algebraic expressions

Algebraic quotients take many different forms. Some may be simplified as in the following cases.

Case 1. The denominator is a factor of each term of the numerator.

(i) $\dfrac{6x^3 - 8x^2y + 4xy^2 + 2x^2}{2x} = \dfrac{6x^3}{2x} - \dfrac{8x^2y}{2x} + \dfrac{4xy^2}{2x} + \dfrac{2x^2}{2x} = 3x^2 - 4xy + 2y^2 + x$

Case 2. The denominator is one of the factors of the numerator.

(ii) $\dfrac{6x^2 + 5xy + y^2}{(2x + y)} = \dfrac{(3x + y)(2x + y)}{(2x + y)} = 3x + y$

Case 3. The denominator divides into the numerator using long division.

(iii) $\dfrac{2x^3 - 9x^2 + 10x - 3}{(x - 3)} = 2x^2 - 3x + 1$ using long division.

Long Division

$$
\begin{array}{r}
2x^2 - 3x + 1 \\
x - 3 \overline{)\,2x^3 - 9x^2 + 10x - 3} \\
\underline{2x^3 - 6x^2} \quad \text{(subtract)} \\
-3x^2 + 10x - 3 \\
\underline{-3x^2 + 9x} \quad \text{(subtract)} \\
x - 3 \\
\underline{x - 3} \quad \text{(subtract)}
\end{array}
$$

... divide $2x^3$ by x to get $2x^2$
... multiply $2x^2$ by denominator
... divide $-3x^2$ by x to get $-3x$
... multiply $-3x$ by denominator
... divide x by x to get 1

Hence, $\dfrac{2x^3 - 9x^2 + 10x - 3}{(x - 3)} = 2x^2 - 3x + 1.$

Example 4

Divide $(2x^3 - 11x + 6)$ by $(2x^2 + 4x - 3)$.

Since this cubic polynomial has no power of x^2, it is good practice to rewrite the polynomial leaving space for the x^2 coefficients as follows;

$$
\begin{array}{r}
x - 2 \\
2x^2 + 4x - 3 \overline{)2x^3 \qquad - 11x + 6} \\
\underline{2x^3 + 4x^2 - 3x} \\
-4x^2 - 8x + 6 \\
\underline{-4x^2 - 8x + 6}
\end{array}
$$

... divide $2x^2$ into $2x^3$ to get x

... multiply x by $2x^2 + 4x - 3$ and then subtract

... divide $2x^2$ into $-4x^2$ to get -2

... multiply -2 by $2x^2 + 4x - 3$ and then subtract

$\therefore \quad (2x^3 - 11x + 6) \div (2x^2 + 4x - 3) = x - 2$

Note also that when we divide $2x^3 - 11x + 6$ by $x - 2$ we get $2x^2 + 4x - 3$.

The factors of the polynomial $2x^3 - 11x + 6$
are $(x - 2)$ and $(2x^2 + 4x - 3)$,

i.e. $2x^3 - 11x + 6 = (x - 2)(2x^2 + 4x - 3)$.

We will use this property more fully in the chapter on factorisation.

$$
\begin{array}{r}
2x^2 + 4x - 3 \\
x - 2 \overline{)2x^3 \qquad - 11x + 6} \\
\underline{2x^3 - 4x^2} \\
4x^2 - 11x + 6 \\
\underline{4x^2 - 8x} \\
-3x + 6 \\
-3x + 6
\end{array}
$$

Exercise 1.1

1. Given the polynomial $4x^3 + 3x^2 - 9x + 5$, write down
   (i) the coefficient of x^2
   (ii) the coefficient of x
   (iii) the term independent of x (the constant term).

2. State the degree of each of the following polynomial expressions.
   (i) $-3x^2 + 5x - 1$ (ii) $4x^3 - 4x^2 + 9x + 3$ (iii) $7 + 3x - 3x^3 - 6x^4$

3. Give two reasons why $3x^2 - \dfrac{4}{x} + x^{\frac{3}{2}}$ is not a polynomial.

4. Simplify each of the following.
   (i) $3x^2 - 6x + 7 + 5x^2 + 2x - 9$ (ii) $x^3 - 4x^2 - 5x + 3x^3 + 6x^2 - x$
   (iii) $x(x + 4) + 3x(2x - 3)$ (iv) $3(x^2 - 7) + 2x(3x - 1) - 7x + 2$

5. Simplify each of the following.
   (i) $3x^2(4x + 2) + 5x^2(2x - 5)$ (ii) $x^3(x - 2) + 4x^3(2x - 6)$
   (iii) $x(x^3 + 4x^2 - 7x) + 3x^2(2x^2 - 3x + 4)$ (iv) $3x(x^2 - 7x + 1) + 2x^2(6x - 5)$

6. Expand each of the following.

(i) $(x + 4)(2x + 5)$ (ii) $(2x + 3)(x - 2)$ (iii) $(3x - 2)(x + 3)$

(iv) $(3x - 2)(4x - 1)$ (v) $(3x - 1)(2x + 5)$ (vi) $(4x + 1)(2x - 6)$

(vii) $(x - 2)(x + 2)$ (viii) $(2x + 5)(2x - 5)$ (ix) $(ax - by)(ax + by)$

7. Expand each of the following perfect squares.

(i) $(x + 2)^2$ (ii) $(x - 3)^2$ (iii) $(x + 5)^2$

(iv) $(a + b)^2$ (v) $(x - y)^2$ (vi) $(a + 2b)^2$

(vii) $(3x - y)^2$ (viii) $(x - 5y)^2$ (ix) $(2x + 3y)^2$

8. Express each of the following in the form $ax^2 + bx + c$.

(i) $(x + \frac{1}{2})^2$ (ii) $8(x - \frac{1}{4})^2$ (iii) $-(1 - x)^2$

9. Which of the following are perfect squares? Explain your answers.

(i) $x^2 + 5x + 25$ (ii) $9x^2 - 6x - 1$ (iii) $4 + 12x + 9x^2$

10. If $px^2 + 4x + 1$ is a perfect square for all values of x, find the value of p.

11. If $25x^2 + tx + 4$ is a perfect square for all values of x, find the value of t.

12. If $9x^2 + 24x + s$ is a perfect square for all values of x, find the value of s.

13. Expand and simplify each of the following.

(i) $(x + 2)(x^2 + 2x + 6)$ (ii) $(x - 4)(2x^2 + 3x - 1)$

(iii) $(2x + 3)(x^2 - 3x + 2)$ (iv) $(3x - 2)(2x^2 - 4x + 2)$

14. Show that $(x + y)(x^2 - xy + y^2) = x^3 + y^3$.

15. Verify that $(x - y)(x^2 + xy + y^2) = x^3 - y^3$.

16. Find the coefficient of x in the expansion of $(2x - 3)(3x^2 - 2x + 4)$.

17. Expand fully and simplify $(x + 3)(x - 4)(2x + 1)$.

18. Expand fully and simplify $(x^2 - 3x - 2)(2x^2 - 4x + 1)$.

19. Find the coefficient of x^2 in the expansion of $(3x^2 + 5x - 1)(2x^2 - 6x - 5)$.

20. Simplify each of the following quotients:

(i) $\dfrac{3x + 6}{3}$ (ii) $\dfrac{x^2 + 2x}{x}$ (iii) $\dfrac{3x^3 - 6x^2}{3x}$ (iv) $\dfrac{15x^2y - 10xy^2}{5xy}$

21. Simplify each of the following quotients:

(i) $\dfrac{6x^2y + 9xy^2 - 3xy}{3xy}$ (ii) $\dfrac{6x^4 - 9x^3 + 12x^2}{3x^2}$

22. Simplify each of the following:

(i) $\dfrac{12a^2b}{3ab}$ (ii) $\dfrac{12a^2bc}{3ac}$ (iii) $\dfrac{4xy^2z}{2xy}$ (iv) $\dfrac{3xy}{2} \times \dfrac{4}{6x^2}$

23. Simplify each of the following:

(i) $\dfrac{2x^2 + 5x - 3}{2x - 1}$ (ii) $\dfrac{2x^2 - 2x - 12}{x - 3}$ (iii) $\dfrac{8x^2 + 8x - 6}{4x - 2}$

24. Divide each of the following:

(i) $x^3 - 8x^2 + 19x - 12 \div (x - 1)$ (ii) $2x^3 - x^2 - 2x + 1 \div (2x - 1)$

(iii) $3x^3 - 4x^2 - 3x + 4 \div (3x - 4)$ (iv) $4x^3 - 7x^2 - 21x + 18 \div (x - 3)$

(v) $x^3 - 22x + 15 \div (x + 5)$ (vi) $2x^3 - x^2 - 12 \div (x - 2)$

25. Perform the following operations:

(i) $x^3 - 2x^2 + 2x - 4 \div (x^2 + 2)$ (ii) $x^3 - 9x^2 + 27x - 27 \div (x^2 - 6x + 9)$

(iii) $3x^3 + 2x^2 - 7x + 2 \div (x^2 + x - 2)$ (iv) $5x^3 + 14x^2 + 7x - 2 \div (5x^2 + 4x - 1)$

26. Divide each of these:

(i) $x^3 - 8 \div (x - 2)$ (ii) $8x^3 - 27y^3 \div (2x - 3y)$

Section 1.2 Polynomial functions, an introduction

Polynomial functions arise as we try to solve day-to-day problems.

Let x cm be the length of a rectangle.

If the width of the rectangle is 5 cm shorter than the length, then $(x - 5)$ cm is the width.

$(x - 5)$ cm   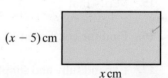

x cm

The area, A, of the rectangle depends on the length and width and by extension depends on x.

The symbol for the area depending on x is written as $A(x)$. _is not multiplied._ _$A(x)$ in this case does not mean A multiplied by x but A depends on x_

Therefore, $A(x) = x(x - 5) = x^2 - 5x$. As x varies, the area A varies. x is called the **independent variable** and $A(x)$ the **dependent variable**. _does the controlling usually plotted on x axis_

$A(x)$ is the quadratic polynomial $x^2 - 5x$ of degree 2.

We note that if $x = 10$ cm, then $A(10) = (10)^2 - 5(10) = 50$ cm^2.

We also note that the width is $(x - 5) \Rightarrow x - 5 > 0$
$$\Rightarrow x > 5 \text{ cm}$$

Like $f(x)$.

Example 1

The length of a rectangle is $(2x + 3)$ cm. If the area of the rectangle is given by the polynomial function $A(x) = 2x^2 + 7x + 6$, find

(a) an expression for the width of the rectangle
(b) an expression for the perimeter, $P(x)$, of the rectangle
(c) the minimum value of x.

Let w be the width of the rectangle.

(a) Area $A(x) = 2x^2 + 7x + 6 = w(2x + 3)$

$$\therefore \quad w = \frac{2x^2 + 7x + 6}{(2x + 3)} = \frac{(2x + 3)(x + 2)}{(2x + 3)} = (x + 2).$$

(b) The perimeter $P(x) = 2(2x + 3) + 2(x + 2) = 4x + 6 + 2x + 4 = 6x + 10.$

(c) Since $(2x + 3)$ is the length of the rectangle,
$$\Rightarrow (2x + 3) > 0$$
$$\Rightarrow x > -1.5$$

Note 1: $A(x)$ must be understood as a single concept and does not imply that A is multiplied by x.
It simply tells us that the quantity A depends on a variable x.

Note 2: Polynomial functions can be added and subtracted as before by collecting like terms and simplifying.

Example 2

Given $f(x) = 3x^3 - 4x^2 - 3x + 4$ and $g(x) = 5x^3 + 14x^2 + 7x - 2$, find

(a) $2f(x) - g(x)$ and state its degree
(b) $f(x) + 2g(x)$ and state its degree.

(a) $2f(x) - g(x) = 2(3x^3 - 4x^2 - 3x + 4) - (5x^3 + 14x^2 + 7x - 2)$
$= 6x^3 - 8x^2 - 6x + 8 - 5x^3 - 14x^2 - 7x + 2$
$= x^3 - 22x^2 - 13x + 10$ which is of degree 3.

(b) $f(x) + 2g(x) = (3x^3 - 4x^2 - 3x + 4) + 2(5x^3 + 14x^2 + 7x - 2)$
$= 3x^3 - 4x^2 - 3x + 4 + 10x^3 + 28x^2 + 14x - 4$
$= 13x^3 + 24x^2 + 11x$ which is of degree 3.

Evaluating polynomial functions

The value of a polynomial function is obtained by substituting a given value for the independent variable and simplifying.

If $p(x) = 2x^2 - 5x + 6$, then $p(1) = 2(1)^2 - 5(1) + 6 = 3$
and $p(-3) = 2(-3)^2 - 5(-3) + 6 = 39.$

A new variable can also be introduced in a similar way.

Given that $p(x) = 2x^2 - 5x + 6$,
$$p(t) = 2t^2 - 5t + 6.$$

Also $\quad p(t^2) = 2(t^2)^2 - 5(t^2) + 6 = 2t^4 - 5t^2 + 6$

Example 3

A paint manufacturer knows that the daily cost (€C) of producing x litres of paint is given by the formula $C(x) = 0.001x^2 + 0.1x + 5$.

(a) State the degree of $C(x)$.
(b) Find the daily cost of producing   (i) $100\,\ell$ of paint   (ii) $400\,\ell$ of paint.

(a) The degree of $C(x)$ is 2.
(b) (i) $C(100) = 0.001(100)^2 + 0.1(100) + 5 = €25$
    (ii) $C(400) = 0.001(400)^2 + 0.1(400) + 5 = €205$.

Example 4

An open box has dimensions $x + 3, x + 1$ and x, where x is the height (in cms) of the box. Find an expression for the external surface area of the box, $S(x)$, and hence find $S(5)$.

Area of the sides $= 2(x)(x + 3) + 2(x)(x + 1)$
$$= 2x^2 + 6x + 2x^2 + 2x = 4x^2 + 8x$$

Area of the base $= (x + 3)(x + 1) = x^2 + 4x + 3$

Total surface area $S(x) = x^2 + 4x + 3 + 4x^2 + 8x$
$$= (5x^2 + 12x + 3)\,\text{cm}^2$$

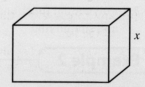

$S(5) = 5(5)^2 + 12(5) + 3 = 188\,\text{cm}^2$

Example 5

Given the function $f(x) = 2x - 4$ for all $x \in R$, find
(a) $f(3), f(-2), f(t)$
(b) for what values of t is $f(t) = t$.

(a) $f(x) = 2x - 4 \Rightarrow f(3) = 2(3) - 4 = 2$
$$f(-2) = 2(-2) - 4 = -8$$
$$f(t) = 2(t) - 4 = 2t - 4$$

(b) $f(t) = t \Rightarrow 2t - 4 = t$
$$t - 4 = 0$$
$$t = 4$$

Note: Polynomial functions with more than one independent variable occur regularly.

The volume of a cylinder $V = \pi.r^2.h$, where r is the radius of the base and h the height of the cylinder.

In function terms: $V(r, h) = \pi.r^2.h$,
that is, the volume of the cylinder depends on both the radius, r, and the height, h.

The volume V depends on two independent variables, r, h.
The degree of this polynomial is 2, the highest power (index) of either variable.

Exercise 1.2

1. A rectangle has one side 4 cm longer than the other.
   Let x be the length of the smaller side.

   Find   (i) an expression for $A(x)$, the area of the rectangle
           (ii) an expression for $P(x)$, the perimeter of the rectangle.

2. The area of a rectangle, $A(x)$, is $6x^2 + 4x - 2$.
   If the length is given by $(3x - 1)$, find

   (i) an expression for the width of the rectangle
   (ii) an expression for the perimeter, $P(x)$, of the rectangle.

3. The dimensions (in cm) of an open rectangular box are given in the diagram. Find

   (a) an expression for the volume, $V(x)$,
   of the box
   (b) an expression for the external surface area, $S(x)$, of the box
   (c) the value of
       (i) $V(x)$ and   (ii) $S(x)$ when $x = 5$.

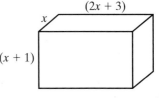

4. If $f(x) = 2x^3 - x^2 - 5x - 4$, find

   (a) $f(0)$ (b) $f(1)$ (c) $f(-2)$ (d) $f(3a)$

5. If $f(x) = x^2 - 3x + 6$, find

   (a) $f(0)$ (b) $f(-5)$ (c) $f\left(-\frac{1}{2}\right)$ (d) $f\left(\frac{a}{4}\right)$

6. A rectangle has length $(x - y)$ and width $(2x + 3y)$.
   Find, in terms of x and y, an expression for the

   (a) area   (b) perimeter   of the rectangle.

7. The width of an open rectangular box is 5 cm shorter than its length and the height of the box is twice the length.
   By letting the length of the box be x cm, find
   (a) an expression for the volume, $V(x)$, of the box
   (b) an expression for the total surface area, $S(x)$ (internal and external), of the box.

8. The number of diagonals, d, in an n-sided polygon is given by the polynomial

$$d(n) = \frac{n^2}{2} - \frac{3n}{2}.$$

Explain what is meant by (i) $d(4)$ (ii) $d(5)$ and find values for $d(4), d(5), d(6)$.

Copy each polygon below and verify your answer in each case.

Explain why $d(3) = 0$.

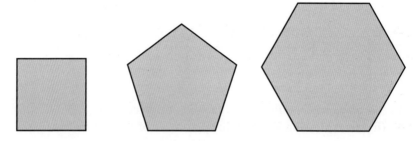

9. If $f(x) = x + 5$, find, in terms of a, $f(a^2) - 3f(a) + 2$.

10. Given $f(x) = x^2 - 3x + 6$, find

(i) $f(-2t)$ (ii) $f(t^2)$ (iii) $f(t - 2)$

State the degree of each of the polynomial functions in t.

11. The volume of a cone, $V(r, h)$, is given by the formula $V(r, h) = \frac{1}{3}\pi r^2 h$, where r is the radius and h is the perpendicular height of the cone. Find

(i) the volume, in terms of π, of a cone with height 21 cm and radius 14 cm

(ii) the volume of a cone, in terms of r and π, if the cone has the same height as the radius r

(iii) the volume of a cone, in terms of h and π, if the radius of the base is twice the height h.

12. If $f(x) = 3x + 6$, find $f(10)$.

If $f(x) = 2x + 8$, find $f(10)$.

By studying the pattern of the results above, if $g(10) = 47$, write $g(x)$ in the form $ax + b$.

13. Use the formula $T = 2\pi\sqrt{\dfrac{l}{g}}$ to find the value of l, in terms of π, if $T = 4\,$s and $g = 10\,\mathrm{m\,s^{-1}}$.

14. Use the formula $V = \frac{4}{3}\pi r^3$ to find the value of r if $V = \frac{792}{7}\,\mathrm{m^3}$ and $\pi = \frac{22}{7}$.

15. In the morning, every student in a classroom shakes hands with every other student as a greeting. The number of handshakes, H, between x students is given by the expression $H(x) = \frac{x}{2}(x - 1)$.

Using this formula, find

  (i) the number of handshakes between 5 students

 (ii) the number of handshakes between 6 students

(iii) the number of handshakes between 10 students.

Using a pattern created by the above, or otherwise, find, if on a particular morning 136 handshakes were given, the number of students in the room.

Section 1.3 Factorising algebraic expressions

An algebraic **factor** divides evenly into a polynomial leaving no remainder.

$(x - 3)$ is a factor of $2x^3 - 9x^2 + 10x - 3$
because $(2x^3 - 9x^2 + 10x - 3) \div (x - 3) = (2x^2 - 3x + 1)$.

$(x - 4)$ and $(x + 3)$ are both factors of $x^2 - x - 12$ because

(i) $(x^2 - x - 12) \div (x - 4) = (x + 3)$ and also   (ii) $(x^2 - x - 12) \div (x + 3) = (x - 4)$.

To solve algebraic equations, we first need to be able to factorise different algebraic expressions.

Several different techniques can be used for factorising expressions and these are shown below.

1. Finding the highest common factor by inspection

  (i) $3x^2 - 9xy = 3x(x - 3y) \Rightarrow$ the factors are $3x$ and $(x - 3y)$

 (ii) $2a^2b - 4ab^2 + 12\,abc = 2ab(a - 2b + 6c) \Rightarrow$ the factors are $2ab$ and $(a - 2ab + 6c)$.

2. Grouping terms

$$6x^2y + 3xy^2 - 12x - 6y = 3xy(2x + y) - 6(2x + y)$$
$$= (2x + y)(3xy - 6)$$
$$\Rightarrow \text{the factors are } (2x + y) \text{ and } (3xy - 6)$$

3. Difference of two squares

Since $(x + y)(x - y) = x^2 - y^2$, the factors of $x^2 - y^2$ are $(x + y)$ and $(x - y)$.

Note: When simplifying quotients, it is important to be able to factorise fully expressions containing the difference of two squares.

   (i) $c^2 - d^2$ $= (c - d)(c + d)$

  (ii) $x^2 - 9y^2 = x^2 - (3y)^2$ $= (x - 3y)(x + 3y)$

 (iii) $x^2 - 8y^2 = x^2 - (\sqrt{8}y)^2$ $= (x - \sqrt{8}y)(x + \sqrt{8}y)$

 (iv) $x - 9 = (\sqrt{x})^2 - 3^2$ $= (\sqrt{x} - 3)(\sqrt{x} + 3)$

Example 1

Factorise fully (i) $x^4 - y^4$ (ii) $12x^2 - 75y^2$

(i) $x^4 - y^4 = (x^2)^2 - (y^2)^2$ ... write as the difference of two squares
$\qquad\qquad = (x^2 - y^2)(x^2 + y^2)$ ... another difference of two squares occurs
$\qquad\qquad = (x - y)(x + y)(x^2 + y^2)$

(ii) $12x^2 - 75y^2 = 3(4x^2 - 25y^2)$ ... find the highest common factor by inspection
$\qquad\qquad\quad = 3[(2x)^2 - (5y)^2]$ ... write as the difference of two squares
$\qquad\qquad\quad = 3(2x - 5y)(2x + 5y)$

Example 2

Simplify $\dfrac{x^2 - 9y^2}{3x + 9y}$

$$\frac{x^2 - 9y^2}{3x + 9y} = \frac{(x - 3y)(x + 3y)}{3(x + 3y)} = \frac{x - 3y}{3}$$

4. Factorising quadratic expressions

We can factorise quadratic expressions of the form $ax^2 + bx + c$ using either

   (i) trial and error   **or**

  (ii) when the coefficients are large or irrational, the quadratic formula.

(i) $x^2 + 3x - 18 = (x \pm ?)(x \pm ?)$ ... checking all the factor pairs of -18
$\qquad\qquad\quad = (x + 6)(x - 3)$ ... $(\pm 1, \pm 18), (\pm 2, \pm 9), (\pm 3, \pm 6)$ ... $(+6, -3)$ is the factor pair
$\qquad\qquad\qquad\qquad\qquad\qquad\qquad$ which, when added, produces $+3$ for the middle term.

(ii) $3x^2 - 17x + 20 = ax^2 + bx + c \rightarrow a = 3, b = -17, c = 20.$

Using $x = \dfrac{-b \pm \sqrt{b^2 - 4ac}}{2a}$,

$\boxed{\text{If } ax^2 + bx + c = 0,}$
$\boxed{\text{then } x = \dfrac{-b \pm \sqrt{b^2 - 4ac}}{2a}}$

$x = \dfrac{17 \pm \sqrt{(-17)^2 - 4.3.20}}{2.3} = \dfrac{17 \pm \sqrt{289 - 240}}{6}$

$\Rightarrow x = \dfrac{17 \pm 7}{6} = \left(\dfrac{24}{6} \text{ or } \dfrac{10}{6}\right) = \left(4 \text{ or } \dfrac{5}{3}\right)$

If $x = 4$, then $(x - 4)$ is the factor.

And if $x = \dfrac{5}{3} \Rightarrow 3x = 5$, therefore the second factor is $(3x - 5)$.

$\therefore$ $3x^2 - 17x + 20 = (3x - 5)(x - 4).$

Example 3

Factorise   (i) $3x^2 + 10x + 8$ (ii) $x^2 - 2\sqrt{2}x - 6$

(i) $3x^2 + 10x + 8 = (3x \pm \;?)(x \pm \;?)$ … the factor pairs of 8 are $(\pm 1, \pm 8), (\pm 2, \pm 4)$

$ = (3x + 4)(x + 2)$ … producing a middle term of $+10x$

(ii) $x^2 - 2\sqrt{2}x - 6 = ax^2 + bx + c \rightarrow a = 1, b = -2\sqrt{2}, c = -6$

$$x = \frac{-b \pm \sqrt{b^2 - 4ac}}{2a} \rightarrow x = \frac{2\sqrt{2} \pm \sqrt{(-2\sqrt{2})^2 - 4(1)(-6)}}{2.1} = \frac{2\sqrt{2} \pm \sqrt{32}}{2}$$

Therefore, $x = \dfrac{2\sqrt{2} \pm 4\sqrt{2}}{2} = \sqrt{2} \pm 2\sqrt{2} = 3\sqrt{2}$ or $(-\sqrt{2})$.

The factors are $(x + \sqrt{2})$ and $(x - 3\sqrt{2})$.

5. Factorising expressions of the form $x^3 - y^3$ and $x^3 + y^3$

We can show by long division that $(x - y)$ is a factor of $x^3 - y^3$, creating a second factor $x^2 + xy + y^2$.

$$\begin{array}{r} x^2 + xy + y^2 \\ x - y \overline{\smash{)}x^3 - y^3} \\ \underline{x^3 - x^2y} \\ + x^2y - y^3 \\ \underline{+ x^2y - xy^2} \\ + xy^2 - y^3 \\ \underline{+ xy^2 - y^3} \end{array}$$

Therefore, we can write
$x^3 - y^3 = (x - y)(x^2 + xy + y^2)$.

Similarly, we have that
$x^3 + y^3 = (x + y)(x^2 - xy + y^2)$.

If we can write a polynomial in one of these forms, we can use these factor pairs as templates to find its factors.

For example, we can write

(i) $27x^3 + y^3 = (3x)^3 + y^3$

(ii) $64x^3 - 125y^3 = (4x)^3 - (5y)^3$.

have to know ✱

difference of 2 cubes ↙

$x^3 - y^3 = (x - y)(x^2 + xy + y^2)$ ↖

$x^3 + y^3 = (x + y)(x^2 - xy + y^2)$ ↘   Also

sum of two cubes

$(ax)^3 - (by)^3 = (ax - by)(a^2x^2 + abxy + b^2y^2)$

$(ax)^3 + (by)^3 = (ax + by)(a^2x^2 - abxy + b^2y^2)$

Example 4

Factorise   (i) $a^3 + 8b^3$ (ii) $64c^3 - 125d^3$

(i) $a^3 + 8b^3 = a^3 + (2b)^3$ ... note: let $x = a$ and $y = 2b$ in the box on previous page

$$= (a + 2b)(a^2 - 2ab + 4b^2)$$

(ii) $64c^3 - 125d^3 = (4c)^3 - (5d)^3$ ... note: let $x = 4c$ and $y = 5d$

$$= (4c - 5d)[(4c)^2 + (4c)(5d) + (5d)^2]$$

$$= (4c - 5d)(16c^2 + 20cd + 25d^2)$$

Exercise 1.3

Using the highest common factor, factorise each of the following:

1. $5x^2 - 10x$
2. $6ab - 12bc$
3. $3x^2 - 6xy$
4. $2x^2y - 6x^2z$
5. $2a^3 - 4a^2 + 8a$
6. $5xy^2 - 20x^2y$
7. $2a^2b - 4ab^2 + 12abc$
8. $3x^2y - 9xy^2 + 15xyz$
9. $4\pi r^2 + 6\pi rh$

Factorise each of the following by grouping terms.

10. $3a(2b - c) - 4(2b - c)$
11. $x^2 - ax + 3x - 3a$
12. $2c^2 - 4cd + c - 2d$
13. $8ax + 4ay - 6bx - 3by$
14. $7y^2 - 21by + 2ay - 6ab$
15. $6xy + 12yz - 8xz - 9y^2$
16. $6x^2 - 3y(3x - 2a) - 4ax$
17. $3ax^2 - 3ay^2 - 4bx^2 + 4by^2$

Using the difference of two squares, factorise the following:

18. $a^2 - b^2$
19. $x^2 - 4y^2$
20. $9x^2 - y^2$
21. $16x^2 - 25y^2$
22. $36x^2 - 25$
23. $1 - 36x^2$
24. $49a^2 - 4b^2$
25. $x^2y^2 - 1$
26. $4a^2b^2 - 16c^2$
27. $3x^2 - 27y^2$
28. $45 - 5x^2$
29. $45a^2 - 20$
30. $(2x + y)^2 - 4$
31. $(3a - 2b)^2 - 9$
32. $a^4 - b^4$

Factorise each of the following quadratic expressions:

33. $x^2 + 9x + 14$
34. $2x^2 + 7x + 3$
35. $2x^2 + 11x + 14$
36. $x^2 - 9x + 14$
37. $x^2 - 11x + 28$
38. $2x^2 - 7x + 3$
39. $3x^2 - 17x + 20$
40. $7x^2 - 18x + 8$
41. $2x^2 - 7x - 15$
42. $3x^2 + 11x - 20$
43. $12x^2 - 11x - 5$
44. $6x^2 + x - 15$
45. $3x^2 + 13x - 10$
46. $6x^2 - 11x + 3$
47. $36x^2 - 7x - 4$
48. $15x^2 - 14x - 8$
49. $6y^2 + 11y - 35$
50. $12x^2 + 17xy - 5y^2$

51. Using the quadratic formula, factorise each of the following:

(i) $x^2 + 3\sqrt{3}x + 6$ (ii) $x^2 + 2\sqrt{5}x - 15$ (iii) $2x^2 - 5\sqrt{2}x - 6$

52. Using both the sum and the difference of two cubes, factorise the following:

(i) $a^3 + b^3$ (ii) $a^3 - b^3$ (iii) $8x^3 + y^3$

Factorise each of the expressions in numbers (53–55):

53. (i) $27x^3 - y^3$ (ii) $x^3 - 64$ (iii) $8x^3 - 27y^3$

54. (i) $8 + 27k^3$ (ii) $64 - 125a^3$ (iii) $27a^3 + 64b^3$

55. (i) $a^3 - 8b^3c^3$ (ii) $5x^3 + 40y^3$ (iii) $(x + y)^3 - z^3$

Section 1.4 Simplifying algebraic fractions

Algebraic fractions are added, subtracted, multiplied and divided in the same way as numerical fractions.

Revision:

(i) $\frac{2}{5} + \frac{3}{7} = \frac{14}{35} + \frac{15}{35} = \frac{29}{35}$ (fractions can only be added or subtracted when they have the same denominator.)

(ii) $\frac{2}{5} \times \frac{3}{7} = \frac{6}{35}$ (fractions are multiplied by multiplying the numerators and denominators separately.)

(iii) $\frac{2}{5} \div \frac{3}{7} = \frac{2}{5} \times \frac{7}{3} = \frac{14}{15}$ (fractions are divided by changing the division into a product.)

Note: $\dfrac{\overset{2}{\cancel{6}} \times 12}{\underset{1}{\cancel{3}}} = 24$ $\dfrac{\overset{2}{\cancel{6}} + \overset{4}{\cancel{12}}}{\underset{1}{\cancel{3}}} = 6$

Similarly with algebraic terms;

(i) $\dfrac{2}{x + 1} - \dfrac{2x}{2x + 3} = \dfrac{2(2x + 3)}{(x + 1)(2x + 3)} - \dfrac{2x(x + 1)}{(x + 1)(2x + 3)}$ ... getting a common denominator

$= \dfrac{4x + 6 - 2x^2 - 2x}{(x + 1)(2x + 3)} = \dfrac{-2x^2 + 2x + 6}{(x + 1)(2x + 3)}$ ... simplifying the numerator

(ii) $\dfrac{2}{x + 1} \times \dfrac{2x}{2x + 3} = \dfrac{4x}{(x + 1)(2x + 3)}$ ... multiplying numerators and multiplying denominators

(iii) $\dfrac{2}{x + 1} \div \dfrac{2x}{2x + 3} = \dfrac{2}{x + 1} \times \dfrac{2x + 3}{2x} = \dfrac{2(2x + 3)}{2x(x + 1)} = \dfrac{(2x + 3)}{x(x + 1)}$ ... changing division to multiplication and then dividing above and below by a common factor

So, in general when dealing with algebraic fractions;

(i) A common denominator is needed to add or subtract fractions.

(ii) A fraction can be reduced (simplified) only if the numerator and denominator have a common factor.

(iii) If the denominator or numerator contain fractions added or subtracted, they must be reduced into a single fraction first before proceeding.

(iv) To divide fractions, we multiply by the denominator inverted.

Example 1

Simplify (i) $\dfrac{5ax}{15a + 10a^2}$ (ii) $\dfrac{t^2 + 3t - 4}{t^2 - 16}$ (iii) $\dfrac{\frac{5}{8} + y}{\frac{1}{8}}$

(i) $\dfrac{5ax}{15a + 10a^2} = \dfrac{(\overset{1}{\cancel{5a}})x}{(\cancel{5a})(3 + 2a)} = \dfrac{x}{3 + 2a}$

(ii) $\dfrac{t^2 + 3t - 4}{t^2 - 16} = \dfrac{(\overset{1}{\cancel{t + 4}})(t - 1)}{(t - 4)(\underset{1}{\cancel{t + 4}})} = \dfrac{t - 1}{t - 4}$

(iii) $\dfrac{\frac{5}{8} + y}{\frac{1}{8}} = \left(\frac{5}{8} + y\right).8 = 5 + 8y$

Example 2

Simplify each of the following

(i) $\dfrac{6y}{x(x + 4y)} - \dfrac{3}{2x}$ (ii) $\dfrac{5}{3x - 4} + \dfrac{2x + 5}{3}$

(i) $\dfrac{6y}{x(x + 4y)} - \dfrac{3}{2x} = \dfrac{2(6y)}{2x(x + 4y)} - \dfrac{3(x+4y)}{2x(x + 4y)}$

$= \dfrac{2(6y) - 3(x+4y)}{2x(x + 4y)} = \dfrac{12y - 3x - 12y}{2x(x + 4y)}$

$= \dfrac{-3x}{2x(x + 4y)} = \dfrac{-3}{2(x + 4y)}$

(i) $\dfrac{5}{3x-4} + \dfrac{2x+5}{3} = \dfrac{3(5)}{3(3x-4)} + \dfrac{(2x+5)(3x-4)}{3(3x-4)}$ ... common denom.: $3(3x-4)$

$$= \dfrac{15 + 6x^2 + 7x - 20}{3(3x-4)}$$

$$= \dfrac{6x^2 + 7x - 5}{3(3x-4)} = \dfrac{(2x-1)(3x+5)}{3(3x-4)}$$

Example 3

Simplify $\dfrac{y - \dfrac{x^2 + y^2}{y}}{\dfrac{1}{x} - \dfrac{1}{y}}$.

$$\dfrac{y - \dfrac{x^2 + y^2}{y}}{\dfrac{1}{x} - \dfrac{1}{y}} = \dfrac{\dfrac{y^2 - (x^2 + y^2)}{y}}{\dfrac{(y-x)}{xy}} = \dfrac{\dfrac{-x^2}{y}}{\dfrac{(y-x)}{xy}} = \dfrac{-x^2}{y} \times \dfrac{xy}{(y-x)}$$

$$= \dfrac{-x^3y}{y(y-x)} = \dfrac{-x^3}{y-x}$$

Division: sub

Exercise 1.4

1. Simplify each of the following fractions:

   (i) $\dfrac{8y}{2y^3}$ (ii) $\dfrac{7a^6b^3}{14a^5b^4}$ (iii) $\dfrac{(2x)^2}{4x}$ (iv) $\dfrac{7y + 2y^2}{7y}$ (v) $\dfrac{5ax}{15a + 10a^2}$

2. Express each of the following as a single fraction:

   (a) $\dfrac{2x}{5} + \dfrac{4x}{3}$ (b) $\dfrac{3x}{5} - \dfrac{x}{2}$ (c) $\dfrac{2x+3}{4} + \dfrac{x}{3}$

   (d) $\dfrac{x+1}{4} + \dfrac{2x-1}{5}$ (e) $\dfrac{3x-4}{6} - \dfrac{2x+1}{3}$ (f) $\dfrac{3x-2}{6} - \dfrac{x-3}{4}$

   (g) $\dfrac{5x-1}{4} - \dfrac{2x-4}{5}$ (h) $\dfrac{3x+5}{6} - \dfrac{2x+3}{4} - \dfrac{1}{12}$ (i) $\dfrac{3x-2}{4} + \dfrac{3}{5} - \dfrac{2x-1}{10}$

   (j) $\dfrac{1}{3x} + \dfrac{1}{5x}$ (k) $\dfrac{3}{4x} - \dfrac{5}{8x}$ (l) $\dfrac{1}{x} + \dfrac{1}{x+3}$

(m) $\dfrac{2}{x+2} + \dfrac{3}{x+4}$ (n) $\dfrac{2}{x-2} + \dfrac{3}{2x-1}$ (o) $\dfrac{5}{3x-1} - \dfrac{2}{x+3}$

(p) $\dfrac{3}{2x-7} - \dfrac{1}{5x+2}$ (q) $\dfrac{2}{3x-5} - \dfrac{1}{4}$ (r) $\dfrac{5}{2x-1} - \dfrac{3}{x-2}$

(s) $\dfrac{x}{x-y} - \dfrac{y}{x+y}$ (t) $\dfrac{3}{x} + \dfrac{4}{3y} - \dfrac{2}{3xy}$ (u) $\dfrac{3}{x} - \dfrac{2}{x-1} - \dfrac{4}{x(x-1)}$

$$(x^2 - a^2) = (x - a)(x + a)$$

3. By factorising the numerator and the denominator fully, simplify each of the following.

(i) $\dfrac{2z^2 - 4z}{2z^2 - 10z}$ (ii) $\dfrac{y^2 + 7y + 10}{y^2 - 25}$ (iii) $\dfrac{t^2 + 3t - 4}{t^2 - 3t + 2}$

(iv) $\dfrac{x}{x^2 - 4} - \dfrac{1}{x+2}$ (v) $\dfrac{2}{a+3} - \dfrac{a+2}{a^2 - 9}$ (vi) $\dfrac{x-1}{x^2 - 4} + \dfrac{1}{x-2}$

4. By factorising the denominator, simplify each of the following:

(i) $\dfrac{10}{2x^2 - 3x - 2} - \dfrac{2}{x-2}$ (ii) $\dfrac{x+2}{2x^2 - x - 1} - \dfrac{1}{x-1}$

5. Simplify the following:

(i) $\dfrac{1}{x^2 - 9} - \dfrac{2}{x^2 - x - 6}$ (ii) $\dfrac{3}{x^2 + x - 2} - \dfrac{2}{x^2 + 3x + 2}$

(iii) $\dfrac{2}{6x^2 - 5x - 4} - \dfrac{3}{9x^2 - 16}$ (iv) $\dfrac{1}{xy - x^2} - \dfrac{1}{y^2 - xy}$

6. Simplify each of the following complex fractions:

(i) $\dfrac{\frac{1}{2} + \frac{3}{4}}{\frac{1}{4}}$ (ii) $\dfrac{\frac{2}{3} + \frac{5}{6}}{\frac{3}{8}}$ (iii) $\dfrac{x - \frac{1}{x}}{1 + \frac{1}{x}}$

7. Simplify each of these:

(i) $\dfrac{\frac{1}{x} + 1}{\frac{1}{x} - 1}$ (ii) $\dfrac{\frac{1}{x^2} - 4}{\frac{1}{x} - 2}$ (iii) $\dfrac{x + y}{\frac{1}{x} + \frac{1}{y}}$

8. By expressing the numerator as a single fraction, simplify the following fractions:

(i) $\dfrac{4y - \frac{3}{2}}{2}$ (ii) $\dfrac{2 - \frac{1}{x}}{2}$ (iii) $\dfrac{3x + \frac{1}{x}}{2}$ (iv) $\dfrac{y + \frac{1}{4}}{\frac{1}{2}}$

9. By expressing the numerator and the denominator as single fractions, write the following fractions in their simplest forms.

(i) $\dfrac{z - \frac{1}{3}}{z - \frac{1}{2}}$ 　　(ii) $\dfrac{2x + \frac{1}{2}}{x + \frac{1}{4}}$ 　　(iii) $\dfrac{z - \frac{1}{2z}}{z - \frac{1}{3z}}$ 　　(iv) $\dfrac{x - \frac{1}{x+1}}{x - 1}$

10. Simplify each of the following.

(i) $\dfrac{1 + \frac{2}{x}}{\frac{x+2}{x-2}}$ 　　(ii) $\dfrac{2 + \frac{1}{x}}{2x^2 + x}$ 　　(iii) $\dfrac{x + \frac{2x}{x-2}}{1 + \frac{4}{(x+2)(x-2)}}$

11. Simplify each of the following.

(i) $\dfrac{\frac{a+b}{a-b} - \frac{a-b}{a+b}}{1 + \frac{a-b}{a+b}}$ 　　(ii) $\dfrac{x + \frac{3}{x}}{x - \frac{9}{x^3}}$ 　　(iii) $\dfrac{9 - \frac{1}{y^2}}{9 + \frac{6}{y} + \frac{1}{y^2}}$

12. Show that $\dfrac{3x - 5}{x - 2} + \dfrac{1}{2 - x}$ simplifies to a constant when $x \neq 2$.

Section 1.5 Algebraic identities

The word identity occurs in many different areas of mathematics. It is used in trigonometry, in sets, in functions and in algebra.

> In an **identity,** all coefficients of like powers are equal.
>
> An identity must be true **for all values** of the independent variable.

If $3x + 7 = ax + b$ **for all values of x**, this is called an **algebraic identity**.

We can conclude that for this to be true, then $a = 3$ and $b = 7$.

When two expressions are equal **for all values of x**, then the resulting equation is an identity. All coefficients of like powers of x in an identity are equal.

Generally, if $ax^3 + bx^2 + cx + d = px^3 + qx^2 + rx + s$ for all values of x,

then $a = p, b = q, c = r, d = s$.

Also, if $ax^3 + bx^2 + cx + d = qx^2 + s$ for all values of x,

then $a = c = 0$ and $b = q, d = s$.

This property is used to find unknown coefficients in certain equations.

Example 1

Find the values of a and b given that $(2x + a)^2 = 4x^2 + 12x + b$, **for all values of x.**

Given $(2x + a)^2 = 4x^2 + 12x + b$ for all values of x,

$4x^2 + 4ax + a^2 = 4x^2 + 12x + b$

$4a = 12$ (comparing like powers of x)   ∴ $a = 3$

and $a^2 = b$ (comparing the constant terms)   ∴ $3^2 = 9 = b$.

Example 2

If $3t^2x - 3px + c - 2t^3 = 0$ **for all values of x**, find c in terms of p.

Given $3t^2x - 3px + c - 2t^3 = 0$ for all values of x,

∴ $(3t^2 - 3p)x + c - 2t^3 = (0)x + (0)$ ... writing both sides as polynomials in x

∴ $3t^2 - 3p = 0$ (comparing like powers of x)   ∴ $t = \sqrt{p}$

and $c - 2t^3 = 0$ (comparing the constant terms)   ∴ $c = 2t^3$

$$\therefore c = 2(\sqrt{p})^3 = 2p^{\frac{3}{2}}$$

Algebraic identities can also be used to create **partial fractions** from a given fraction.

For example, $\dfrac{1}{(x + 1)(x - 2)} = \dfrac{A}{(x + 1)} + \dfrac{B}{(x - 2)}$ where A and $B \in Q$.

Example 3

Given $\dfrac{1}{(x + 1)(x - 2)} = \dfrac{A}{(x + 1)} + \dfrac{B}{(x - 2)}$ for all values of x, find the values of A and B.

$$\frac{1}{(x + 1)(x - 2)} = \frac{A}{(x + 1)} + \frac{B}{(x - 2)} = \frac{A(x - 2) + B(x + 1)}{(x + 1)(x - 2)}$$

∴ $1 = A(x - 2) + B(x + 1)$ for all values of x.

We can find values of A and B using two different methods.

Method 1: Since this equation must be true for all values of x, by picking two suitable values of x, A and B can be easily evaluated.

Since $1 = A(x - 2) + B(x + 1)$

Let $x = 2$ ∴ $1 = A(0) + B(2 + 1)$ ∴ $B = \frac{1}{3}$

Let $x = -1$ ∴ $1 = A(-1 - 2) + B(0)$ ∴ $1 = -3A \Rightarrow A = -\frac{1}{3}$

Method 2: Equating coefficients of like powers and then solve using simultaneous equations.

$$1 = A(x - 2) + B(x + 1)$$
$$1 = Ax - 2A + Bx + B$$
$$1 = Ax + Bx - 2A + B$$
$$1 = x(A + B) - 2A + B$$
$$x(0) + 1 = x(A + B) - 2A + B \text{ for all values of } x.$$

$\therefore \quad 0 = A + B$ and $1 = -2A + B$ ... equating like powers of x and constant terms

$\therefore \quad A = -B$ and using substitution, $1 = -2(-B) + B = 3B$.

$\therefore \quad B = \frac{1}{3}$ and $A = -\frac{1}{3}$

$$\therefore \quad \frac{1}{(x + 1)(x - 2)} = \frac{A}{(x + 1)} + \frac{B}{(x - 2)} = \frac{-1}{3(x + 1)} + \frac{1}{3(x - 2)}$$

Algebraic identities and factors

If $x^2 - ax + b$ is a factor of $x^3 + 2ax^2 + 4bx + c$,
using **algebraic identities** we can find a relationship between the coefficients a, b and c.

It is important to realise that when a factor is divided into an expression, there can be no remainder by definition of a factor.

$$\begin{array}{r} x + 3a \\ x^2 - ax + b \overline{)x^3 + 2ax^2 + 4bx + c} \\ \underline{x^3 - ax^2 + bx} \\ 3ax^2 + 3bx + c \\ \underline{3ax^2 - 3a^2x + 3ab} \\ \end{array}$$

$$\text{Remainder} = x(3b + 3a^2) + c - 3ab$$

Since there can be no remainder, we can conclude that **for all values of x,**

(i) $3b + 3a^2 = 0$, i.e. $b = -a^2$ and

(ii) $c - 3ab = 0$, i.e. $c = 3ab$

The same results can be obtained by letting the missing factor $= (x + k)$.

$$\therefore \quad (x + k)(x^2 - ax + b) = x^3 + 2ax^2 + 4bx + c$$

Expanding the left-hand side we get,

$$x^3 - ax^2 + bx + kx^2 - akx + bk = x^3 + 2ax^2 + 4bx + c \text{ ... for all values of } x.$$
$$\therefore \quad x^3 + (k - a)x^2 + (b - ak)x + bk = x^3 + 2ax^2 + 4bx + c \text{ ... grouping like terms.}$$

Comparing coefficients of x^2: $\quad (k - a) = 2a$, hence $k = 3a$ as above.

Comparing coefficients of x: $\quad (b - ak) = 4b$
$$(b - 3a^2) = 4b, \text{ hence } 3b = -3a^2, \text{ i.e. } b = -a^2 \text{ as above.}$$

Finally, comparing constant terms: $\quad bk = c$
$$\therefore \quad 3ab = c, \text{ again the same as above.}$$

Example 4

Given that $(x - t)^2$ is a factor of $x^3 + 3px + c$, show that $p = -t^2$ and $c = 2t^3$.

$(x - t)^2 = x^2 - 2xt + t^2$ and using long division we get;

$$
\begin{array}{r}
x + 2t \\
x^2 - 2xt + t^2 \overline{\smash{)}x^3 \qquad\quad + 3px + c} \\
\underline{x^3 - 2tx^2 + t^2x} \\
2tx^2 - t^2x + 3px + c \\
2tx^2 + (3p - t^2)x + c \\
\underline{2tx^2 - 4t^2x + 2t^3} \\
(3p + 3t^2)x + c - 2t^3
\end{array}
$$

(note: there is no x^2 term)

(= remainder)

Since we should get no remainder, $(3p + 3t^2)x + c - 2t^2 = 0$ **for all values of x.**

$\therefore \quad (3p + 3t^2)x + c - 2t^3 = (0)x + 0 \qquad$ for all values of x.

$\therefore \quad 3p + 3t^2 = 0 \rightarrow p = -t^2$

and $\quad +c - 2t^3 = 0 \rightarrow c = 2t^3$.

(Note: The factors of $x^3 + 3px + c$ are $x^2 - 2xt + t^2$ and $x + 2t$.)

Example 5

$2x - \sqrt{3}$ is a factor of $4x^2 - 2(1 + \sqrt{3})x + \sqrt{3}$; find the second factor.

Let the second factor take the form $(ax + b)$.
(Note: a needs to be introduced because the coefficient of x^2 is 4; it should be clear that $a = 2$)

Then $(2x - \sqrt{3})(ax + b) = 4x^2 - 2(1 + \sqrt{3})x + \sqrt{3}$

$\qquad 2ax^2 + 2bx - \sqrt{3}ax - \sqrt{3}b = 4x^2 - 2(1 + \sqrt{3})x + \sqrt{3}$

$\qquad 2ax^2 + (2b - \sqrt{3}a)x - \sqrt{3}b = 4x^2 - 2(1 + \sqrt{3})x + \sqrt{3}$

Equating coefficients of like powers,

(i) $(x^2) \ldots 2a = 4 \Rightarrow a = 2$

(ii) $(x) \ldots + (2b - \sqrt{3}a) = -2(1 + \sqrt{3})$
 since $a = 2$, $\Rightarrow 2b - 2\sqrt{3} = -2 - 2\sqrt{3}$
 $\therefore \quad b = -1$

(iii) (comparing the constants) $\ldots -\sqrt{3}b = \sqrt{3}$, verifying that $b = -1$.
 Therefore the second factor is $2x - 1$.

Exercise 1.5

1. If $ax^2 + bx + c = (2x - 3)(3x + 4)$ for all values of x, find the values of a, b and c.

2. If $(3x - 2)(x + 5) = 3x^2 + px + q$ for all values of x, find the values of p and q.

3. If $x^2 + 6x + 16 = (x + a)^2 + b$ for all values of x, find the values of a and b.

4. Find the real numbers a and b such that $x^2 + 4x - 6 = (x + a)^2 + b$ for all $x \in R$.

5. If $2x^2 + 5x + 6 = p(x + q)^2 + r$ for all values of x, find the values of p, q and r.

6. Find the values of a and b if $(2x + a)^2 = 4x^2 + 12x + b$, for all x.

7. If $x^2 - 4x - 5 = (x - n)^2 - m$ for all x, find the values of m and n.

8. The volume of this closed box, V, is given by the function $V(x) = ax^3 + bx^2 + cx + d$, where a, b, c and $d \in Z$.

   (i) Find the values for a, b, c and d.

   The external surface area, $S(x)$, is given by the equation $S(x) = px^2 + qx + r$, where p, q and $r \in Z$.

   (ii) Find the values of p, q and r.

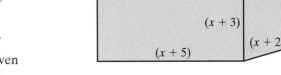

9. If $3(x - p)^2 + q = 3x^2 - 12x + 7$ for all x, find the values of p and q.

10. The volume of a solid box is given by
    $$V(x) = x^3 + 12x^2 + bx + 30.$$

    If the top of the box has an area of $x^2 + cx + 4$ and the height is $x + a$, find the values of a, b and c.

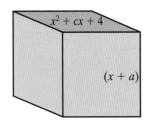

11. If $(x - 4)^3 = x^3 + px^2 + qx - 64$ for all x, find the values of the constants p and q.

12. If $(x + a)(x^2 + bx + 2) = x^3 - 2x^2 - x - 6$ for all x, find the values of the constants a and b.

13. Find the values of b and c given that $(x - 2)(x^2 + bx + c) = x^3 + 2x^2 - 5x - 6$ for all values of x.

14. Given that $(5a - b)x + b + 2c = 0$ for all values of x, find a in terms of c.

15. If $(4x + r)(x^2 + s) = 4x^3 + px^2 + qx + 2$ for all x, find a value for pq.

16. $(x + s)(x - s)(ax + t) = ax^3 + bx^2 + cx + d$ for all values of x.

Using this identify, show that $bc = ad$.

17. If $\dfrac{1}{(x + 1)(x - 1)} = \dfrac{A}{(x + 1)} + \dfrac{B}{(x - 1)}$ for all x, find values for A and B.

18. If $\dfrac{1}{(x + 2)(x - 3)} = \dfrac{C}{(x + 2)} + \dfrac{D}{(x - 3)}$ for all x, find values for C and D.

19. Write $\dfrac{1}{(x + 1)(x + 4)}$ as the partial fractions $\dfrac{A}{(x + 1)} + \dfrac{B}{(x + 4)}$.

20. If $(x - 3)^2$ is a factor of $x^3 + ax + b$, find the value of a and the value of b.

21. If $(x - 2)^2$ is a factor of $x^3 + px + q$, find the value of p and the value of q.

22. Given that $(x^2 - 4)$ is a factor of $x^3 + cx^2 + dx - 12$, find the values of the coefficients c and d.

Hence factorise the cubic polynomial fully.

23. If $(x^2 + b)$ is a factor of $x^3 - 3x^2 + bx - 15$, find the value of b.

24. If $x^2 - px + 9$ is a factor of $x^3 + ax + b$, express   (i) a (ii) b in terms of p.

Hence find the values of p for which $a + b = 17$.

25. If $x^2 - kx + 1$ is a factor of $ax^3 + bx + c$, show that $c^2 = a(a - b)$.

26. If $(x - a)^2$ is a factor of $x^3 + 3px + c$, show that   (i) $p = -a^2$ (ii) $c = 2a^3$.

27. If $x^2 + ax + b$ is a factor of $x^3 - k$, show that   (i) $a^3 = k$ (ii) $b^3 = k^2$.

28. Show by long division that $2x - \sqrt{3}$ is a factor of $4x^2 - 2(1 + \sqrt{3})x + \sqrt{3}$ and hence find the second factor.

29. Find the values of A, B and C such that

$5x + 3 = Ax(x + 3) + Bx(x - 1) + C(x - 1)(x + 3)$ for all values of x.

Section 1.6 Manipulating formulae

The area of a disc is given by the formula $A = \pi r^2$.

A is said to be defined **in terms of** r (r is the independent variable).

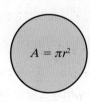

$A = \pi r^2$

If we know r, we can find A.

For example, if $r = 3$, then $A = 9\pi$; if $r = 8$, then $A = 64\pi$, etc..

In some cases we may need to find r in terms A, i.e. make r the **subject** of the equation.

$\therefore \quad \pi r^2 = A \Rightarrow r^2 = \dfrac{A}{\pi} \Rightarrow r = \sqrt{\dfrac{A}{\pi}} \ \dots \ r$ is now defined in terms of A.

Thus, if we know the area of the circle, we can find the radius.

For example, if $A = 9\pi$, then $r = \sqrt{\dfrac{A}{\pi}} \Rightarrow r = \sqrt{\dfrac{9\pi}{\pi}} = \sqrt{9} = 3$.

Example 1

(i) If $v^2 = u^2 + 2as$, express a in terms of v, u and s.

(ii) If $\sqrt{\dfrac{x+y}{x-y}} = \dfrac{1}{2}$, express y in terms of x. Hence find the value of y when $x = 5$.

(i) $\qquad v^2 = u^2 + 2as$

$u^2 + 2as = v^2$

$\qquad 2as = v^2 - u^2$

$\qquad \therefore a = \dfrac{v^2 - u^2}{2s}$

(ii) $\sqrt{\dfrac{x+y}{x-y}} = \dfrac{1}{2}$

$\dfrac{x+y}{x-y} = \dfrac{1}{4} \qquad \dots$ squaring both sides

$4(x+y) = x - y \ \dots$ multiplying both sides by $4(x - y)$

$4x + 4y = x - y \ \dots$ expanding the left-hand side

$y + 4y = x - 4x \ \dots$ gathering only y terms on the left-hand side

$5y = -3x$

$y = \dfrac{-3x}{5} \ \dots$ finding y in terms of x

When $x = 5$, $\quad y = \dfrac{-3(5)}{5} = -3$.

Example 2

A container in the shape of an inverted cone is used to hold liquid.

Given $\tan \theta = \dfrac{r}{h}$, express the volume, V, in terms of the depth, h, of the liquid and the angle θ.

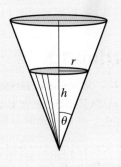

Volume of a cone, $V = \tfrac{1}{3}\pi r^2 h$

But $\tan \theta = \dfrac{r}{h} \Rightarrow h \tan \theta = r$

$V = \tfrac{1}{3}\pi r^2 h = \dfrac{\pi}{3}(h \tan \theta)^2 h = \dfrac{\pi}{3}h^3 \tan^2 \theta$

Example 3

Given $x = \dfrac{t + 4}{3t + 1}$, find t in terms of x.

$$x = \dfrac{t + 4}{3t + 1}$$

$x(3t + 1) = t + 4$ ... multiplying both sides by $3t + 1$

$3tx + x = t + 4$ ... expanding the left-hand side

$3tx - t = 4 - x$ ... gathering only t terms on the left-hand side

$t(3x - 1) = 4 - x$ ... factorising

$t = \dfrac{4 - x}{3x - 1}$ ... dividing both sides by $3x - 1$

Exercise 1.6

1. In each of the following, express x in terms of the other variables.

   (i) $3x - 2y = 4$ (ii) $2x - b = 4c$ (iii) $5x - 4 = \dfrac{y}{2}$

   (iv) $5(x - 3) = 2y$ (v) $3y = \dfrac{x}{3} - 2$ (vi) $xy = xz + yz$

2. Express x in terms of the other variables in each of the following:

   (i) $2x - \dfrac{y}{3} = \dfrac{1}{3}$ (ii) $z = \dfrac{y - 2x}{3}$ (iii) $\dfrac{a}{x} - b = c$

3. (a) The volume of a cylinder is given by $V = \pi r^2 h$.
      Find the radius r in terms of V and h.

   (b) The curved surface area of a cylinder is given
      by $A = 2\pi r h$.
      Find the radius r in terms of A and h.

   (c) Hence show that $A^2 = 4\pi h V$.

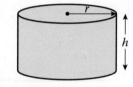

4. A circle of radius r is drawn inside a square as shown.

   (a) Find the area of the circle, A.
   (b) Find the area of the square in terms of r.
   (c) Hence find an expression for the area of the shaded
      corners in terms of r.
   (d) If the side of the square is doubled while the radius
      of the circle is halved, find an expression for the
      shaded area in terms of r.
   (e) If a circle is circumscribed around the original square,
      prove that the area of the outer disc is twice the area of the
      inner disc.

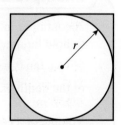

5. A speed camera measures the change in frequency of waves from f to f', caused by a moving car, using the formula $f' = \dfrac{fc}{c - u}$, where c is the speed of the waves and u the speed of the car. Find

   (i) the speed of the car, u, in terms of the other variables f', f and c.

   (ii) the speed of the waves, c, in terms of the other variables f', f and u.

6. The time taken for one complete cycle of a pendulum is given by $T = 2\pi\sqrt{\dfrac{l}{g}}$, where l is the length of the pendulum and g the acceleration due to gravity.

   (i) Find l in terms of the other variables.

   (ii) Given that $T = 3\,\text{s}$ and $g = 10\,\text{m s}^{-2}$, calculate the length of the pendulum correct to one decimal place.

7. In each of the following, express a in terms of the other variables:

   (i) $\dfrac{x}{y} = \dfrac{a + b}{a - b}$ (ii) $bc - ac = ac.$

8. Express v in terms of the other variables in each of the following:

   (i) $y = \dfrac{3(u - v)}{4}$ (ii) $S = \dfrac{t}{2}(u + v)$

9. The future value of €P, invested for 3 years at $i\%$, is given by the formula $A = P\left(1 + \dfrac{i}{100}\right)^{3}$. Find i in terms of P and A.

If €2500 invested 3 years ago has a present value of €2650, find the rate of interest, i (correct to one place of decimals).

10. Write c in terms of the other variables in each of the following.

   (i) $d = \sqrt{\dfrac{a - b}{ac}}$ (ii) $b = \dfrac{2c - 1}{c - 1}$

11. A cone has a radius r cm and a vertical height h cm. If the slant height $l = 15\,\text{cm}$, and using Pythagoras' theorem:

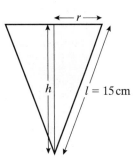

   (i) Express h in terms of r.

   (ii) Hence find the value of h when $r = 5\,\text{cm}$.

   (iii) At what value of h will the radius r be equal to half the slant height l?

        Give your answer correct to the nearest cm.

12. A farmer has 300 metres of fencing and wants to make a rectangular paddock against an existing wall, as shown, using all of this fencing.

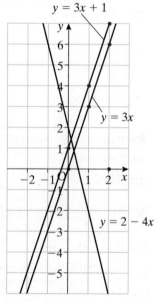

    (i) Find the length (L) of the paddock in terms of the width (W).

    (ii) Hence find the area of the paddock (A) in terms of the width only.

    (iii) Find the dimensions of the paddock if the maximum allowable area is 10,000 m².

Section 1.7 Algebraic patterns, an introduction

1. Linear Each polynomial function creates a pattern which can be studied both numerically and graphically.

Patterns such as 0, 3, 6, 9, ... can be described by the function
$f(x) = (y) = 3x$, where $x \geqslant 0$.

Similarly, 1, 4, 7, 10, ... can be described by the function
$f(x) = (y) = 3x + 1$, where $x \geqslant 0$.

Also, 2, −2, −6, −10 ... can be represented by the function
$f(x) = (y) = 2 − 4x$, where $x \geqslant 0$.

Each of these number patterns has a constant amount added or subtracted between terms and each, when graphed, produces a straight line as shown.

Functions of the form $f(x) = y = mx + c$ are called **linear** functions.

In a linear pattern, the difference between consecutive terms (called the 1st difference) gives m, the slope of the line.

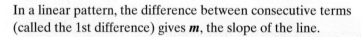

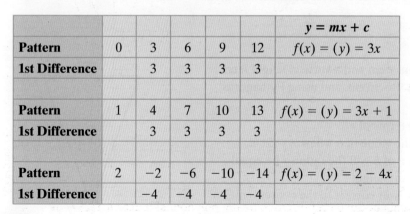

						$y = mx + c$
Pattern	0	3	6	9	12	$f(x) = (y) = 3x$
1st Difference		3	3	3	3	
Pattern	1	4	7	10	13	$f(x) = (y) = 3x + 1$
1st Difference		3	3	3	3	
Pattern	2	−2	−6	−10	−14	$f(x) = (y) = 2 − 4x$
1st Difference		−4	−4	−4	−4	

The starting point of each pattern determines c, the constant term. We note that when $x = 0$, geometrically, we get the y-axis intercept, c.

2. Quadratic   Patterns such as $0, 1, 4, 9, 16 \dots$ do not have a constant amount added or subtracted between terms.

Studying the 1ˢᵗ differences between terms, we get $1, 3, 5, 7, \dots$.

The **2nd difference** $(3 - 1), (5 - 3), \dots$ however is a constant, 2.

Such patterns can be represented by the function $f(x) = (y) = x^2$ for $x \geqslant 0$.

Functions of the form $\boldsymbol{f(x) = x^2 + b}$ create similar patterns.

Pattern	0	1	4	9	16	25	$f(x) = (y) = x^2$
1st Difference		1	3	5	7	9	
2nd Difference			2	2	2	2	

Pattern	2	3	6	11	18	27	$f(x) = (y) = x^2 + 2$
1st Difference		1	3	5	7	9	
2nd Difference			2	2	2	2	

Pattern	-3	-2	1	6	13	22	$f(x) = (y) = x^2 - 3$
1st Difference		1	3	5	7	9	
2nd Difference			2	2	2	2	

Pattern	2	1	-2	-7	-14	-23	$f(x) = (y) = 2 - x^2$
1st Difference		-1	-3	-5	-7	-9	
2nd Difference			-2	-2	-2	-2	

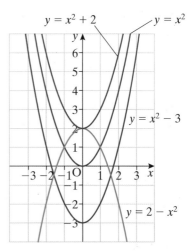

As can be seen from the graphs, the curves are symmetrical about the line $x = 0$ (y-axis).

Patterns of the form $f(x) = x^2 + b$ are $\cup$-shaped.

Patterns of the form $f(x) = b - x^2$ are $\cap$-shaped.

Consider the following pattern.

Pattern	4	7	16	31	52	79
1st Difference		3	9	15	21	27
2nd Difference			6	6	6	6

Because the 2nd difference is a constant, we know this is a quadratic pattern of the form

$ax^2 + b, x \geqslant 0.$

The starting value is 4, i.e. when $x = 0, b = 4$.

When $x = 1, ax^2 + b = a(1) + 4 = 7 \Rightarrow a = 3.$

(We also note that the second difference is 6, i.e. $2 \times 3 = 2a$)

> If $f(x) = ax^2 + bx + c$, the second difference $= 2a$.

Thus this pattern of numbers can be represented by the polynomial function $f(x) = 3x^2 + 4$.

Example 1

Examine each of the following patterns of numbers and determine if there is a linear or quadratic relationship between the terms.

Write an algebraic expression for each set of numbers:

(a) $-2, 1, 4, 7, \ldots$ (b) $3, 5, 11, 21, \ldots$

Pattern	-2	1	4	7
1st Difference		3	3	3

(a) Since the first difference is a constant, this indicates a linear relationship $f(x) = ax + b$.
$a = 3$ and $b = -2$,
$\therefore \; f(x) = 3x - 2, x \geqslant 0.$

Pattern	3	5	11	21
1st Difference		2	6	10
2nd Difference			4	4

(b) Since the second difference is a constant, this indicates a quadratic relationship
$f(x) = ax^2 + b.$
$4 = 2a \Rightarrow a = 2$ and $b = 3$,
$\therefore \; f(x) = 2x^2 + 3, x \geqslant 0.$

More complex quadratic patterns of the form $ax^2 + bx + c$ can be formed in two stages; first to identify the quadratic element x^2, then subtracting this from the pattern to form the linear element $bx + c$.

Example 2

Single matchsticks were used to form a sequence of patterns as shown.
Find an algebraic quadratic expression for the number of matchsticks needed for each pattern.
How many matchsticks are needed for the 10th pattern?

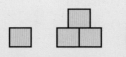 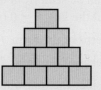

Counting the matchsticks needed for the first four patterns, we get the number pattern $4, 10, 18, 28, \ldots$

Pattern	4	10	18	28
1st Difference		6	8	10
2nd Difference			2	2

The 2nd difference produces $2, 2, 2, \ldots$ etc.

So there is a quadratic element (x^2) to this pattern.

Trying $f(x) = x^2 + 4$ for $x \geqslant 0$, we get the pattern $4, 5, 8, 13$, which is not the required pattern.

Subtracting $f(x) = x^2 = 0, 1, 4, 9, \ldots$ for $x \geqslant 0$ from $4, 10, 18, 28, \ldots$ produces the new pattern $4, 9, 14, 19, \ldots$

Pattern	4	10	18	28
x^2	0	1	4	9
New Pattern	4	9	14	19
1st Difference		5	5	5

The first difference in this sequence is 5.
– a linear relation of the form $5x + 4$ for $x \geqslant 0$.

Combining the two relationships, we get $f(x) = x^2 + 5x + 4$ for $x \geqslant 0$.

To get the 10th pattern, we let $x = 9$ (since our equation is true for $x \geqslant 0$, i.e. it starts at 0). $\therefore f(9) = 9^2 + 5(9) + 4 = 130$ matchsticks are needed.

[Note: If $x \geqslant 1$, we would subtract $1, 4, 9$, etc. creating a new sequence $3, 6, 9, \ldots$ with a linear relationship $3x$. Combining, we get $f(x) = x^2 + 3x$ for $x \geqslant 1$, and using this formula, $f(10) = 10^2 + 3(10) = 130$ again.]

Note: Linear and quadratic patterns are studied in greater depth in chapter 4.

Exercise 1.7

1. Examine each of the following patterns of numbers and determine if the pattern has a linear or quadratic relationship.

   (a) $4, 7, 10, 13, 16, \ldots$ (b) $-2, 2, 6, 10, 14, \ldots$
   (c) $-4, -3, 0, 5, 12, \ldots$ (d) $2, 1, -2, -7, -14, -23, \ldots$
   (e) $2, 7, 22, 47, \ldots$ (f) $3, 1, -5, -15, -29, \ldots$
   (g) $1, -4, -19, -44, -79, \ldots$ (h) $3, -2, -7, -12, -17, \ldots$
   (i) $0, 3, 12, 27, 48, \ldots$ (j) $5, 17, 37, 65, 101, \ldots$

2. Write an algebraic expression to represent each of the followings number patterns.
   (a) $-1, 3, 15, 35, 63, \ldots$ (b) $4, 3, 0, -5, -12, -21, -32, \ldots$

3. Each of the following number patterns can be written in the form $f(x) = ax + b, x \geqslant 0$. Find the values of a and b.
   (i) $2, 7, 12, 17, 22, \ldots$ (ii) $-6, -2, 2, 6, 10, \ldots$
   (iii) $3, 2, 1, 0, -1, -2, \ldots$ (iv) $-2, -7, -12, -17, -22, -27, \ldots$
   (v) $3, 3.5, 4, 4.5, 5, \ldots$ (vi) $-1, -0.8, -0.6, -0.4, -0.2, \ldots$

4. If $x \geqslant 3$, find an algebraic linear expression for the pattern $11, 13, 15, 17, 19, \ldots$

5. If $x \geqslant -2$, find a and b such that $f(x) = ax + b$ represents the number pattern $1, 3, 5, 7, 9, \ldots$

6. Convert each of the following designs to number patterns. By finding an algebraic linear expression for the number of matchsticks needed for each design, find the number of matchsticks needed to make the 15th element of each design.

(a)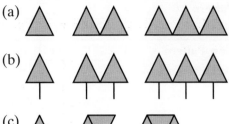

(b)

(c)

7. A company offers two different billing plans for the purchase of a TV over a number of months. Plan A where the repayments are €35.00 per month with a down-payment of €70.00, or Plan B with repayments of €24.00 per month with a down-payment of €125.00. If x represents the number of months of the plan, write an expression for each billing plan. Write a number sequence representing the cost per month of each plan (A and B) for the first four months. After how many months would both plans have repaid the same amount?

8. A biologist counted the number of bacteria cells growing in a culture every hour. The pattern 4, 7, 14, 25, 40, ... was recorded for the first four hours, with 4 being the initial number present. Show that this sequence contains both a linear and a quadratic element. Find an expression for the number of bacteria after t hours, i.e. find $f(t)$. Using your expression for $f(t)$, and trial and error, find in which hour the colony will have reached 529.

Section 1.8 Solving equations

To solve an equation, we need to find the values of the given variable that satisfy the equation.

If $4x - 12 = 0$, then $x = 3$ is the only solution of this equation.
If $x^2 - 5x + 6 = 0$, then $x = 2$ and $x = 3$ are both solutions of this equation.
If $y = 4x - 12$, then $(x, y) = (4, 4)$ is one of the many values of (x, y) that satisfy this equation.

Given $f(x) = 4x - 12$,
then $x = 3$ is the value that makes $f(x) = 0$.

Therefore, $(x, y) = (3, 0)$ is the solution of $y = 4x - 12$.

Similarly, $(2, 0)$ and $(3, 0)$ are solutions of $y = x^2 - 5x + 6$.

The values of x that make $y = 0$ are called the **roots** of an equation.

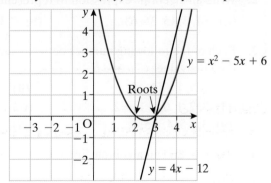

If a graph of the function is plotted, the roots are those points where the graph crosses the x-axis.

Solving linear equations

Any equation of the form $y = ax + b$, when plotted, creates a straight line.

Such equations are called **linear equations**.

To solve the equation $2x + 1 = 0$, we need to find the value of x that makes $y = 0$, i.e. where the line crosses the x-axis.

$$2x + 1 = 0$$

$$\Rightarrow \quad x = \frac{-1}{2} = -0.5$$

Similarly, to solve the equation $2x + 1 = 2$, we have to find the value of x that makes $y = 2$, i.e. where the line crosses the line $y = 2$.

$$2x + 1 = 2$$

$$\Rightarrow \quad x = \frac{1}{2} = 0.5$$

In each case, there is only one value of x (one root) produced.

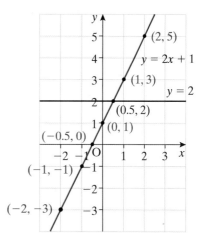

Example 1

Solve the linear equation $\dfrac{2t - 3}{5} + \dfrac{1}{20} = \dfrac{t - 1}{4}$.

$$\frac{2t - 3}{5} + \frac{1}{20} = \frac{t - 1}{4}$$

$$\frac{4(2t - 3)}{20} + \frac{1}{20} = \frac{5(t - 1)}{20} \qquad \text{... finding the lowest common denominator}$$

$$4(2t - 3) + 1 = 5(t - 1)$$

$$8t - 12 + 1 = 5t - 5 \qquad \text{... expanding}$$

$$3t = 6$$

$$t = 2$$

Exercise 1.8

1. Explain why each of the following is a **non-linear** equation.

   (i) $y = 2x^2 + 2x - 1$

   (ii) $y = \dfrac{2}{(x - 1)} = 2(x - 1)^{-1}$

   (iii) $y^2 = 3x + 4$

2. Solve each of the following equations.

    (i) $5x - 3 = 32$ (ii) $3x + 2 = x + 8$ (iii) $2 - 5x = 8 - 3x$

3. Solve each of these equations.

    (i) $2(x - 3) + 5(x - 1) = 3$ (ii) $2(4x - 1) - 3(x - 2) = 14$
    (iii) $3(x - 1) - 4(x - 2) = 6(2x + 3)$ (iv) $3(x + 5) + 2(x + 1) - 3x = 22$

4. Solve each of the following equations:

    (i) $\dfrac{2x + 1}{5} = 1$ (ii) $\dfrac{3x - 1}{4} = 8$ (iii) $\dfrac{x - 3}{4} = \dfrac{x - 2}{5}$

5. Find the value of the unknown in each of the following equations:

    (i) $\dfrac{2a}{3} - \dfrac{a}{4} = \dfrac{5}{6}$ (ii) $\dfrac{b + 2}{4} - \dfrac{b - 3}{3} = \dfrac{1}{2}$ (iii) $\dfrac{3c - 1}{6} - \dfrac{c - 3}{4} = \dfrac{4}{3}$

6. Find the value of the unknown in each of the following equations:

    (i) $\dfrac{x - 2}{5} + \dfrac{2x - 3}{10} = \dfrac{1}{2}$ (ii) $\dfrac{3y - 12}{5} + 3 = \dfrac{3(y - 5)}{2}$

    (iii) $\dfrac{3p - 2}{6} - \dfrac{3p + 1}{4} = \dfrac{2}{3}$ (iv) $\dfrac{3r - 2}{5} - \dfrac{2r - 3}{4} = \dfrac{1}{2}$

7. Solve each of the following:

    (i) $\frac{3}{4}(2x - 1) - \frac{2}{3}(4 - x) = 2$ (ii) $\frac{2}{3}(x - 1) - \frac{1}{5}(x - 3) = x + 1$

Section 1.9 Solving simultaneous linear equations ———

1. Solving simultaneous linear equations with two variables

The linear equation $y = \frac{2}{3}x - 3$ can be rearranged as follows:

$$y = \tfrac{2}{3}x - 3$$
$$3y = 2x - 9$$

Standard form of the equation of a line:

$$ax + by + c = 0$$

$2x - 3y - 9 = 0$ is the equation of the same line, expressed in standard form.

This equation has two variables (x, y) for which there are many solutions.
However, if we have two equations in x and y, they are either

(a) parallel, with no point of intersection or
(b) they intersect at a point (x_1, y_1), common to both lines.

In this diagram, the lines $2x - y + 1 = 0$ and $3x + y - 4 = 0$ are plotted.

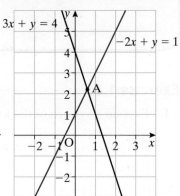

They have a point of intersection $A(x, y) = \left(\frac{3}{5}, \frac{11}{5}\right)$ which satisfies both equations at the same time, i.e. simultaneously.

We can solve two linear equations (i.e. find their point of intersection) by:

(i) substitution   (ii) elimination   (iii) graphically (as above).

Example 1

Solve the equations $3x - y = 1$ and $x - 2y = -8$.

Take $x - 2y = -8$ and rearrange the terms, finding **x in terms of y**,

$$\rightarrow x = -8 + 2y$$

Substitute this expression for x into the second linear equation.

$$3x - y = 1 \text{ becomes } 3(-8 + 2y) - y = 1$$
$$-24 + 6y - y = 1 \quad \text{... expanding}$$
$$5y = 25$$
$$y = 5$$

If $y = 5$, then $x = -8 + 2y$ becomes $x = -8 + 2(5) = 2$

Therefore $(x, y) = (2, 5)$ is the point of intersection.

[Note: Since $3(2) - (5) = 1$ and $(2) - 2(5) = -8$, the point $(2, 5)$ is on both lines.]

Note 1:   The technique for solving equations by substitution will be used later to find the point(s) of intersection of a line and a curve.

Note 2:   Either variable can be substituted.
(Always choose the variable that is easiest to isolate.)

Example 2

Solve the equations $2x - 5y = 9$ and $3x + 2y = 4$.

Let A be $2x - 5y = 9$
Let B be $3x + 2y = 4$

$\therefore$ 3A: $6x - 15y = 27$
and   2B: $\underline{6x + 4y = 8}$
$$-19y = 19 \quad \text{... Subtracting to } \underline{\text{eliminate}} \ x$$
$$y = -1$$

Now substituting $y = -1$ into A, we get $2x - 5(-1) = 9$
$$2x = 4$$
$$x = 2$$

The point of intersection is $(x, y) = (2, -1)$.

[Note: $2(2) - 5(-1) = 9$ and $3(2) + 2(-1) = 4$ and so this point is on both lines.]

2. Solving simultaneous equations with three variables

$x + y + z = 6$ is an equation with three variables (three dimensions).

To plot this equation we need three axes, x, y and z-axes, at right angles to one another.

When plotted, this equation represents a plane of points.

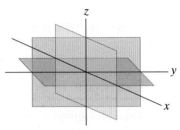

If three planes are plotted on the same axes, there will be one point of intersection $(x, y, z,)$ provided none of the planes are parallel.

To solve an equation with three unknowns,

  (i) reduce the three equations to two by eliminating one of the unknowns
  (ii) choose an unknown that is easy to isolate
  (iii) eliminate this unknown from all three equations, taking them two at a time
  (iv) solve these two equations as before
  (v) use your values for these unknowns in one of the original equations to solve for the third unknown
  (vi) check your solutions in all equations.

Example 3

Solve the simultaneous equations:
  A: $x + y + z = 6$
  B: $2x + y - z = 1$
  C: $4x - 3y + 2z = 4$

Eliminating z from all three equations we get,

A: $x + y + z = 6$ 2B: $4x + 2y - 2z = 2$
B: $\underline{2x + y - z = 1}$ C: $\underline{4x - 3y + 2z = 4}$
D: $3x + 2y\quad = 7$ ... adding A and B   E: $8x - y\quad\quad = 6$ ... adding 2B and C

  D: $3x + 2y = 7$
2E: $\underline{16x - 2y = 12}$
  $\quad 19x\quad\quad = 19$ ... adding D and 2E

  $\quad\quad x = 1$ $\therefore$ Using D: $3(1) + 2y = 7$
                            $2y = 4$
                            $y = 2$

Finally, using A: $(1) + (2) + z = 6$
                $z = 3$ $\therefore$ the point of intersection is
                    $(x, y, z) = (1, 2, 3)$

[**Note:** A: $(1) + (2) + (3) = 6$, and
        B: $2(1) + (2) - (3) = 1$, and
        C: $4(1) - 3(2) + 2(3) = 4$ and so this point satisfies all three equations]

3. Simultaneous equations in context

Example 4

An opera was attended by 240 people. Two ticket prices, €31 and €16, were available. If the total takings on the night were €5595, find using this data

  (i) two linear equations connecting the two types of tickets sold
  (ii) the number of €31 tickets sold
  (iii) the number of €16 tickets sold.

Let x represent the number of €16 tickets sold and y represent the number of €31 tickets sold.

  (i) Since 240 people attended altogether, then   A: $x + y = 240$
       If the receipts were €5595, then   B: $16x + 31y = 5595$

  (ii) Solving, we get 16A: $16x + 16y = 3840$
                        B: $\underline{16x + 31y = 5595}$
                            $-15y = -1755$ (subtracting)
                            $y = 117$, i.e. 117 €31 tickets were sold

  (iii)   Using $y = 117$: $x + (117) = 240$

                            $x = 123$, i.e. 123 €16 tickets were sold.

Example 5

Fifty, twenty and ten cent coins are collected from a coin machine and counted. The total value of the coins is €32. When counting, the cashier noted that twice the number of twenty cent coins, added to the number of ten cent coins, equalled three times the number of fifty cent coins. She then noticed that four times the number of fifty cent coins, added to the number of ten cent coins, equalled six times the number of twenty cent coins.
Find the number of each type of coin in the machine.

Let x = the number of 50 cent coins
Let y = the number of 20 cent coins
Let z = the number of 10 cent coins.

  (i) $50x + 20y + 10z = 3200$ ... €32 = 3200c
  (ii) $2y + z = 3x$
  (iii) $4x + z = 6y$

Rearranging the equations into standard form, we get   A: $50x + 20y + 10z = 3200$
                                                        B: $3x - 2y - z = 0$
                                                        C: $4x - 6y + z = 0$

Adding B and C eliminates z $\therefore$ B + C $\Rightarrow 7x - 8y = 0$.

Adding A and 10B also eliminates z (and y in this case) $\therefore$ A: $50x + 20y + 10z = 3200$

$$10B: 30x - 20y - 10z = 0$$

$$A + 10B \Rightarrow 80x = 3200$$

$$\therefore x = 40$$

Since $7x - 8y = 0 \Rightarrow 7(40) - 8y = 0$
$$\Rightarrow 280 - 8y = 0$$
$$\Rightarrow y = 35$$

Also, $3x - 2y - z = 0 \Rightarrow 3(40) - 2(35) - z = 0 \quad \therefore z = 120 - 70 = 50.$

$\therefore (x, y, z) = (40, 35, 50).$

There are forty 50c coins, thirty-five 20c coins and fifty 10c coins in the machine.

Exercise 1.9

1. Find the point of intersection of each of the following pairs of lines.

   (i) $3x - 2y = 8$
   $x + y = 6$

   (ii) $3x - y = 1$
   $x - 2y = -8$

   (iii) $2x - 5y = 1$
   $4x - 3y - 9 = 0$

2. Solve each of the following pairs of simultaneous equations.

   (i) $4x - 5y = 22$
   $7x + 3y - 15 = 0$

   (ii) $\dfrac{x}{2} - \dfrac{y}{6} = \dfrac{1}{6}$
   $x - 2y = -8$

   (iii) $\dfrac{4x - 2}{5} = \dfrac{8y}{10}$
   $18x - 20y = 4$

3. Solve for x and y given that $\dfrac{2x - 5}{3} + \dfrac{y}{5} = 6$ and $\dfrac{3x}{10} + 2 = \dfrac{3y - 5}{2}$.

4. Given that $y = 3x - 23$ and $y = \dfrac{x}{2} + 2$, find the values of y and x.

5. Solve the following equations with three unknowns.

   (i) $2x + y + z = 8$
   $5x - 3y + 2z = 3$
   $7x + y + 3z = 20$

   (ii) $2x - y - z = 6$
   $3x + 2y + 3z = 3$
   $4x + y - 2z = 3$

   (iii) $2x + y - z = 9$
   $x + 2y + z = 6$
   $3x - y + 2z = 17$

6. Find the point of intersection of each of the following sets of planes.

   (i) $2a + b + c = 8$
   $5a - 3b + 2c = -3$
   $7a - 3b + 3c = 1$

   (ii) $x + y + 2z = 3$
   $4x + 2y + z = 13$
   $2x + y - 2z = 9$

   (iii) $x + y + z = 2$
   $2x + 3y + z = 7$
   $\dfrac{x}{2} - \dfrac{y}{6} + \dfrac{z}{3} = \dfrac{2}{3}$

7. Find the solution (x, y, z) for
   $6x + 4y - 2z - 5 = 3x - 2y + 4z + 10 = 5x - 2y + 6z + 13 = 0.$

8. The curve $f(x) = y = ax^2 + bx + c$ passes through the three points $(1, 2)$, $(2, 4)$ and $(3, 8)$. Use these points to find three equations in a, b and c and hence solve to find $f(x)$.

9. A curve of the form $f(x) = y = ax^2 + bx + c$ is drawn as shown.
   By using any three points on the curve, form three equations connecting the coefficients a, b and c and hence solve to find $f(x)$.

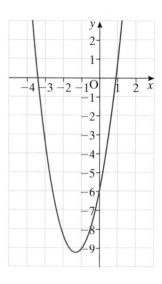

10. 44 000 people attended a match in Croke Park. The two ticket prices on the day were €30 and €20. The total receipts for the game came to €1.2 million.
    How many people paid the higher ticket price?

11. Three years from now, Callum will be twice as old as Lydia was five years ago.
    At the moment, half their combined ages is 16. Find their ages.

12. Find the equation of the line AB in the form, $y = ax + b$, by forming two simultaneous equations in a and b using the two given points on the line.
    Verify that your line passes through a selected point between A and B.

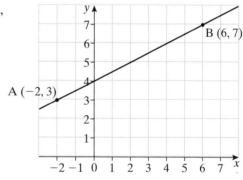

13. Two forces, N_1 and N_2, act on a hemisphere at rest.
    If $\frac{1}{4}N_1 - N_2 = 0$ and $N_1 + \frac{1}{2}N_2 - 99 = 0$,
    find the values of N_1 and N_2.

14. If $\dfrac{a}{x-2} + \dfrac{b}{x+2} = \dfrac{4}{(x-2)(x+2)}$ for all values of x,

    using algebraic identities, write down two equations in terms of a and b only.
    Hence solve for a and b.
    Verify your answers using the original equation.

15. If $\dfrac{c}{z-3} + \dfrac{d}{z+2} = \dfrac{4}{(z-3)(z+2)}$ for all values of z, solve for c and d.

Verify your answers by substitution.

16. How many litres of 70% alcohol need to be added to 50 litres of 40% alcohol to make a 50% solution?

17. The sum of two numbers is 26.

If five times the smaller number is taken from four times the larger number, the result is 5.

Let x be the bigger number and y the smaller number.

   (i) Write down two equations in x and y.

   (ii) Solve these equations for x and y.

   (iii) Verify your answers by substitution.

18. A student studied a car rolling down an inclined plane and took measurements of its speed at two different times.

After 7 seconds, it had a speed of 2 m/sec and after 13 seconds, the speed increased to 5 m/sec.

Using the equation $v = u + at$, where v is the speed and t is the time, write down two linear equations in u and a.

Solve these equations to find values for u and a.

19. A farmer builds a long narrow pen for sheep using 60 m of fencing.

If he doubles the width and halves the length, he only needs to use 42 m of fencing.

Find the dimensions of the two pens.

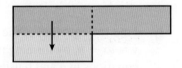

(As can be seen from the diagram, the areas of the two pens remain the same. Explain why less fencing is needed in the second pen.)

20. The curve $y = ax^2 + bx + c$ contains the points $(0, 1)$, $(2, 9)$ and $(4, 41)$.

   (i) Using these points, write three simultaneous equations in a, b and c.

   (ii) Hence solve the equations to find the values of a, b and c.

21. Solve the simultaneous equations.

   (i) $y - z = 3$

         $x - 2y + z = -4$

         $x + 2y = 11$

   (ii) $\dfrac{x}{3} + \dfrac{y}{2} - z = 7$

         $\dfrac{x}{4} - \dfrac{3y}{2} + \dfrac{z}{2} = -6$

         $\dfrac{x}{6} - \dfrac{y}{4} - \dfrac{z}{3} = 1$

22. The circle $x^2 + y^2 + ax + by + c = 0$ passes through the points $(1, 0)$, $(1, 2)$ and $(2, 1)$.

Find the values of a, b, and c.

Revision Exercise 1 (Core)

1. Simplify each of the following algebraic expressions.

   (i) $\dfrac{12m^2n^3}{(6m^4n^5)^2}$

   (ii) $\dfrac{3 + \dfrac{1}{x}}{\dfrac{5}{x} + 4}$

   (iii) $\dfrac{2 + \dfrac{x}{2}}{x^2 - 16}$

2. Solve for x and y:

   (i) $y = x + 4$
   $5y + 2x = 6$

   (ii) $3x + y = 7$
   $x^2 + y^2 = 13$

3. Using long division, find $x^3 - x^2 - 7x + 3 \div x - 3$.

4. Divide $3x^4 - 9x^2 + 27x - 66$ by $x - 2$.

5. Solve the equations.

   (i) $x^4 - 9x^2 = 0$

   (ii) $(2x - 1)^3(2 - x) = 0$

6. Given that $4x^2 + 20x + k$ is a perfect square, find k.

7. Find the integers a and b such that

   (i) $(3 - \sqrt{2})^2 = a - b\sqrt{2}$

   (ii) $\left(\dfrac{1 - \sqrt{2}}{1 + \sqrt{2}}\right) = a\sqrt{2} - b.$

8. Factorise $x^3 - 27$.

9. If $p(x - q)^2 + r = 2x^2 - 12x + 5$ for all values of x, find the values of p, q and r.

10. Solve the simultaneous equations $3x + 5y - z = -3$
    $2x + y - 3z = -9$
    $x + 3y + 2z = 7.$

11. Simplify $(b + 1)^3 - (b - 1)^3$.

12. Find the rule (i.e. the nth term) for each of the following quadratic patterns.

    (i) $3, 12, 27, 48, 75 \ldots$
    (ii) $5, 20, 45, 80, 125 \ldots$
    (iii) $0.5, 2, 4.5, 8, 12.5 \ldots$

13. Find the rule for the pattern $6, 12, 20, 30, 42$ using first and second differences. Hence find the 100th term of this pattern.

14. Three times the width of a certain rectangle exceeds twice the length by 3 cm. Four times the length is 12 cm more than its perimeter. Find the dimensions of the rectangle.

15. The formula for a spherical mirror of radius r cm is given by $\frac{1}{u} + \frac{1}{v} = \frac{2}{r}$, where u cm is the object distance and v cm is the image distance to the mirror.

The magnification in the mirror is given by $m = \frac{v - r}{r - u}$.

(i) Find r in terms of u and v.
(ii) Find m in terms of v and u only.

Revision Exercise 1 (Advanced)

1. By converting the number of squares in the following designs into a number pattern, write down a rule for the pattern. Use the rule to find out how many bricks are needed to build the 49th design.

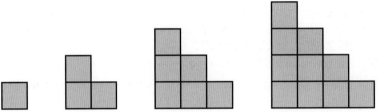

2. How much soil containing 55% sand needs to be added to 1 m³ of soil containing 25% sand to make soil containing 35% sand?

Hint: let x m³ be the amount of soil needed.

3. A metallurgist needs to make 8.4 kg of an alloy containing 50% gold. He is going to melt two metal alloys, one containing 60% gold with a second metal alloy that contains 40% gold.

(i) Let x kg and y kg be the amounts needed of each metal alloy. Write two equations linking the unknowns x and y.
(ii) Solve the equations to find the amount of each metal needed.

4. If, for all values of x, $(3p - 2t)x + r - 4t^2 = 0$, show that $r = 9p^2$.

5. Simplify the equation $\frac{x + y^2}{x^2} + \frac{x - 1}{x} = -1$ and hence find the ratio of x^2 to y^2.

6. In a chemistry class, a group of students need a 15% acid solution to complete a test. The lab only has 10% acid solution and 30% acid solution.
The students decide to mix the two solutions to get the 15% solution they require.
If the students need 10 litres of the new solution, find

(i) the number of litres of the 10% solution they require
(ii) the number of litres of the 30% solution they require.

7. Brian and Luke race over 50 metres. Brian runs so that it takes him a seconds to run 1 metre. Luke runs so that it takes him b seconds to run 1 metre. Luke wins the race by 1 second. The next day, they race again over 50 metres (and again at the same speeds) but Luke gives Brian a 3-metre start so that Brian only runs 47 metres. Luke wins this race by 0.1 seconds. Find

(i) the values of a and b　　(ii) Luke's speed.

Revision Exercise 1 (Extended-Response Questions)

1. A football club wanted to organise a family day as a fund-raiser.
   They decided to pre-sell tickets at €5.00 for adults and €2.50 for children aged 6 years or younger.
   Last year, when they held a similar event 13 000 attended.
   Last year they had only one ticket-price.
   The organisers wanted to estimate the expected revenue for the day. They decided to use the information obtained from the pre-sold tickets to arrive at this estimate.
   However, the members selling the tickets did not record the numbers of adult and children separately. It was known however that 548 tickets in total were sold and that €2460 was collected.

   (a) By setting up suitable equations, find
      (i) the number of adult tickets pre-sold
      (ii) the number of children tickets pre-sold
      (iii) the proportion of adult tickets sold.

   (b) Based on the same attendance for this year, estimate the revenue expected for the coming fund-raiser.

2. A factory makes two types of sofa. The standard sofa requires 2 hours of work in the manufacturing section and 1 hour in the finishing section.
   The deluxe sofa requires 2.5 hours in the manufacturing section and 1.5 hours of finishing work.
   Each day, there is a maximum of 48 hours of worker-time available in the manufacturing section and a maximum of 26 hours available in the finishing section.

   (i) If x standard sofas and y deluxe sofas are made per day, and the manufacturing section is worked to its capacity, explain why $2x + 2.5y = 48$.
   (ii) Find a second equation in x and y if the finishing section is also used to its capacity.
   (iii) How many of each sofa can be produced if each section is used to its capacity?

3. A closed rectangular box has a square base of length x cm and height h cm.
   The volume of the box is $40\,\text{cm}^3$.
   (i) Write an expression for h in terms of x.
   (ii) Show that the surface area, $S\,\text{cm}^2$, of this box is given by

   $$S = 2x^2 + \frac{160}{x}.$$

   (iii) Sketch a graph of S against x, for $0 \leqslant x \leqslant 10$.
   (iv) Estimate from the graph the possible values of x and h for which this box has a surface area of $72\,\text{cm}^2$.

4. A game made by a company sells for €11.50. The cost of production consists of an initial cost of €3500 and then €10.50 for each game produced.
   Let x be the number of games produced.

   (i) If $C(x)$ is the cost of producing x games, find an expression for $C(x)$ in terms of x.
   (ii) If $I(x)$ represents the income received for selling x games, find an expression for $I(x)$ in terms of x.

(iii) Plot the graphs of $I(x)$ and $C(x)$ on the same axes. (Scale the x-axis in units of 500 and the y-axis in units of 10,000.)

(iv) How many games need to be sold to recoup the production costs?

(v) Let $P = I - C$. What does P represent?

(vi) How many games need to be sold to make a profit of €2000?

5. Celine has 15 days to complete her quilt for sale at the country market. She can sew blue squares in the quilt at a rate of 4 squares per day and white squares at a rate of 7 squares per day. The quilt is to have a total of 96 squares. The blue fabric costs €0.80 per square and the white fabric costs €1.20 per square.

   (a) Find the cost of the quilt.

   (b) The 96 squares are used to form a rectangle whose length and width are to be in the ratio $3:2$.

   Celine decides to have a rectangle of blue squares in the centre of the quilt surrounded by white squares.

   Draw an arrangement of blue and white squares that creates a symmetrical design.

6. A small company manufactures wheelbarrows for the garden-supply market.
   The company has overheads of €30 000 per year.
   It costs €40 to manufacture each wheelbarrow.

   (i) Write a rule which determines the total cost, €C, of manufacturing x wheelbarrows per year.

   (ii) If the average production is 6000 wheelbarrows per year, what is the overall cost per wheelbarrow?

   (iii) How many wheelbarrows must be made so that the average cost is €46 per wheelbarrow?

   (iv) The wheelbarrows are sold to retailers at €80 each. Write a rule which determines the revenue, €R, from the sale of x wheelbarrows to the retailers.

   (v) Plot the graphs for C and R on the same axes, with the number of wheelbarrows, x, on the horizontal axis.

   (vi) What is the minimum number of wheelbarrows that have to be sold to make a profit each year?

   (vii) Write a rule that determines the profit, €P, from the manufacture and sale of x wheelbarrows.

7. Sean joins the end of a long queue to get into a concert. Every time one customer is admitted, Sean skips forward (a) two places or (b) three places.

   By completing the following table, form a pattern of numbers for the number of people admitted before Sean, based on the length of the queue.

   Using the pattern formed, find the number of people admitted before Sean if there are 70 people in the queue when he joins.

Number of people in the queue before Sean joined	(a) Number of people admitted before Sean. Skipping two	(b) Number of people admitted before Sean. Skipping three
4		
5		
6		
7		
8		
9		
10		
11		
12		
13		
14		
15		
70		

Key words

substitution   discriminant   completing the square   real and distinct

imaginary   rational   vertex   parabola   maximum   minimum   surd

irrational   rationalising the denominator

Section 2.1 Quadratic equations

As mentioned already, when the highest power of a variable in a polynomial is two, the resulting expression is called a quadratic expression.

The following are examples of quadratic equations:

(i) $3x^2 + 4x - 5 = 0$ (ii) $6 = 3t + 8t^2$ (iii) $A = 2\pi rh + 2\pi r^2$

Each quadratic equation has two solutions (or roots).

Solving quadratic equations

Techniques for solving quadratic equations include

(i) factorising   (ii) quadratic formula   (iii) graphical methods   (iv) substitution.

(i) Factorising methods (as in Chapter 1)

If an equation which equates to zero can be factorised, then at least one of its factors must equal zero.

If $(a)(b) = 0$, then $a = 0$ or $b = 0$.

Example 1

Use factors to solve   (i) $x^2 - 5x - 6 = 0$ (ii) $y^2 - 5y = 0$ (iii) $4t^2 - 100 = 0$

(i) $x^2 - 5x - 6 = 0$	(ii) $y^2 - 5y = 0$	(iii) $4t^2 - 100 = 0$
$(x - 6)(x + 1) = 0$	$y(y - 5) = 0$	$4(t^2 - 25) = 0$
$\therefore x - 6 = 0 \rightarrow x = 6$	$\therefore y = 0$	$4(t - 5)(t + 5) = 0$
or $x + 1 = 0 \rightarrow x = -1$	or $y - 5 = 0 \rightarrow y = +5$	$\therefore t - 5 = 0 \rightarrow t = +5$
		or $t + 5 = 0 \rightarrow t = -5$

Solutions (roots)   (i) $x = (6, -1)$ (ii) $y = (0, +5)$ (iii) $t = (+5, -5)$

(ii) Quadratic formula

The quadratic formula $x = \dfrac{-b \pm \sqrt{b^2 - 4ac}}{2a}$ can be used to solve any quadratic equation of the form $ax^2 + bx + c = 0$.

> If $ax^2 + bx + c = 0$,
>
> then $x = \dfrac{-b \pm \sqrt{b^2 - 4ac}}{2a}$

It is good practice to write out the coefficients a, b, and c separately before applying the formula.

Example 2

Solve $x - 6 = \dfrac{3}{x}$.   (Note: It is not always obvious that we are dealing with an equation of the form $ax^2 + bx + c = 0$.)

$$x - 6 = \frac{3}{x}$$

Rearranging $\rightarrow x^2 - 6x = 3 \Rightarrow x^2 - 6x - 3 = 0$

$\therefore$ $a = 1, b = -6, c = -3$, hence $x = \dfrac{-b \pm \sqrt{b^2 - 4ac}}{2a} = \dfrac{6 \pm \sqrt{(-6)^2 - 4(1)(-3)}}{2(1)}$

$$x = \frac{6 \pm \sqrt{48}}{2} = \frac{6 \pm 4\sqrt{3}}{2} = 3 \pm 2\sqrt{3}$$

$\therefore$ $x = 3 + 2\sqrt{3}$ or $x = 3 - 2\sqrt{3}$ are the roots (solutions) of the equation.

(iii) Graphical methods

Graphing the expression $y = x^2 - 5x + 1, 0 \leqslant x \leqslant 5$, we get the points
$(0, 1), (1, -3), (2, -5), (3, -5), (4, -3), (5, 1)$,
which, when plotted, produce the familiar
U-shaped curve.

To solve $y = x^2 - 5x + 1 = 0$ graphically, we must find the points on the curve where $y = 0$, i.e. the points $G(0.2, 0)$ and $H(4.8, 0)$.

$\therefore$ The roots are 0.2 and 4.8.

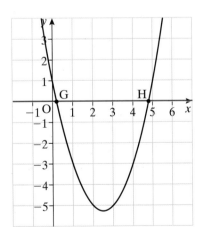

When the expression $y = -x^2 - 3x + 2$ is plotted, a ∩-shaped graph results.

Again, the roots of the equation $-x^2 - 3x + 2 = 0$ occur where the curve intersects the x-axis (i.e. where $y = 0$), i.e. the points $G(-3.6, 0)$ and $H(0.6, 0)$.

Graphical methods can only give approximate values for the roots of an equation.

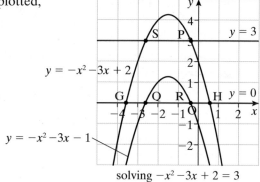

solving $-x^2 - 3x + 2 = 3$

To solve the equation $-x^2 - 3x + 2 = 3$, we can consider two approaches;

(i) To find the points on the curve $y = -x^2 - 3x + 2$ where $y = 3$ (i.e. S, P) **or**

(ii) To create the new curve $y = -x^2 - 3x + 2 - 3 = -x^2 - 3x - 1$ and solve $-x^2 - 3x - 1 = 0$.

Both are different curves but with the same solutions (roots), $Q = S = (x, y) \cong (-2.6, 0)$ and $P = R = (x, y) \cong (-0.4, 0)$.

(iv) Substitution

The following types of equations can be solved by choosing a suitable substitution which creates a new quadratic equation in standard form.

(i) $\left(t - \dfrac{6}{t}\right)^2 - 6\left(t - \dfrac{6}{t}\right) + 5 = 0$ let $u = \left(t - \dfrac{6}{t}\right)$,   then $u^2 - 6u + 5 = 0$

(ii) $x^4 + x^2 - 6 = 0$ let $u = x^2$,   then $u^2 + u - 6 = 0$

(iii) $2x + 3\sqrt{x} = 5$ let $u = \sqrt{x}$,   then $2u^2 + 3u - 5 = 0$

Once the values for u have been found, the values for x can then be obtained.

Example 3

Solve $x^4 + x^2 - 6 = 0$ for $x \in R$.

Let $u = x^2, \Rightarrow u^2 = x^4$.

$$x^4 + x^2 - 6 = 0 \Rightarrow u^2 + u - 6 = 0$$
$$\Rightarrow (u + 3)(u - 2) = 0$$
$$u + 3 = 0 \Rightarrow u = -3 \Rightarrow x^2 = -3 \Rightarrow x = \pm\sqrt{(-3)}$$
$$\textbf{or } \ u - 2 = 0 \Rightarrow u = 2 \Rightarrow x^2 = 2 \Rightarrow x = \pm\sqrt{(2)}$$

$x = \pm\sqrt{(-3)}$, two imaginary roots which are not required.

∴ $x = +\sqrt{(2)}, -\sqrt{(2)}$ are the solutions.

[Note: $(+\sqrt{(2)})^4 + (+\sqrt{(2)})^2 - 6 = 0$ and $(-\sqrt{(2)})^4 + (-\sqrt{(2)})^2 - 6 = 0$]

Example 4

Solve $2x + 3\sqrt{x} = 5$ for $x \in R$.

Let $u = \sqrt{x} \Rightarrow u^2 = x \Rightarrow 2x + 3\sqrt{x} = 5 \Rightarrow 2u^2 + 3u - 5 = 0$

$$\Rightarrow 2u^2 + 3u - 5 = (u - 1)(2u + 5) = 0$$

$$\Rightarrow u = 1 \text{ or } u = \frac{-5}{2}$$

Therefore, $\sqrt{x} = 1 \Rightarrow x = 1$

$$\text{or } \sqrt{x} = \frac{-5}{2} \Rightarrow x = \frac{25}{4}$$

Validating solutions; $x = 1 \Rightarrow 2x + 3\sqrt{x} = 2(1) + 3(\sqrt{1}) = 5$

Also, $x = \frac{25}{4} \Rightarrow 2x + 3\sqrt{x} = 2\left(\frac{25}{4}\right) + 3\left(\sqrt{\frac{25}{4}}\right) \neq 5$

Therefore the only real solution is $x = 1$.

Exercise 2.1

1. Use factors to solve the following equations:
   (a) (i) $(x - 4)(x + 5) = 0$ (ii) $x^2 - 7x + 12 = 0$ (iii) $x^2 - 4x - 5 = 0$
   (b) (i) $x^2 - 2x - 15 = 0$ (ii) $2x^2 + 7x - 15 = 0$ (iii) $3x^2 - 13x - 10 = 0$
   (c) (i) $5x^2 - 13x - 6 = 0$ (ii) $9x^2 + 3x - 20 = 0$ (iii) $8x^2 - 2x - 15 = 0$
   (d) (i) $x^2 - 9 = 0$ (ii) $3x^2 - 10x = 0$ (iii) $5x^2 - 8x = 0$
   (e) (i) $15 - 7x - 2x^2 = 0$ (ii) $10 + x - 3x^2 = 0$ (iii) $12 - 6x - 6x^2 = 0$
   (f) (i) $(x + 5)(x^2 - 16) = 0$ (ii) $(x - 3)(4x^2 - 4) = 0$
   (g) (i) $(x^2 - 4)(3x + 4) = 0$ (ii) $(2x + 8)(x^2 - 2x - 15) = 0$

2. Use the quadratic formula to solve each of the following, giving your answers correct to one place of decimals:
   (a) (i) $x^2 - 2x - 2 = 0$ (ii) $x^2 + 3x - 2 = 0$ (iii) $2x^2 - 6x + 3 = 0$
   (b) (i) $x^2 - 6x + 3 = 0$ (ii) $3x^2 - 8x + 1 = 0$ (iii) $2x^2 + 4x - 5 = 0$

3. Use the quadratic formula to solve each of the following, leaving your answers in surd form:
   (a) (i) $3x^2 + 4x - 5 = 0$ (ii) $2x^2 - 12x - 5 = 0$ (iii) $(2x - 3)^2 = 8$
   (b) (i) $x^2 + 4x - 8 = 0$ (ii) $5x^2 + 4x - 2 = 0$ (iii) $x^2 - x - 1 = 0$

4. Solve the following equations:
   (a) (i) $\dfrac{x + 7}{3} + \dfrac{2}{x} = 4$ (ii) $\dfrac{1}{x - 1} + \dfrac{4}{x} = 3$ (iii) $\dfrac{3}{x - 1} - \dfrac{2}{x + 1} = 1$

   (b) (i) $\dfrac{1}{x} + \dfrac{2}{x - 2} = 3$ (ii) $\dfrac{x + 2}{x - 4} = \dfrac{2x + 1}{x - 2}$ (iii) $\dfrac{2}{x - 2} + \dfrac{3}{x} = \dfrac{5}{x - 4}$

5. By finding a suitable substitution, solve each of the following:

(a) (i) $x^4 - 7x^2 + 10 = 0, x \in R$ (ii) $(x+1)^2 + 3(x+1) - 2 = 0$
    (iii) $x^4 - 2x^2 - 2 = 0$ (iv) $2(k-2)^2 - 3(k-2) - 4 = 0$

(b) (i) $(2y-1)^2 - 3(2y-1) - 28 = 0$ (ii) $(2y-3)^2 - 1 = 0$

(c) $\left(y + \dfrac{4}{y}\right)^2 - 9\left(y + \dfrac{4}{y}\right) + 20 = 0$

(d) $\left(2t - \dfrac{5}{t}\right)^2 - 12\left(2t - \dfrac{5}{t}\right) + 27 = 0$

6. Solve $2x^2 - \sqrt{3}x - 3 = 0$.

7. Using the graphs, find *approximate* solutions to each of the following equations.

(a) $x^2 + 3x - 5 = 0$ (b) $-x^2 - x + 1 = -2$ (c) $p(x) = 0$ (d) $g(x) > 0$
(e) $-x^2 - x + 1 = 0$ (f) $g(x) = f(x)$ (g) $h(x) = 5$ (h) $p(x) > h(x)$

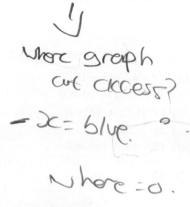

where graph
cut across?
- $x =$ blue.

where $= 0$.

-3
-1 ist

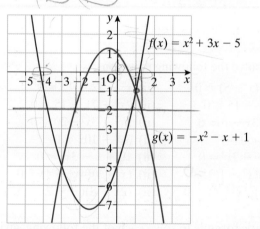

$f(x) = x^2 + 3x - 5$

$g(x) = -x^2 - x + 1$

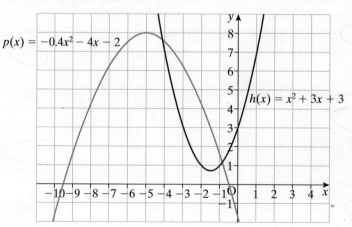

$p(x) = -0.4x^2 - 4x - 2$

$h(x) = x^2 + 3x + 3$

8. Using the graphs above, explain why $x^2 + 3x + 3 = 0$ has no real solutions.

9. If x_1 and x_2 are the roots of the equation $f(x) = 0.2x^2 + 5x + 9 = 0$ and $x_1 > x_2$, using the graph, find an approximate value for

   (a) $(x_2 - x_1)$
   (b) $(x_2 + x_1)$

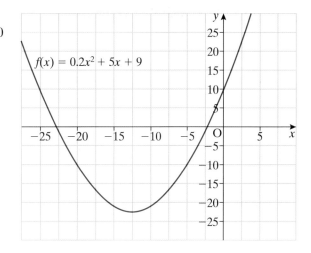

10. The graphs of the functions

    $$f(x) = 2x^2 - 3x - 2 \text{ and } g(x) = \frac{4x + 3}{5}$$

    are drawn as shown. Using the graphs, estimate the solutions of the following equations

    (a) $f(x) = 0$
    (b) $g(x) = 0$
    (c) $f(x) = g(x)$.

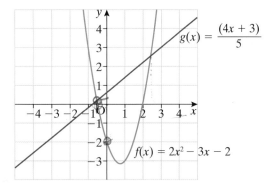

11. By using the substitution $u = \sqrt{x}$, solve each of the following equations. Explain why there is only one solution for each equation.

    (i) $2x + 3\sqrt{x} = 5$ (ii) $x - 3\sqrt{x} - 4 = 0$

    when you have a √ in an equation you must check the solution.

12. Solve each of the following equations, giving your answers in surd form.
    (i) $x^2 - \sqrt{7}x - 14 = 0$ (ii) $2x^2 + 7\sqrt{5}x + 15 = 0$

Section 2.2 Nature of quadratic roots

1. The discriminant

We have used the formula $x = \dfrac{-b \pm \sqrt{b^2 - 4ac}}{2a}$ to solve quadratic equations of

the form $ax^2 + bx + c = 0$, where $a, b, c \in R$.

The value of the expression $(b^2 - 4ac)$ will determine the nature of the roots of this equation and is called the **discriminant** of the equation.

$(b^2 - 4ac) = $ discriminant

2. Real and distinct roots

Real distinct roots occur when $(b^2 - 4ac) > 0$.

e.g. $3x^2 + 5x - 2 = 0$; $a = 3, b = 5, c = -2$;
$\therefore (b^2 - 4ac) = [5^2 - 4(3)(-2)] = 49 > 0$.

$$x = \frac{-b \pm \sqrt{b^2 - 4ac}}{2a} \rightarrow x = \frac{-5 \pm \sqrt{49}}{6}$$

$$\rightarrow x = \frac{-5 + 7}{6}, \frac{-5 - 7}{6} = (0.33, -2)$$

In this case, the graph crosses the x-axis at two distinct places, $(-2, 0)$ and $(0.33, 0)$.

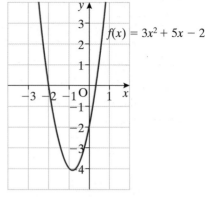

$$b^2 - 4ac > 0$$

3. Real and equal roots

Real and equal roots occur when $(b^2 - 4ac) = 0$.

e.g. $4x^2 - 12x + 9 = 0$; $a = 4, b = -12, c = 9$;
$\therefore (b^2 - 4ac) = [144 - 4(4)(9)] = 0$.

$$x = \frac{-b \pm \sqrt{b^2 - 4ac}}{2a} \rightarrow x = \frac{12 \pm \sqrt{(0)}}{2.4}$$

$$= \frac{12}{8} = \frac{3}{2}$$

Only one solution occurs and the graph touches the x-axis at this point $- A(\frac{3}{2}, 0)$.

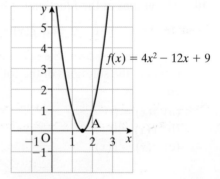

$$b^2 - 4ac = 0$$

4. Imaginary roots

Imaginary roots occur when $(b^2 - 4ac) < 0$.

e.g. $x^2 - 4x + 5 = 0$; $a = 1, b = -4, c = 5$;
$\therefore (b^2 - 4ac) = [16 - 4(1)(5)] = -4 < 0$.

$$x = \frac{-b \pm \sqrt{b^2 - 4ac}}{2a} \rightarrow x = \frac{4 \pm \sqrt{(-4)}}{2.1}$$

$$\rightarrow x = \frac{4 + \sqrt{-4}}{2}, \frac{4 - \sqrt{-4}}{2}$$

If we let $\sqrt{-1} = i$, then we can rewrite the solutions as follows:

$$x = \frac{4 + 2i}{2}, \frac{4 - 2i}{2} = 2 + i, 2 - i$$

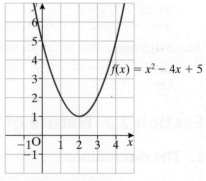

$$b^2 - 4ac < 0$$

These points cannot be represented on the real plane. (We will study these types of numbers further in the next chapter on complex numbers.)

We note that the curve does not cut (cross) the x-axis.

5. Rational roots

If $(b^2 - 4ac)$ is a perfect square then $\sqrt{(b^2 - 4ac)}$ is a rational number and this means that the equation has rational roots.

(Perfect squares are 1, 4, 9, 16, 25, 36, etc.)

e.g. $3x^2 + 5x + 2 = 0$; $a = 3, b=5, c = 2$;

$\therefore (b^2 - 4ac) = [25 - 4(3)(2)] = 1$ which is a perfect square.

$f(x) = 3x^2 + 5x + 2$

$$x = \frac{-b \pm \sqrt{b^2 - 4ac}}{2a} \Rightarrow x = \frac{-5 \pm \sqrt{(25 - 24)}}{2.3}$$

$$\Rightarrow x = \frac{-5 \pm 1}{6} = \frac{-6}{6}, \frac{-4}{6} = \left(-1, -\tfrac{2}{3}\right)$$

In summary

1. If $(b^2 - 4ac) > 0 \Rightarrow$ two different (distinct) real roots
2. If $(b^2 - 4ac) = 0 \Rightarrow$ two equal real roots
3. If $(b^2 - 4ac) < 0 \Rightarrow$ two imaginary roots
4. If $(b^2 - 4ac)$ is a perfect square $\rightarrow$ rational roots

Note: When the phrase "has **real roots**" is used in questions, then this must be taken to mean "has *either* two real distinct roots *or* two equal (repeated) roots".

Roots are **real** if $(b^2 - 4ac) \geqslant 0$

Example 1

Evaluate the discriminant of each of the following, stating whether the equation has

(i) two distinct real roots   (ii) two identical real roots   (iii) no real roots.

(a) $3x^2 + 5x - 1 = 0$ (b) $49x^2 + 42x + 9 = 0$
(c) $2x^2 + 8x + 9 = 0$ (d) $2x^2 + 7x + 4 = 0$

(a) $3x^2 + 5x - 1 = 0 \rightarrow a = 3, b = 5, c = -1.$
$\therefore (b^2 - 4ac) = 25 - 4(3)(-1) = 37 > 0$ $\therefore$ two distinct real roots.

(b) $49x^2 + 42x + 9 = 0 \rightarrow a = 49, b = 42, c = 9.$
$\therefore (b^2 - 4ac) = 1764 - 4(49)(9) = 0$ $\therefore$ two identical real roots.

(c) $2x^2 + 8x + 9 = 0 \rightarrow a = 2, b = 8, c = 9.$
$\therefore (b^2 - 4ac) = 64 - 4(2)(9) = -8 < 0$ $\therefore$ no real roots.

(d) $2x^2 + 7x + 4 = 0 \rightarrow a = 2, b = 7, c = 4.$
$\therefore (b^2 - 4ac) = 49 - 4(2)(4) = 17 > 0$ $\therefore$ two distinct real roots.

Example 2

Find the values of k so that $-8 + kx - 2x^2 = 0$ has equal roots.

$$-8 + kx - 2x^2 = 0 \Rightarrow a = -2, b = k, c = -8.$$

For equal roots, we have that $(b^2 - 4ac) = 0$

$\therefore \quad (b^2 - 4ac) = [k^2 - 4(-2)(-8)]$

$\therefore \quad k^2 - 64 = 0 \qquad \therefore \quad k = \pm 8$

Example 3

Given the equation $px^2 + (p + q)x + q = 0$.
  (i) Show that the roots are real for all values of p and $q \in R$.
  (ii) Show that the roots are rational.
  (iii) Hence find
        (a) the roots, in terms of p and q
        (b) the factors, in terms of p and q.

$$px^2 + (p + q)x + q = 0 \rightarrow a = p, b = (p + q), c = q.$$

(i) For real roots, we need to show that $(b^2 - 4ac) \geqslant 0$.

$$\begin{aligned} \therefore \quad (b^2 - 4ac) &= (p + q)^2 - 4(p)(q) \\ &= p^2 + 2pq + q^2 - 4pq \\ &= p^2 - 2pq + q^2 = (p - q)^2 \end{aligned}$$

Since (any real quantity)^2 cannot be negative $\Rightarrow (p - q)^2 \geqslant 0$.

$\therefore \quad (b^2 - 4ac) \geqslant 0$

$\therefore \quad$ the roots are real.

(ii) For rational roots, $(b^2 - 4ac)$ must be a perfect square.

Since $(b^2 - 4ac) = (p - q)^2$, i.e. a perfect square,

$\therefore \quad$ the roots are also rational.

(iii) (a) The roots are $x = \dfrac{-b \pm \sqrt{b^2 - 4ac}}{2a} = \dfrac{-(p + q) \pm \sqrt{(p - q)^2}}{2p}$

$$= \dfrac{-(p + q) \pm (p - q)}{2p}$$

$$\therefore \quad x = \left(\dfrac{-2q}{2p}, \dfrac{-2p}{2p}\right) = \left(\dfrac{-q}{p}, -1\right)$$

(b) The factors are $x + \dfrac{q}{p}$ and $x + 1$,

i.e. $\dfrac{(xp + q)}{p}$ and $(x + 1)$.

Exercise 2.2

1. By inspection, state which of the curves – f, g and h – have

   (i) real and distinct roots
   (ii) real and equal roots
   (iii) imaginary roots.
   (iv) In the case of real roots, estimate from the graph the roots of each equation.

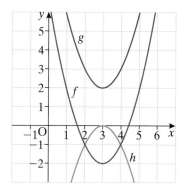

2. The curve shown has equation of the form
   $$ax^2 + bx + c = 0.$$

   Find, in terms of a, b, and c, the coordinates of the points A and B.

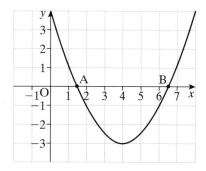

3. Find the discriminant of each of the following equations and state if the roots are
   (a) real and different   (b) real and equal   (c) imaginary.

   (i) $2x^2 + x + 5 = 0$ (ii) $-2x^2 + 3x + 1 = 0$ (iii) $3x^2 + 2x - 1 = 0$
   (iv) $-3 + 2x - x^2 = 0$ (v) $x^2 + 8x + 16 = 0$ (vi) $25 - 10x + x^2 = 0$

4. Draw a sketch of any quadratic curve that is positive for all values of x.
   Given that $3x^2 - kx + 12$ is positive for all values of x, find the range of possible values of k.

5. For what value(s) of k does each of the following equations have equal roots?
   (i) $x^2 - 10x + k = 0$ (ii) $4x^2 + kx + 9 = 0$ (iii) $x^2 - x(2k + 2) + 5k + 1 = 0$

6. Find the values of k if the equation $k^2x^2 + 2(k + 1)x + 4 = 0$ has equal roots.

7. Given that (any real number)$^2 \geqslant 0$, prove that the following equations have real roots for all values of $k \in R$.
   (i) $x^2 - 3kx - k^2 = 0$ (ii) $kx^2 + 2x + (2 - k) = 0$

8. Show that the roots of the equation $x^2 - 3x + 2 - c^2 = 0$ are real for all values of $c \in R$.

9. Prove that the equation $(k - 2)x^2 + 2x - k = 0$ has real roots, whatever the value of k.

10. Find the value of k for which the equation $(k - 2)x^2 + x(2k + 1) + k = 0$ has equal roots.

11. Show that the equation $(m + 3)x^2 + (6 - 2m)x + m - 1 = 0$ has equal roots if $m = \frac{3}{2}$.

12. If the equation $ax^2 + bx + 1 = 0$ has equal roots, express a in terms of b.
Hence write down the root of the equation in terms of b.

13. Show that the equation $x^2 - 2px + 3p^2 + q^2 = 0$ cannot have real roots for $p, q \in R$.

Section 2.3 Solving quadratic and linear equations

To find the point(s) of intersection between a line and a curve, we use the technique of **substitution**. We have used this method already when solving simultaneous linear equations.

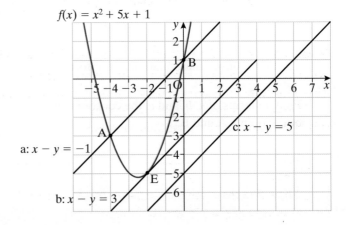

We note that in this case, the line may
(i)   intersect the curve at two points
(ii) intersect at one point
(iii) or not intersect the curve at all.

If there is just one point of intersection, the line is said to be a **tangent** to the curve.

The line $x - y = -1$ intersects the curve $y = x^2 + 5x + 1$ at two points, A(−4, −3) and B(0, 1).
The line $x - y = 3$ is a tangent to the curve $y = x^2 + 5x + 1$ at the point E(−2, −5).
The line $x - y = 5$ does not intersect the curve.

Example 1

Find the point(s) of intersection between
   (i) $x - y = -1$ (ii) $x - y = 3$ and the curve $y = x^2 + 5x + 1$.

(i) Since $x - y = -1$ Substituting $y = (1 + x)$ into $y = x^2 + 5x + 1$,
   $\rightarrow -y = -1 - x$ we get $(1 + x) = x^2 + 5x + 1$.
   $\rightarrow y = (1 + x)$ $\therefore \quad 0 = x^2 + 5x + 1 - 1 - x = x^2 + 4x$.
                                  $\therefore \quad 0 = x(x + 4)$
                                  $\therefore \quad (x + 4) = 0$ or $x = 0$,   i.e. $x = -4$ or 0.
                                  $\therefore \quad y = 1 - 4 = -3 \rightarrow (x, y) = (-4, -3)$
                                  and $y = 1 - 0 = 1 \rightarrow (x, y) = (0, 1)$
   $\therefore$ the points of intersection for $x - y = -1$ are $(-4, -3)$ and $(0, 1)$.

(ii) $x - y = 3$

$\rightarrow -y = 3 - x$

$\rightarrow y = (-3 + x)$

Substituting $y = (-3 + x)$ into $y = x^2 + 5x + 1$,

$\therefore \quad (-3 + x) = x^2 + 5x + 1$

$0 = x^2 + 5x + 1 + 3 - x = x^2 + 4x + 4$

$\therefore \quad (x + 2)(x + 2) = 0$

$\therefore \quad x = -2 \quad$ (a repeated solution)

$\therefore \quad y = -3 - 2 = -5 \rightarrow (x, y) = (-2, -5)$

$\therefore \quad$ the point of intersection for $x - y = 3$ is $(-2, -5)$.

$\therefore \quad x - y = 3$ is a **tangent** to the curve $y = x^2 + 5x + 1$ at the point $(-2, -5)$.

In summary, to find the point(s) of intersection between a line and a curve,

(i) isolate one of the variables in the equation of the line, e.g. $y = ax + b$.

(ii) Substitute this expression for y into the equation for the curve $y = cx^2 + dx + e$,
   i.e. $ax + b = cx^2 + dx + e$ and simplify.

(iii) Solve the resulting quadratic equation.

Example 2

Show that there are no point(s) of intersection between the line $x - y = 5$ and the curve $y = x^2 + 5x + 1$.

$x - y = 5$

$\rightarrow -y = 5 - x$

$\rightarrow \quad y = (-5 + x)$

Substituting $y = (-5 + x)$ into $y = x^2 + 5x + 1$,
we get $(-5 + x) = x^2 + 5x + 1$.

$\therefore \quad 0 = x^2 + 5x + 1 + 5 - x$

$0 = x^2 + 4x + 6.$

If there are no points of intersection, this implies that $0 = x^2 + 4x + 6$ has no real roots.

$\therefore \quad (b^2 - 4ac) < 0$

$0 = x^2 + 4x + 6 \rightarrow a = +1, b = +4, c = +6.$

$\therefore \quad (b^2 - 4ac) = [4^2 - 4(1)(6)] = (16 - 24) = -8 < 0.$

$\therefore \quad$ the line $x - y = 5$ does not intersect the curve $y = x^2 + 5x + 1$.

Exercise 2.3

Solve the following pairs of simultaneous equations, one linear and one quadratic.

1. $y = x^2$
   $2x + y = 3$

2. $x^2 + y^2 = 5$
   $x - y + 1 = 0$

3. $4x^2 - y = 0$
   $2x + y = 2$

4. $y = x^2 - 6x + 5$
   $x + y - 1 = 0$

5. $x^2 + y^2 = 25$
   $x + y = 7$

6. $3x^2 - y^2 = 3$
   $2x - y = 1$

7. $y = x^2 - 4x + 6$
   $y = 3x - 4$

8. $x^2 + y^2 - 4x + 2 = 0$
   $x + y - 4 = 0$

9. $x^2 + 4y^2 = 4$
   $x + 2y - 2 = 0$

y in terms of x

10. $xy = 4$
$2x - y + 2 = 0$

11. $y^2 + xy = 2$
$2x + y = 3$

12. $x^2 + y^2 + 2x - 4y + 3 = 0$
$x - y + 3 = 0$

13. $s = 2t - 1$
$3t^2 - 2ts + s^2 = 9$

14. $2s^2 = t^2 + 1$
$2s = t - 3$

15. $2t - 3s = 1$
$t^2 + ts - 4s^2 = 2$

Section 2.4 Quadratic and linear equations in context ——

Algebraic methods can be used to solve many real-life problems.
If we can represent an unknown or variable with a symbol, and write the relationship between the variables in the form of a linear or quadratic equation, then the resulting equations can be solved using the techniques discussed earlier.

Example 1

A right-angled triangle is to be made from a rope 24 m long. If the hypotenuse of the triangle, AB, has to be 10 m, find

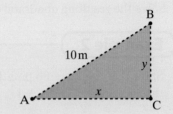

(i) an equation in terms of x and y for the perimeter of the triangle
(ii) an equation in terms of x and y for the hypotenuse of the triangle.
(iii) Solve the equations to find possible lengths of the base (x) and height (y) of the triangle.

(i) The perimeter of the triangle $= x + y + 10$.
$\Rightarrow x + y + 10 = 24 \Rightarrow x + y = 14$.

(ii) The (hypotenuse)$^2 = x^2 + y^2 = 10^2$.

(iii) Since $x + y = 14 \Rightarrow x = 14 - y$.

$\therefore \quad (14 - y)^2 + y^2 = 10^2$

$\therefore \quad 196 - 28y + y^2 + y^2 = 10^2$

$\therefore \quad 2y^2 - 28y + 96 = 0$

$\therefore \quad y^2 - 14y + 48 = 0$

$\qquad (y - 6)(y - 8) = 0$

$\therefore \quad y = 6 \text{ or } y = 8$

When $y = 6$
$\Rightarrow x = 14 - y = 14 - 6 = 8$.

Also, if $y = 8$
$\Rightarrow x = 14 - y = 14 - 8 = 6$.

$\therefore$ if the base is 8 m, the height is 6 m, or vice versa.

Example 2

A satellite is on a fact-finding mission to the moons of Pluto. The equation $x - y = 3$ represents its path. A comet is discovered moving in a curve in the same plane as the satellite. If the path of the comet is determined to be $x^2 + y^2 - 36x + 224 = 0$, decide if their paths will cross.

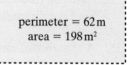

$x - y = 3$
(path of satellite)

$x^2 + y^2 - 36x + 224 = 0$
(path of comet)

If the paths are to collide, then the intersection of the two equations must have real solution(s).

  i.e. $b^2 - 4ac \geqslant 0$.

  If $x - y = 3$,
    then $y = x - 3$.   Substituting into $x^2 + y^2 - 36x + 224 = 0$,
                  we get $x^2 + (x - 3)^2 - 36x + 224 = 0$
                  $\therefore \quad 2x^2 - 42x + 233 = 0$ ... must have real solutions.

$\therefore \quad a = 2, b = -42, c = 233$.
$\therefore \quad b^2 - 4ac = [(-42)^2 - 4(2)(233)] = -100 < 0$

$\therefore \quad$ There are no real solutions and the paths do not cross.

Exercise 2.4

1. Find the values of two consecutive numbers, the sum of the squares of which equals 61.

2. Find two consecutive **even** numbers, the sum of the squares of which equals 52.

3. 62 m of fencing is used to form a rectangular pen of area 198 m².

   (i) Find two equations linking the length and width of the rectangle.

   (ii) Solve the equations to find the dimensions of the rectangle.

   perimeter = 62 m
   area = 198 m²

4. A right-angled triangle is to be made using three consecutive integer numbers as sides.

   Find the length of the perimeter of the triangle.

5. The distance s travelled by a car is given by the formula $s = 12t - t^2$.
   Find the two times at which the car passes a point 25 m away, giving your answers correct to two places of decimals.

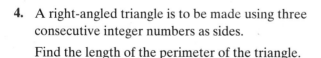

59

6. The square of a number is reduced by 15. The resulting value is twice the original number. Find the number(s).

7. A football is kicked up into the air. The height of the ball can be modelled by the equation $h = -16t^2 + 24t + 1$, where h = the height in metres and t = time in seconds.
   At what times will the ball be at a height of 6 m?

8. One side of a right-angled triangle is 4 cm longer than the other side. The hypotenuse is 20 cm long. Find the shortest side of the triangle.

9. The product of two consecutive odd integers is 1 less than four times their sum. Find the two integers.

10. The hypotenuse of a right-angled triangle is 6 cm longer than the shortest side. The third side is 3 cm longer than the shortest side. Find the length of the shortest side.

11. The length of a rectangular garden is 4 metres longer than its width. If the area of the garden is 60 m², find the dimensions of the garden.

12. Find three consecutive integers such that three times their sum equals the product of the larger two.

13. A circular swimming pool with a diameter of 28 metres has a wooden deck around its edge.
    If the deck has an area of 60π m², find the width of the deck.

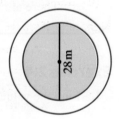

14. If one side of a square is doubled and the adjacent side is decreased by 2 cm, the resulting rectangle has an area that is 96 cm² larger than the original square. Find the dimensions of the rectangle.

15. A skateboard ramp is in the shape of a curve with equation
    $h = 0.1x^2 - x + 2.5$.
    Two platforms represent the starting and finishing points as shown.

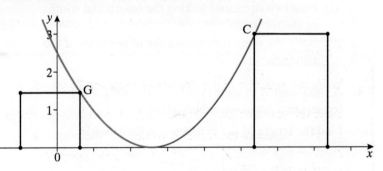

    If the starting point C is at a height of 3 m and G, the finishing point, is at a height of 1.5 m, calculate the distance between the bases of the two platforms, correct to two places of decimals.

60

16. A rocket travels along a path given by the equation $3t - s = 4$, where t represents time and s represents distance from the ground.
A comet is travelling along a path represented by the equation $2t^2 + s^2 = 43$.
Determine the point where the paths cross.
Suggest a reason why there is only one solution, i.e. one point of intersection.

17. A plane is travelling along a path given by the equation $x + 3y = 5$. A weather front is reported in the path of the plane. If the front is modelled using the equation $x^2 + 6y^2 = 40$, determine if the plane will cross this front. If the path of the plane is given by $x + 3y = k$, find the minimum value of k so that the plane will avoid the weather front.

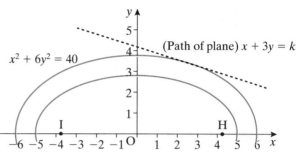

Section 2.5 Forming quadratic equations from their roots

If we know the roots of an equation, we can find the equation by

   (i) finding the factors of the equation

   (ii) multiplying the factors to get the equation.

Generally, if we let $x = r_1$ and $x = r_2$ be the roots of a quadratic equation,

then $(x - r_1)$ and $(x - r_2)$ are the factors

and $(x - r_1)(x - r_2) = 0$ is the equation.

i.e. $x^2 - xr_2 - xr_1 + r_1r_2 = 0$

$x^2 - x(r_2 + r_1) + r_1r_2 = 0.$

> Given r_1, r_2 as the roots of an equation, then the equation is
> $$x^2 - x(r_1 + r_2) + r_1r_2 = 0,$$
> i.e. $x^2 - x$ (sum of the roots) + product of the roots = 0.

Example 1

Write the equation of a curve whose roots are 7 and -5.

Since the equation has only two roots, it must be a quadratic equation.

∴ $x^2 - x$ (sum of the roots) + product of the roots = 0

∴ $x^2 - x[7 + (-5)] + [(7)(-5)] = 0$ is the equation.

∴ $x^2 - x(2) - 35 = 0$

The equation is $x^2 - 2x - 35 = 0.$

Example 2

If $x = \sqrt{3}$ and $x = \dfrac{-\sqrt{3}}{2}$ are the roots of a quadratic equation $ax^2 + bx + c = 0$, find a, b and c.

We have that $x^2 - x$ (sum of the roots) + product of the roots = 0.

$$\Rightarrow x^2 - x\left(\sqrt{3} + \frac{-\sqrt{3}}{2}\right) + \sqrt{3}\left(\frac{-\sqrt{3}}{2}\right) = 0 \text{ is the equation.}$$

$$\Rightarrow x^2 - x\left(\frac{2\sqrt{3}}{2} - \frac{\sqrt{3}}{2}\right) - \frac{3}{2} = 0$$

$$\Rightarrow x^2 - x\left(\frac{\sqrt{3}}{2}\right) - \frac{3}{2} = 0$$

$2x^2 - \sqrt{3}x - 3 = 0$ ... multiplying both sides of the equation by 2

$\therefore \quad a = 2, b = -\sqrt{3}$ and $c = -3$.

Exercise 2.5

1. State (i) the sum and (ii) the product of the roots of each of the following quadratic equations.

   (a) $x^2 + 9x + 4 = 0$ 　　　　　　(b) $x^2 - 2x - 5 = 0$
   (c) $x^2 - 7x + 2 = 0$ 　　　　　　(d) $x^2 - 9x - 3 = 0$
   (e) $2x^2 - 7x + 1 = 0$ 　　　　　　(f) $7x^2 + x - 1 = 0$
   (g) $3x^2 + 10x - 2 = 0$ 　　　　　(h) $5x^2 + 10x + 1 = 0$
   (i) $3 - 2x - x^2 = 0$ 　　　　　　(j) $-5 + 3x - 4x^2 = 0$

2. In the following table, you are given both the sum and the product of the roots of quadratic equations. In each case, find the quadratic equation in the form $ax^2 + bx + c = 0$, with a, b and c taking integer values.

	(a)	(b)	(c)	(d)	(e)	(f)	(g)	(h)
Sum	-3	6	7	$-\frac{2}{3}$	$-\frac{5}{2}$	$-\frac{3}{2}$	$-\frac{1}{4}$	$-1\frac{2}{3}$
Product	-1	-4	-5	$-\frac{7}{3}$	-2	-5	$-\frac{1}{3}$	$\frac{1}{2}$

3. Find the quadratic equations that have the following pairs of roots (r_1, r_2).

   (i) $(4, 6)$ 　　　(ii) $(2, -3)$ 　　　(iii) $(-5, -1)$ 　　　(iv) $(\sqrt{5}, 4)$

   (v) $(a, 3a)$ 　　(vi) $\left(\frac{2}{5}, \frac{3}{5}\right)$ 　　(vii) $\left(\frac{2}{b}, \frac{3}{b}\right)$ 　　(viii) $\left(\frac{5}{2}, \frac{3}{5}\right)$

Section 2.6 Max and Min of Quadratic graphs

The quadratic expression $x^2 - 6x + 11$ can be rewritten as

$$x^2 - 6x + 9 - 9 + 11$$
$$= (x - 3)(x - 3) - 9 + 11 = (x - 3)^2 + 2.$$
$$\therefore \quad x^2 - 6x + 11 = (x - 3)^2 + 2.$$

This is called **completing the square**.

This form of a quadratic expression can give us very useful information about the behaviour of the quadratic function.

(i) **Maximum or minimum values.**
At $x = 3, (x - 3) = 0$.
$\therefore (x - 3)^2 + 2 = 2$ is the minimum value of this expression.

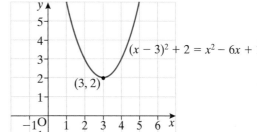

$(x - 3)^2 + 2 = x^2 - 6x + 11$

$(3, 2)$

(ii) **Real or imaginary roots.**
Let $(x - 3)^2 + 2 = 0$ to find the roots.
Then $(x - 3)^2 = -2$
$x - 3 = \pm\sqrt{-2}$
$x = 3 \pm \sqrt{-2} \Rightarrow$ Imaginary roots.

(iii) **Values of x which make the function positive or negative.**
$(x - 3)^2$ is positive for all $x \in R$.
$\therefore (x - 3)^2 + 2$ is positive for all $x \in R$.

(iv) Each graph has a turning point called a **vertex.**
This vertex is the maximum or minimum point of the graph.

(v) Each graph has an **axis of symmetry** parallel to the y-axis through its vertex.

(vi) The graph of a quadratic function is called a **parabola.**

Example 1

Complete the square on each of the following quadratic expressions.
Hence find the minimum value of each expression.
(i) $x^2 - 8x + 10$ (ii) $4x^2 + 4x + 2$

(i) $x^2 - 8x + 10$
$= x^2 - 8x + 16 - 16 + 10$
$= (x - 4)(x - 4) - 6$
$= (x - 4)^2 - 6$
Minimum value $= -6$

(ii) $4x^2 + 4x + 2$
$= 4(x^2 + x + \frac{1}{2})$
$= 4(x^2 + x + \frac{1}{4} - \frac{1}{4} + \frac{1}{2})$
$= 4[(x + \frac{1}{2})^2 + \frac{1}{4}]$
$= 4(x + \frac{1}{2})^2 + 1$
Minimum value $= +1$

Generally, to complete the square of expressions of the form $x^2 + bx + c$, **add and subtract (half the coefficient of x)^2** to the expression and isolate the perfect square portion.

$$x^2 + bx + c = \left(x + \frac{b}{2}\right)^2 - \left(\frac{b}{2}\right)^2 + c$$

i.e. $x^2 + bx + c = x^2 + bx + \left(\frac{b}{2}\right)^2 - \left(\frac{b}{2}\right)^2 + c = \left(x + \frac{b}{2}\right)^2 - \left(\frac{b}{2}\right)^2 + c$

Note: If the coefficient of x^2 is not 1, the x^2 coefficient must be factored out before proceeding, e.g.,

(i) $\quad x^2 + 2x + 5 = x^2 + 2x + 1 - 1 + 5$
$\qquad\qquad\qquad = (x + 1)^2 + 4$

(ii) $\quad 4 - 2x - x^2 = 4 - (x^2 + 2x) = 4 - (x^2 + 2x + 1 - 1) = 4 - [(x + 1)^2 - 1]$
$\qquad\qquad\qquad\qquad = 5 - (x + 1)^2$

(iii) $\quad 3x^2 - 3x + 2 = 3(x^2 - x + \frac{2}{3}) = 3(x^2 - x + \frac{1}{4} - \frac{1}{4} + \frac{2}{3})$
$\qquad\qquad\qquad\qquad\qquad = 3[(x - \frac{1}{2})^2 + \frac{5}{12}] = 3(x - \frac{1}{2})^2 + \frac{5}{4}$

All quadratic expressions $(ax^2 + bx + c)$ can be written in the form of

$\quad a(x - p)^2 + q$, a $\cup$-shaped graph

or $\quad q - a(x - p)^2$, a $\cap$-shaped graph.

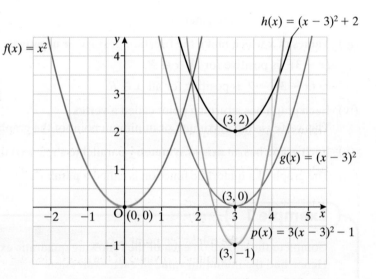

$h(x) = (x - 3)^2 + 2$
$f(x) = x^2$
$g(x) = (x - 3)^2$
$p(x) = 3(x - 3)^2 - 1$
$(3, 2)$
$(3, 0)$
$(0, 0)$
$(3, -1)$

ICT: Using a graphics calculator or computer software (e.g. Geogebra), sketches of the following curves can be compared, identifying the minimum points and the axes of symmetry for each.

	Min
$f(x) = x^2 = (x - 0)^2 + 0$	$(0, 0)$
$g(x) = x^2 - 6x + 9 = (x - 3)^2 + 0$	$(3, 0)$
$h(x) = x^2 - 6x + 11 = (x - 3)^2 + 2$	$(3, 2)$
$p(x) = 3x^2 - 18x + 26 = 3(x - 3)^2 - 1$	$(3, -1)$

The point (p, q) is the **minimum point** of the curve $a(x - p)^2 + q$.

At $x = p$, $(x - p) = 0$.

$\Rightarrow a(x - p)^2 + q = 0 + q = q$, the minimum value.

Similarly, a quadratic equation in the form $q - a(x - p)^2$ has a **maximum point** at (p, q) and a maximum value q at the point $x = p$.

When quadratic expressions can be written as $a(x - p)^2 + q$, there is a **minimum** point (p, q). When quadratic expressions can be written as $q - a(x - p)^2$, there is a **maximum** point (p, q).

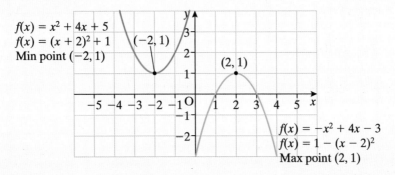

$f(x) = x^2 + 4x + 5$
$f(x) = (x + 2)^2 + 1$
Min point $(-2, 1)$

$f(x) = -x^2 + 4x - 3$
$f(x) = 1 - (x - 2)^2$
Max point $(2, 1)$

Example 2

Write the quadratic equation $x^2 + 4x + 1$ in the form $(x - p)^2 + q$ and hence,

(i) find the minimum point and minimum value of $x^2 + 4x + 1$

(ii) solve the equation $x^2 + 4x + 1 = 0$, leaving your answer in surd form.

(i) $x^2 + 4x + 1 = x^2 + 4x + \mathbf{4} - \mathbf{4} + 1$
$\qquad\qquad\quad = (x + 2)^2 - 3$

$\qquad\qquad \Rightarrow$ the minimum point is $(-2, -3)$
$\qquad\qquad \Rightarrow$ the minimum value of the expression is -3.

(ii) Solving $x^2 + 4x + 1 = 0$,
$\qquad\quad \Rightarrow (x + 2)^2 - 3 = 0$
$\qquad\quad \Rightarrow (x + 2)^2 = 3$
$\qquad\quad \Rightarrow x + 2 = \pm\sqrt{3}$
$\qquad\quad \Rightarrow x = -2 \pm \sqrt{3}$.

(**Note:** It should be verified that the same result is obtained using the quadratic formula.)

Example 3

(i) Write the equation of the graph provided in the form $y = q - a(x - p)^2$, where (p, q) is the maximum point of the curve and a is a constant.

(ii) By choosing any suitable point on the curve, find a.

(iii) Hence write the equation in the form $y = ax^2 + bx + c$.

(i) The maximum point $= (-1, 3) = (p, q)$.
$$y = q - a(x - p)^2$$
$$\therefore \quad y = 3 - a(x + 1)^2$$

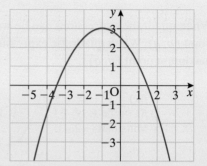

(ii) Selecting $(x, y) = (1, 1)$,
$$\Rightarrow 1 = 3 - a(1 + 1)^2$$
$$= 3 - 4a$$
$$\Rightarrow a = \tfrac{1}{2}$$

(iii) $\therefore \quad y = 3 - \left(\tfrac{1}{2}\right)(x + 1)^2$

$\therefore \quad y = 3 - \dfrac{x^2}{2} - x - \dfrac{1}{2}$

$= -\dfrac{x^2}{2} - x + 2\tfrac{1}{2}$

Exercise 2.6

1. Find the value of c that completes the square in each of the following:
   (i) $a^2 + 28a + c$
   (ii) $x^2 - 6x + c$
   (iii) $y^2 - 5y + c$

2. Complete the square in each of the following:
   (i) $x^2 - 8x - 3 = 0$
   (ii) $x^2 - 2x - 5 = 0$
   (iii) $x^2 - 2x + 1 = 0$

3. Write each of the following in the form $(x - p)^2 + q = 0$.
   (i) $x^2 + 4x - 6 = 0$
   (ii) $x^2 + 9x + 4 = 0$
   (iii) $x^2 - 7x - 3 = 0$

4. The graph of $y = a(x - p)^2 + q$ has a minimum point (p, q).
   By completing the square, find the minimum point of each of the following quadratic equations:
   (i) $2x^2 + 4x - 5 = 0$
   (ii) $3x^2 - 6x - 1 = 0$
   (iii) $4x^2 + x + 3 = 0$

5. Complete the square of the expression $x^2 - 6x + k$.
   Find the minimum value of k such that $x^2 - 6x + k$ is positive for all values of x.

6. Express $2x^2 - 12x + 7$ in the form $a(x - b)^2 + c$.

7. Given that $g(x) = x^2 + 8x + 20$, show that $g(x) \geqslant 4$ for all values of x.

8. (i) Write down the coordinates (p, q) of the minimum point of each of these graphs.
   (ii) Write the equation of each graph in the form
   (a) $y = (x - p)^2 + q$
   (b) $y = ax^2 + bx + c$.
   (iii) By picking a suitable point on each graph (other than the minimum point), verify each equation.

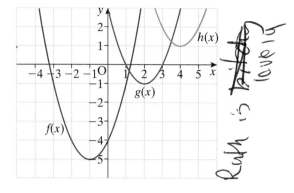

9. If $f(x) = x^2 + 4x + 7$, find
   (i) the smallest possible value of $f(x)$
   (ii) the value of x at which this smallest value occurs
   (iii) the greatest possible value of $\dfrac{1}{(x^2 + 4x + 7)}$.

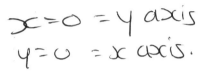

10. The path of a golf ball is given by the equation $y = -x^2 + 6x$.
By completing the square, find the maximum point of the path and hence the greatest height reached. Sketch the curve in the domain $0 < x < 6$ to validate your result.

11. Identify the graphs of the equations
   (i) $y = x^2 - 6x + 8$
   (ii) $y = x^2 - 6x + 9$
   (iii) $y = x^2 - 6x + 10$.

   Express each equation in the form
   $y = a(x - p)^2 + q$.

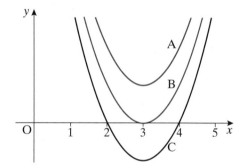

12. Each of the curves C and D can be represented by equations in the form
   $$p - a(x - q)^2.$$
   Find the values of p, a and q for each curve.

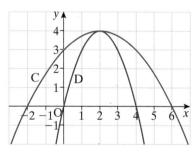

13. A parabola has x-axis intercepts of 6 and -3 and passes through the point $(1, 10)$. Find the equation of the parabola.

14. A parabola has a minimum vertex with coordinates $(-1, 3)$ and y-axis intercept 4. Find the equation of the parabola.

15. The path of a golf ball is given below.
    (i) Using the maximum point of the path (p, q), complete the equation
        $f(x) = q - 0.1(x - p)^2$ for this curve.
    (ii) Solve the equation $f(x) = 0$ to find the point from which the ball started, and the
         point where the ball finished on level ground (leaving your answer in square root
         form).
    (iii) Hence find the horizontal distance travelled by the ball, giving your answer in
          the form $a\sqrt{b}$.

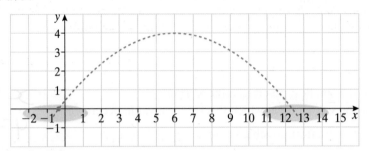

Section 2.7 Surds

A surd is a **square root** which cannot be reduced to a whole number, e.g. $\sqrt{2}, \sqrt{3}, \sqrt{5}, \sqrt{6}, \sqrt{7}, \ldots$

If $x^2 = 2$, then $x = \sqrt{2} \cong \pm 1.414213562\ldots$ A surd therefore is an **irrational number**, a
number which cannot be expressed as a fraction.

$\sqrt{1}, \sqrt{4}, \sqrt{9}, \sqrt{16}, \ldots$ are not surds since 1, 4, 9, 16, etc. are perfect squares and have square roots.

Note: $x = \pm\sqrt{2}$ is an exact answer.

$x = \pm 1.414\,213\,562$ is an approximate or corrected answer and should be only
given when asked for.

1. Reducing surds to their lowest form

$\sqrt{5}, \sqrt{6}, \sqrt{7}$ cannot be simplified further,

but $\sqrt{8} = \sqrt{4 \times 2} = \sqrt{4} \times \sqrt{2} = 2\sqrt{2}$,

since 8 has a factor that is a perfect square.

$$\sqrt{ab} = \sqrt{a} \times \sqrt{b}$$

2. Simplifying surd quotients

$$\sqrt{\frac{50}{64}} = \frac{\sqrt{50}}{\sqrt{64}} = \frac{\sqrt{25} \times \sqrt{2}}{8} = \frac{5\sqrt{2}}{8}$$

$$\sqrt{\frac{a}{b}} = \frac{\sqrt{a}}{\sqrt{b}}$$

3. Adding or subtracting surds

$2\sqrt{3} + 4\sqrt{3} = 6\sqrt{3}$.

$\sqrt{27} - \sqrt{12} = \sqrt{9 \times 3} - \sqrt{4 \times 3} = 3\sqrt{3} - 2\sqrt{3} = \sqrt{3}$.

$$a\sqrt{b} \pm c\sqrt{b} = (a \pm c)\sqrt{b}$$

4. Multiplying surds

$\sqrt{4} \times \sqrt{4} = (\sqrt{4})^2 = 4.$

$\sqrt{5} \times \sqrt{6} = \sqrt{30}.$

$(7 - \sqrt{2})(7 + \sqrt{2}) = 49 + 7\sqrt{2} - 7\sqrt{2} - 2 = 47.$

$$\sqrt{a} \times \sqrt{b} = \sqrt{ab}$$

5. Dividing by surds

It is normal practice not to leave a surd (an irrational number) in the denominator of a quotient, hence the practice of "**rationalising the denominator**".

$$\frac{5}{\sqrt{3}} = \frac{5}{\sqrt{3}} \cdot \frac{\sqrt{3}}{\sqrt{3}} = \frac{5\sqrt{3}}{3} \quad \left(\textbf{Note: } \text{Multiplying by } \frac{\sqrt{3}}{\sqrt{3}} \text{ is equivalent to multiplying by 1.} \right)$$

$$\frac{1}{7 - \sqrt{2}} = \frac{1}{7 - \sqrt{2}} \cdot \frac{7 + \sqrt{2}}{7 + \sqrt{2}}$$

$$= \frac{7 + \sqrt{2}}{7^2 - \sqrt{2}^2} = \frac{7 + \sqrt{2}}{47}$$

To rationalise the denominator:

$$\frac{1}{a - \sqrt{b}} = \frac{1}{a - \sqrt{b}} \cdot \frac{a + \sqrt{b}}{a + \sqrt{b}}$$

Example 1

(i) Express $\sqrt{80}$ in the form $a\sqrt{5}$, where a is an integer.

(ii) Express $(4 - \sqrt{5})^2$ in the form $b + c\sqrt{5}$, where b and c are integers.

(i) $\sqrt{80} = \sqrt{16 \times 5} = 4\sqrt{5}$

(ii) $(4 - \sqrt{5})^2 = (4 - \sqrt{5})(4 - \sqrt{5}) = 16 - 8\sqrt{5} + 5 = 21 - 8\sqrt{5}$

Example 2

Simplify (i) $\dfrac{\sqrt{12}}{5\sqrt{3} - \sqrt{27}}$ (ii) $\dfrac{7}{\sqrt{13} - \sqrt{11}}$

(i) $\dfrac{\sqrt{12}}{5\sqrt{3} - \sqrt{27}} = \dfrac{\sqrt{4 \times 3}}{5\sqrt{3} - \sqrt{9 \times 3}} = \dfrac{2\sqrt{3}}{5\sqrt{3} - 3\sqrt{3}} = \dfrac{2\sqrt{3}}{2\sqrt{3}} = 1$

(ii) $\dfrac{7}{\sqrt{13} - \sqrt{11}} = \dfrac{7}{\sqrt{13} - \sqrt{11}} \cdot \dfrac{\sqrt{13} + \sqrt{11}}{\sqrt{13} + \sqrt{11}} = \dfrac{7(\sqrt{13} + \sqrt{11})}{13 - 11} = \dfrac{7(\sqrt{13} + \sqrt{11})}{2}$

Exercise 2.7

1. Simplify each of the following:

   (i) $\sqrt{8}$ (ii) $\sqrt{27}$ (iii) $\sqrt{45}$ (iv) $\sqrt{200}$ (v) $3\sqrt{18}$

2. Express each of the following in its simplest form:

   (i) $2\sqrt{2} + 6\sqrt{2} - 3\sqrt{2}$ (ii) $2\sqrt{2} + \sqrt{18}$ (iii) $\sqrt{32} + \sqrt{18}$

   (iv) $\sqrt{27} + \sqrt{48} - 2\sqrt{3}$ (v) $\sqrt{8} + \sqrt{200} - \sqrt{18}$ (vi) $7\sqrt{5} + 2\sqrt{20} - \sqrt{80}$

3. In each of the following quotients, rationalise the denominator.

   (i) $\dfrac{1}{\sqrt{3}}$ (ii) $\dfrac{2}{\sqrt{8}}$ (iii) $\dfrac{2}{5\sqrt{2}}$ (iv) $\dfrac{20}{\sqrt{50}}$ (v) $\dfrac{8}{\sqrt{128}}$

4. Simplify each of the following:

   (i) $\sqrt{8} \times \sqrt{12}$ (ii) $3\sqrt{2} \times 5\sqrt{2}$ (iii) $\sqrt{2}(\sqrt{6} + 3\sqrt{2})$

   (iv) $(5 - \sqrt{3})(5 + \sqrt{3})$ (v) $(\sqrt{7} + \sqrt{5})(\sqrt{7} - \sqrt{5})$ (vi) $(a + 2\sqrt{b})(a - 2\sqrt{b})$

5. By rationalising the denominator, express each of the following in its simplest form.

   (i) $\dfrac{4}{\sqrt{5} + 1}$ (ii) $\dfrac{12}{3 - \sqrt{2}}$ (iii) $\dfrac{2 - \sqrt{5}}{2 + \sqrt{5}}$ (iv) $\dfrac{1}{\sqrt{8} - \sqrt{2}}$

6. Simplify each of the following.

   (i) $\dfrac{1}{\sqrt{2} - 1} - \dfrac{1}{\sqrt{2} + 1}$ (ii) $\dfrac{1}{2 + \sqrt{3}} + \dfrac{1}{2 - \sqrt{3}}$

7. Simplify

   (i) $(2\sqrt{3} - \sqrt{5})(2\sqrt{3} + \sqrt{5})$ (ii) $\dfrac{4}{2 - \sqrt{5}} + \dfrac{2}{2 + \sqrt{5}}$

8. Letting $X = \dfrac{4 + \sqrt{3}}{\sqrt{2}}$ and $Y = \dfrac{4 - \sqrt{3}}{\sqrt{2}}$, find in its simplest form:

   (i) $X + Y$ (ii) $X - Y$ (iii) XY (iv) $\dfrac{X}{Y}$

9. Show that $(2\sqrt{5} - 3\sqrt{2})(2\sqrt{5} + 3\sqrt{2}) = 2$.

10. Simplify $\dfrac{5}{2 + \sqrt{3}}$.

11. Simplify $\dfrac{(2 + \sqrt{2})(3 + \sqrt{5})(\sqrt{5} - 2)}{(\sqrt{5} - 1)(1 + \sqrt{2})}$.

Section 2.8 Algebraic surd equations

Expressions such as $\sqrt{2x + 1}$ occur often in algebra.

To solve the equation $\sqrt{2x + 1} = 5$, we proceed as follows.

$$(\sqrt{2x + 1})^2 = 5^2 \ \ldots \text{ squaring both sides to remove the square root}$$
$$2x + 1 = 25$$
$$2x = 24$$
$$\Rightarrow \quad x = 12$$

Note: With surds, it is important to check all solutions in the original equation as some may result in imaginary solutions.

At $x = 12$, $\sqrt{2x + 1} = \sqrt{2.12 + 1} = \sqrt{25} = 5$, which is correct.

Example 1

Solve $\dfrac{1}{\sqrt{x + 2}} - \dfrac{1}{\sqrt{4x + 8}} = 2$.

$$\frac{1}{\sqrt{x + 2}} - \frac{1}{\sqrt{4x + 8}} = 2$$

$$\frac{1}{\sqrt{x + 2}} - \frac{1}{\sqrt{4(x + 2)}} = 2 \ \ldots \text{ simplifying the denominator before getting a common denominator}$$

$$\frac{1}{\sqrt{x + 2}} - \frac{1}{2\sqrt{x + 2}} = 2$$

$$\frac{2}{2\sqrt{x + 2}} - \frac{1}{2\sqrt{x + 2}} = 2$$

$$\frac{2 - 1}{2\sqrt{x + 2}} = 2 \ \ldots \text{ getting a common denominator}$$

$$1 = 4(\sqrt{x + 2}) \ \ldots \text{ multiplying both sides by } 2\sqrt{x + 2}$$
$$1 = 16(x + 2) \ \ldots \text{ squaring both sides}$$
$$1 = 16x + 32$$
$$16x = -31 \qquad \therefore \quad x = \frac{-31}{16}$$

Checking the answer, we get

$$\frac{1}{\sqrt{\dfrac{-31}{16} + 2}} - \frac{1}{\sqrt{\dfrac{4(-31) + 8}{16}}} = \frac{1}{\sqrt{\dfrac{1}{16}}} - \frac{1}{\sqrt{\dfrac{1}{4}}} = 2 \ (\textbf{true}).$$

- If there is **only one surd**, isolate it on one side and then square both sides and solve.
- If there are **two surds**, move one to each side of the equation. Square both sides and isolate any remaining surds. Square both sides again to remove any remaining surd.
- Solve the resulting equation.
- Check your answers.

Example 2

Solve $\sqrt{5x + 6} - \sqrt{2x} = 2$.

$$\sqrt{5x + 6} - \sqrt{2x} = 2$$
$$\sqrt{5x + 6} = \sqrt{2x} + 2 \quad \text{... place one surd on each side}$$
$$(\sqrt{5x + 6})^2 = (\sqrt{2x} + 2)^2 \quad \text{... square both sides}$$
$$5x + 6 = 2x + 4\sqrt{2x} + 4$$
$$3x + 2 = 4\sqrt{2x} \quad \text{... isolate the surd on one side of the equation}$$
$$(3x + 2)^2 = (4\sqrt{2x})^2 \quad \text{... square both sides again}$$
$$9x^2 + 12x + 4 = (16)2x$$
$$9x^2 - 20x + 4 = 0$$
$$(9x - 2)(x - 2) = 0.$$
$$\therefore \quad x = 2 \text{ or } x = \tfrac{2}{9}$$

Note: It is important to check the validity of both solutions in the original equation,

i.e. $\sqrt{5.2 + 6} = \sqrt{2.2} + 2$ and $\sqrt{5.\tfrac{2}{9} + 6} = \sqrt{2.\tfrac{2}{9}} + 2$

$4 = 4$ **(true)** $\qquad \sqrt{\tfrac{64}{9}} = \sqrt{\tfrac{4}{9}} + 2$

$$\tfrac{8}{3} = \tfrac{2}{3} + 2 = \tfrac{8}{3} \text{ (true)}$$

Exercise 2.8

1. One side of a rectangular park is $(x + 2)$ m long and the other $(x - 2)$ m wide. Find an expression for the length of the diagonal, leaving your answer in surd form.

2. (a) Find the length of the diagonal [AC] of the rectangular field ABCD.

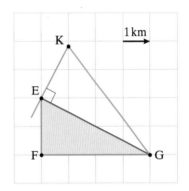

(b) One runner completes a full circuit ABCDA on a path, at a rate of $1.5\,\text{ms}^{-1}$.
A second runner runs from A to C and then back to A across the field at a rate of $1.4\,\text{ms}^{-1}$.

 (i) Express, in surd form, the difference in the distances travelled by the two runners.

 (ii) Calculate the time difference between the two runners, correct to the nearest second.

3. Martin starts at G and walks along a path towards a point F. At F, he takes the perpendicular path to E. He then takes the path EK, which is the same length as [EF] and is at right angles to [EG]. From K, he returns directly to G.
Find exactly, in surd form, the distance travelled by Martin.

4. Show that $\dfrac{-1 + \sqrt{3}}{1 + \sqrt{3}} = 2 - \sqrt{3}$.

5. Express $\dfrac{\sqrt{3}}{1 - \sqrt{3}} - \dfrac{1}{\sqrt{3}}$ as a single fraction and simplify by rationalising the denominator.

6. If $x = \sqrt{a} + \dfrac{1}{\sqrt{a}}$ and $y = \sqrt{a} - \dfrac{1}{\sqrt{a}}$ and $a > 0$, find (i) $x + y$ (ii) $x - y$.

 Hence find the value of $\sqrt{x^2 - y^2}$.

7. Solve the following equations and check your solutions in each case:

 (i) $\sqrt{2x + 1} = 3$ (ii) $\sqrt{3x + 10} = x$ (iii) $\sqrt{2x - 1} = \sqrt{x + 8}$

 (iv) $\sqrt{3x - 5} = x - 1$ (v) $\sqrt{2x + 5} = x + 1$ (vi) $\sqrt{2x^2 - 7} = x + 3$

8. Solve each of these equations and check each solution:

 (i) $\sqrt{x + 5} = 5 - \sqrt{x}$ (ii) $\sqrt{5x + 6} = \sqrt{2x} + 2$

 (iii) $\sqrt{x + 7} + \sqrt{x} = 7$ (iv) $\sqrt{3x - 2} = \sqrt{x - 2} + 2$

9. If $x = \sqrt{a} + \dfrac{1}{\sqrt{a}} + 1$ where $a > 0$, express $x^2 - 2x$ in terms of a.

10. Given that $(a + \sqrt{3})(b - \sqrt{3}) = 7 + 3\sqrt{3}$, and that a and b are positive integers, find the values of a and b.

11. The length of an open rectangular box is 2 m longer than its height. The width is 2 m shorter than its height. Let x be the height in metres and find an expression for
    (i) the diagonal [IC]
    (ii) the diagonal [ID].
    If $|ID| = \sqrt{56}$, find x.

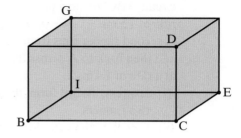

Section 2.9 The factor theorem

In Chapter 1 we revised techniques for factorising algebraic expressions.
The factor theorem is a more general technique that can be applied to expressions of higher orders.
Using long division, we can divide $f(x) = x^3 + 3x^2 - 4x - 12$ by $x + 3$ as before.

$$
\begin{array}{r}
x^2 - 4 \\
x + 3 \overline{)x^3 + 3x^2 - 4x - 12} \\
x^3 + 3x^2 \\
\hline
-4x - 12 \\
-4x - 12 \\
\hline
\text{no remainder}
\end{array}
$$

$\therefore \ f(x) = x^3 + 3x^2 - 4x - 12 = (x^2 - 4)(x + 3)$.

$\therefore$ the factors of $f(x)$ are $(x^2 - 4)$ and $(x + 3)$.

$\therefore$ the roots of $f(x)$ are $(x + 3) = 0 \Rightarrow x = -3$
and $(x^2 - 4) = 0 \Rightarrow x = \pm 2$.

Evaluating the function at $x = -3, +2, -2$;

$$f(-3) = (-3)^3 + 3(-3)^2 - 4(-3) - 12 = 0$$
$$f(-2) = (-2)^3 + 3(-2)^2 - 4(-2) - 12 = 0$$
$$f(2) = (2)^3 + 3(2)^2 - 4(2) - 12 = 0 \text{, as we would expect of every root.}$$

Generalising this for every polynomial $f(x)$; if $f(k) = 0$, then $x - k$ is a factor.

Conversely, if $x - k$ is a factor, then $f(k) = 0$.

> **The Factor Theorem:**
>
> If $f(k) = 0$, then $(x - k)$ is a factor.
>
> Conversely, if $(x - k)$ is a factor, then $f(k) = 0$.
>
> Also, if $(ax - k)$ is a factor, then $f\left(\dfrac{k}{a}\right) = 0$.

Example 1

Show that $(2x - 3)$ is a factor of $2x^3 - 5x^2 + 5x - 3$.

Given $(2x - 3)$ is a factor, then $(2x - 3) = 0$ is a root, i.e. $x = \frac{3}{2}$ is a root.
If $(2x - 3)$ is a factor, then $f(\frac{3}{2})$ must equal 0.

$$f(x) = 2x^3 - 5x^2 + 5x - 3$$
$$f(\tfrac{3}{2}) = 2(\tfrac{3}{2})^3 - 5(\tfrac{3}{2})^2 + 5(\tfrac{3}{2}) + 3 = (\tfrac{27}{4}) - (\tfrac{45}{4}) + (\tfrac{15}{2}) - 3 = 0.$$

$\therefore$ $(2x - 3)$ is a factor of $f(x) = 2x^3 - 5x^2 + 5x - 3$.

Example 2

If $(x - 2)$ and $(x + 1)$ are both factors of $ax^3 + 3x^2 - 9x + b$, find the values a and b.

If $(x - 2)$ is a factor, then $f(2) = 0$.
If $(x + 1)$ is a factor, then $f(-1) = 0$.

(i) $f(2) = a(2)^3 + 3(2)^2 - 9(2) + b = 0$

$\Rightarrow a.8 + 3.4 - 18 + b = 0$

$\Rightarrow 8a + 12 - 18 + b = 0$

$\Rightarrow 8a + b = 6$

Using simultaneous equations,

$\Rightarrow 8a + b = 6$

$ a - b = 12$

$ 9a = 18$

$ a = 2$

(ii) $f(-1) = a(-1)^3 + 3(-1)^2 - 9(-1) + b = 0$

$\Rightarrow a(-1) + 3.1 + 9 + b = 0$

$\Rightarrow -a + 3 + 9 + b = 0$

$\Rightarrow -a + b = -12$

$\Rightarrow a - b = 12$

$\therefore$ $a = 2$ and $b = -10$.

1. Factorising cubic expressions

We can now use the **factor theorem** to factorise higher-order polynomials, e.g. cubic polynomials of the form $f(x) = ax^3 + bx^2 + cx + d$ that have at least one integer root.

Using trial and error, we evaluate $f(0), f(1), f(-1), f(2), f(-2), f(3) \ldots$ etc., until we get a value of zero.
This is the integer root.

If $f(-2) = 0$, then $(x + 2)$ is a factor.
If $f(3) = 0$, then $(x - 3)$ is a factor.

Dividing by this factor produces a quadratic expression which can be factorised separately using factor pairs or using the quadratic formula.

Example 3

Factorise $f(x) = 2x^3 + x^2 - 13x + 6$.

$f(x) = 2x^3 + x^2 - 13x + 6$

$f(0) = 0 + 0 - 0 + 6 = 6 \neq 0$

$f(1) = 2(1)^3 + (1)^2 - 13(1) + 6 = -4 \neq 0$

$f(-1) = 2(-1)^3 + (-1)^2 - 13(-1) + 6$
$\qquad = +18 \neq 0$

$f(2) = 2(2)^3 + (2)^2 - 13(2) + 6 = 0$

$\therefore \quad (x - 2)$ is a factor.

Dividing $2x^3 + x^2 - 13x + 6$ by $(x - 2)$,

$$
\begin{array}{r}
2x^2 + 5x - 3 \\
x - 2 \overline{)2x^3 + x^2 - 13x + 6} \\
2x^3 - 4x^2 \\
\hline
5x^2 - 13x + 6 \\
5x^2 - 10x \\
\hline
-3x + 6 \\
-3x + 6 \\
\hline
0 + 0
\end{array}
$$

$\Rightarrow$ the factors of $f(x)$ are $(x - 2)(2x^2 + 5x - 3)$

$\Rightarrow$ the factors of $f(x)$ are $(x - 2)(x + 3)(2x - 1)$.

2. Solving cubic equations

To solve cubic equations of the form $f(x) = ax^3 + bx^2 + cx + d = 0$, we first find the factors as in the above example and then equate each factor to zero to find the roots(solutions).

Example 4

Solve the equation $\quad 2x^3 - 4x^2 - 22x + 24 = 0$.

Let $f(x) = 2x^3 - 4x^2 - 22x + 24$

$\Rightarrow f(0) = 2(0)^3 - 4(0)^2 - 22(0) + 24 = 24$

$\Rightarrow f(1) = 2(1)^3 - 4(1)^2 - 22(1) + 24 = 0$

$\Rightarrow (x - 1)$ is a factor.

The factors are $(x - 1)(2x^2 - 2x - 24)$

Factorising further ; $(x - 1)(2x + 6)(x - 4)$

Dividing we get,

$$
\begin{array}{r}
2x^2 - 2x - 24 \\
x - 1 \overline{)2x^3 - 4x^2 - 22x + 24} \\
2x^3 - 2x^2 \\
\hline
-2x^2 - 22x + 24 \\
-2x^2 + 2x \\
\hline
-24x + 24 \\
-24x + 24
\end{array}
$$

$\therefore \quad f(x) = 0 \Rightarrow (x - 1) = 0 \Rightarrow x = 1$.

Also, $(2x + 6) = 0 \Rightarrow x = -3$

and $(x - 4) = 0 \Rightarrow x = 4$.

The solutions are $x = (1, -3, 4)$

Exercise 2.9

1. Show that $(x - 3)$ is a factor of $x^2 - 8x + 15$.

2. Show that $(x - 1)$ is a factor of $x^3 - x^2 - 9x + 9$.

3. Show that $(x + 2)$ is a factor of $x^3 + 6x^2 + 11x + 6$.

4. Show that $(x - 2)$ is a factor of $2x^3 - 3x^2 - 12x + 20$.

5. Investigate if $(x - 2)$ is a factor of $x^3 - 5x^2 + 8x - 4$.

6. Show that $(2x - 1)$ is a factor of $2x^3 + 7x^2 + 2x - 3$.

7. Investigate if $(2x + 1)$ is a factor of $2x^3 - x^2 - 5x - 2$.

8. If $(x - 1)$ is a factor of $x^3 + kx^2 - x - 8$, find the value of k.

9. Find p if $(x + 2)$ is a factor of $x^3 + 6x^2 + px + 6$.

10. Show that $(x - 3)$ is a factor of $x^3 - 2x^2 - 5x + 6$ and find the other two factors.

11. Show that $(x + 3)$ is a factor of $x^3 - 2x^2 - 9x + 18$ and find the other two factors.

12. Use the *factor theorem* to factorise fully each of the following:
    (i) $x^3 - 4x^2 - x + 4$ (ii) $x^3 - 8x^2 + 19x - 12$
    (iii) $x^3 + 6x^2 - x - 30$ (iv) $3x^3 - 4x^2 - 3x + 4$
    (v) $2x^3 - 3x^2 - 8x - 3$ (vi) $2x^3 - 3x^2 - 12x + 20$.

13. Given $f(x) = 2x^3 + 13x^2 + 13x - 10$.
    Show that $f(-2) = 0$ and hence find the three factors of $f(x)$.

14. If $(x + 2)$ is a factor of $x^3 + ax^2 - x - 2$, find a and hence find the other two factors.

15. Factorise fully $x^3 - x^2 - 14x + 24$.
    Hence solve the equation $x^3 - x^2 - 14x + 24 = 0$.

16. Show that $x = 1$ is a root of the equation $x^3 + 5x^2 + 2x - 8 = 0$ and find the other two roots.

17. Solve each of the following equations
    (i) $x^3 - 4x^2 - x + 4$ (ii) $x^3 + 2x^2 - 11x - 12$
    (iii) $3x^3 - 4x^2 - 3x + 4$ (iv) $x^3 - 7x - 6$.

18. If $(x + 1)$ and $(x + 3)$ are both factors of $2x^3 + ax^2 + bx - 3$, find the values of a and b.
    Find the third factor and hence solve the equation $2x^3 + ax^2 + bx - 3 = 0$.

19. If $(x + 1)$ is a factor of $x^3 + 5x^2 + kx - 12$, find the value of k and the other two factors of the cubic expression.

20. If $(x + 2)$ and $(x - 3)$ are both factors of $2x^3 + ax^2 - 17x + b$, find the values of a and b.

Hence find the third factor.

21. Given that the expression $ax^3 + 8x^2 + bx + 6$ is exactly divisible by $x^2 - 2x - 3$, find the values of a and b.

Hence solve the equation $ax^3 + 8x^2 + bx + 6 = 0$.

22. Solve the following equations for x:

(i) $ax^3 - b = c$ 　　　　　　　　　(ii) $a(x + b)^3 = c$

Section 2.10 Graphs of cubic polynomials

The coefficients of a cubic polynomial $f(x) = ax^3 + bx^2 + cx + d$ determine the final shape of each graph. Some important features need to be noted and emphasised.

ICT: *Input* each of the following functions using a graphics calculator or computer software (e.g. Geogebra). Examine the effect of changing coefficients on the shape of each graph.

Note: The factor form of each function is very suitable in some cases.

1. Three real roots

$f(x) = 2x^3 - 4x^2 - 22x + 24$
$f(x) = (x - 1)(2x + 6)(x - 4)$

This graph has three real roots, $-3, 1, 4$.

As the graph passes through a root, the value of the function changes from
$(-)^{ve}$ to $(+)^{ve}$ or $(+)^{ve}$ to $(-)^{ve}$.

The graph has two turning points, a local maximum and a local minimum.

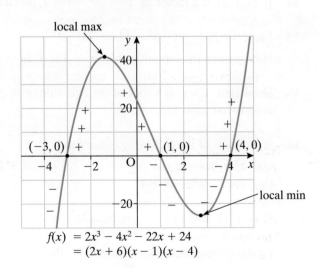

$$f(x) = 2x^3 - 4x^2 - 22x + 24$$
$$= (2x + 6)(x - 1)(x - 4)$$

2. Three real roots, two of which repeat

$f(x) = x^3 - x^2 - 8x + 12$
$\quad = (x + 3)(x - 2)^2$

This graph again has three real roots, $-3, 2, 2$, but one of the roots is repeated.

This graph only crosses the x-axis once because of the repeated root.

The graph has two turning points.

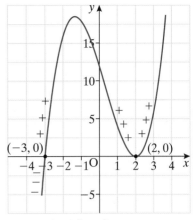

$f(x) = x^3 - x^2 - 8x + 12$
$\quad = (x + 3)(x - 2)(x - 2)$
$\quad = (x + 3)(x - 2)^2$

3. One real, two imaginary roots

$f(x) = x^3 - 2x - 4$
$\quad = (x - 2)(x^2 + 2x + 2)$
$\quad = (x - 2)(x + 1 - \sqrt{-1})(x + 1 + \sqrt{-1})$ ... using the
$\qquad\qquad\qquad\qquad\qquad\qquad\qquad\qquad$ quadratic formula

This polynomial has only one real root and two imaginary roots.

It crosses the x- axis once and has two turning points.

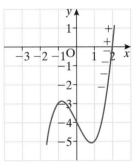

$f(x) = x^3 - 2x - 4$
$\quad = (x - 2)(x^2 + 2x + 2)$

4. Comparing $f(x) = x^3 - 3x^2 + 2x$ and $g(x) = 2x^3 - 6x^2 + 4x = 2f(x)$

Both polynomials have the same roots, $x = 0, 1, 2$.
$\therefore$ the polynomials have common factors (x), $(x - 1)$ and $(x - 2)$.

But $g(x)$ has an integer factor 2 as well that multiplies each value of the curve, except where the value is zero at the roots.

This integer factor acts as an amplification factor.

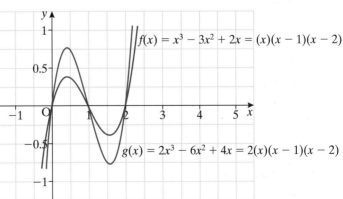

$f(x) = x^3 - 3x^2 + 2x = (x)(x - 1)(x - 2)$

$g(x) = 2x^3 - 6x^2 + 4x = 2(x)(x - 1)(x - 2)$

5. Comparing $f(x) = x^3 - 3x^2 + 2x$ and $g(x) = -x^3 + 3x^2 - 2x = -f(x)$

Again, both polynomials have the same roots and hence common factors. The graphs are symmetrical across the x-axis.

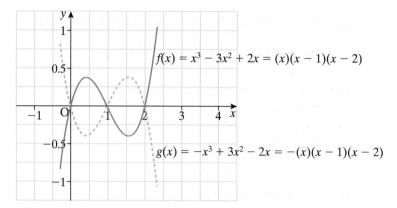

$f(x) = x^3 - 3x^2 + 2x = (x)(x - 1)(x - 2)$

$g(x) = -x^3 + 3x^2 - 2x = -(x)(x - 1)(x - 2)$

$g(x) = -x^3 + 3x^2 - 2x = -(x^3 - 3x^2 + 2x) = -f(x)$.

Multiplying by a minus inverts the graph.

6. The graphs of $f(x) = ax^3$

All the graphs pass through $(0, 0)$.
For $a > 0$, the graphs are all increasing, and as a increases, the graphs rise more steeply.
For $a < 0$, the graphs are decreasing.

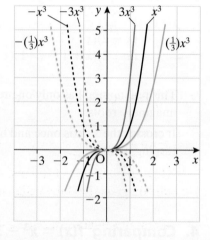

Note:

(i) If $f(x) = 3x^3$ and $g(x) = -3x^3$,
$\Rightarrow f(x) = -g(x)$, i.e. $f(x)$ is the reflection of $g(x)$ in the x-axis.

(ii) $f(-x) = g(x)$, i.e. $f(x)$ and $g(x)$ reflect each other in the y-axis.

Note: There are no local maximum or minimum points as in the previous graphs.

Summary:

(i) Every cubic polynomial crosses the x-axis at least once, i.e. has one real root.

(ii) Each root produces a factor of the polynomial.

(iii) Some polynomials have repeated roots.
The graph touches, but does not cross, the x-axis at this point.

(iv) If the coefficient of x^3 is positive, the graph starts below the x-axis, i.e. starts with a negative y-value and increases with increasing x-values.

(v) If the coefficient of x^3 is negative, the graph starts above the x-axis, i.e. starts with a positive y-value and decreases with increasing x-values.

(vi) Some cubic graphs have local maximum and minimum turning points.

(vii) When forming a polynomial from its roots, check for an integer factor.

Example 1

By examining the graph, find an expression for this cubic polynomial.

(i) The graph crosses the x-axis at $x = -2$.

(ii) $\Rightarrow x = -2$ is a root
$\Rightarrow (x + 2)$ is a factor.

(iii) The graph touches the x-axis at $x = 1$.
$\Rightarrow x = 1$ is a repeated root
$\Rightarrow (x - 1)^2$ is a factor.

(iv) The graph may contain an integer factor,
i.e. $f(x) = a(x + 2)(x - 1)^2$.

From the sketch of this graph, when $x = 0$, $f(x) = 4$.

∴ $4 = a(2)(1)^2 = 2a$

∴ $a = 2$.

∴ $f(x) = 2(x + 2)(x - 1)^2 = 2x^3 - 6x + 4$.

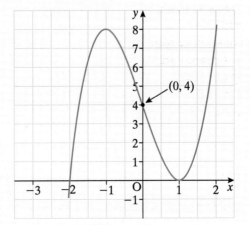

---

7. Higher-order polynomials

Example 2

The graph of the polynomial $f(x) = a(x + b)(x + c)(x + d)(x + d)$ is given in the diagram. Find the values of a, b, c and d.

From the diagram, the roots are $x = -2, -1, 3$.

A double root occurs at $x = 3$.

Hence the factors are $(x + 2), (x + 1), (x - 3)$ and $(x - 3)$.

∴ $f(x) = a(x + 2)(x + 1)(x - 3)(x - 3)$.

At $x = 0$, $f(x) = 18$.

∴ $18 = a(0 + 2)(0 + 1)(0 - 3)(0 - 3) = 18a$

∴ $a = 1$

∴ $a = 1, b = 2, c = 1, d = -3$.

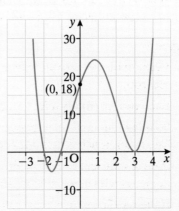

Exercise 2.10

1. Find a cubic expression for each of the following graphs, giving your answers in the form $f(x) = ax^3 + bx^2 + cx + d$.

(i)

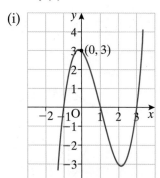

(ii)

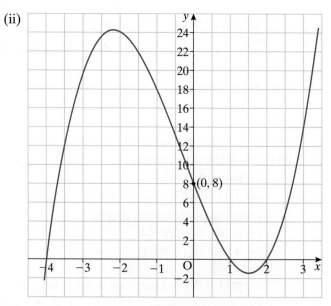

2. Write a polynomial expression for each of the following cubic graphs.

(i)

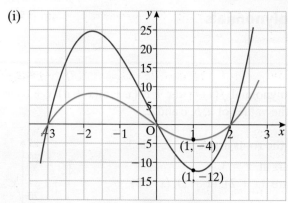

(ii)

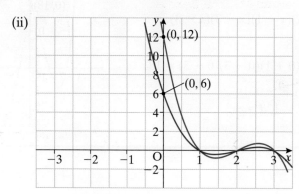

3. The graph of $y = f(x) = ax^3 + bx^2 + cx + d$ crosses the x-axis at $x = 1, x = -2$ and $x = \frac{1}{2}$. It also crosses the y-axis at the point $(0, 6)$.

   Find the coefficients a, b, c and d.

4. The factors of a given polynomial $f(x)$ are $(x - 3), (x + 1)$ and $(x + 2)$.

   If $f(x) = x^3 + ax^2 + bx + c$, find the values of a, b and c.

5. Identify the graphs of the three polynomial expressions,
   - (i) $x^3 + 2$
   - (ii) x^3
   - (iii) $2x^3$, given in this diagram.

   Find the coordinates of the point A.

   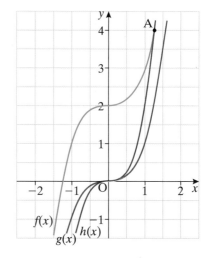

   ICT: Note that several answers in this exercise can be verified using a graphing calculator or computer software (e.g. Geogebra).

6. Given that $f(x) = (x)(x - 4)(x - 6)$, find the values of $f(2)$ and $f(5)$.

   Hence draw a rough sketch of the curve.

7. Given $f(x) = (x + 2)(x - 1)(x - 3)$, find the values of $f(0), f(\frac{1}{2})$ and $f(2)$.

   Hence draw a rough sketch of the curve.

8. The graph of a polynomial $f(x) = ax^4 + bx^3 + cx^2 + dx + e$ is given in the diagram.
   - (i) Find the factors of the expression.
   - (ii) Hence find the values of a, b, c, d and e.

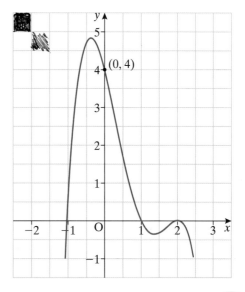

9. The graphs of two functions $f(x)$ and $g(x)$ are given in the following diagram.

   If $f(x) = ag(x)$,

   (i) find the value of a

   (ii) find equations for $f(x)$ and $g(x)$.

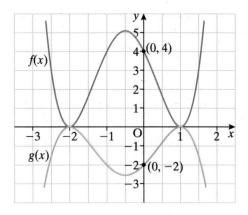

10. Write, in the form $ax^3 + bx^2 + cx + d = 0$, a cubic equation with the following roots:

    (i) $-1, 2, 5$ (ii) $-3, -1, 0$ (iii) $-2, \frac{1}{4}, 3$ (iv) $\frac{1}{2}, 2, 4$.

11. Find a cubic expression for each of the following curves.

    (i)

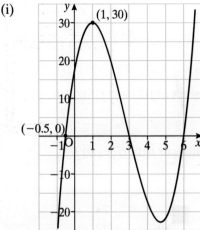

    (ii)

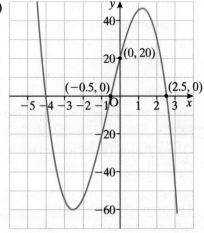

12. The diagram shows a graph of the function $f(x) = -3x^3 + 17x^2 + bx - 8$.

    The graph crosses the x-axis at the points $a, 2$ and 4.

    Find the values of a and b.

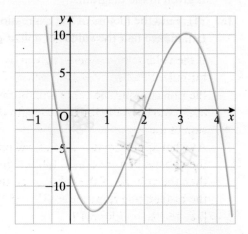

13. The diagram shows a graph of $f(x) = x^3 - x^2 - 2x$ and $g(x) = x$.

Use the graph to solve

    (i) $f(x) = 0$

    (ii) $f(x) = g(x)$.

    (iii) By solving the equations, correct to one place of decimals, check the accuracy of your answers.

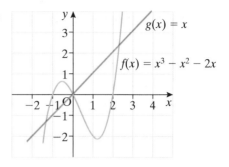

14. A box has dimensions x cm, $(x + 1)$ cm and $(x - 1)$ cm, as shown.

    (i) Find the volume of the box in terms of x.

    (ii) If the volume of the box is 24 cm³, and using the *factor theorem*, find the value of x.

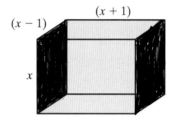

15. The volume of a cylinder is given by $V = \pi r^2 h$, where r is the radius and h is the height.

Given that the diameter is equal to the height, show that the volume can be written as

$$V = ah^3.$$

Taking $\pi = 3.14$, find the value of a correct to two places of decimals.

Using this function, calculate the volume of a cylinder with a diameter of 11 cm.

Find the diameter of a cylinder whose volume is 215.58 cm³, correct to one place of decimals.

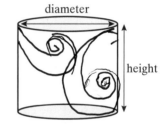

16. The contents of a spherical container of radius 3 cm completely fill a cube of side x cm.

If the volume of a sphere is given by the formula $V = \frac{4}{3}\pi x^3 \cong 4.19x^3$, where x is the radius, using the cubic graphs, find an approximate value for x, the length of the side of the cube.

At what approximate value of x would the volume of a sphere be 150 cm³ greater than the volume of the cube, given that the broken line represents $(V - 150)$ cm³ ? [i.e. $(4.19x^3 - 150)$ cm³]

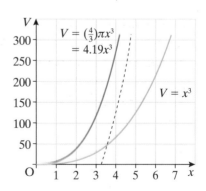

Revision Exercise 2 (Core)

1. Solve the equation $x^2 - 6x + 5 = 0$.

   Hence solve fully the equation

   $$\left(t - \frac{6}{t}\right)^2 - 6\left(t - \frac{6}{t}\right) + 5 = 0.$$

2. Find the roots of the equation $2(x + 1)(x - 4) - (x - 2)^2 = 0$, leaving your answer in surd form.

3. Find the range of values of p for which $px^2 + 2x + 1 = 0$ has no solutions.

4. Show that the roots of the equation $x^2 - (a + d)x + (ad - b^2) = 0$ are real.

5. Given that $(x + 1)$ and $(x - 2)$ are factors of $6x^4 - x^3 + ax^2 - 6x + b$, find the values of a and b.

6. Using trial and error, find
   (i) a root of the polynomial $f(x) = x^3 - 4x^2 - 11x + 30$
   (ii) the factors of $f(x)$, and
   (iii) hence solve the equation $x^3 - 4x^2 - 11x + 30 = 0$.

7. By using the discriminant, determine the nature of the roots of each of the following:
   (i) $x^2 - 2x - 5 = 0$ (ii) $x^2 - 4x + 6 = 0$ (iii) $-6 + 4x - x^2 = 0$

8. Using the substitution $y = 3^x$, write the equation $3^{2x} - 12(3^x) + 27 = 0$ in terms of y. Hence solve the equation for x.

Revision Exercise 2 (Advanced)

1. Express $2x^2 - 4x - 5$ in the form $a(x + h)^2 + k$ and hence,
   (i) solve the equation $2x^2 - 4x - 5 = 0$
   (ii) find the minimum point of this curve.

2. Expand $(2\sqrt{2} - \sqrt{3})^2$.

3. Simplify and then rationalise the denominator of $\dfrac{\sqrt{7} + \sqrt{5}}{\sqrt{80} + \sqrt{5}}$.

4. Solve $\sqrt{x + 2} = x - 4$.

5. The motion of a car is given by the equation $8t^2 + 4t = s$, where s is the distance travelled in metres.
   (i) By inspection, *estimate* the time, t, taken for the car to pass a point 10 metres away.
   (ii) Find, correct to two places of decimals, the time taken and explain why there is only one such time.
   (iii) Calculate the percentage error in correcting the answer to two places of decimals.

6. The standard error, σ, of the proportion p of a sample, is given by the formula

$\sigma = \dfrac{\sqrt{p(1+p)}}{n}$, where p is the proportion and n the number in the sample.

Using the quadratic formula, find p, the proportion, in terms of σ and n.

7. Complete the table by stating whether each quantity is positive $(+)^{ve}$ or negative $(-)^{ve}$.

	$k < 0$	$0 < k < \frac{1}{4}$	$k > \frac{1}{4}$
k	Negative		Positive
$4k$			
$4k - 1$			
$k(4k - 1)$			

Using this table, find the range of values of k so that the quadratic expression $x^2 + 4kx + k$ is positive for all values of x.

8. $a, b,$ and c are positive constants and the roots of $ax^2 + 2bx + c$ and $bx^2 + 2cx + a$ are all real and unequal (unique). Show that the roots of $cx^2 + 2ax + b = 0$ are not real.

9. Given $f(x) = -x^2 + 5x + 3$
and $g(x) = x^2 + 5x - 1$.

Find the coordinates of
the points A and B,
leaving your answers
in surd form.

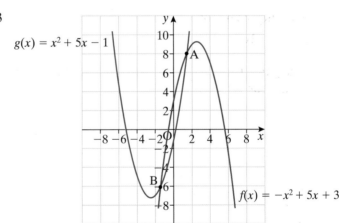

10. Find the range of values of k so that $kx^2 - 2kx - 3k - 12 = 0$ has real roots.

11. If r_1 and r_2 are the roots of the equation $x^2 - \sqrt{3}x - 6 = 0$, evaluate $r_1 r_2$.

12. Solve the simultaneous equations $3x + y = -1$ and $x^2 + y^2 = 53$.

13. If the length of a rectangular kitchen is half the square of its width and its perimeter is 48 m, find the dimensions of the kitchen.

14. If x is real, find the set of possible values of the function $y = \dfrac{x^2}{x + 1}$.

15. Find the equation of the quadratic curve that passes through the points
$(-2, -1), (1, 2), (3, -16)$.

16. (i) State what you understand by the "*Factor Theorem*" and its converse.

   (ii) Given that $f(x) = x^3 - 6x^2 + 11x - 6$, find the values of
   $f(0), f(1), f(2), f(3), f(4)$ and hence, solve the equation $x^3 - 6x^2 + 11x - 6 = 0$.

   (iii) Sketch the curve.

17. A section of the graph of a polynomial
$$f(x) = ax^3 + bx^2 + cx + d$$
is drawn in this diagram.

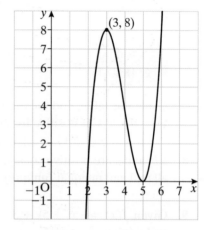

   (i) Find the roots of the equation $f(x) = 0$.

   (ii) Write an expression for $f(x)$ in terms of the factors of this polynomial.

   (iii) Find the values of a, b, c and d.

   (iv) Find an expression for the reflected image of this curve in the x-axis.

   (v) Find an expression for the reflected image of this curve in the y-axis.

Revision Exercise 2 (Extended-Response Questions)

1. A person who contracts a particular disease requires treatment with a certain drug. The concentration C of that drug in the bloodstream, t hours after taking a dose of the drug, is given by the equation $C(t) = 0.02t - at^3$. The concentration C is measured as 0.075, five hours after taking the first dose.

   (i) Find the value of the constant a.

   (ii) For how many hours is some of the drug still in the bloodstream?

   (iii) Explain why the graph of $C(t)$ is approximately linear up to $t = 10$ hours.

2. A large rectangular poster is subdivided into 6 purple squares of side x m, with dividing strips y m wide as shown.

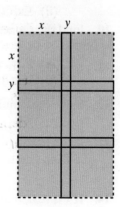

   (i) Find the area of the full poster in terms of x and y.

   (ii) If the area of the dividing strips can be written in the form $kxy + 2y^2$, find k.

   (iii) If the total area of the purple is 1.5 m², and the area of the dividing strips is 1 m², find x and hence find an equation for y and solve it.

3. A TY project consists of making a reinforced box, as shown in diagram. The plan for the box is as follows:

- Squares of side x cm are cut from the four corners of a rectangular piece of cardboard that measures 48 cm by 96 cm.
- The fold lines are indicated by dotted lines.
- Two flaps are then folded with a double thickness of card at each end.

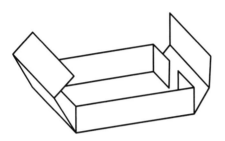
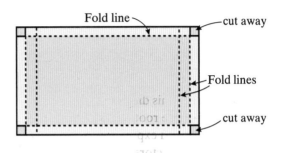

(a) Find an expression for the volume V of the open box.

(b) A section of the graph of this expression is given in the diagram shown.

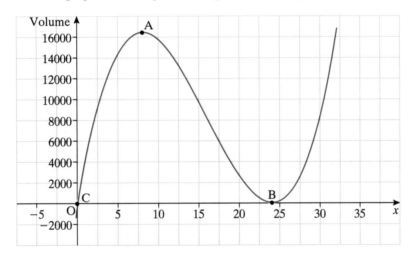

   (i) What domain set of values of x are valid for making this box?
   (ii) Explain the significance of the points A, B and C.
   (iii) Estimate from the graph the maximum volume of the box and the value of x at which this occurs.
   (iv) Find the volume of the box when $x = 10$ cm.
   (v) It is decided that $0 < x < 5$ cm. Find the maximum volume possible.
   (vi) If $5 \leqslant x \leqslant 15$ cm, what is the minimum volume of the box?

(c) The external surface area of the box can be given by the formula
$A = a(b - x)(c + x)$; find the values of a, b and c.

4. Riding stables need temporary additional paddock space for an upcoming horse show. There is sufficient funding to rent 120 m of temporary chain-link fencing. The plan is to form two paddocks with a shared fence running down the middle.

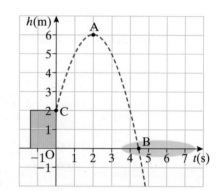

Paddock 1

Paddock 2

   (i) Show that the area of the paddocks can be represented by the quadratic equation $A = -\frac{3}{2}w^2 + 60w$, where A stands for the area and w for the width of the paddock.
   (ii) Find the roots of this equation and hence draw a rough sketch of the curve.
   (iii) By completing the square of the equation for the area A, find the maximum area of the paddock, and
   (iv) the value of w at which this maximum area occurs.
   (v) Hence find the dimensions of each of the paddocks.

5. A golf ball is hit from the top of a 2 m-high tee. If the height of the ball, h, above ground level is given by the equation $h = 2 + 4t - t^2$, where t is the time measured in seconds,

   (a) estimate from the graph:
       (i) the times, t, at which the ball is 5 m above ground level,
       (ii) the time the ball takes to land on the ground.

   (b) Find, correct to two places of decimals, the time taken by the ball to reach the ground.

   (c) The equation $h = 2 + 4t - t^2$ can be written in the form $q - (t - p)^2$ for all values of t, where q is the highest point of the ball above ground, at time p. Find (p, q).

6. You have managed a bike-rental scheme in a seaside holiday resort for the summer. You found that if you charged €12.00 per bike per day, then on average you did 36 rentals per day.
   For every 50 cent increase in the rental price, the average number of rentals decreased by 2 rentals per day.
   Complete the following table.

No. of price hikes	Price per rental	Number of rentals	Total income (I)
	€12	36	
1 price hike			
2 price hikes			
3 price hikes			
x price hikes			

(i) Write an equation in terms of x for the income I.

(ii) Write this equation in the form $q - (x - p)^2$, where (p, q) is the maximum point of the curve.

(iii) Use this information to find the maximum income.

(iv) What should you change to increase income?

7. The plan of a garden against a wall is shown. The rectangle GCED is of length y m and width x m. The garden is to have two borders, each a quarter circle, at each end. The radius of the circle is x m. A fence is to be erected along BCEF.

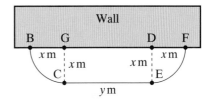

(a) Write an expression for the area A of the garden in terms of x and y.

(b) If the length of the fence is to be 100 m, find

(i) y in terms of x

(ii) A in terms of x

(iii) the maximum domain for the values of x for the area A in (ii).

(c) Find, correct to one place of decimals, the values of x for a garden of area 1000 m².

(d) It is decided to build the garden up to a height of $\frac{x}{50}$ m. If the length of the fence is 100 m, find correct to one place of decimals,

(i) the volume V m³ of soil needed in terms of x,

(ii) the volume of soil needed for a garden of area 1000 m²,

(iii) the value(s) of x for which 500 m³ of soil is required.

8. Examine the graph supplied.

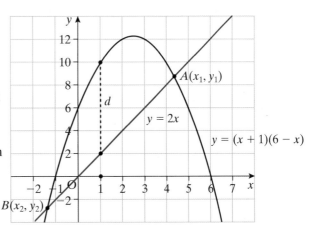

(a) Using the information contained in the graph, find the coordinates of the points $A(x_1, y_1)$ and $B(x_2, y_2)$, giving your answers in surd form.

(b) Write an expression for the "vertical distance", d, between the graphs, in terms of x.

(c) On separate axes, draw a sketch of the distance $d(x)$ between the two graphs.

(d) Write the equation for $d(x)$ in the form $y = q - a(x - p)^2$ by completing the square.

(e) Write down the coordinates of the maximum point (p, q) of this graph and interpret the meaning of the coordinates (p, q).

(f) Find the range of values of $d(x)$.

9. Examine the curve $y = \sqrt{x - b} + c$.

(i) Show that if the line $y = x$ intersects this curve at the point (a, a), then
$a^2 - a(2c + 1) + c^2 + b = 0$.

(ii) If the line is a tangent to the curve, show that $c = \dfrac{4b - 1}{4}$.

(iii) Sketch the graph $y = \sqrt{x} - \frac{1}{4}$ for the domain $0 \leqslant x \leqslant 4$, indicating the x and y intercepts.

(iv) Find the coordinates at which the line $y = x$ is a tangent to $y = \sqrt{x} - \frac{1}{4}$.

(v) Find the values of k for which $y = x + k$ meets the curve $y = \sqrt{x} - \frac{1}{4}$:

(a) twice   (b) once   (c) not at all.

Complex numbers

Section 3.1 Irrational numbers

In your study of maths so far, you will have met these number systems:

  (i)   Natural numbers: $N = \{1, 2, 3, 4, \ldots\ldots\}$ … whole positive numbers.

 (ii)   Integers: $Z = \{\ldots\ldots-3, -2, -1, 0, 1, 2, 3, \ldots\ldots\}$ … whole, positive and negative numbers including zero.

(iii)   Rational numbers: $Q = \{\frac{a}{b} \mid a, b \in Z, b \neq 0\}$, i.e. fractions, e.g. $\frac{1}{2}, \frac{7}{3}, \frac{-3}{5}, \frac{6}{1}, \frac{10}{9}, \frac{-4}{2}$ etc.

   Note: The set Q includes decimals that can be written as fractions.

If we try to solve the equation $x^2 + 2 = 7$, we get
$$x^2 = 7 - 2 = 5$$
$$x = \sqrt{5}$$

$\sqrt{5}$ is a number that is not an element of any of the above sets of numbers.

Using a calculator, we find $\sqrt{5} = 2.236067978\ldots\ldots$, a non-repeating, non-terminating decimal.

Because $\sqrt{5}$ cannot be written as a ratio (fraction), it is called an **irrational number**.

Examples of irrational numbers are $\sqrt{2}, \sqrt{3}, \sqrt{5}, \sqrt{6}, \sqrt{7}$ …

Note: We have already described these numbers as **surds**.

One of the most famous irrational numbers is π, the ratio of the circumference of a circle to its diameter.

$$\pi = 3.141592654\ldots\ldots$$

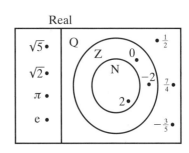

Another is Euler's number, **e**, the base number of the natural logarithms.

$$e = 2.71828182845\ldots\ldots$$

Definition: An irrational number is any real number that **cannot** be expressed in the form $\frac{a}{b}$, where a and b are integers, and b is not zero.

Since there can be no numbers common to the rational and irrational sets, together the sets of natural numbers, integers, rational and irrational numbers form the **partitioned** set of Real numbers (R).

It is clear that $N \subset Z \subset Q$.

Also, $R \setminus Q$ = the set of irrational numbers.

Note: Not all square roots are irrational numbers, e.g. $\sqrt{4} = 2$, $\sqrt{9} = 3$ etc.

As outlined in the section on surds, irrational numbers can be simplified by finding a pair of factors, one factor of which is a perfect square.

E.g. $\sqrt{18} = \sqrt{9 \times 2} = \sqrt{9} \times \sqrt{2} = 3\sqrt{2}$.

Example 1

Simplify each of the following, giving your answers in the form $a\sqrt{b}$, $a, b \in Z$.

   (i) $\sqrt{48} + \sqrt{75}$ (ii) $\sqrt{180} - \sqrt{20}$

(i)
$$\sqrt{48} = \sqrt{16 \times 3} = \sqrt{16} \times \sqrt{3} = 4\sqrt{3}$$
$$\sqrt{75} = \sqrt{25 \times 3} = \sqrt{25} \times \sqrt{3} = 5\sqrt{3}$$
$$\therefore \quad \sqrt{48} + \sqrt{75} = 4\sqrt{3} + 5\sqrt{3} = 9\sqrt{3}$$

(ii)
$$\sqrt{180} = \sqrt{36 \times 5} = 6\sqrt{5}$$
$$\sqrt{20} = \sqrt{4 \times 5} = 2\sqrt{5}$$
$$\therefore \quad \sqrt{180} - \sqrt{20} = 6\sqrt{5} - 2\sqrt{5} = 4\sqrt{5}$$

Constructing a line of length $\sqrt{2}$

Although $\sqrt{2} = 1.414214...$ is a non-terminating decimal, it is possible to construct a line of length $\sqrt{2}$ on the number line as the following example shows.

Example 2

Using a compass and straightedge only, construct a line segment of length $\sqrt{2}$ and hence mark $\sqrt{2}$ on the number line.

  (i) Using a straightedge, draw a line segment [AM].

  (ii) Starting at A, mark equal spaces 0, 1, 2... (A, B, C) using a compass.

  (iii) Using a compass, construct the perpendicular bisector of [AC], that is, draw a perpendicular line through B.

  (iv) Join D and E.

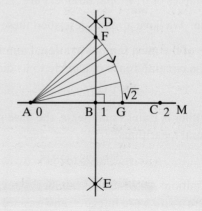

(v) Mark the point F on [DE] so that |AB| = |BF|.

(vi) Using A as the centre and |AF| as radius, draw an arc FG to the number line.

(vii) Mark G on the number line, $\sqrt{2}$.

Proof: Consider the triangle *ABF*:

$|AB| = 1, |BF| = 1, ABF = 90°$

Using Pythagoras' theorem: $|AF|^2 = |AB|^2 + |FB|^2$

$\therefore |AF|^2 = 1^2 + 1^2 = 2$

$\therefore |AF| = \sqrt{2} \Rightarrow |AG| = \sqrt{2}$

Note: Using similar constructions, other irrational numbers can be plotted on the number line.

  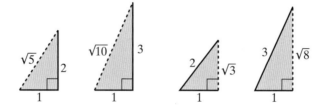

Example 3

Construct a line segment of length $\sqrt{3}$ on the number line.

(i) Mark a point A on a straight line AB.

(ii) Using a compass, mark equal spaces |AJ| and |JC| (each 1 unit) along AB.

(iii) Using A as centre and |AC| as radius, draw an arc.

(iv) Using C as centre and |CA| as radius, draw an arc.

(v) Join the points of intersection of the arcs HI.

(vi) From our geometry theorems, we know that HI is perpendicular to AB and bisects [AC] at J.

Consider the triangle AJH.

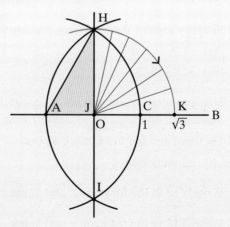

$$|AJ| = 1, |AH| = 2, \angle AJH = 90°$$

$$\therefore \quad |AH|^2 = |AJ|^2 + |JH|^2 \quad \text{...using Pythagroas's theorem}$$

$$\therefore \quad 2^2 = 1^2 + |JH|^2$$

$$\therefore \quad 4 = 1 + |JH|^2$$

$$\therefore \quad 3 = |JH|^2 => JH = \sqrt{3}$$

Using J as centre and |JH| as radius, draw an arc HK intersecting the horizontal line at K. $\quad |JK| = \sqrt{3}$

Exercise 3.1

1. By finding factors, one of which is a perfect square, write each of the following in its simplest form:

    (i) $\sqrt{18}$ (ii) $\sqrt{12}$ (iii) $\sqrt{45}$ (iv) $\sqrt{28}$

2. Simplify each of the following, giving your answer in the form $a\sqrt{b}, a, b \in Z$.

    (i) $\sqrt{18} + \sqrt{50}$ (ii) $\sqrt{48} + \sqrt{147}$

3. Given that N is the set of natural numbers,

         Z is the set of integers,

           Q is the set of rational numbers,

             and R is the set of real numbers, give two elements of each of the following sets:

    (i) $Z \backslash N$ (ii) $Q \backslash Z$ (iii) $R \backslash Q$

4. Describe in words each of the following sets:

    (i) Z (ii) $Q \backslash Z$ (iii) $Q \backslash N$ (iv) $R \backslash Z$ (v) $R \backslash Q$

5. Simplify each of the following, leaving your answer in the form $a\sqrt{b}, a, b \in Z$:

    (i) $\sqrt{125} - \sqrt{20}$ (ii) $\sqrt{32} - \sqrt{18} - \sqrt{8}$

    (iii) $3\sqrt{8} + 5\sqrt{2}$ (iv) $4\sqrt{18} - 2\sqrt{27} + 3\sqrt{3} - \sqrt{288}$

6. Using a compass and straightedge, construct two line segments each of length 12 cm. Mark each line segment in *units of 4 cm* (0, 1, 2, 3).

    On these number lines, mark a point

    (i) $\sqrt{3}$ units from 0   (ii) $\sqrt{2}$ units from 0.

7. Write $\sqrt{18}$ in the form $a\sqrt{2}$ and hence draw a line $\sqrt{18}$ in length.

8. Write $\sqrt{12}$ in the form $a\sqrt{3}$ and hence draw a line $\sqrt{12}$ in length.

9. Given a line segment [AB] of length $\sqrt{2}$, describe how to make a line segment of length $\sqrt{3}$ using a compass and straightedge only.

10. Find the length of the perimeter of this triangle.

Give your answer in the form $a\sqrt{b}$, $a, b \in N$.

11. Which of the following are irrational numbers:

$$\sqrt{3}, \ \pi, \ \tfrac{1}{3}, \ e, \ 0, \ \sqrt[5]{2}, \ \tfrac{22}{7}, \ \sqrt{36}$$

12. Find the length of each of the sides a, b, c, d, e, f and g.

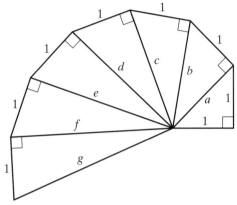

Which of these lengths is not an irrational number?

13. A stairs makes an angle of 45° with the horizontal.

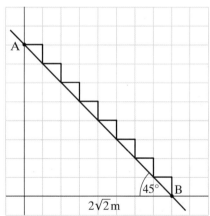

If the base of the stairs measures $2\sqrt{2}$ m, as shown, find the length of the carpet needed to cover the stairs from A to B. Give your answer in the form $a\sqrt{2}$.
If the angle of the stairs is increased to 60°, find how much extra carpet is needed.
Give your answer in the form $2(\sqrt{a} - \sqrt{b})$.

14. (i) Write down one value of x for which the expression $\sqrt{3 - x}$ is rational.

(ii) Describe in words the set of values of x for which the expression $\sqrt{3 - x}$ is rational.

Section 3.2 Complex numbers

To solve an equation such as $x^2 - 9 = 0$, we could proceed as follows:

$$x^2 - 9 = 0$$
$$x^2 = 9$$
$$x = \sqrt{9} = \pm 3$$

However, if $x^2 + 9 = 0$

$$x^2 = -9$$
$$x = \sqrt{-9}$$ and since no real number multiplied by itself gives -9, no real number can satisfy this equation.

To deal with the square root of a negative number, a new number $\sqrt{-1}$ is created. This number is called **i**.

Hence, $\sqrt{-9} = \sqrt{9 \times -1} = \sqrt{9} \times \sqrt{-1} = \pm 3i$.

Similarly, $\sqrt{-16} = \sqrt{16 \times -1} = \sqrt{16} \times \sqrt{-1} = \pm 4i$

and $\sqrt{-5} = \sqrt{5 \times -1} = \sqrt{5} \times \sqrt{-1} = \pm\sqrt{5}i$.

$$i = \sqrt{-1}$$
$$\Rightarrow i^2 = -1$$

Square roots of negative numbers are called **imaginary numbers** and are written in the form of bi, where b is a real number, e.g. $3i$.

Example 1

Solve the equation $x^2 + 25 = 0$.

$$x^2 + 25 = 0$$
$$x^2 = -25$$
$$x = \sqrt{-25} = \sqrt{25 \times -1} = \sqrt{25} \times \sqrt{-1}$$
$$x = \pm 5i$$

Example 2

Solve the equation $x^2 + 2x + 2 = 0$.

Using the quadratic formula, we have $a = 1, b = 2, c = 2$.

Hence, $x = \dfrac{-b \pm \sqrt{b^2 - 4ac}}{2a}$

$$x = \frac{-2 \pm \sqrt{2^2 - 4(1)(2)}}{2(1)}$$

$$x = \frac{-2 \pm \sqrt{-4}}{2} = \frac{-2 \pm \sqrt{4 \times -1}}{2} = \frac{-2 \pm 2i}{2}$$

$$x = -1 \pm i$$

Therefore, $x = -1 + i, -1 - i$.

Numbers such as $-1 + i$ are called **complex numbers** and are normally denoted by the letter z.

A complex number such as $z = 3 + 6i$, has two parts (dimensions); a **real part** and an **imaginary part**.

The first part of this complex number is the real constant 3.

The second part of this complex number is imaginary; the real constant 6 multiplied by i.

3 is referred to as the real part and is given by **Re(z) = 3**.

6 is referred to as the imaginary part and is given by **Im(z) = 6**.

The set of complex numbers is denoted by **C**.

> Complex number (z):
> $z = x + iy$
> $\text{Re}(z) = x$ and $\text{Im}(z) = y$

Complex number (z)	Real part, Re(z)	Imaginary part, Im(z)
$4 + 3i$	4	3
$3 - i$	3	-1
-5	-5	0
$2i$	0	2
$3 - \sqrt{5}i$	3	$-\sqrt{5}$

Adding and subtracting complex numbers

When adding or subtracting complex numbers, we add (or subtract) the real and imaginary parts separately.

For example: (i) $(4 + 3i) + (3 - 2i) = 4 + 3i + 3 - 2i$
$$= (4 + 3) + (3i - 2i)$$
$$= 7 + i$$

(ii) $(3 + 7i) - (4 - 5i) = 3 + 7i - 4 + 5i$
$$= 3 - 4 + 7i + 5i$$
$$= -1 + 12i$$

Multiplying complex numbers

For example: (i) $(3 + 5i)(4 - 3i) = 3(4 - 3i) + 5i(4 - 3i)$
$$= 12 - 9i + 20i - 15i^2$$
$$= 12 - 9i + 20i - 15(-1)$$
$$= 12 - 9i + 20i + 15$$
$$= 12 + 15 - 9i + 20i$$
$$= 27 + 11i$$

> $i^2 = -1$

(ii) $(2 + 4i)(2 - 4i) = 2(2 - 4i) + 4i(2 - 4i)$
$$= 4 - 8i + 8i - 16i^2$$
$$= 4 - 16(-1)$$
$$= 20$$

Example 3

If $z_1 = 2 + 3i$, $z_2 = 3 - 4i$ and $z_3 = 1 + 5i$, express each of the following complex numbers in the form $a + bi$.

(i) $z_1 + z_3$ (ii) $z_2 . z_3$ (iii) $z_1(z_2 + z_3)$

(i) $z_1 + z_3 = 2 + 3i + 1 + 5i$
$$= 2 + 1 + 3i + 5i = 3 + 8i$$

(ii) $z_2 . z_3 = (3 - 4i)(1 + 5i)$
$$= 3 + 15i - 4i - 20i^2$$
$$= 3 + 20 + 15i - 4i = 23 + 11i$$

(iii) $z_1(z_2 + z_3) = (2 + 3i)(3 - 4i + 1 + 5i)$
$$= (2 + 3i)(4 + i)$$
$$= 8 + 2i + 12i + 3i^2$$
$$= 8 - 3 + 2i + 12i \quad \dots + 3i^2 = -3$$
$$= 5 + 14i$$

Exercise 3.2

1. Write each of the following numbers in terms of i:

   (i) $\sqrt{-4}$ (ii) $\sqrt{-36}$ (iii) $\sqrt{-27}$ (iv) $\sqrt{-20}$

2. Solve each of the following equations, giving your answer in the form bi, where b is a real number.

    (i) $x^2 + 9 = 0$ (ii) $x^2 + 12 = 0$

3. Express each of the following in the form $a + bi$:

    (i) $(3 + 2i) + (5 - i)$ (ii) $(7 - 2i) + (3 - 4i)$ (iii) $(-3 + 4i) + (6 - 4i)$
    (iv) $(-3 - i) + (-2 + 6i)$ (v) $(5 - 3i) + (-5 + 6i)$ (vi) $(1 + i) + (2 - 3i)$

4. Simplify each of the following:

    (i) $(2 + 6i) - (1 + 4i)$ (ii) $(3 - 5i) - (2 + 4i)$ (iii) $(4 - 7i) - (-1 + 3i)$
    (iv) $3 - (1 + 4i)$ (v) $(3 - 6i) - 4i$ (vi) $(-3 - 2i) - (4 - 7i)$

5. Multiply each of the following complex numbers and give your answer in the form $a + bi$, $a, b \in R$:

    (i) $(3 + 2i)(2 + 3i)$ (ii) $(4 + i)(3 - 5i)$ (iii) $(5 - 2i)(3 - 5i)$
    (iv) $(3 + 4i)(3 - 4i)$ (v) $(5 - i)(5 + i)$ (vi) $(3 - 2i)^2$

6. If $z_1 = 2 + 4i$, $z_2 = 3 - i$ and $z_3 = 4 - 2i$, express each of the following in the form of $a + bi$, $a, b \in R$.

    (i) $3z_1$ (ii) $z_2 + z_3$ (iii) $2z_1 + z_2$ (iv) $-3z_2$
    (v) $z_1 . z_2$ (vi) $z_2 . z_3$ (vii) $i(z_3)$ (viii) $z_2(z_1 - z_2)$

7. Solve each of the following equations using the quadratic formula and give your answer in the form $a + bi, a, b \in R$:

$$x = \frac{-b \pm \sqrt{b^2 - 4ac}}{2a}$$

   (i) $x^2 - 2x + 17 = 0$ (ii) $x^2 - 4x + 13 = 0$

   (iii) $x^3 - 10x + 26 = 0$ (iv) $x^2 - 8x + 52 = 0$

8. Solve the equation $2z^2 - 8z + 9 = 0$.

9. Complete the table, given that $i = \sqrt{-1}$ and $i^2 = -1$.

   i $= i^1 = i$

   $i \times i$ $= i^2 = -1$

   $i \times i \times i$ $= i^3 = -i$

   $i \times i \times i \times i$ $= i^4 = $ 1

   $i \times i \times i \times i \times i$ $= i^5 = $ i

   $i \times i \times i \times i \times i \times i = i^6 = $ -1

   Describe the pattern formed from this sequence.

   What strategy could be used to simplify $i^n, n \in N$? [e.g., i^{29} and i^{32}.]
   Divide power/index by four and write i to power of remainder

10. Simplify each of the following:

   (i) i^{30} (ii) i^{11} (iii) i^{19} (iv) i^{21} (v) i^{-4}

11. Simplify the following:

   (i) $i^{16} + i^{10} + i^6 - i^{12}$ (ii) $i^3 - i^{11} + i^{17} - i^{29}$

12. Simplify the following:

   (i) $i^2.i^6.i^5$ (ii) $3i^3.2i^5.4i^2$ (iii) $(2i^7)^3$

13. Write $4i^3 + 7i^9$ in the form bi where $b \in Z$.

Section 3.3 Division of complex numbers

Complex numbers can be divided by a real number as follows.

$$\frac{2 + 5i}{2} = \frac{2}{2} + \frac{5}{2}i = 1 + \frac{5}{2}i$$

To divide a complex number by another complex number, we must change the denominator into a real number using a **complex conjugate**.

Complex conjugate

Given any complex number $z = a + bi$, then the complex conjugate of z, written $\bar{z}$, is $a - bi$.

For example, if $z = 3 + 4i$,

        then $\bar{z} = 3 - 4i$, where $\bar{z}$ is the complex conjugate of z.

The product $z.\bar{z} = (3 + 4i)(3 - 4i)$

$$= 9 - \cancel{12}i + \cancel{12}i - 16i^2$$
$$= 9 + 16$$
$$= 25, \text{ a real number}$$

Complex conjugate: If $z = a + bi$, then $\bar{z} = a - ib$

and $z\bar{z} = (a + bi)(a - bi)$

$$= a^2 + b^2$$

Note:

z	$\bar{z}$
$3 + 7i$	$3 - 7i$
$2 - 4i$	$2 + 4i$
$-3 + i$	$-3 - i$
$+4i$	$-4i$

Using the complex conjugate, we can divide complex numbers as shown in the following example.

Example 1

Write $\dfrac{3 + 4i}{2 - 5i}$ in the form $a + bi$.

$$\frac{3 + 4i}{2 - 5i} = \frac{3 + 4i}{2 - 5i} \times \frac{2 + 5i}{2 + 5i}$$

$$= \frac{6 + 15i + 8i + 20i^2}{4 + \cancel{10}i - \cancel{10}i - 25i^2}$$

$$= \frac{6 + 23i - 20}{4 + 25} \quad \text{...since } i^2 = -1$$

$$= \frac{-14 + 23i}{29} = -\frac{14}{29} + \frac{23i}{29}$$

Equality of complex numbers

For two complex numbers to be equal, their real parts must be equal and their imaginary parts must be equal.

If $(x + 2) + 4i = 6 + (y - 2)i,$

then $x + 2 = 6$ and $4 = y - 2$

$\Rightarrow x = 4$ and $6 = y$

If $a + bi = x + yi,$

then $a = x$ and $b = y$

Example 2

Find x and y if $x + 2i + 2(3 - 5yi) = 8 - 13i$.

$$x + 2i + 2(3 - 5yi) = 8 - 13i$$

$\Rightarrow \quad x + 2i + 6 - 10yi = 8 - 13i$

$\Rightarrow \quad x + 6 + (2 - 10y)i = 8 - 13i$

Equating the real parts:

$\quad x + 6 = 8$

$\quad\quad x = 2$

Equating the imaginary parts:

$\quad 2 - 10y = -13$

$\quad\quad -10y = -15$

$\quad\quad 10y = 15$

$\quad\quad y = \frac{15}{10} = \frac{3}{2}$

Example 3

Given that $(z + 1)(2 - i) = 3 - 4i$, find z in the form $x + yi$, where $x, y \in R$.

$$(z + 1)(2 - i) = 3 - 4i$$

$\Rightarrow \quad z + 1 = \dfrac{3 - 4i}{2 - i} \times \dfrac{2 + i}{2 + i}$

$\quad\quad\quad = \dfrac{3 - 4i}{2 - i} \times \dfrac{2 + i}{2 + i} = \dfrac{6 + 3i - 8i - 4i^2}{4 + 2i - 2i - i^2}$

$\quad\quad\quad = \dfrac{10 - 5i}{5}$

$z + 1 = 2 - i$

$\therefore \quad z = 2 - i - 1$

$\quad\quad = 1 - i$

Example 4

Express $\sqrt{5 + 12i}$ in the form of $a + bi$, where $a, b \in R$.

Let $\quad\quad a + bi = \sqrt{5 + 12i}$

$\quad\quad (a + bi)^2 = 5 + 12i$

$\Rightarrow a^2 + 2abi + b^2i^2 = 5 + 12i$

$\Rightarrow \quad a^2 - b^2 + 2abi = 5 + 12i$

$\therefore \quad a^2 - b^2 = 5$ and $2ab = 12$

$\quad\quad\quad \Rightarrow \quad a = \dfrac{12}{2b} = \dfrac{6}{b}$

$$\therefore \quad \left(\frac{6}{b}\right)^2 - b^2 = 5$$

$$6^2 - b^4 = 5b^2$$

$$\Rightarrow \quad b^4 + 5b^2 - 36 = 0$$

$$(b^2 + 9)(b^2 - 4) = 0 \quad \Rightarrow \quad b^2 = -9 \quad \text{or} \quad b^2 = 4$$

$$b = \sqrt{-9} \qquad b = \pm 2$$

$$b = \pm 3i$$

Since $a = \dfrac{6}{b}$, when $b = +2, a = \dfrac{6}{2} = 3$ \qquad [Note: $b \neq 3i$ since $b \in R$]

when $b = -2, a = \dfrac{6}{-2} = -3$

$$\therefore \quad \sqrt{5 + 12i} = (3 + 2i) \quad \text{or} \quad (-3 - 2i)$$

Exercise 3.3

1. Write down the complex conjugate of each of the following complex numbers.

   (i) $3 + 4i$ \qquad (ii) $2 - 6i$ \qquad (iii) $-5 - 2i$ \qquad (iv) $-8 + 3i$

2. Given z, find $\bar{z}$ in each of the following cases.

   (i) $z = 2 + 5i$ \qquad (ii) $z = -3 - 4i$ \qquad (iii) $z = 1 + 7i$ \qquad (iv) $z = -5 + i$

3. Express each of the following in the form of $a + bi$, where $a, b \in R$:

   (i) $\dfrac{2 + 3i}{4 - i}$ \qquad (ii) $\dfrac{4 + 3i}{5 + i}$ \qquad (iii) $\dfrac{8 - i}{2 + 3i}$ \qquad (iv) $\dfrac{2 + 5i}{-3 + 2i}$

4. If $z = 2 + 6i$, express each of the following in the form of $a + bi$, where $a, b \in R$:

   (i) $z.\bar{z}$ \qquad (ii) $z + \bar{z}$ \qquad (iii) $z - \bar{z}$ \qquad (iv) z^2

5. Simplify each of the following.

   (i) $\dfrac{(3 + 4i) + (2 + i)}{4 - i}$ \qquad\qquad (ii) $\dfrac{(2 - 6i) - (3 + 2i)}{2 + 2i}$

   (iii) $\dfrac{3(2 + 4i)}{5i}$ \qquad\qquad (iv) $\dfrac{(2 + i) + (3 - 2i)}{(4 + i) - (3 + 2i)}$

   (v) $\dfrac{(3 + 2i)(1 - i)}{2 + 4i}$ \qquad\qquad (vi) $\dfrac{(3 + i)(2 - i)}{(4 + i)(2 + i)}$

6. Find the values of x and y in each of the following:

   (i) $x + yi = 4 - 2i$ \qquad\qquad (ii) $x + yi = (2 + i)(3 - 2i)$

   (iii) $x + yi = \dfrac{7 + i}{2 - i}$ \qquad\qquad (iv) $x + yi = (2 - 3i)^2$

7. Find the values of a and b in each of the following:
    (i) $a + bi + 3 - 2i = 4(-2 + 5i)$
    (ii) $a(1 + 2i) - b(3 + 4i) = 5$

8. If $z = x + yi$ and $3(z - 1) = i(3 + i)$, find the values of x and y.

9. If $z_1 = -3 + 4i$ and $z_2 = 1 + 2i$ are two complex numbers and $z_1 + (p + iq)z_2 = 0$ where $p, q \in R$, find the values of p and q.

    Hint: $0 = 0 + 0i$

10. Given $z = \sqrt{3 + 4i}$, find z in the form of $a \pm bi$, where $a, b \in R$.

11. If $(x + iy)^2 = 8 - 6i$, find the values of x and y, $x, y \in R$.

12. Express each of the following in the form $a + bi$, $a, b \in R$:
    (i) $\sqrt{-12 - 16i}$
    (ii) $\sqrt{-15 + 8i}$
    (iii) $\sqrt{9 - 40i}$

13. Given $z_1 = 2 + 3i$ and $z_2 = -1 - 5i$, find
    (i) $\overline{z_1 + z_2}$
    (ii) $\overline{z_1 z_2}$

Section 3.4 Argand diagram – Modulus

The **Argand diagram** gives a geometric representation of a complex number as a point in the complex plane.

Real numbers can be plotted on a single number line but complex numbers, with two parts consisting of a real part and an imaginary part, need a plane of points to represent them.

The complex plane is similar to the Cartesian plane, with the real part Re(z) of a complex number represented by the x-axis, and the imaginary part Im (z) represented by the y-axis.

In this diagram we have plotted the complex numbers
    (i) $z_1 = 5 + 2i$
    (ii) $z_2 = 0 + 4i = 4i$
    (iii) $z_3 = 2 + 0i = 2$
    (iv) $z_4 = -2 - 4i$
    (v) $\overline{z_1} = 5 - 2i$

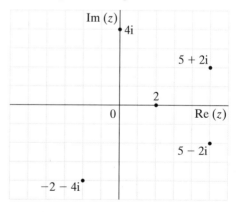

Modulus of a complex number

The **modulus** of a complex number is the distance from the origin to the point in the plane representing the number.

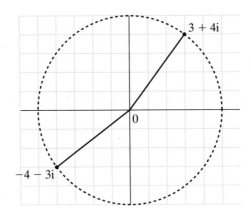

3 + 4i

−4 − 3i

0

The modulus of $z_1 = 3 + 4i$ is given by:

$$|z_1| = \sqrt{3^2 + 4^2}$$
$$= \sqrt{25} = 5$$

> If $z = a + bi$, then the modulus of z, written as $|z|$, is given by
> $$|z| = \sqrt{a^2 + b^2}.$$

Notice that the modulus of $z_2 = -4 - 3i$, is

$$|z_2| = \sqrt{(-4)^2 + (-3)^2}$$
$$= \sqrt{16 + 9}$$
$$= \sqrt{25} = 5$$

This shows that $3 + 4i$ and $-4 - 3i$ have equal moduli and hence lie on the circumference of the same circle.

Example 1

Given that $z_1 = 4 + i$ and $z_2 = -2 + 2i$, plot the following on an Argand diagram:

$$0, z_1, z_2 \text{ and } (z_1 + z_2).$$

Also calculate $|z_1|, |z_2|$ and $|z_1 + z_2|$.
Is $|z_1| + |z_2| = |z_1 + z_2|$?

$z_1 = 4 + i \Rightarrow |z_1| = \sqrt{4^2 + 1^2}$
$\qquad\qquad\qquad = \sqrt{17}$

$z_2 = -2 + 2i \Rightarrow |z_2| = \sqrt{(-2)^2 + (2)^2}$
$\qquad\qquad\qquad\quad = \sqrt{4 + 4}$
$\qquad\qquad\qquad\quad = \sqrt{8}$

$z_1 + z_2 = 4 + i + (-2 + 2i)$
$\qquad\quad = 2 + 3i$
$|z_1 + z_2| = \sqrt{2^2 + 3^2}$
$\qquad\quad\; = \sqrt{13}$

$\Rightarrow |z_1| + |z_2| = \sqrt{17} + \sqrt{8}$
$\qquad |z_1 + z_2| = \sqrt{13}$

$\Rightarrow |z_1| + |z_2| \neq |z_1 + z_2|.$

(Argand diagram showing Im(z) and Re(z) axes with points z_1, z_2, $z_1 + z_2$, and 0.)

Exercise 3.4

1. Plot each of the following complex numbers on an Argand diagram:

   (i) $z_1 = 3 + 5i$ (ii) $z_2 = -3 + i$ (iii) $z_3 = 5i$ (iv) $z_4 = -1 - 3i$

2. Given $z_1 = 2 + i$ and $z_2 = -4 + 3i$, plot each of the following numbers on an Argand diagram:

   (i) z_1 (ii) z_2 (iii) $\bar{z}_1$ (iv) $\bar{z}_2$

   (v) $z_1 + z_2$ (vi) $z_1 - z_2$ (vii) $z_1 z_2$ (viii) $\dfrac{z_1}{z_2}$

3. If $z_1 = 3 - i$ and $z_2 = 2 + 4i$, plot each of the following numbers on an Argand diagram:

   (i) $z_1 . \bar{z}_1$ (ii) $z_1 + \bar{z}_1$ (iii) $\dfrac{1}{z_1}$ (iv) $z_1 z_2$

4. (a) Given $z_1 = 3 + i$ and $z_2 = -1 + 3i$, plot the numbers z_1, z_2 and $z_1 + z_2$ on an Argand diagram. Join the points $0, z_1, z_2$, and $z_1 + z_2$.

   (b) Given $z_3 = 2 - 2i$ and $z_4 = -1 - 4i$, plot the numbers z_3, z_4 and $z_3 + z_4$ on an Argand diagram. Join the points $0, z_3, z_4$, and $z_3 + z_4$.

   (c) What geometrical observation could you make about the relationship between $0, z_1, z_2$, and $z_1 + z_2$?

5. If $z = 1 + 3i$, plot each of the following complex numbers on an Argand diagram.

   (i) 2 (ii) $2 + z$ (iii) $3i$ (iv) $3i + z$
   (v) $1 + i$ (vi) $1 + i + z$ (vii) $-3i + z$ (viii) $-2 - i + z$

   What geometrical observation can be made about adding the same complex number z to other complex numbers?

6. If $z = 3 + 2i$, find each of the following complex numbers in the form $a + bi$: on scve diagram.

   (i) iz (ii) $i^2 z$ (iii) $i^3 z$

   Plot the complex numbers $z, iz, i^2 z, i^3 z$.

7. Find the modulus of each of the following complex numbers:

   (i) $5 + 2i$ (ii) $4 - 2i$ (iii) $-2 - 4i$ (iv) $-3 + i$

8. Plot the number $z_1 = 2 + 5i$.

   Write down three different complex numbers that have the same modulus as z_1.

9. Evaluate each of the following:

   (i) $\left| \dfrac{3 + i}{-2 - 3i} \right|$ (ii) $|(4 + 2i)(3 - i)|$ (iii) $\left| \dfrac{1}{3 + 5i} \right|$

10. Given $z_1 = -2 - 3i$ and $z_2 = 3 + i$, find the complex number $\dfrac{z_1}{z_2}$.

   Investigate if $\dfrac{|z_1|}{|z_2|} = \left| \dfrac{z_1}{z_2} \right|$

11. The complex numbers u, v and w are related by the equation

$$\frac{1}{u} = \frac{1}{v} + \frac{1}{w}.$$

Given that $v = 3 + 4i$ and $w = 4 - 3i$, find u in the form $x + yi$.

12. If $z = 4 - 2i$, find $|z|, |2z|$ and $|3z|$. Is $2|z| = |2z|$?

Explain your answer.

13. Investigate if $|z| = |\bar{z}|$ for all $z \in C$.

14. Let $z_1 = s + 8i$ and $z_2 = t + 8i$, where $s, t \in R$ and $i^2 = -1$.

(i) Given that $|z_1| = 10$, find the value of s.
(ii) Given that $|z_2| = 2|z_1|$, find the value of t.

15. Find the modulus of $\dfrac{i}{1-i}$.

16. Describe the set of solutions of $|z - 1||z - 1| = 1$.

17. Given any two complex numbers z_1, and z_2 as shown.
Indicate on an Argand diagram z_1, z_2 and $(z_1 + z_2)$.
Under what conditions would $|z_1 + z_2| = |z_1| + |z_2|$?

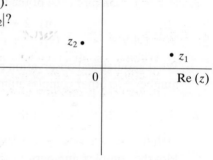

ICT: Use computer software such as Geogebra to investigate Q17.
Take the y-axis as the imaginary axis.
Use the polygon function to plot $0, z_1, z_2$ and $(z_1 + z_2)$ as a parallelogram.
By moving $(z_1 + z_2)$, investigate the conditions under which $|z_1 + z_2| = |z_1| + |z_2|$.

Section 3.5 Transformations of complex numbers

1. Multiplying a complex number by a real number

If a complex number $z_1 = 3 + 2i$ is multiplied by 4,
we get $4z_1 = 4(3 + 2i) = 12 + 8i$.
The real part is increased by a factor of 4 and the
imaginary part is also increased by a factor of 4.

The complex number appears to be **stretched**
along a line from the origin by a factor of 4.
For example, $3 + 2i$ is mapped onto $12 + 8i$.

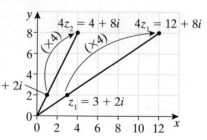

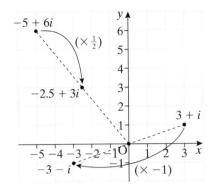

If the complex number is multiplied by $\frac{1}{2}$, a **contraction** occurs.
For example, $(-5 + 6i)$ is mapped onto $-2.5 + 3i$.

Multiplying by (-1) **changes the direction**, that is, the number is reflected through the origin. For example, $(3 + i) \times (-1)$ is mapped onto $-3 - i$.

> If $z = x + iy$, then the transformation az has the following results:
>
> (i) $|a| > 1$, results in stretching away from the origin
> (ii) $0 < |a| < 1$, results in a contraction towards the origin
> (iii) $a < 0$, then az is reflected in the origin and stretched or contracted as in (i) or (ii)

2. Adding complex numbers

(i) When a complex number z is added separately to other complex numbers – z_1, z_2, z_3 – it creates a **translation of the plane.**

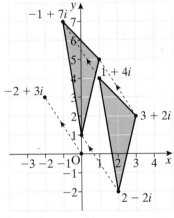

Let $z = -2 + 3i$
and $z_1 = 3 + 2i$, $z_2 = 1 + 4i$, $z_3 = 2 - 2i$.
Then $z + z_1 = -2 + 3i + 3 + 2i = 1 + 5i$
$z + z_2 = -2 + 3i + 1 + 4i = -1 + 7i$
$z + z_3 = -2 + 3i + 2 - 2i = i$

Notice that the complex number z_1 translates to $z_1 + z$.

Translation mapping $z_1 \longrightarrow z_1 + z$

(ii) When z_1 is added to z_2 to create the new complex number $(z_1 + z_2)$, the three complex numbers form a parallelogram with the origin $(0 + 0i)$.

109

Let $z_1 = -2 + 2i$ and $z_2 = 3 + 2i$,

then $z_1 + z_2 = -2 + 2i + 3 + 2i$

$= 1 + 4i$.

$0 + 0i, -2 + 2i, 3 + 2i$ and $1 + 4i$ form a parallelogram, as shown.

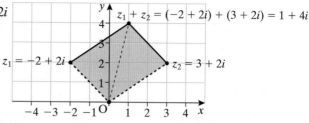

$z_1 + z_2 = (-2 + 2i) + (3 + 2i) = 1 + 4i$

$z_1 = -2 + 2i$

$z_2 = 3 + 2i$

3. Multiplying complex numbers

(i) When a complex number such as $4 + i$ is multiplied by i, the complex number **rotates anti-clockwise about the origin by a quarter of a turn.**

For example, $(4 + i).i = 4i + i^2$

$= 4i - 1$

$= -1 + 4i$

... a rotation of $90°$

Also, $(4 + i)(i^2) = (4 + i)(i)(i)$

$(-1 + 4i)(i) = -i + 4i^2$

$= -i - 4$

$= -4 - i$

... a rotation of $180°$

Note: $(-4 - i)(-i) = +4i + i^2$

$= +4i - 1$

$= -1 + 4i$

... a rotation of $-90°$

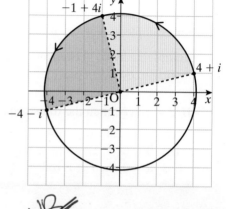

$-1 + 4i$

$4 + i$

$-4 - i$

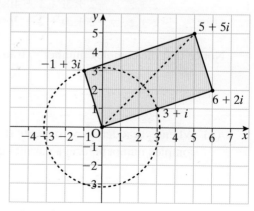

NB

$z \times i$, z rotates by $90°$

$z \times (i)^2$, z rotates by $180°$

$z \times (i)^3$, z rotates by $270°$

$z \times (i)^4$, z rotates by $360°$

$z \times (-i)$, z rotates by $(-90°)$

(ii) When $z_1 = 2 + i$ is multiplied by $z_2 = 3 + i$, the product can be seen as a combination of a stretching and rotation transformation as follows.

$z_1 z_2 = (2 + i)(3 + i)$

$= 2(3 + i) + i(3 + i)$

$2(3 + i)$ produces a **stretching effect** from $(3 + i)$ to $6 + 2i$.

$i(3 + i)$ produces a **rotation** of $90°$ from $(3 + i)$ to $-1 + 3i$.

$2(3 + i) + i(3 + i) = 6 + 2i + 3i - 1$

$= 5 + 5i$

This combines both transformations.

$5 + 5i$

$-1 + 3i$

$6 + 2i$

$3 + i$

Example 1

(i) Plot the complex numbers $z_1 = 3 + 2i$, $z_2 = 3 + 3i$, $z_3 = 4 + 2i$ on the Argand diagram.

(ii) Using the same axes, plot the complex numbers $3z_1$, $3z_2$ and $3z_3$.

(iii) Plot the rotation $z_1(i)^2$, $z_2(i)^2$ and $z_3(i)^2$.

(iv) The complex numbers $4 - i$, 4, $5 - i$ are the images of z_1, z_2, z_3 by the translation $a + bi$. Find the values of a and b.

(i)

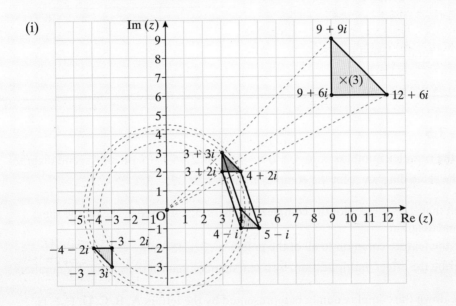

(ii) If $z_1 = 3 + 2i$, $3z_1 = 9 + 6i$

If $z_2 = 3 + 3i$, $3z_2 = 9 + 9i$

If $z_3 = 4 + 2i$, $3z_3 = 12 + 6i$

(iii) $z_1(i)^2 = (3 + 2i)(-1) = -3 - 2i$

$z_2(i)^2 = (3 + 3i)(-1) = -3 - 3i$

$z_3(i)^2 = (4 + 2i)(-1) = -4 - 2i$

(iv) $z_1 + a + bi = 4 - i$

$\qquad a + bi = 4 - i - z_1$

$\qquad a + bi = 4 - i - (3 + 2i)$

$\qquad\qquad = 1 - 3i$

$\qquad \Rightarrow \quad a = 1, b = -3$

[Checking z_3: $4 + 2i + (1 - 3i) = 5 - i$ ... which is correct.]

Example 2

Describe the transformation in each of the following:

(i) $z_1, z_2 \longrightarrow z_3, z_4$

(ii) $z_1, z_2 \longrightarrow z_5, z_6$

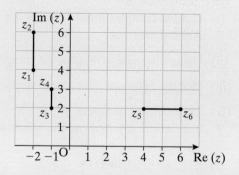

Solution:

(i) $z_1, z_2 \longrightarrow z_3, z_4$

a contraction by $\frac{1}{2}$

$\therefore \quad z_3 = \left(\frac{1}{2}\right)z_1$

(ii) $z_1, z_2 \longrightarrow z_5, z_6$

a rotation clockwise by $90°$

$\therefore \quad z_5 = (-i)z_1$

Exercise 3.5

1. Plot the complex numbers $z_1 = 1 + i$, $z_2 = 3 + 2i$, $z_3 = 4 - i$ on an Argand diagram. On the same diagram, plot the complex numbers $3z_1, 3z_2, 3z_3$.

2. Given that $z_1 = 2 - i$, plot the complex numbers $3z_1, 4z_1$ and $-2z_1$ on the same Argand diagram.

   State the feature common to all of the points $z_1, 3z_1, 4z_1$ and $-2z_1$.

   Describe the effect multiplication, by a real number, has on these complex numbers.

3. Write down the complex numbers represented by the letters A, B, C, D, E, F, N.

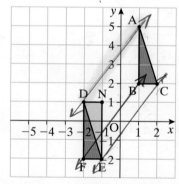

   (i) What transformation in the complex plane moves the triangle ABC onto DEF?
   (ii) Copy this diagram and indicate the image of ABC by the transformation (ABC)(i).
   (iii) What rotation followed by a translation is needed to transform ABC onto DEN?

4. Plot the complex numbers, $z_1 = 4 + i$, $z_2 = 7 + 2i$, $z_3 = 5 + 5i$.
   If $w = -3 - 4i$, plot the complex numbers $z_1 + w, z_2 + w, z_3 + w$.
   State the transformation generated here.

5. Plot the complex number (i) $z_1 = 6 - 2i$ (ii) $z_2 = (z_1)i$ (iii) $z_3 = (z_1)i^2$.

What transformation is created by this multiplication?

6. Given that

(i) $z_2 = a z_1$, find the value of a

(ii) $z_3 = b z_1$, find the value of b

(iii) $z_4 = c z_1$, find the value of c.

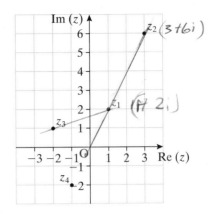

7. Copy this diagram and plot the complex number, w.

Plot the complex number, $-w$, and hence plot the complex number $z - w$.

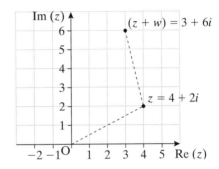

8. Describe each of the following transformations of the complex plane.

(i) $z \longrightarrow z + k$, where $k = a + bi$.

(ii) $z \longrightarrow k z$, where $k \in R, k \neq 0$.

(iii) $z \longrightarrow k z$, where $k \in C, k \neq 0$.

9. A rectangle is represented in the complex plane by the numbers z_1, z_2, z_3, z_4.

Copy this diagram and mark in the diagram the image of this rectangle under the following transformations

(i) $z \longrightarrow 2 z$

(ii) $z \longrightarrow (i) z$

(iii) $z \longrightarrow (2 + i) z$

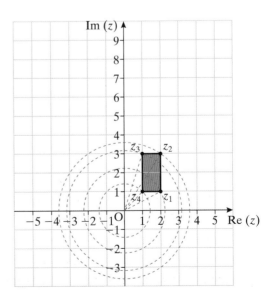

10. A triangle formed by the complex numbers z_1, z_2, z_3 is shown in the diagram.

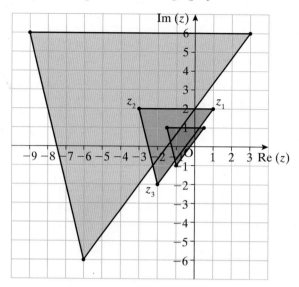

Describe the transformations needed to create the other triangles.

Section 3.6 Conjugate roots theorem

When dealing with complex numbers, it is usual to use z instead of x as a variable. The quadratic equation then takes the form $az^2 + bz + c = 0$.

Consider the quadratic equation $z^2 + 2z + 2 = 0$.

Using the quadratic formula where $a = 1$, $b = 2$ and $c = 2$.

$$\Rightarrow z = \frac{-b \pm \sqrt{b^2 - 4ac}}{2a}$$

$$= \frac{-2 \pm \sqrt{2^2 - 4(1)(2)}}{2(1)}$$

$$= \frac{-2 \pm \sqrt{-4}}{2} = \frac{-2 \pm 2i}{2} = -1 \pm i$$

The roots of this equation are $z_1 = -1 + i$ and $z_2 = -1 - i$ which we note are the complex conjugates of each other.

The sum of the roots $= (-1 + i) + (-1 - i) = -2$ (a real number).

The product of the roots $= (-1 + i)(-1 - i) = 1 + i - i - i^2$

$$= 1 + 1$$

$$= 2 \text{ (a real number)}.$$

$\therefore \quad z^2 - (\text{Sum of roots})z + (\text{Product of roots}) = z^2 - (-2)z + 2 = 0$

$$= z^2 + 2z + 2 = 0.$$

Therefore, the roots of a quadratic equation with real coefficients occur in conjugate pairs.

Example 1

If $z = 1 + 5i$ is a root of the equation $az^2 + bz + c = 0$, where $a, b, c \in R$, find the values of a, b, c.

Given $1 + 5i$ is one root and since the coefficients are real, therefore the roots occur in conjugate pairs; the other root is $1 - 5i$.

$\therefore$ the two roots are $1 + 5i$ and $1 - 5i$

$\therefore \quad z^2 - (\text{Sum of roots})z + \text{Product of roots} = 0$

$\Rightarrow \quad z^2 - (1 + 5i + 1 - 5i)z + (1 + 5i)(1 - 5i) = 0$

$\Rightarrow \quad z^2 - 2z + 1 - 5i + 5i - 25i^2 = 0$

$\quad\quad z^2 - 2z + 26 = 0$

$\therefore \quad a = 1, b = -2$ and $c = 26$

Example 2

Given that $z = 2 + i$ is a root of $z^2 - 4z + 5 = 0$, show that $\bar{z}$ is also a root.

$z = 2 + i \Rightarrow \bar{z} = 2 - i$

Since $f(z) = z^2 - 4z + 5 = 0$

$\Rightarrow \quad f(2 - i) = (2 - i)^2 - 4(2 - i) + 5$

$\quad\quad\quad\quad = 4 - 4i + i^2 - 8 + 4i + 5$

$\quad\quad\quad\quad = 4 - 1 - 8 + 5 = 0$

$\therefore \quad 2 - i$ is also a root of $z^2 - 4z + 5 = 0$.

We can now generalise this result to include all polynomials with real coefficients and state the conjugate roots theorem as follows:

Conjugate roots theorem $\rightarrow$ polynominal

if you are told the root of an equation is $(-1 + i)$ then we can say $(-1 - i)$ is also a root provided the coefficient in the equation are real.

If z is a root of $az^n + bz^{n-1} + \ldots dz + c = 0$ where $a, b, c, d, \ldots$ are all $\in R$, then $\bar{z}$ is also a root of this equation.

Example 3

Given that $z = 1 + 2i$ is a root of $z^3 - z^2 + 3z + 5 = 0$, show that $\bar{z}$ is also a root. Hence find the third root.

Since the coefficients are real, $z = 1 + 2i$ is a root

$\Rightarrow \quad \bar{z} = 1 - 2i$ is also a root.

Proof: $f(z) = z^3 - z^2 - 3z + 5$

$$f(1 - 2i) = (1 - 2i)^3 - (1 - 2i)^2 + 3(1 - 2i) + 5$$
$$= -11 + 2i - (-3 - 4i) + 3 - 6i + 5$$
$$= -\cancel{11} + \cancel{2i} + \cancel{3} + \cancel{4i} + \cancel{3} - \cancel{6i} + \cancel{5}$$
$$= 0$$

$\therefore$ $1 - 2i$ is also a root.

If $1 + 2i$ and $1 - 2i$ are roots $\Rightarrow z^2 - (1 + 2i + 1 - 2i)z + (1 + 2i)(1 - 2i) = 0$

$\Rightarrow z^2 - 2z + 5 = 0$ is a quadratic equation formed from two of the roots.

$\therefore$ The third factor can be obtained by dividing the cubic expression by the quadratic expression.

$$\begin{array}{r} z + 1 \\ z^2 - 2z + 5 \overline{\smash{\big)}\, z^3 - z^2 + 3z + 5} \\ \underline{z^3 - 2z^2 + 5z} \\ z^2 - 2z + 5 \\ \underline{z^2 - 2z + 5} \\ 0 \end{array}$$

or $(z + a)(z^2 - 2z + 5)$
$\equiv z^3 - z^2 + 3z + 5$

$\Rightarrow 5a \equiv 5$ ... equating coefficients
$a = 1$

$\therefore$ $z + 1 = 0$

and $z = -1$ is the third root.

Exercise 3.6

1. Show that $-2 + 4i$ is a root of the equation $z^2 + 4z + 20 = 0$ and write down the second root.

2. Solve these equations, giving your answers in the form $a \pm bi, a, b \in R$.

   (i) $z^2 - 2z + 17 = 0$ (ii) $z^2 + 4z + 7 = 0$

3. Form a quadratic equation, given a pair of roots in each case.

   (i) $1 \pm 3i$ (ii) $-2 \pm i$ (iii) $4 \pm 2i$ (iv) $\pm 5i$

4. If $z = 4 - i$ is a root of the equation $z^2 - 8z + 17 = 0$, show that $\bar{z}$ is also a root.

5. Show that $-2 + 2i$ is a root of the equation $z^3 + 3z^2 + 4z - 8 = 0$ and find the other roots.

6. Given that $2 + 3i$ is one root of the equation $2z^3 - 9z^2 + 30z - 13 = 0$, find the other two roots.

7. Show that $1 + 2i$ is a root of the equation $z^2 + (-1 + 5i)z + 14 - 7i = 0$. Show also that the conjugate $1 - 2i$ is not a root of this equation. Explain why.

8. $\dfrac{1+2i}{1-2i}$ is a root of $az^2 + bz + 5 = 0$, where $a, b \in R$. Find a value for a and for b.

9. Given that $z^3 - 1 = (z - 1)(z^2 + az + b)$, find a and b and hence solve the equation $z^3 - 1 = 0$, giving the complex roots in the form $a + bi$.

10. Form the quadratic equation whose roots are $-2 \pm i$. If $-2 + i$ is a root of $z^3 + z^2 - 7z - 15 = 0$, find the other two roots.

11. Form the quadratic equation whose roots are $-3 \pm 2i$.

    Hence form the cubic equation whose roots are $-3 \pm 2i$ and 2.

12. Form a cubic equation with real coefficients, two of whose roots are 2 and $-1 + i$.

13. The roots of the equation $z = 1^{\frac{1}{3}}$ are called the cube roots of unity. If these roots are $1, \alpha, \beta$, find α and β and prove that

    (i) $\alpha^2 = \beta$ (ii) $1 + \alpha + \beta = 0$

    Hint: see Q9.

Section 3.7 Polar form of a complex number

By studying this diagram, we can see that there are two ways to locate a point in the complex plane.

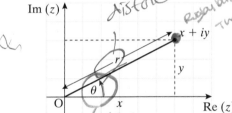

(i) Cartesian coordinates (x, y) or   (ii) Polar coordinates (r, θ)

$$\sin \theta = \frac{y}{r} \implies y = r \sin \theta$$

$$\cos \theta = \frac{x}{r} \implies x = r \cos \theta$$

Therefore, any complex number $x + yi$ can be written as $r \cos \theta + ri \sin \theta$.

$$\implies x + iy = r(\cos \theta + i \sin \theta)$$

We note also from the diagram that

(i) $r = \sqrt{x^2 + y^2}$ = modulus of the number

(ii) $\tan \theta = \dfrac{y}{x}$

$$\implies \theta = \tan^{-1}\left(\frac{y}{x}\right),$$ where θ is called the **argument** of the number.

Rectangular form / Cartesian form: $x + iy$

Polar form / Modulus argument form: $r(\cos \theta + i \sin \theta)$

Example 1

Express in the form $x + iy$ these complex numbers:

(a) $z_1 = 12\left(\cos\dfrac{\pi}{6} + i\sin\dfrac{\pi}{6}\right)$ \qquad (b) $z_2 = 5\left(\cos\dfrac{\pi}{8} + i\sin\dfrac{\pi}{8}\right)$

(a) $\cos\dfrac{\pi}{6} = \dfrac{\sqrt{3}}{2}$ and $\sin\dfrac{\pi}{6} = \dfrac{1}{2}$ \quad ... (*Formulae and Tables*, p. 13)

$$z_1 = 12\left(\cos\dfrac{\pi}{6} + i\sin\dfrac{\pi}{6}\right)$$
$$= 12\left(\dfrac{\sqrt{3}}{2} + i\dfrac{1}{2}\right)$$
$$= 6\sqrt{3} + 6i$$

(b) $\sin\dfrac{\pi}{8} = 0.382$ and $\cos\dfrac{\pi}{8} = 0.924$

Remember to use rad mode on calculator when using π.

$$z_2 = 5\left(\cos\dfrac{\pi}{8} + i\sin\dfrac{\pi}{8}\right)$$
$$= 5[0.924 + i(0.382)]$$
$$= 4.62 + 1.92i$$

Example 2

Express $(-1 + i\sqrt{3})$ in the form $r(\cos\theta + i\sin\theta)$.

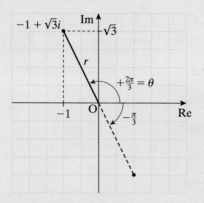

$r = \sqrt{x^2 + y^2} = \sqrt{(-1)^2 + (\sqrt{3})^2} = \sqrt{4} = 2$

$\theta = \tan^{-1}\left(\dfrac{y}{x}\right) = \tan^{-1}\left(\dfrac{\sqrt{3}}{-1}\right) = -\dfrac{\pi}{3}$ or $+\dfrac{2\pi}{3}$

$\left[\text{Note: } \tan\left(-\dfrac{\pi}{3}\right) = \tan\left(\pi - \dfrac{\pi}{3}\right) = \tan\left(\dfrac{2\pi}{3}\right) = -1.7321\right]$

By plotting the complex number, we see that the argument required is $\dfrac{2\pi}{3}$.

$\therefore \ r(\cos\theta + i\sin\theta) = 2\left(\cos\dfrac{2\pi}{3} + i\sin\dfrac{2\pi}{3}\right).$

Note 1: When calculating the argument of a complex number, the principal value of θ is taken to be between $-\pi$ and $+\pi$, that is, $-\pi < \theta < +\pi$.

Note 2: When using a calculator to find the argument (θ), it is important to check that the angle given by the calculator locates the correct quadrant for the particular complex number.

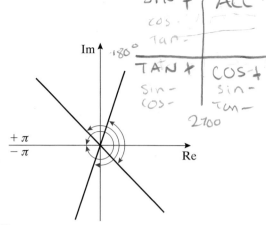

By first plotting the complex number on an Argand diagram, it can help to solve this problem.

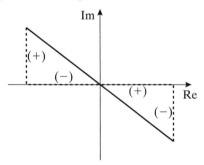

The tan ratio is negative in both 2nd and 4th quadrants.

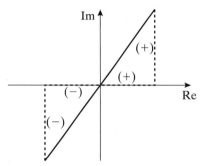

The tan ratio is positive in both the 1st and 3rd quadrants.

Example 3

Write the complex number $1 - i\sqrt{3}$ in modulus/argument form.

$x + iy = 1 - i\sqrt{3}$

Modulus $r = \sqrt{x^2 + y^2}$
$= \sqrt{1^2 + (-\sqrt{3})^2}$
$= \sqrt{4} = 2$

Argument $\theta = \tan^{-1}\dfrac{y}{x}$
$= \tan^{-1}\dfrac{-\sqrt{3}}{1}$
$= \dfrac{-\pi}{3}$

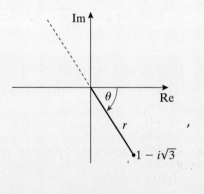

Since the complex number is in the 4th quadrant, $\dfrac{-\pi}{3}$ is the correct argument.

$\Rightarrow \quad (r, \theta) = \left(2, \dfrac{-\pi}{3}\right)$

$\therefore \quad 1 - i\sqrt{3} = \left[2\cos\left(\dfrac{-\pi}{3}\right) + i\sin\left(\dfrac{-\pi}{3}\right)\right]$

Example 4

Write $-\sqrt{3} - i$ in polar form.

$$x + iy = -\sqrt{3} - i$$

Modulus $r = \sqrt{x^2 + y^2}$

$$= \sqrt{(-\sqrt{3})^2 + (-1)^2}$$

$$= \sqrt{3 + 1} = 2$$

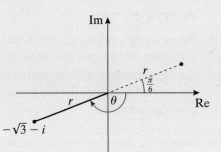

$-\sqrt{3} - i$

Argument $\theta = \tan^{-1}\dfrac{y}{x}$

$$= \frac{-1}{-\sqrt{3}} = \frac{1}{\sqrt{3}}$$

$$= \frac{\pi}{6} \; (30°) \;\ldots\ldots$$

$$\left(\begin{array}{l} \text{since the number is in the 3rd quadrant,} \\ \theta = \dfrac{\pi}{6} - \pi = \dfrac{-5\pi}{6} \end{array} \right)$$

$$\Rightarrow \qquad \theta = \frac{-5\pi}{6} \; (-150°)$$

$$\therefore \quad -\sqrt{3} - i = 2\left[\cos\left(\frac{-5\pi}{6}\right) + i\sin\left(\frac{-5\pi}{6}\right)\right]$$

Exercise 3.7

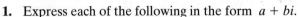

argument is the angle of the positive relax.

angle

1. Express each of the following in the form $a + bi$.

   (i) $4\left(\cos\dfrac{\pi}{2} + i\sin\dfrac{\pi}{2}\right)$

   (ii) $2\left(\cos\dfrac{5\pi}{6} + i\sin\dfrac{5\pi}{6}\right)$

   (iii) $\sqrt{2}\left(\cos\dfrac{3\pi}{4} + i\sin\dfrac{3\pi}{4}\right)$

   (iv) $2\left(\cos\dfrac{\pi}{3} + i\sin\dfrac{\pi}{3}\right)$

2. Represent each of the following complex numbers on an Argand diagram, indicating the modulus and argument of each number.

   (i) $2 + 2i$ (ii) $-3i$ (iii) 4 (iv) $-\sqrt{3} + i$

3. Express each of the following complex numbers in polar form.

   (i) $1 + i$ (ii) $\sqrt{3} + i$ (iii) $-2 + \sqrt{2}i$ (iv) $-2 - \sqrt{2}i$

   (v) $4i$ (vi) -5 (vii) $-3i$ (viii) $\dfrac{1}{2} - \dfrac{\sqrt{3}}{2}i$

Modulus =

4. Simplify each of the following, giving your answer in the form $r(\cos\theta + i\sin\theta)$.

   (i) $(1 + \sqrt{3}i)^2$

   (ii) $\dfrac{-2}{-\sqrt{3} + i}$

5. If $z = 1 + \sqrt{3}i$, find the complex numbers:

   (i) iz (ii) i^2z (iii) i^3z

   Plot each of the numbers z, iz, i^2z and i^3z on an Argand diagram.

   Find the argument (θ) of each number: (i) z (ii) iz (iii) i^2z (iv) i^3z

   What geometrical observation can be made about multiplying a complex number by i?

We always look at the angle to complex axis we never look at the angle

6. Express each of the following in polar form:

    (i) $2i$ (ii) $-3 - \sqrt{3}i$ (iii) $\dfrac{2}{-1 + i}$

7. Solve the equation $z^2 - 2z + 2 = 0$ and express your answer in the form $r(\cos\theta + i\sin\theta)$.

8. Let $z_2 = t + 8i,\, t \in \mathbb{R}$ and $i^2 = -1$. Given that $\arg(z_2) = \dfrac{3\pi}{4}$, find the value of t.

Section 3.8 Products and quotients of complex numbers in polar form

Consider the complex numbers $z_1 = r_1(\cos\theta_1 + i\sin\theta_1)$ and $z_2 = r_2(\cos\theta_2 + i\sin\theta_2)$.

Then $z_1.z_2 = r_1(\cos\theta_1 + i\sin\theta_1).r_2(\cos\theta_2 + i\sin\theta_2)$

$\quad = r_1 r_2[\cos\theta_1\cos\theta_2 + i\cos\theta_1\sin\theta_2 + i\sin\theta_1\cos\theta_2 + i^2\sin\theta_1\sin\theta_2]$

$\quad = r_1 r_2[\cos\theta_1\cos\theta_2 - \sin\theta_1\sin\theta_2 + i(\sin\theta_1\cos\theta_2 + \cos\theta_1\sin\theta_2)]$

$\quad = r_1 r_2[\cos(\theta_1 + \theta_2) + i\sin(\theta_1 + \theta_2)]$ ...(*Formulae and Tables*, p. 15)

$\Rightarrow$ Modulus of $z_1.z_2 = r_1.r_2$ and argument of $z_1.z_2 = \theta_1 + \theta_2$

Also, $\dfrac{z_1}{z_2} = \dfrac{r_1(\cos\theta_1 + i\sin\theta_1)}{r_2(\cos\theta_2 + i\sin\theta_2)}$

$\quad = \dfrac{r_1(\cos\theta_1 + i\sin\theta_1)}{r_2(\cos\theta_2 + i\sin\theta_2)} \times \dfrac{(\cos\theta_2 - i\sin\theta_2)}{(\cos\theta_2 - i\sin\theta_2)}$

$\quad = \dfrac{r_1}{r_2}\dfrac{[\cos\theta_1\cos\theta_2 - i\cos\theta_1\sin\theta_2 + i\sin\theta_1\cos\theta_2 - i^2\sin\theta_1\sin\theta_2]}{[\cos^2\theta_2 - i\cos\theta_2\sin\theta_2 + i\sin\theta_2\cos\theta_2 - i^2\sin^2\theta_2]}$

$\quad = \dfrac{r_1}{r_2}\left[\dfrac{\cos\theta_1\cos\theta_2 + \sin\theta_1\sin\theta_2 + i(\sin\theta_1\cos\theta_2 - \cos\theta_1\sin\theta_2)}{\cos^2\theta_2 + \sin^2\theta_2}\right]$

$\quad = \dfrac{r_1}{r_2}\left[\dfrac{\cos(\theta_1 - \theta_2) + i\sin(\theta_1 - \theta_2)}{1}\right]$ ...(*Formulae and Tables*, p. 15)

$\Rightarrow$ Modulus of $\dfrac{z_1}{z_2} = \dfrac{r_1}{r_2}$ and the argument of $\dfrac{z_1}{z_2} = \theta_1 - \theta_2$.

> If $z_1 = r_1(\cos\theta_1 + i\sin\theta_1)$
>
> and $z_2 = r_2(\cos\theta_2 + i\sin\theta_2)$,
>
> then $z_1.z_2 = r_1.r_2[\cos(\theta_1 + \theta_2) + i\sin(\theta_1 + \theta_2)]$
>
> and $\dfrac{z_1}{z_2} = \dfrac{r_1}{r_2}[\cos(\theta_1 - \theta_2) + i\sin(\theta_1 - \theta_2)]$.

Note: $\dfrac{z_1}{z_2} = z_1\left(\dfrac{1}{z_2}\right) = \dfrac{r_1}{r_2}[\cos(\theta_1 - \theta_2) + i\sin(\theta_1 - \theta_2)]$

$\Rightarrow \quad \dfrac{1}{z_2} = \dfrac{1}{r_2}[\cos(-\theta_2) + i\sin(-\theta_2)]$

> If $z = r(\cos\theta + i\sin\theta)$, $\dfrac{1}{z} = \dfrac{1}{r}[\cos(-\theta) + i\sin(-\theta)]$

Handwritten margin notes:
when we multiply complex numbers we multiply the moduli And add the angles

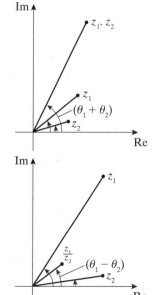

when we divide complex numbers we divide the moduli and subtract the angles

Example 1

If $z_1 = 2\left(\cos \frac{\pi}{4} + i \sin \frac{\pi}{4}\right)$ and $z_2 = 5\left(\cos \frac{5\pi}{12} + i \sin \frac{5\pi}{12}\right)$, find

(i) $z_1 z_2$ (ii) $\frac{z_2}{z_1}$ in the form $a + ib$.

(i) $z_1 z_2 = \left[2\left(\cos \frac{\pi}{4} + i \sin \frac{\pi}{4}\right)\right] \cdot \left[5\left(\cos \frac{5\pi}{12} + i \sin \frac{5\pi}{12}\right)\right]$

$$= (2 \times 5)\left[\cos \left(\frac{\pi}{4} + \frac{5\pi}{12}\right) + i \sin\left(\frac{\pi}{4} + \frac{5\pi}{12}\right)\right]$$

$$= 10\left(\cos \frac{2\pi}{3} + i \sin \frac{2\pi}{3}\right) = 10\left(-\frac{1}{2} + \frac{\sqrt{3}}{2} i\right)$$

$$= -5 + 5\sqrt{3}i$$

(ii) $\dfrac{z_2}{z_1} = \dfrac{5\left(\cos \frac{5\pi}{12} + i \sin \frac{5\pi}{12}\right)}{2\left(\cos \frac{\pi}{4} + i \sin \frac{\pi}{4}\right)}$

$$= \left(\frac{5}{2}\right)\left[\cos \left(\frac{5\pi}{12} - \frac{\pi}{4}\right) + i \sin \left(\frac{5\pi}{12} - \frac{\pi}{4}\right)\right]$$

$$= \frac{5}{2}\left[\cos \frac{\pi}{6} + i \sin \frac{\pi}{6}\right] = \frac{5}{2}\left(\frac{\sqrt{3}}{2} + i \frac{1}{2}\right)$$

$$= \frac{5\sqrt{3}}{4} + \frac{5}{4} i$$

Exercise 3.8

1. If $z_1 = 4\left(\cos \frac{3\pi}{4} + i \sin \frac{3\pi}{4}\right)$ and $z_2 = 2\left(\cos \frac{\pi}{4} + i \sin \frac{\pi}{4}\right)$, find

   (i) $z_1 . z_2$ (ii) $\frac{z_1}{z_2}$, giving your answer in the form $r(\cos \theta + i \sin \theta)$.

2. Given $z = 2\left(\cos \frac{\pi}{3} + i \sin \frac{\pi}{3}\right)$, find z^2 in the form $r(\cos \theta + i \sin \theta)$.

3. Given $z_1 = 3\left(\cos \frac{\pi}{2} + i \sin \frac{\pi}{2}\right)$ and $z_2 = 4\left(\cos \frac{\pi}{3} + i \sin \frac{\pi}{3}\right)$, find the modulus and argument of

   (i) z_1 (ii) z_2 (iii) $z_1 . z_2$ (iv) $\frac{z_1}{z_2}$

4. Multiply $4\left(\cos \frac{\pi}{6} + i \sin \frac{\pi}{6}\right)$ by $3\left(\cos \frac{\pi}{3} + i \sin \frac{\pi}{3}\right)$.

5. Divide $9\left(\cos \frac{5\pi}{6} + i \sin \frac{5\pi}{6}\right)$ by $6\left(\cos \frac{\pi}{3} + i \sin \frac{\pi}{3}\right)$.

6. Simplify $2\left(\cos\frac{\pi}{9} + i \sin \frac{\pi}{9}\right) \cdot \frac{1}{3}\left(\cos \frac{\pi}{9} + i \sin \frac{\pi}{9}\right) \cdot 6\left(\cos\frac{\pi}{9} + i \sin \frac{\pi}{9}\right)$, giving your answer in the form $a + bi$.

7. Simplify $\left(\cos \frac{3\pi}{7} + i \sin \frac{3\pi}{7}\right)\left(\cos \frac{2\pi}{7} + i \sin \frac{2\pi}{7}\right)^2$.

8. Simplify (a) $\left[2\left(\cos\frac{\pi}{3} + i\sin\frac{\pi}{3}\right)\right]^3$ (b) $\left[2\left(\cos\frac{\pi}{3} + i\sin\frac{\pi}{3}\right)\right]^4$

9. If $z = 3(\cos\pi + i\sin\pi)$, express $\frac{1}{z}$ in the form

(i) $r(\cos\theta + i\sin\theta)$ (ii) $a + bi$.

10. Express $z = -2 + 2\sqrt{3}i$ in polar form.

Hence express (a) z^2 (b) z^3 in (i) polar form   (ii) cartesian form.

11. Show that if $z = \cos\theta + i\sin\theta$, then $\frac{1}{z} = \bar{z}$.

12. Given $z.\left(\cos\frac{\pi}{4} + i\sin\frac{\pi}{4}\right) = 1$, find z in the form $a + ib$.

13. If $z = \cos\theta + i\sin\theta$, show that $z + \frac{1}{z} = 2\cos\theta$.

Section 3.9 De Moivre's theorem

In the previous section, we saw that

$$(\cos\theta_1 + i\sin\theta_1)(\cos\theta_1 + i\sin\theta_1) = \cos(\theta_1 + \theta_1) + i\sin(\theta_1 + \theta_1)$$
$$= \cos 2\theta_1 + i\sin 2\theta_1$$

That is $(\cos\theta_1 + i\sin\theta_1)^2 = \cos 2\theta_1 + i\sin 2\theta_1$

Also, $(\cos\theta_1 + i\sin\theta_1)^3 = \cos 3\theta_1 + i\sin 3\theta_1$

The general case of this result is known as **de Moivre's theorem**.

De Moivre's theorem

$$(\cos\theta + i\sin\theta)^n \equiv \cos n\theta + i\sin n\theta,$$
for all real values of n.

Proof of de Moivre's Theorem by Induction

A: When n is a positive integer, prove $(\cos\theta + i\sin\theta)^n = (\cos n\theta + i\sin n\theta)$

(i) Let $n = 1 \Rightarrow (\cos\theta + i\sin\theta)^1 = \cos\theta + i\sin\theta$ ... which is true

(ii) Assume that $(\cos\theta + i\sin\theta)^k = \cos k\theta + i\sin k\theta$

(iii) Prove true for $n = k + 1$, i.e.,

$$(\cos\theta + i\sin\theta)^{k+1} = [\cos(k + 1)\theta + i\sin(k + 1)\theta]$$

Proof: $(\cos\theta + i\sin\theta)^{k+1} = (\cos\theta + i\sin\theta)^k (\cos\theta + i\sin\theta)$

$= (\cos k\theta + i\sin k\theta)(\cos\theta + i\sin\theta)$... assumed

$= \cos k\theta\cos\theta + i\cos k\theta\sin\theta + i\sin k\theta\cos\theta - \sin k\theta\sin\theta$

$= \cos k\theta\cos\theta - \sin k\theta\sin\theta + i(\cos k\theta\sin\theta + \sin k\theta\cos\theta)$

$= \cos(k + 1)\theta + i\sin(k + 1)\theta$

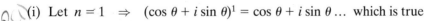

Therefore, if it is true for $n = k$, it is true for $n = k + 1$.

But it is true for $n = 1$.

Thus, it is true for $n = 1 + 1 = 2$.

Therefore, the theorem is true for $n = 1, 2, 3, \ldots$ i.e. for all positive integers.

B: When n is a negative integer,

let $n = -p$ where p is a positive integer.

We now prove that $(\cos \theta + i \sin \theta)^n = (\cos n\theta + i \sin n\theta)$

$$\Rightarrow \quad (\cos \theta + i \sin \theta)^{-p} = \frac{1}{(\cos \theta + i \sin \theta)^p}$$

$$= \frac{1}{\cos p\theta + i \sin p\theta} \quad \ldots \text{ using de Moivre's theorem}$$

$$= \frac{1}{\cos p\theta + i \sin p\theta} \cdot \frac{\cos p\theta - i \sin p\theta}{\cos p\theta - i \sin p\theta}$$

$$= \frac{\cos p\theta - i \sin p\theta}{\cos^2 p\theta + \sin^2 p\theta}$$

$$= \cos p\theta - i \sin p\theta$$

But $p = -n$.

$\therefore \quad (\cos \theta + i \sin \theta)^n = \cos(-n\theta) - \sin(-n\theta)$

$$= \cos n\theta + i \sin n\theta$$

$$\boxed{\begin{aligned} \cos(-\theta) &= \cos \theta \\ \sin(-\theta) &= -\sin \theta \end{aligned}}$$

(Formulae and Tables, p. 13)

$\therefore \quad (\cos \theta + i \sin \theta)^n = \cos n\theta + i \sin n\theta$ for all negative integers.

Note: For $n = 0$, $(\cos \theta + i \sin \theta)^n = (\cos n\theta + i \sin n\theta)$

becomes $(\cos \theta + i \sin \theta)^0 = (\cos 0 + i \sin 0)$

$$1 = 1$$

Therefore, $(\cos \theta + i \sin \theta)^n = (\cos n\theta + i \sin n\theta)$ for all integer values.

If $z = r (\cos \theta + i \sin \theta)$, then using de Moivre's Theorem:

$$z^n = [r(\cos \theta + i \sin \theta)]^n$$
$$= r^n(\cos n\theta + i \sin n\theta) \text{ for all } n \in Z.$$

Example 1

Find the value of $\left(\cos \frac{\pi}{6} + i \sin \frac{\pi}{6}\right)^3$.

$$\left(\cos \frac{\pi}{6} + i \sin \frac{\pi}{6}\right)^3 = \cos \frac{3\pi}{6} + i \sin \frac{3\pi}{6}$$

$$= \cos \frac{\pi}{2} + i \sin \frac{\pi}{2}$$

$$= 0 + i = i$$

Example 2

Write $1 + \sqrt{3}i$ in polar form and hence find the value of $(1 + \sqrt{3}i)^9$.

$$x + iy = 1 + \sqrt{3}i$$

Modulus $r = \sqrt{x^2 + y^2} = \sqrt{1^2 + (\sqrt{3})^2} = 2$

Argument $\theta = \tan^{-1}\dfrac{y}{x} = \tan^{-1}\dfrac{\sqrt{3}}{1} = \dfrac{\pi}{3}$

$\therefore \quad z = 1 + \sqrt{3}i = 2\left(\cos\dfrac{\pi}{3} + i\sin\dfrac{\pi}{3}\right)$

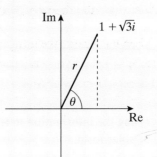

$$\therefore \quad z^9 = (1 + \sqrt{3}i)^9 = 2^9\left(\cos\dfrac{\pi}{3} + i\sin\dfrac{\pi}{3}\right)^9$$

$$= 2^9\left(\cos\dfrac{9\pi}{3} + i\sin\dfrac{9\pi}{3}\right)$$

$$= 2^9\left(\cos 3\pi + i\sin 3\pi\right)$$

$$= 2^9\left(-1 + i.0\right)$$

$$= -2^9$$

Exercise 3.9

1. Use de Moivre's theorem to simplify each of the following, expressing your answers in the form $a + bi$:

   (i) $\left(\cos\left(\dfrac{\pi}{8}\right) + i\sin\left(\dfrac{\pi}{8}\right)\right)^4$

   (ii) $\left(\cos\left(\dfrac{\pi}{6}\right) + i\sin\left(\dfrac{\pi}{6}\right)\right)^7$

   (iii) $\left(\cos\dfrac{\pi}{12} + i\sin\dfrac{\pi}{12}\right)^8$

   (iv) $\left(\cos\dfrac{2\pi}{3} + i\sin\dfrac{2\pi}{3}\right)^3$

   (v) $\left(\cos\dfrac{\pi}{4} + i\sin\dfrac{\pi}{4}\right)^{-6}$

   (vi) $\left(\cos\dfrac{2\pi}{5} + i\sin\dfrac{2\pi}{5}\right)^{10}$

   (vii) $\left(\cos\dfrac{-\pi}{18} + i\sin\dfrac{-\pi}{18}\right)^9$

   (viii) $\left(\cos\dfrac{\pi}{6} + i\sin\dfrac{\pi}{6}\right)^{-3}$

2. Given $z = \sqrt{2}\left(\cos\dfrac{\pi}{3} + i\sin\dfrac{\pi}{3}\right)$, express z^4 in the form $a + bi$.

3. Given $z = 3\left(\cos\dfrac{\pi}{10} + i\sin\dfrac{\pi}{10}\right)$, express z^5 in the form $a + bi$.

4. Express (i) $\left(\cos\dfrac{\pi}{3} + i\sin\dfrac{\pi}{3}\right)^2$ (ii) $\left(\cos\dfrac{2\pi}{3} + i\sin\dfrac{2\pi}{3}\right)^4$ in the form $\cos\theta + i\sin\theta$.

   Hence express $\left(\cos\dfrac{\pi}{3} + i\sin\dfrac{\pi}{3}\right)^2\left(\cos\dfrac{2\pi}{3} + i\sin\dfrac{2\pi}{3}\right)^4$ in the form $a + bi$.

5.

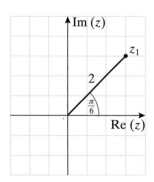

Using the information in the Argand diagrams above, express each of the following in polar form.

(i) z_1

(ii) z_2

(iii) $\bar{z}_1$

(iv) $\bar{z}_2$

(v) $z_1.z_2$

(vi) $\dfrac{z_1}{z_2}$

6. Change each of the following to polar form and then use de Moivre's theorem to express your answers in the form $a + bi$:

(i) $(1 - i)^4$

(ii) $(1 + \sqrt{3}i)^3$

(iii) $(-2 - 2i)^4$

7. Find the value of $(1 + i)^4$.

8. Express $4 - 4i$ in polar form.

Hence find the value of $\dfrac{1}{(4 - 4i)^3}$.

9. Simplify   (i) $(3 - \sqrt{3}i)^6$ (ii) $(2 + 2\sqrt{3}i)^6$.

10. Express $\dfrac{\sqrt{3} + i}{1 + \sqrt{3}i}$ in the form $r(\cos \theta + i \sin \theta)$.

Hence evaluate $\left(\dfrac{\sqrt{3} + i}{1 + \sqrt{3}i}\right)^6$.

Section 3.10 Applications of de Moivre's Theorem ———

Simplifying expressions of the form $(\cos \theta - i \sin \theta)^n$ ———

de Moivre's theorem applies to $(\cos \theta + i \sin \theta)$ and not to $(\cos \theta - i \sin \theta)$.

However, since $-\sin \theta = \sin (-\theta)$ and $\cos \theta = \cos (-\theta)$,

then $\cos \theta - i \sin \theta = \cos (-\theta) + i \sin (-\theta)$.

Hence, $(\cos \theta - i \sin \theta)^n = [\cos (-\theta) + i \sin (-\theta)]^n$

$$= [\cos (-n\theta) + i \sin (-n\theta)]$$

Example 1

Simplify $\left(\cos \frac{\pi}{3} - i \sin \frac{\pi}{3}\right)^6$, giving your answer in rectangular form.

$$\cos \frac{\pi}{3} - i \sin \frac{\pi}{3} = \cos \left(-\frac{\pi}{3}\right) + i \sin \left(-\frac{\pi}{3}\right)$$

$$\Rightarrow \left(\cos \frac{\pi}{3} - i \sin \frac{\pi}{3}\right)^6 = \left(\cos \left(-\frac{\pi}{3}\right) + i \sin \left(-\frac{\pi}{3}\right)\right)^6$$

$$= \cos \left(-\frac{6\pi}{3}\right) + i \sin \left(-\frac{6\pi}{3}\right)$$

$$= \cos (-2\pi) + i \sin (-2\pi)$$

$$= 1 + i.0$$

$$= 1$$

Expressing $\cos n\theta$ and $\sin n\theta$ in terms of $\cos \theta$ and $\sin \theta$

Example 2

Express   (a) $\cos 2\theta$ in terms of $\cos \theta$ (b) $\sin 3\theta$ in terms of $\sin \theta$.

(a) $\cos 2\theta$: $(\cos \theta + i \sin \theta)^2 = \cos 2\theta + i \sin 2\theta$

$$\Rightarrow \quad \cos 2\theta + i \sin 2\theta = (\cos \theta + i \sin \theta)^2$$

$$= \cos^2 \theta + 2i \cos \theta \sin \theta + i^2 \sin^2 \theta$$

$$\cos 2\theta + i \sin 2\theta = \cos^2 \theta - \sin^2 \theta + i(2 \cos \theta \sin \theta)$$

Equating real parts: $\cos 2\theta = \cos^2 \theta - \sin^2 \theta$

$$= \cos^2 \theta - [1 - \cos^2 \theta] \quad \dots [\sin^2 \theta + \cos^2 \theta = 1]$$

$$\cos 2\theta = 2 \cos^2 \theta - 1$$

(**Note:** If we need $\sin 2\theta$, we equate the imaginary parts.)

(b) $\sin 3\theta$: $(\cos \theta + i \sin \theta)^3 = \cos 3\theta + i \sin 3\theta$

$$\Rightarrow \quad \cos 3\theta + i \sin 3\theta = (\cos \theta + i \sin \theta)^3$$

$$= \cos^3 \theta + 3i \cos^2 \theta \sin \theta$$
$$+ 3i^2 \cos \theta \sin^2 \theta + i^3 \sin^3 \theta$$

$$= \cos^3 \theta - 3 \cos \theta \sin^2 \theta$$
$$+ i(3 \cos^2 \theta \sin \theta - \sin^3 \theta)$$

Equating imaginary parts:

$$\sin 3\theta = 3 \cos^2 \theta \sin \theta - \sin^3 \theta$$

$$= 3[1 - \sin^2 \theta] \sin \theta - \sin^3 \theta \quad \dots [\cos^2 \theta = 1 - \sin^2 \theta]$$

$$= 3 \sin \theta - 3 \sin^3 \theta - \sin^3 \theta$$

$$\sin 3\theta = 3 \sin \theta - 4 \sin^3 \theta$$

How to find the nth root of a complex number

If $z^n = a + bi \Rightarrow z = (a + bi)^{\frac{1}{n}}$, the nth root of $a + bi$.

Then (i) $z^3 = 1 + i \Rightarrow z = (1 + i)^{\frac{1}{3}}$, the cube root of $(1 + i)$

 (ii) $z^4 = 0 + 8i \Rightarrow z = (0 + 8i)^{\frac{1}{4}}$, the fourth root of $8i$.

To use de Moivre's theorem to find the nth root of a complex number, we need to express the complex number in **general** polar form.

Because the trigonometric functions cosine and sine are periodic functions, with period 2π,

$$\cos \theta = \cos(\theta + 2n\pi) \text{ and}$$

$$\sin \theta = \sin(\theta + 2n\pi) \text{ for } n \in N.$$

$$\therefore \ a + bi = r[\cos(\theta + 2n\pi) + i \sin(\theta + 2n\pi)].$$

> Given $z = a + bi$,
> then $z = r[\cos(\theta + 2n\pi) + i\sin(\theta + 2n\pi)]$
> where $n \in N$ is the **general polar form** of z.

Example 3

Solve the equation $z^3 = 8i$.

$$z^3 = 8i \Rightarrow z = (8i)^{\frac{1}{3}}$$

Modulus $r = \sqrt{x^2 + y^2}$

$$= \sqrt{0^2 + 8^2} = 8$$

Argument $\theta = \dfrac{\pi}{2}$

$$\therefore \ 0 + 8i = 8\left(\cos \frac{\pi}{2} + i \sin \frac{\pi}{2}\right) \quad \text{... in polar form.}$$

$$8i = 8\left(\cos\left(\frac{\pi}{2} + 2n\pi\right) + i \sin\left(\frac{\pi}{2} + 2n\pi\right)\right)$$

   ... in general polar form.

$$\Rightarrow z = (8i)^{\frac{1}{3}} = 8^{\frac{1}{3}}\left(\cos\left(\frac{\pi}{2} + 2n\pi\right) + i \sin\left(\frac{\pi}{2} + 2n\pi\right)\right)^{\frac{1}{3}}$$

$$= 2\left(\cos\frac{1}{3}\left(\frac{\pi}{2} + 2n\pi\right) + i \sin\frac{1}{3}\left(\frac{\pi}{2} + 2n\pi\right)\right) \quad \text{... using de Moivre's theorem}$$

Let $n = 0$: $z = 2\left(\cos\frac{1}{3}\left(\frac{\pi}{2}\right) + i \sin\frac{1}{3}\left(\frac{\pi}{2}\right)\right) = 2\left(\cos\frac{\pi}{6} + i \sin\frac{\pi}{6}\right)$

$$= 2\left(\frac{\sqrt{3}}{2} + i\frac{1}{2}\right)$$

$$= \sqrt{3} + i$$

Let $n = 1$: $z = 2\left(\cos\frac{1}{3}\left(\frac{\pi}{2} + 2\pi\right) + i \sin\frac{1}{3}\left(\frac{\pi}{2} + 2\pi\right)\right)$

$$= 2\left(\cos\left(\frac{5\pi}{6}\right) + i \sin\left(\frac{5\pi}{6}\right)\right)$$

$$= 2\left(\frac{-\sqrt{3}}{2} + i\frac{1}{2}\right)$$

$$= -\sqrt{3} + i$$

Let $n = 2$: $z = 2\left(\cos \frac{1}{3}\left(\frac{\pi}{2} + 4\pi\right) + i \sin \frac{1}{3}\left(\frac{\pi}{2} + 4\pi\right)\right)$

$$= 2\left(\cos \frac{9\pi}{6} + i \sin \frac{9\pi}{6}\right)$$

$$= 2\left(\cos \frac{3\pi}{2} + i \sin \frac{3\pi}{2}\right)$$

$$= 2(0 + i(-1))$$

$$= -2i$$

The cube roots of $8i$ are

$$\sqrt{3} + i, \quad -\sqrt{3} + i, \quad -2i.$$

Example 4

Solve the equation $z^2 = -2 - 2\sqrt{3}i$.

$$z^2 = -2 - 2\sqrt{3}i \quad \Rightarrow \quad z = (-2 - 2\sqrt{3}i)^{\frac{1}{2}}$$

Modulus $\quad r = \sqrt{x^2 + y^2}$

$$= \sqrt{(-2)^2 + (-2\sqrt{3})^2} = 4$$

Argument $\theta = \tan^{-1} \dfrac{y}{x}$

$$= \tan^{-1} \frac{-2\sqrt{3}}{-2} = \tan^{-1}\sqrt{3} = \frac{\pi}{3}$$

Tan θ is positive in the first and third quadrants.

$$\Rightarrow \quad \theta = -\frac{2\pi}{3}$$

$$-2 - 2\sqrt{3}i = 4\left(\cos\left(-\frac{2\pi}{3}\right) + i \sin\left(-\frac{2\pi}{3}\right)\right)$$

$$z = (-2 - 2\sqrt{3}i)^{\frac{1}{2}} = 4^{\frac{1}{2}}\left(\cos\left(-\frac{2\pi}{3} + 2n\pi\right) + i \sin\left(-\frac{2\pi}{3} + 2n\pi\right)\right)^{\frac{1}{2}}$$

$$= 2\left(\cos \frac{1}{2}\left(-\frac{2\pi}{3} + 2n\pi\right) + i \sin \frac{1}{2}\left(-\frac{2\pi}{3} + 2n\pi\right)\right)$$

Let $n = 0$: $\quad z = 2\left(\cos \frac{1}{2}\left(-\frac{2\pi}{3}\right) + i \sin \frac{1}{2}\left(-\frac{2\pi}{3}\right)\right)$

$$= 2\left(\cos\left(-\frac{2\pi}{6}\right) + i \sin\left(-\frac{2\pi}{6}\right)\right) = 2\left(\frac{1}{2} - \frac{i\sqrt{3}}{2}\right) = 1 - \sqrt{3}i$$

Let $n = 1$: $\quad z = 2\left(\cos \frac{1}{2}\left(-\frac{2\pi}{3} + 2\pi\right) + i \sin \frac{1}{2}\left(-\frac{2\pi}{3} + 2\pi\right)\right)$

$$= 2\left(\cos\left(\frac{2\pi}{3}\right) + i \sin\left(\frac{2\pi}{3}\right)\right) = 2\left(-\frac{1}{2} + \frac{i\sqrt{3}}{2}\right) = -1 + \sqrt{3}i$$

$$\therefore \quad z = 1 - \sqrt{3}i, \ -1 + \sqrt{3}i$$

Exercise 3.10

1. Simplify each of the following, giving your answer in the form $a + bi$:

   (i) $(\cos \pi - i \sin \pi)^5$

   (ii) $\left(\cos \dfrac{\pi}{5} - i \sin \dfrac{\pi}{5}\right)^{10}$

   (iii) $\dfrac{1}{\left(\cos \dfrac{\pi}{3} - i \sin \dfrac{\pi}{3}\right)^3}$

   (iv) $\left(\cos \dfrac{\pi}{2} - i \sin \dfrac{\pi}{2}\right)^4$

2. Using de Moivre's theorem, express

   (i) $\sin 2\theta$ in terms of $\sin \theta$ and $\cos \theta$

   (ii) $\cos 3\theta$ in terms of $\cos \theta$.

3. Use the identity $(\cos 4\theta + i \sin 4\theta) = (\cos \theta + i \sin \theta)^4$ to show that

   (i) $\cos 4\theta = 8 \cos^4 \theta - 8 \cos^2 \theta + 1$

   (ii) $\sin 4\theta = 4 \cos^3 \theta \sin \theta - 4 \cos \theta \sin^3 \theta$.

4. Use de Moivre's theorem to solve the equation $z^3 = 8$.

5. Find the values of z for which $z^3 = -8$, giving your answer in $a + bi$ form.

6. Plot the point $2 + 2\sqrt{3}i$ on an Argand diagram.

   Use this diagram to express $2 + 2\sqrt{3}i$ in the form $r(\cos \theta + i \sin \theta)$

   Hence find the solution set of $z^2 = 2 + 2\sqrt{3}i$.

7. The complex number $z = 1$ is plotted on this Argand diagram.

   Write down the modulus and argument of this number.

   (a) Express $z = 1$ in general polar form and hence find the cube roots of unity, that is, find the values of z for which $z = 1^{\frac{1}{3}}$.

   (b) Prove that the sum of these roots is zero.

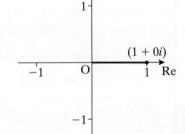

8. Find the cube roots of $27i$.

9. Use de Moivre's theorem to solve,

   (i) $z^2 = 1 + \sqrt{3}i$

   (ii) $z^2 = 2 - 2\sqrt{3}i$

   (iii) $z^2 = 4i$.

10. Use de Moivre's theorem to find, in polar form, the five roots of the equation $z^5 = 1$.

    Choose one of the roots w, where $w \neq 1$, and prove that $w^2 + w^3$ is real.

Revision Exercise 3 (Core)

1. Simplify $\sqrt{80} - \sqrt{20}$, expressing your answer in the form $a\sqrt{b}$ where $a, b \in \mathbb{N}$.

2. $(x - 1) + yi = y + 4i$; find x and y.

3. Solve the equation $z^2 + 4z + 3 = 0$, giving your answer in the form $a + bi$.

4. Given $z_1 = 5 + i$ and $z_2 = -2 + 3i$.
   (i) Find $(z_1)^2$ (ii) Show that $|z_1|^2 = 2|z_2|^2$

5. Let z be the complex number $-1 + \sqrt{3}i$.
   (i) Express z^2 in the form $a + bi$.
   (ii) Find the value of the real number p such that $z^2 + pz$ is real.

6. Express the complex number $z = 1 + i$ in the form $r(\cos \theta + i \sin \theta)$ and hence find a value for z^4 in the form $p + qi$ where $p, q \in R$.

7. Express $-1 + \sqrt{3}i$ in the form $r(\cos \theta + i \sin \theta)$.

8. Show that $2 + 3i$ is a root of $z^2 - 4z + 13 = 0$.
   Hence find the other root.

9. If $z_1 = 2 + 3i$ and $z_2 = 1 - 4i$, investigate if $|z_1|.|z_2| = |z_1.z_2|$

10. Write $\dfrac{5 - 5i}{2 + i}$ in the form $a + bi, a, b \in R$.

11. Simplify $4i^{13} + 3i^3$.

12. Given that $f(z)$ has roots $z_1 = 2 + 3i$ and $z_2 = -1 + 4i$, find $f(z)$.

13. Plot the complex numbers $a = 3 + 3i$ and $b = 1 - 2i$ on an Argand diagram.
    Plot the complex number $a + b$ on the same diagram.
    Find the complex number, c, that would translate
    (i) a to $a + b$ (ii) b to $a + b$ (iii) a to b.

14. In this diagram, describe the transformations needed for these:
    (i) R $\rightarrow$ S
    (ii) S $\rightarrow$ T
    (iii) If $z \in R$, find z_1 so that $zz_1 \in S$.
    (iv) If $z \in R$, find z_3 so that $zz_1 + z_3 \in T$.

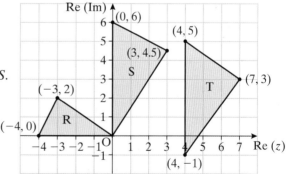

Revision Exercise 3 (Advanced)

1. If $z = x + iy$ and $3(z - 1) = i(z + 1)$, find the value of x and the value of y.

2. Given that $2 + 3i$ is a root of $2z^3 - 9z^2 + 30z - 13 = 0$, find the other two roots.

3. Express $\sqrt{3} + i$ in the form $r(\cos \theta + i \sin \theta)$.
   Use de Moivre's theorem to simplify $(\sqrt{3} + i)^{11}$.

4. The roots of the quadratic equation $z^2 + pz + q = 0$ are $1 + i$ and $4 + 3i$. Find the values of p and q.

5. If $w_1 = -\dfrac{1}{2} + \dfrac{\sqrt{3}}{2}i$ and $w_2 = (w_1)^2$, find w_2.
   Prove that $w_1 + w_2 = -1$.

6. If $p = 2\left(\cos\dfrac{\pi}{3} + i\sin\dfrac{\pi}{3}\right)$, find $\bar{p}$, the complex conjugate of p. Prove that $p\bar{p}$ is a real number.

7. Express $\dfrac{(1 + 2i)^2}{1 - i}$ in the form $a + bi$.

8. Find the value of k if the real part of $\dfrac{-3 + i}{1 + ki}$ is -3, $k \neq 0$.

9. Simplify $\left(\cos\dfrac{\pi}{3} + i\sin\dfrac{\pi}{3}\right)\left(\cos\dfrac{\pi}{12} + i\sin\dfrac{\pi}{12}\right)^2$.

10. Show that $1 + 2i$ is a root of the equation $z^2 - (3 + 3i)z + 5i = 0$ and find the other root.

11. Simplify the following expression giving your answer in the form $a + bi$, $a, b \in R$:
$$\left(\cos\dfrac{\pi}{3} + i\sin\dfrac{\pi}{3}\right)^2 \left(\cos\dfrac{2\pi}{3} + i\sin\dfrac{2\pi}{3}\right)^4$$

12. One of the roots of $z^3 + z^2 + 4z + \rho = 0$, where ρ is real, is $1 - 3i$.
    Find the value of ρ and the other two roots.

13. Given $x + iy = \sqrt{8 - 6i}$.
    By squaring both sides of this equation, use simultaneous equations to find the values of x and y.

14. Find the value of t for which ti is a solution of the equation
    $$z^4 - 2z^3 + 7z^2 - 4z + 10 = 0.$$
    Hence find all the solutions of this equation.

15. Given that $\bar{z}$ is the conjugate of z and $z = a + bi$ where a and b are real, find the possible values of z if $z\bar{z} - 2iz = 7 - 4i$.

16. Determine the real p and q for which $(p + iq)^2 = 15 - 8i$.
    Hence solve the equation $(1 + i)z^2 + (-2 + 3i)z - 3 + 2i = 0$

Revision Exercise 3 (Extended-Response Questions)

1. Given that $p = 3\left(\cos\dfrac{\pi}{6} + i\sin\dfrac{\pi}{6}\right)$ and $q = 2 - 2\sqrt{3}i$.
   (i) Find pq in the form $a + bi$.　　(ii) Find $|p|, |q|, |pq|, |p + q|$.

2. The complex number $z = \dfrac{1 + i\sqrt{3}}{1 - i\sqrt{3}}$.

    (i) Express z in the form $a + bi$.   (ii) Plot z on an Argand diagram.

    (iii) Express z in the form of $r(\cos\theta + i\sin\theta)$.   (iv) Show that $z^3 = 1$.

3. The complex number $z = (1 + 3i)(p + qi)$, where p and $q \in R$ and $p > 0$.

    (i) Write z in the form $a + bi$.

        Given that the argument of $z = \dfrac{\pi}{4}$, show that $p + 2q = 0$.

    (ii) Given also that $|z| = 10\sqrt{2}$, find the values of p and q.

4. $z_1 = 3\left(\cos\dfrac{\pi}{6} + i\sin\dfrac{\pi}{6}\right)$ and $z_2 = \left(\cos\dfrac{\pi}{4} + i\sin\dfrac{\pi}{4}\right)$; find

    (i) $|z_1 z_2|$ (ii) $\arg(z_1 z_2)$ (iii) $|z_1|^2$

    (iv) $|z_2|^2$ (v) $\arg(z_1{}^2)$ (vi) $\arg(z_2{}^2)$

    (vii) Determine if each of the following statements is true or false for any two complex numbers $z, w \in C$.

        (a) $|zw| = |z||w|$ (b) $\arg(zw) = \arg(z) + \arg(w)$

5. If $z = 2\left(\cos\dfrac{\pi}{6} + i\sin\dfrac{\pi}{6}\right)$, find z^2, z^4 and z^6.

    (i) Plot z^2, z^4, z^6.

    (ii) Describe the transformation that occurs as z^2 is multiplied each time.

6. Express $\dfrac{\sqrt{3} + i}{1 + \sqrt{3}i}$ in the form $r(\cos\theta + i\sin\theta)$. Hence evaluate $\left(\dfrac{\sqrt{3} + i}{1 + \sqrt{3}i}\right)^6$.

7. Plot any two complex numbers z_1, z_2.

    By completing the parallelogram, find the complex number $z_1 + z_2$.

    Using this parallelogram, describe geometrically a proof for the triangle inequality $|z_1 + z_2| \leqslant |z_1| + |z_2|$.

    Under what conditions is $|z_1 + z_2| = |z_1| + |z_2|$?

8. z is said to be the reciprocal of w if $zw = 1$.

    (i) By letting $z = a + bi$ and $w = c + di$, find two algebraic relationships between the real parts and imaginary parts a, b, c and d.

    (ii) Using simultaneous equations, find a and b in terms of c and d.

    (iii) Prove that $\dfrac{1}{z} = \dfrac{\bar{z}}{|z|^2}$.   (iv) Plot $z, \dfrac{1}{z}$ and $\bar{z}$ on the same Argand diagram.

    (v) Prove that $\dfrac{1}{z}$ and $\bar{z}$ are always collinear with $0 + 0i$.

9. Prove that

    (i) the conjugate of a sum of complex numbers is equal to the sum of the conjugates

    (ii) the conjugate of the difference of complex numbers is equal to the difference of the conjugates

    (iii) the conjugate of a quotient of complex numbers is equal to the quotient of the conjugates.

    (iv) the conjugate of a product of complex numbers is equal to the product of the conjugates.

10. **(a)** Given $w = -1 + \sqrt{3}i$, where $i^2 = -1$.

    (i) Write w in polar form.

    (ii) Use de Moivre's theorem to solve $z^2 = -1 + \sqrt{3}i$, giving your answer in rectangular form.

(b) Four complex numbers z_1, z_2, z_3 and z_4 are shown on an Argand diagram. They satisfy the following conditions:

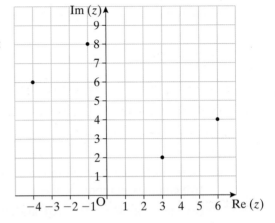

    $z_2 = i z_1$

    $z_3 = k z_1$, where $k \in R$

    $z_4 = z_2 + z_3$.

(Note: the same scale was used on both axes.)

    (i) Identify which number is which by labelling each point in the diagram.

    (ii) Write down an appropriate value of k.

    (iii) State which condition helped to identify the numbers first. Explain your answer.   (Adapted from SEC *project maths* paper 1, 2011)

11. **(a)** **(i)** Write the complex number $1 - i$ in polar form.

    (ii) Use de Moivre's theorem to evaluate $(1 - i)^9$, giving your answer in rectangular form.

(b) A complex number z has a modulus greater than 1. The three numbers z, z^2 and z^3 are shown on an Argand diagram. One of them lies on the imaginary axis, as shown.

    (i) Label the points to show which point corresponds to which number.

    (ii) Find θ, the argument of z.

    (iii) Explain the significance of knowing that the modulus of z is greater than 1.

(c) Consider the complex number $z = a + ai$, $a > 1$, $a \in R$.

    (i) Find the complex numbers z^2, z^4, z^6, etc., giving your answers in rectangular form.

    (ii) Describe geometrically the pattern formed by z, z^2, z^4, z^6, ...

    (Adapted from SEC *project maths* paper 1, 2010)

12. **(i)** Given $z = \cos\theta + i\sin\theta$, use de Moivre's theorem to write down an expression for z^k in terms of θ, where k is a positive integer.

(ii) Hence show that $\dfrac{1}{z^k} = \cos k\theta - i\sin k\theta$.

(iii) Deduce expressions for $\cos k\theta$ and $\sin k\theta$ in terms of z^k.

(iv) Show that $\cos^2\theta\sin^2\theta = \dfrac{-1}{16}\left(z^2 - \dfrac{1}{z^2}\right)^2$.

(v) Hence show that $\cos^2\theta\sin^2\theta = a + b\cos 4\theta$, where a and b are constants.

Sequences –Series – Patterns

chapter 4

Key words

number sequence   arithmetic sequence   series   sigma (Σ)

geometric sequence   exponential sequence   geometric series   recurring decimal

finite difference   composite function   quadratic function

Section 4.1 Sequences

A **number sequence** is a set of numbers written down in a definite order.
All the terms of the sequence are connected by a rule.

Examine the following sequences and state in words the rule that connects one term to the next. Hence find the next two terms of each sequence.

(i)   1, 3, 5, 7, ...

(ii)   2, 5, 8, 11, ...

(iii) $\frac{1}{3}, \frac{1}{6}, \frac{1}{12}, \frac{1}{24}, \ldots$

(iv)   1, 2, 4, 8, ...

(v) $1^3, 2^3, 3^3, 4^3, \ldots$

(vi) $\frac{1}{2}, \frac{2}{3}, \frac{3}{4}, \frac{4}{5}, \ldots$

(vii)   1, 4, 9, 16, ...

(viii)   1, 2, 6, 24, 120, ...

(ix) $1, \frac{2}{3}, \frac{3}{9}, \frac{4}{27}, \ldots$

(x)   4, 2, 0, -2, ...

(xi)   1, -1, 1, -1, ...

(xii) $1, -\frac{1}{2}, \frac{1}{4}, -\frac{1}{8}, \ldots$

The most basic number sequence is the set of natural numbers, $N = \{1, 2, 3, 4, \ldots n\}$; all other sequences can be compared to it.

Consider the natural numbers   1,   2,   3,   4,   5, ... n

and compare them with the sequence $\rightarrow$ 1,   3,   5,   7,   9, ... $2n - 1$

                    $T_1,$ $T_2,$ $T_3,$ $T_4,$ $T_5,$ ...... T_n

The first term is T_1 ; the second term is T_2.

T_n is called the nth term and it gives us the rule needed to find any term of the sequence.

     $T_n = 2n - 1$

Let $n = 1,$ $T_1 = 2(1) - 1 = 1$

Let $n = 2,$ $T_2 = 2(2) - 1 = 3$ Hence the rule $T_n = 2n - 1$ produces

Let $n = 3,$ $T_3 = 2(3) - 1 = 5$ the sequence 1, 3, 5, 7, ...

Let $n = 4,$ $T_4 = 2(4) - 1 = 7$ etc.

Sequences are often derived from patterns created by different processes. In biology the arrangement of leaves on a stem can be described by the 'Fibonacci sequence' 0, 1, 1, 2, 3, 5, 8, 13, ...

Sequences are used in computational software. In physics they occur in the study of waves; sequence patterns control robot movements and are used extensively in digital technology.

Consider the following patterns and describe how to add two more elements to each pattern.

(i)   ......

(ii)   ......

(iii)   ......

Example 1

Write down the first four terms of each of the following sequences:

(i) $T_n = n^2 + n$ (ii) $T_n = 2^n - 3n$

(i) $T_n = n^2 + n$

Let $n = 1$, $T_1 = 1^2 + 1 = 2$
     $n = 2$, $T_2 = 2^2 + 2 = 6$
     $n = 3$, $T_3 = 3^2 + 3 = 12$
     $n = 4$, $T_4 = 4^2 + 4 = 20$

The sequence is $2, 6, 12, 20$.

(ii) $T_n = 2^n - 3n$

Let $n = 1$, $T_1 = 2^1 - 3(1) = -1$
     $n = 2$, $T_2 = 2^2 - 3(2) = -2$
     $n = 3$, $T_3 = 2^3 - 3(3) = -1$
     $n = 4$, $T_4 = 2^4 - 3(4) = 4$

The sequence is $-1, -2, -1, 4$.

Example 2

The following rectangular patterns are made from two sets of coloured tiles.

(i) Draw the next two patterns of tiles.
(ii) Write a number sequence for the blue tiles used in each of these patterns.
(iii) Write a number sequence for the total number of tiles used in each of these patterns.
(iv) Write a number sequence for the white tiles used in each of these patterns.
(v) Write out the next 3 terms in each sequence found in (ii), (iii), (iv).

(i)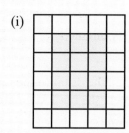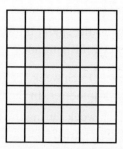

(ii) 6, 10, 14, 18, 22 is the sequence for the blue tiles
(iii) 6, 12, 20, 30, 42 is the sequence for the total number of tiles
(iv) 0, 2, 6, 12, 20 is the sequence for the white tiles.

$$+4 \quad +4 \quad +4 \quad +4$$

(v) (ii) We notice that 6, 10, 14, 18, 22, ... each term increases by 4.

$\Rightarrow$ the next three terms are $\quad 22 + 4 = 26$
$26 + 4 = 30$ $\Big\}$ 26, 30, 34
$30 + 4 = 34$

$$+6 \quad +8 \quad +10 \quad +12$$

(iii) 6, 12, 20, 30, 42, ... each term increases according to the pattern 6, 8, 10, 12 ..., i.e. the gap between terms is increasing by 2.

$\Rightarrow$ the next three terms are $\quad 42 + 14 = 56$
$56 + 16 = 72$ $\Big\}$ 56, 72, 90
$72 + 18 = 90$

(iv) The white tile sequence is 0, 2, 6, 12, 20, ... and has a rectangular property (0×1), (1×2), (2×3), (3×4), (4×5), ...

$\Rightarrow$ the next three terms are $\quad (5 \times 6)$, (6×7), (7×8)
$\quad\quad\quad = 30 \quad\quad 42 \quad\quad 56$

[Note: This sequence could also be found by subtracting sequence (ii) from sequence (iii)]

Exercise 4.1

1. Write down the next three terms of each of the following sequences:

(i) 6, 12, 18, 24, ...
(ii) 7, 12, 17, 22, ...
(iii) 4.7, 5.9, 7.1, 8.3, ...
(iv) 2, −1, −4, −7, ...
(v) 2, 3, 6, 11, 18, 27, ...

(vi) 78, 70, 62, 54, ...
(vii) 10, 5, 0, −5, −10, ...
(viii) −64, −55, −46, −37, ...
(ix) 2, 6, 18, ...
(x) 2, 6, 12, 20, ...

(xi) $\frac{3}{4}$, $\frac{1}{4}$, $-\frac{1}{4}$
(xii) 1, 2, 4, 7, 11, ...
(xiii) 0, 3, 8, 15, 24, ...
(xiv) 3, −6, 12, −24, ...
(xv) $\frac{1}{2}$, $\frac{1}{6}$, $\frac{1}{12}$, $\frac{1}{20}$, ...

2. Find the first four terms of the following sequences, given the nth term (T_n) in each case.

(i) $T_n = 4n - 2$
(ii) $T_n = (n + 1)^2$
(iii) $T_n = n^2 - 2n$

(iv) $T_n = (n + 3)(n + 1)$
(v) $T_n = n^3 - 1$
(vi) $T_n = \dfrac{n}{n + 2}$

(vii) $T_n = 2^n$
(viii) $T_n = (-3)^n$
(ix) $T_n = n.2^n$

3. A spider is climbing up a wall. It crawled 5 cm in the first minute. Every minute after the first, it crawled 4 cm further than the previous minute.

    (i) Write a sequence to show how far the spider crawled every minute.

    (ii) How far did the spider crawl in the fifth minute?

4. Joan was training for a marathon race. Each week she increased the distance she ran in the previous week by 1, 2, 3, 4, 5, ... kilometres. In the first week, she ran 1 kilometre.

    (i) Write down how far she ran each week during the first 6 weeks.

    (ii) In which week did she run 29 kilometres?

5. If $T_n = 4n - 3$, find T_1, T_5, T_{10}.

6. If $T_n = (-2)^{n+1}$, find T_1, T_6, T_{11}.

7. By inspection, draw the next three patterns of each of the following sequences. Write a number sequence for each set of patterns.

    (i)    ......

    (ii)  ......

    (iii)   ......

8. Match each nth term (T_n) with one of the sequences given:

    (i) $T_n = 4n - 2$ A: 2, 4, 8, 16, ...

    (ii) $T_n = 2n^2$ B: 2, 8, 18, 32, ...

    (iii) $T_n = n(n + 1)$ C: 2, 6, 10, 14, ...

    (iv) $T_n = 2^n$ D: 2, 6, 12, 20, ...

9. Given the set of natural numbers, N = 1, 2, 3, 4, 5, ... n. By inspection, find the nth term (T_n) of each of the following sequences:

    (i) 5, 6, 7, 8, 9, ...   (vi) −1, 1, −1, 1, −1, ...

    (ii) 2, 4, 6, 8, 10, ...   (vii) 1, 5, 9, 13, 17, ...

    (iii) 2, 5, 8, 11, 14, ...   (viii) $1, \frac{1}{2}, \frac{1}{3}, \frac{1}{4}, \frac{1}{5}, \ldots$

    (iv) 1, 4, 9, 16, 25, ...   (ix) $\frac{2}{3}, \frac{3}{4}, \frac{4}{5}, \frac{5}{6}, \frac{6}{7}, \ldots$

    (v) 2, 5, 10, 17, 26, ...   (x) (2×3), (3×4), (4×5), (5×6), ...

10. The first eight terms of the Fibonacci sequence are given below. Describe in words how the sequence is formed and hence write out the next four terms of the sequence.

         0, 1, 1, 2, 3, 5, 8, 13, 21, ...

11. Shown opposite are the first 5 rows of 'Pascal's triangle'.

Copy these 5 rows and, by finding the pattern, continue 'Pascal's triangle' up to row 8.

By examining the triangle, find the nth term, T_n, for

Row 1				1				
Row 2			1		1			
Row 3		1		2		1		
Row 4	1		3		3		1	
Row 5	1	4		6		4		1

   (i) the sequence formed by the second numbers in each row
   (ii) the sequence of numbers produced by the third numbers in each row
   (iii) the sequence given by the sum of the numbers in each row
   (iv) the sequence created by adding the second and third numbers in each row.

Section 4.2 Arithmetic sequences

A sequence in which each term changes by the same fixed amount is called an **arithmetic sequence**.

For example, $\overset{+4 \quad +4 \quad +4}{3, \quad 7, \quad 11, \quad 15, \ldots}$ each term increases by 4.

$\overset{-2 \quad -2 \quad -2}{3, \quad 1, \quad -1, -3, \ldots}$ each term decreases by 2.

If we let the first term be a ($= T_1$), and the difference between consecutive terms be d (called the common difference), then every arithmetic sequence can be represented by

$$\overset{+d \qquad +d \qquad +d}{\begin{array}{cccccc} T_1, & T_2, & T_3, & T_4 & \ldots & T_n \\ a, & a+d & a+2d, & a+3d, & \ldots & a+(n-1)d \end{array}}$$

For the sequence: $3, 7, 11, 15, \ldots$

$\left. \begin{array}{l} a = 3 \\ d = 7 - 3 = 4 \end{array} \right\}$

$\begin{aligned} T_n &= a + (n-1)d \\ &= 3 + (n-1)4 \\ &= 3 + 4n - 4 \\ T_n &= 4n - 1. \end{aligned}$

> In every arithmetic sequence,
> $T_1 = a$
> $T_2 - T_1 = d$
> $T_n - T_{n-1} = d$
> $T_n = a + (n-1)d$

Example 1

Find the nth term (T_n) of the arithmetic sequence:
   $-2, \quad 3, \quad 8, \quad 13, \ldots$
and hence find (i) T_{20} (ii) T_{21} (iii) $T_{21} - T_{20}$.

$\left. \begin{array}{l} a = -2 \\ d = 3 - (-2) = 5 \\ \text{(also, } d = 8 - 3 = 5) \end{array} \right\}$
$\begin{aligned} T_n &= a + (n-1)d \\ T_n &= -2 + (n-1)5 \\ &= -2 + 5n - 5 \\ T_n &= 5n - 7 \end{aligned}$

$\therefore \quad T_{20} = 5(20) - 7 \quad$ and $\quad T_{21} = 5(21) - 7$
       $= 93 \qquad\qquad\qquad\quad = 98$

$\Rightarrow \quad T_{21} - T_{20} = 98 - 93 = 5 \ (=d).$

The sequence $3, 1, -1, -3, \ldots.$ has an infinite number of terms.

The sequence $3, 1, -1, -3, \ldots. \ -35$ has a finite number of terms.

If we are given $T_n = -35$, we can find the number of terms (n) in the sequence if we know the formula for T_n.

Example 2

Find the number of terms in the sequence
$$1, \quad -3, \quad -7, \quad -11, \quad \ldots\ldots \quad -251.$$

In this sequence, $\quad a = 1$
$$\left. \begin{array}{l} a = 1 \\ d = -3 - 1 = -4 \\ T_n = -251 \end{array} \right\} \qquad T_n = a + (n-1)d$$
$$-251 = 1 + (n-1)(-4)$$
$$-251 = 1 - 4n + 4$$
$$4n = 256$$
$$n = \tfrac{256}{4} = 64$$

There are 64 terms in this sequence.

Example 3

In an arithmetic sequence, $T_4 = 6$ and $3T_2 = T_{10}$, find the values of a and d and hence write out the first 6 terms of the sequence.

$$T_n = a + (n-1)d$$
$$T_4 = a + (4-1)d = a + 3d$$
$$T_2 = a + (2-1)d = a + d$$
$$T_{10} = a + (10-1)d = a + 9d$$

$$\qquad T_4 = 6 \qquad \text{and} \qquad 3T_2 = T_{10}$$
$$\Rightarrow \quad a + 3d = 6 \qquad\qquad 3(a + d) = a + 9d$$
$$3a + 3d = a + 9d$$
$$2a - 6d = 0$$
$$\Rightarrow \quad a - 3d = 0$$

Using simultaneous equations,

$$\begin{array}{l} a - 3d = 0 \\ a + 3d = 6 \\ \hline 2a \quad\;\; = 6 \ldots \text{adding both lines} \\ \quad a = 3 \end{array} \qquad\qquad \begin{array}{l} \text{Also,} \quad a - 3d = 0 \\ \quad\;\; 3 - 3d = 0 \\ \quad\; -3d = -3 \\ \quad\quad d = \left(\tfrac{-3}{-3}\right) = 1 \end{array}$$

The sequence is $3, 4, 5, 6, 7, 8, \ldots$

> Given an arithmetic sequence $T_1, T_2, T_3, T_4, T_5, \ldots\ldots T_n$,

$$T_3 - T_2 = T_4 - T_3 = T_5 - T_4 = \text{the common difference } (d).$$

In general terms:

$$T_{n+1} - T_n = d \text{ (the common difference)}.$$

A corollary to this is as follows:

To prove that a sequence is arithmetic, we must show that $T_{n+1} - T_n$ is a constant.

> Also, if $T_{n+1} - T_n > 0$, then the sequence is increasing

if $T_{n+1} - T_n < 0$, then the sequence is decreasing.

Note, to find T_{n+1}, substitute $(n + 1)$ for n in T_n.

If $T_n = 3n + 1$,

$$T_{n+1} = 3(n + 1) + 1 = 3n + 4.$$

Example 4

If $p + 2$, $2p + 3$ and $5p - 2$ are three consecutive terms of an arithmetic sequence, find the value of $p, p \in R$.

Because we have three consecutive terms of an arithmetic sequence,

$$
\begin{aligned}
\Rightarrow \quad (2p + 3) - (p + 2) &= (5p - 2) - (2p + 3) \\
2p + 3 - p - 2 &= 5p - 2 - 2p - 3 \\
p + 1 &= 3p - 5 \\
-2p &= -6 \\
p &= \left(\frac{-6}{-2}\right) = 3.
\end{aligned}
$$

Note: The three terms of the sequence are $5, 9, 13$.

Example 5

Given (i) $T_n = \dfrac{n + 1}{2}$

(ii) $T_n = \dfrac{2}{n + 1}$, determine whether

(a) the sequence is arithmetic or not

(b) the sequence is increasing or decreasing.

(i) $$T_n = \frac{n+1}{2}$$

$$T_{n+1} = \frac{(n+1)+1}{2}$$

$$= \frac{n+2}{2}$$

$$T_{n+1} - T_n = \frac{n+2}{2} - \frac{n+1}{2}$$

$$= \frac{\not{n}+2-\not{n}-1}{2}$$

$$T_{n+1} - T_n = \frac{1}{2}$$

∴ $T_{n+1} - T_n$ is a constant

∴ T_n is an arithmetic sequence

Also, since $T_{n+1} - T_n = \frac{1}{2}$,

i.e. > 0,

$\Rightarrow$ T_n is an increasing sequence.

(ii) $$T_n = \frac{2}{n+1}$$

$$T_{n+1} = \frac{2}{(n+1)+1} = \frac{2}{n+2}$$

$$T_{n+1} - T_n = \frac{2}{n+2} - \frac{2}{n+1}$$

$$= \frac{2(n+1) - 2(n+2)}{(n+2)(n+1)}$$

$$= \frac{2\not{n}+2-2\not{n}-4}{(n+2)(n+1)}$$

$$T_{n+1} - T_n = \frac{-2}{(n+2)(n+1)}$$

$\neq$ constant ... since the value depends on n.

∴ T_n is not arithmetic

Also,

$$T_{n+1} - T_n = \frac{-2}{(n+2)(n+1)} < 0.$$

Since $n \in N$ and is always positive,

∴ T_n is a decreasing sequence.

Exercise 4.2

1. Find T_n, the nth term of the following arithmetic sequences.
   Hence find T_{22} for each sequence.

   (i) 8, 13, 18, 23, ...   (ii) 16, 36, 56, 76, ...   (iii) 10, 7, 4, 1, ...

2. The nth term of an arithmetic sequence is given by $T_n = 5n - 2$.
   Write down the first four terms.

3. Find the number of terms in each of the following arithmetic sequences:

   (i) $-5, -1, 3, 7, \ldots\ldots 75$ (ii) $2, 5, 8, 11, \ldots\ldots 59$ (iii) $-\frac{3}{2}, -1, -\frac{1}{2}, 0, \ldots\ldots 14$.

4. In an arithmetic sequence, $T_1 = 4$ and $T_7 = 22$. Using simultaneous equations, find

   (i) the values of a and d (ii) the first five terms of the sequence   (iii) T_{20}.

5. Niamh made wall hangings using the following designs:

Design 1   Design 2   Design 3

(i) How many red and orange tiles will she need for design 8?

(ii) Will any of her designs need 38 tiles? Explain your answer.

6. In an arithmetic sequence, $T_{13} = 27$ and $T_7 = 3T_2$. Find expressions in terms of n for T_{13}, T_7 and T_2 and hence find the values of a and d.
Write down the first six terms of the sequence. *example u*

7. (i) If $2k + 2, 5k - 3$ and $6k$ are three consecutive terms of an arithmetic sequence, find the value of $k, k \in \mathbb{Z}$.

(ii) Given that $4p, -3 - p$ and $5p + 16$ are three consecutive terms of an arithmetic sequence, find the value of $p, p \in \mathbb{Z}$.

8.

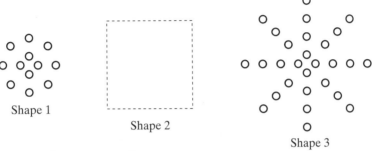

Shape 1

Shape 2

Shape 3

Three shapes were drawn on a wall.
The second shape was removed accidentally. Given that the shapes were drawn in arithmetic sequence, draw shape 2.

(i) Write a number sequence for the number of circles used in each shape and hence find T_n for the sequence.

(ii) How many circles are needed for shape 15?

(iii) Which shape requires 164 circles?

9. The nth term of a sequence is given by $T_n = 4n - 2$.
Verify that the sequence is arithmetic. *be able to do.*

10. If $T_n = n(n + 2)$ for a given sequence, verify that the sequence is not arithmetic.

11. Continue the following pattern by adding two more shapes.

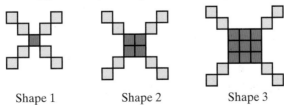

Shape 1   Shape 2   Shape 3

(i) How many light-coloured tiles will be needed for shape 7?

(ii) How many dark-coloured tiles will be needed for shape 7?

(iii) By inspection, write down an expression for T_n, the number of tiles needed for the nth shape.

(iv) Prove that the sequence generated is not arithmetic.

12. Sandrine made the following hexagon patterns with matchsticks.

| 1 hexagon | 2 "hexagons" | 3 "hexagons" |

She hoped to continue this pattern and find an expression for T_n.
Copy and complete the following table.

Number of "hexagons"	1	2	3	4	...	...	10	...	( )	...	...	...	30
Perimeter	6	10	( )	( )	...	...	( )	...	82	...	...	...	( )

(i) Having finished a number of "hexagons", Sandrine counted 87 matchsticks left over. Has she enough to complete other designs with no matchsticks left over? Explain your answer.

(ii) Prove that the sequence formed by the number of sticks in the shapes generates an arithmetic sequence.

(iii) Sandrine then decided to change her design to create a stacked hexagon pattern, removing the matchsticks in the centre.

 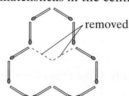
removed

How many completed levels could she make with 122 matchsticks, and how many matchsticks would be left over?

13. After knee surgery, your trainer changes your jogging programme slowly. He suggests jogging for 12 minutes each day for the first week. Each week thereafter, he suggests that you increase that time by 6 minutes a day.
In which week will you be jogging 60 minutes a day?

Section 4.3 Arithmetic series

When the terms of a sequence are added, a **series** is formed.

$T_1, T_2, T_3, T_4, ... T_n$ is a sequence ;   e.g. $3, 6, 9, 12, ...$

$T_1 + T_2 + T_3 + T_4, ... + T_n$ is a series ;   e.g. $3 + 6 + 9 + 12 + ...$

We use S_n to represent the sum of n terms of a series,

i.e. $S_n = T_1 + T_2 + T_3 + T_4 + ... T_n$

To find an expression for S_n, we note that in an arithmetic sequence,

$T_n = a + (n - 1)d$ (where $a = T_1$, the first term, and d = the common difference)

$\Rightarrow \quad T_{n-1} = a + [(n - 1) - 1]d$
$\qquad\qquad = a + (n - 2)d$
$\qquad T_3 = a + 2d$
$\qquad T_2 = a + d$
$\qquad T_1 = a$

Hence, $S_n =$	T_1	T_2	T_3	$... T_{n-1}$	T_n
$\Rightarrow$ $S_n =$	a	$+ a + d$	$+ a + 2d$	$.... + a + (n-2)d$	$+ a + (n-1)d$
Also, $S_n =$	$a + (n-1)d$	$+ a + (n-2)d$	$a + (n-3)d$	$... + a + d$	$+ a$ (reversing the order)
$\Rightarrow$ $2S_n =$	$2a + (n-1)d$	$+ 2a + (n-1)d$	$2a + (n-1)d$	$.... + 2a + (n-1)d$	$+ 2a + (n-1)d$

$\Rightarrow 2S_n = n[2a + (n-1)]d$ ... since there are n identical terms in the sum.

$\Rightarrow S_n = \frac{n}{2}[2a + (n-1)]d$ ... where a is the first term, d is the common difference, n is the number of terms.

Example 1

Find the sum of the series $4 + 11 + 18 + 25 + ... + 144$.

Examining the series, we find: $a = 4$
$$d = 11 - 4 = 7$$

To find n, the number of terms up to the term 144, we use

$$T_n = a + (n-1)d$$
$$144 = 4 + (n-1)7 = 4 + 7n - 7$$
$$144 = 7n - 3$$
$$7n = 147$$
$$n = \left(\frac{147}{7}\right) = 21 \text{ ... i.e. there are 21 terms in this sequence.}$$
$$\therefore \quad S_n = \frac{n}{2}\{2a + (n-1)d\}$$
$$S_{21} = \frac{21}{2}\{2(4) + (21-1)7\}$$
$$S_{21} = 1554.$$

Example 2

To celebrate the birth of his niece, an uncle offers to open a savings account with a deposit of €50. He also offers to every year add €10 more than he did the previous year until his niece is 21 years of age.
(i) Find an expression for S_n, the sum of money on deposit after n years.
(ii) Find S_{21}, the total saved after 21 years.

$$\left. \begin{array}{l} a = €50 \\ d = €10 \end{array} \right\} \quad S_n = \frac{n}{2}\{2a + (n-1)d\}$$
$$= \frac{n}{2}\{2(50) + (n-1)10\}$$
$$= \frac{n}{2}\{100 + 10n - 10)\}$$
$$\Rightarrow S_n = \frac{n}{2}\{10n + 90\}$$
$$S_{21} = \frac{21}{2}\{10(21) + 90\} = €3150$$

We note that

$$S_1 = T_1$$
$$S_2 = T_1 + T_2$$
$$\underline{S_3 = T_1 + T_2 + T_3 \text{ etc.}}$$
$$\therefore \quad S_3 - S_2 = \qquad T_3$$

Generally, $\qquad S_n - S_{n-1} = T_n$

Given S_n to find T_n :
$$S_n - S_{n-1} = T_n$$

Example 3

Given $S_n = n^2 - 4n$, find an expression for T_n and hence determine if the sequence is arithmetic.

$$S_n = n^2 - 4n$$
$$S_{n-1} = (n-1)^2 - 4(n-1) \quad \text{... replace } n \text{ with } n-1$$
$$= n^2 - 2n + 1 - 4n + 4$$
$$\Rightarrow \quad S_{n-1} = n^2 - 6n + 5$$

$$T_n = S_n - S_{n-1} = n^2 - 4n - (n^2 - 6n + 5)$$
$$= n^2 - 4n - n^2 + 6n - 5.$$
$$T_n = 2n - 5$$

If a sequence is arithmetic, $T_n - T_{n-1}$ must be a constant.
$$\Rightarrow \quad T_n - T_{n-1} = 2n - 5 - [2(n-1) - 5]$$
$$= 2n - 5 - (2n - 7)$$
$$= 2n - 5 - 2n + 7$$
$$= 2 \text{ , i.e. a constant.}$$

Therefore the sequence is arithmetic.

Example 4

A lighting company is making a sequence of light panels with the number of bulbs per panel in arithmetic sequence.

For the first 10 panels, 165 bulbs were used.

If the third panel is as shown in the diagram, find a, the first term of the sequence, and d, the common difference.

3rd panel (9 bulbs)

Hence draw a diagram of the first four panels.

$T_n = a + (n - 1)d$ Also, $S_n = \frac{n}{2}\{2a + (n - 1)d\}$

$T_3 = a + (3 - 1)d$

$T_3 = a + 2d = 9$ ..... we know that $S_n = 165$ when $n = 10$

$$\Rightarrow\; S_{10} = \frac{10}{2}\{2a + (10 - 1)d\}$$

$$S_{10} = 10a + 45d = 165.$$

$a + 2d = 9$

$\Rightarrow\quad 10a + 20d = 90$

and $10a + 45d = 165$

$\qquad\quad -25d = -75$ ... subtracting

$$\Rightarrow\qquad d = \left(\frac{-75}{-25}\right) = 3$$

If $d = 3$, then $a + 2(3) = 9$

$$\Rightarrow\quad a\quad = 3$$

The sequence of bulbs in the panels is 3, 6, 9, 12.

   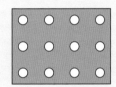

Sigma (Σ) notation

An efficient way of representing a series is to use the sigma notation.

$$S_n = T_1 + T_2 + T_3 + T_4 + \ldots\ldots T_n$$

$$= \sum_{r=1}^{n} T_r \text{ which reads as the sum of all the values of } T_r \text{ as } r \text{ changes from 1 to } n.$$

$$\sum_{r=1}^{6} (2r + 1) = 3 + 5 + 7 + 9 + 11 + 13 \;(n = 6 \text{ terms})$$

$$\sum_{r=2}^{5} \frac{r^2}{3} = \frac{4}{3} + \frac{9}{3} + \frac{16}{3} + \frac{25}{3} \;(n = 4 \text{ terms})$$

$$\sum_{r=0}^{4} r(r + 1) = 0(0 + 1) + 1(1 + 1) + 2(2 + 1) + 3(3 + 1) + 4(4 + 1)$$
$$\qquad\qquad = \quad 0 \quad + \quad 2 \quad + \quad 6 \quad + \quad 12 \quad + \quad 20 \quad (n = 5 \text{ terms})$$

$$\sum = \text{ the sum of}$$

$$\sum_{r=1}^{4} T_r \text{ is the sum of } T_1 + T_2 + T_3 + T_4$$

Example 5

(i) Use the sigma notation ($\sum$) to represent $2 + 6 + 10 + 14 + \ldots$ for 45 terms.

(ii) For what value of n is $\displaystyle\sum_{r=1}^{n} 3r - 5 = 90$?

(iii) Find the value of $\displaystyle\sum_{r=1}^{8} 4r - 1$.

(i) $2 + 6 + 10 + \ldots \quad \left.\begin{array}{l} a = 2 \\ d = 4 \end{array}\right\}$ $\qquad$ $\begin{aligned} T_n &= a + (n-1)d \\ &= 2 + (n-1)4 \\ T_n &= 4n - 2 \\ \Rightarrow \quad T_r &= 4r - 2. \end{aligned}$

$\therefore \quad 2 + 6 + 10 + \ldots \text{ for 45 terms} = \displaystyle\sum_{r=1}^{r=45} (4r - 2)$

(ii) $\displaystyle\sum_{r=1}^{n} (3r - 5) = [3(1) - 5] + [3(2) - 5] + [3(3) - 5)] + \ldots 3n - 5$

$\qquad\qquad\quad = \quad -2 \quad + \quad 1 \quad + \quad 4 \quad + \ldots 3n - 5.$

$\Rightarrow \quad \left.\begin{array}{l} a = -2 \\ d = 1 - (-2) = 3 \\ S_n = 90 \end{array}\right\}$ $\qquad$ $S_n = \dfrac{n}{2}\{2a + (n-1)d\}$

$\qquad\qquad\qquad\qquad\qquad\qquad 90 = \dfrac{n}{2}\{2(-2) + (n-1)(3)\}$

$\qquad\qquad\qquad\qquad\qquad 180 = n(-4 + 3n - 3)$

$\qquad\qquad\qquad\qquad\qquad 180 = n(3n - 7)$

$\qquad\qquad\qquad\qquad \Rightarrow \quad 3n^2 - 7n - 180 = 0$

$\qquad\qquad\qquad\qquad\quad (3n + 20)(n - 9) = 0$

$\Rightarrow \quad n - 9 = 0 \quad \text{or} \quad 3n + 20 = 0$

$\therefore \qquad n = 9 \quad \text{or} \qquad n = \dfrac{-20}{3}$

$\therefore \qquad n = 9 \quad \text{since} \quad n \in N$

(iii) $\displaystyle\sum_{r=1}^{8} 4r - 1 = 3 + 7 + 11 + \ldots (n = 8 \text{ terms})$

$\qquad\qquad \left.\begin{array}{l} a = 3 \\ d = 7 - 3 = 4 \end{array}\right\}$ $\qquad \therefore \quad S_n = \dfrac{n}{2}\{2a + (n-1)d\}$

$\qquad\qquad\qquad\qquad\qquad\qquad S_8 = \dfrac{8}{2}\{2(3) + (8-1)4\}$

$\qquad\qquad\qquad\qquad\qquad\qquad\quad = 4(34) = 136$

$\therefore \quad \displaystyle\sum_{r=1}^{8} 4r - 1 = 136$

Exercise 4.3

1. Find S_n and S_{20} of each of the following arithmetic series:
   (i) $1 + 5 + 9 + 13 + \dots$
   (ii) $50 + 48 + 46 + 44 + \dots$
   (iii) $1 + 1.1 + 1.2 + 1.3 + \dots$
   (iv) $-7 - 3 + 1 + 5 + \dots$

2. Find the sum of each of the following:
   (i) $6 + 10 + 14 + 18 + \dots + 50$
   (ii) $1 + 2 + 3 + 4 + \dots + 100$
   (iii) $80 + 74 + 68 + 62 + \dots -34$

3. How many terms of the series $5 + 8 + 11 + 14 + \dots$ must be added to make a total of 98?

4. Given $T_n = 5 - 3n$, write down the first term a, and the common difference d.
   Hence find S_{10}.

5. Anna saves money each week to buy a printer which costs €190. Her plan is to start with €10 and to put aside €2 more each week (i.e. €12, €14, etc.) until she has enough money to buy the printer.
   At this rate, how many weeks will it take Anna to save for the printer?

6. Evaluate (i) $\sum_{r=1}^{6} (3r + 1)$ (ii) $\sum_{r=0}^{5} (4r - 1)$ (iii) $\sum_{r=1}^{100} r$

7. Write each of the following series in sigma notation.
   (i) $4 + 8 + 12 + 16 + \dots + 124$
   (ii) $-10 - 9\frac{1}{2} - 8 - 7\frac{1}{2} + \dots + 4$
   (iii) $10 + 10.1 + 10.2 + 10.3 + \dots + 50$

8. In an arithmetic series, $T_4 = 15$ and $S_5 = 55$.
   Find the first five terms of the series.

9. The third term of an arithmetic sequence is 18 and the seventh term is 30.
   Find the sum of the first 33 terms.

10. In an Art class, a student experiments with a design for a dreamcatcher using rings and threads. The first three designs are shown below.
    He wishes to continue his pattern of designs. How many rings will he need for
    (i) design 10 (ii) design 20?
    How many rings in total will he need to make all 20 designs?

Design 1

Design 2

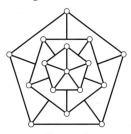
Design 3

11. The first term of an arithmetic sequence is -12 and the last term is 40. If the sum of the series is 196, find the number of terms in the sequence and the common difference.

12. Show that the sum of the natural numbers from 1 to n is $\frac{n}{2}(n+1)$ and use the formula to find the sum of $1 + 2 + 3 + 4 + \ldots\ldots 99$.

13. The twenty-first term of an arithmetic sequence is $5\frac{1}{2}$ and the sum of the first twenty-one terms is $94\frac{1}{2}$.

Find the first term and the common difference.

Hence find S_{30}, the sum of the first thirty terms.

14. In an arithmetic sequence, $T_{21} = 37$ and $S_{20} = 320$. Find the sum of the first ten terms.

15. Show that $S_n = \dfrac{n(a+l)}{2}$ is the sum to n terms of an arithmetic sequence where l is the last term.

16. Explain why S_∞ (the sum to infinity) for an arithmetic sequence cannot be found.

Section 4.4 Geometric sequences

A **geometric sequence** is formed when each term of the sequence is obtained by multiplying the previous term by a fixed amount.

For example, $\overset{\times 3}{\overgroup{}}\ \overset{\times 3}{\overgroup{}}\ \overset{\times 3}{\overgroup{}}$

2, 6, 18, 54, $\ldots\ldots$ each term increasing by a factor of 3.

$\overset{\times \frac{1}{2}}{\overgroup{}}\ \overset{\times \frac{1}{2}}{\overgroup{}}\ \overset{\times \frac{1}{2}}{\overgroup{}}$

4, 2, 1, $\frac{1}{2}$, $\ldots\ldots$ each term decreasing by a factor of $\frac{1}{2}$.

For any geometric sequence, the first term is denoted by a and the ratio between consecutive terms is r (called the common ratio); then every geometric sequence can be represented by

$$
\begin{array}{cccccc}
\overset{+r}{\overgroup{}} & \overset{+r}{\overgroup{}} & \overset{+r}{\overgroup{}} & \overset{+r}{\overgroup{}} & & \\
T_1, & T_2, & T_3, & T_4, & T_5, & \ldots\ldots \quad T_n \\
a, & ar, & ar^2, & ar^3, & ar^4, & \ldots\ldots \quad ar^{n-1}
\end{array}
$$

Consider the sequence:

$$
\left.
\begin{array}{cccccc}
& 2, & 6, & 18, & 54, & \ldots\ldots \ a.r^{n-1} \\
= & 2, & 2\times 3, & 2\times 3^2, & 2\times 3^3, & \ldots\ldots \ 2\times 3^{n-1}
\end{array}
\right\}
\begin{array}{l}
a = 2 \\
r = \frac{6}{2} = 3 \\
T_n = ar^{n-1} \\
T_n = 2.3^{n-1}
\end{array}
$$

Example 1

Find T_n and T_{10} of the geometric sequence $1, \frac{1}{4}, \frac{1}{16}, \frac{1}{64}, \ldots$

$$\left.\begin{array}{c} a = 1 \\[2mm] r = \dfrac{\frac{1}{4}}{1} = \dfrac{1}{4} \end{array}\right\}$$

$$\begin{aligned} T_n &= a.r^{n-1} \\ &= 1.\left(\tfrac{1}{4}\right)^{n-1} \\ &= \frac{1}{4^{n-1}} \\ T_n &= 4^{-n+1} = 4^{1-n} \\ T_{10} &= 4^{1-10} = 4^{-9} = \frac{1}{262\,144} \end{aligned}$$

In every geometric sequence:

$$T_1 = a$$
$$\frac{T_2}{T_1} = r$$
$$T_n = ar^{n-1}$$
$$\frac{T_{n+1}}{T_n} = r$$

Example 2

In a geometric sequence, $T_3 = 32$ and $T_6 = 4$.

Find a and r and hence write down the first six terms of the sequence.

$$\begin{aligned} T_n &= a.r^{n-1} \\ T_3 &= a.r^{3-1} = ar^2 = 32 \\ T_6 &= a.r^{6-1} = ar^5 = 4 \end{aligned}$$

Dividing these terms:

$$\frac{\cancel{a}r^5}{\cancel{a}r^2} = \frac{4}{32}$$
$$r^3 = \frac{1}{8}$$
$$r = \sqrt[3]{\frac{1}{8}} = \frac{1}{2}$$

If $\quad r = \frac{1}{2}$,

then $\quad ar^2 = 32$

$\Rightarrow \quad a.\left(\frac{1}{4}\right) = 32$

$\qquad\qquad a = 128.$

The sequence is $128, 64, 32, 16, 8, 4$.

Note:

➤ Given three consecutive terms of a geometric sequence, T_1, T_2, T_3, we note that
$$\frac{T_2}{T_1} = \frac{T_3}{T_2} = (\text{common ratio, } r).$$

➤ We also note that $\frac{a}{r}, a, ar$ are three consecutive terms of a geometric sequence, with first term $\frac{a}{r}$ and common ratio r.

Multiplying these terms gives $\frac{a}{\cancel{r}} \times a \times a\cancel{r} = a^3$, i.e. the cube of the middle term.

For example: $2, 6, 18$ are in geometric sequence,

$$\Rightarrow \quad 2 \times 6 \times 18 = 216 = 6^3$$

Also, $\quad 1, \frac{1}{4}, \frac{1}{16}$ are in geometric sequence,

$$\Rightarrow \quad 1 \times \frac{1}{4} \times \frac{1}{16} = \frac{1}{64} = \left(\frac{1}{4}\right)^3$$

Example 3

$3, x, x + 6, \ldots$ are the first three terms of a geometric sequence of positive terms.

Find
  (i) the value of x (ii) the tenth term of the sequence.

(i) For a geometric sequence, $\dfrac{T_2}{T_1} = \dfrac{T_3}{T_2}$, i.e., $\dfrac{x}{3} = \dfrac{x + 6}{x}$

$\therefore\quad x^2 = 3x + 18$

$\therefore\quad x^2 - 3x - 18 = 0$

$\therefore\quad (x - 6)(x + 3) = 0$

$\Rightarrow\quad x = 6 \text{ or } x = -3.$

$x = 6$ since the terms are positive $\Rightarrow$ sequence is $3, 6, 12, \ldots$

(ii) $T_n = a.r^{n-1}$

$T_{10} = a.r^{10-1} = a.r^9 = 3.2^9 = 1536$

Example 4

The product of the first three terms of a geometric sequence is 216 and their sum is 21. Given that the common ratio r is less than 1, find the first three terms of the sequence.

Let $\dfrac{a}{r}, a, ar$ be the first three terms.

$\Rightarrow\quad \dfrac{a}{r} \times a \times ar = a^3 = 216$

$\Rightarrow\quad a = \sqrt[3]{216} = 6$

Also, $\dfrac{a}{r} + a + ar = 21$

$\dfrac{6}{r} + 6 + 6r = 21$

$\dfrac{6}{r} + 6r - 15 = 0$

$6 + 6r^2 - 15r = 0$

$\therefore\quad 6r^2 - 15r + 6 = 0$

$(2r - 1)(r - 2) = 0$

$\Rightarrow\quad r = \tfrac{1}{2} \text{ or } r = 2.$

Since $r < 1 \Rightarrow r = \tfrac{1}{2}.$

Therefore the first three terms are $\dfrac{a}{r}, a, ar = \dfrac{6}{\left(\frac{1}{2}\right)}, 6, 6\left(\tfrac{1}{2}\right) = 12, 6, 3.$

Example 5

Find the number of terms in the geometric sequence $81, 27, 9, \ldots \frac{1}{27}$.

$$\left. \begin{array}{l} a = 81 \\ r = \dfrac{27}{81} = \dfrac{1}{3} \end{array} \right\}$$

Let $T_n = \dfrac{1}{27}$

$$T_n = a.r^{n-1}$$

$$= 81.\left(\dfrac{1}{3}\right)^{n-1} = \dfrac{1}{27}$$

$$\Rightarrow \quad \dfrac{1}{3^{n-1}} = \dfrac{1}{27 \times 81}$$

$$\Rightarrow \quad 3^{n-1} = 27 \times 81$$

$$\Rightarrow \quad 3^{n-1} = 3^3 \times 3^4 = 3^7$$

$$\therefore \quad n - 1 = 7$$

$$n = 8 \quad \Rightarrow \quad \text{there are eight terms in the sequence.}$$

Note: When solving an equation such as $4^{n-1} = 4096$, we can use two different methods.

Method A: Express 4096 as a power of 4 using a calculator and trial and error.

$$\therefore \quad 4^{n-1} = 4096 = 4^6$$

$$n - 1 = 6$$

$$n = 7$$

Method B: Using logs.

$$4^{n-1} = 4096$$

$$\Rightarrow \quad \log 4^{n-1} = \log 4096$$

$$\therefore \quad (n - 1) \log 4 = \log 4096$$

$$n - 1 = \dfrac{\log 4096}{\log 4} = 6$$

$$\therefore \quad n = 7$$

(See chapter 7).

Exponential sequences

Exponential functions of the form $y = Aa^x$, where A is the initial value and a the multiplier or common ratio, produce geometric sequences.

Consider a ball dropping from a height of 10 m.

If the ball bounces back to $\frac{2}{3}$ of its original height on each bounce, the height of the ball is given by the following pattern:

After 1 bounce: $\quad 10 \times \frac{2}{3} = 10\left(\frac{2}{3}\right)^1$

After 2 bounces: $\quad 10 \times \frac{2}{3} \times \frac{2}{3} = 10\left(\frac{2}{3}\right)^2$

After 3 bounces: $\quad 10 \times \frac{2}{3} \times \frac{2}{3} \times \frac{2}{3} = 10\left(\frac{2}{3}\right)^3$

After n bounces: $\quad 10 \times \left(\frac{2}{3}\right)^n$

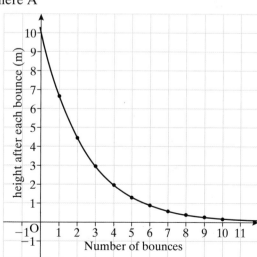

Example 6

A ball is dropped from a height of 27 m and loses $\frac{2}{3}$ of its height on each bounce.

(i) Find the height of the ball on each of its first four bounces.
(ii) Hence write down the height of the ball after the 10th bounce.
(iii) After which bounce will the ball be at most 2.5 m above the ground?

(i) After the 1st bounce, the ball is $27 \times \frac{1}{3} = 9$ m above the ground.

After the 2nd bounce, the ball is $27 \times \frac{1}{3} \times \frac{1}{3} = 3$ m.

After the 3rd bounce, the ball is $27 \times \frac{1}{3} \times \frac{1}{3} \times \frac{1}{3} = 1$ m.

After the 4th bounce, the ball is $27 \times \frac{1}{3} \times \frac{1}{3} \times \frac{1}{3} \times \frac{1}{3} = \frac{1}{3}$ m.

(ii) After the 10th bounce, the ball is $27 \times \left(\frac{1}{3}\right)^n = 27 \times \left(\frac{1}{3}\right)^{10} = 0.00046$ m.

(iii) To find n, the number of bounces needed to produce a height of 2.5 m,

let $27 \times \left(\frac{1}{3}\right)^n = 2.5$

$\left(\frac{1}{3}\right)^n = 0.093$

$\ln\left(\frac{1}{3}\right)^n = \ln(0.093)$

$n\ln\left(\frac{1}{3}\right) = \ln(0.093) \Rightarrow n = \left(\frac{\ln(0.093)}{\ln\left(\frac{1}{3}\right)}\right) = 2.16$ bounces.

Since the number of bounces of a ball has to be a discrete (whole) number, after two bounces the ball *will* be above 2.5 m.

Therefore it will require three bounces of the ball to guarantee the ball is below 2.5 m.

Exercise 4.4

1. Determine which of the following sequences are geometric.

   Find the common ratios of these sequences and write down the next two terms of each sequence.

   (i) 3, 9, 27, 81, ...
   (ii) 1, $\frac{1}{3}$, $\frac{1}{9}$, $\frac{1}{27}$, ...
   (iii) −1, 2, −4, 8, ...
   (iv) 1, −1, 1, −1, ...
   (v) 1, $1\frac{1}{2}$, $1\frac{1}{4}$, $1\frac{1}{8}$, ...
   (vi) a, a^2, a^3, a^4, ...
   (vii) 1, 1.1, 1.21, 1.331, ...
   (viii) $\frac{1}{2}$, $\frac{1}{6}$, $\frac{1}{12}$, $\frac{1}{36}$, ...
   (ix) 2, 4, −8, −16, ...
   (x) $\frac{3}{4}$, $\frac{9}{2}$, 27, 162, ...

2. Each of the following sequences is geometric.
   Find a and r and hence find the indicated term.

   (i) 5, 10, ... (T_{11})
   (ii) 10, 25, ... (T_7)
   (iii) 1.1, 1.21, ... (T_8)
   (iv) 24, −12, 6, ... (T_{10})

3. Given $T_2 = 12$ and $T_5 = 324$, find a and r and hence write down the first five terms of the sequence.

4. Find the value of r given that the third term is 6 and the eighth term is 1458.

5. Write down the first five terms of the geometric sequence that has a second term 4 and a fifth term $-\frac{1}{16}$.

6.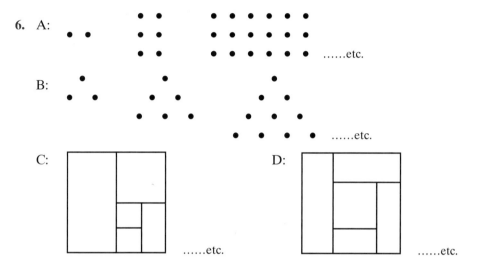

A:

B:

C:

D:

By inspection, decide which of the above patterns generate a geometric sequence. Draw the next pattern of those that are geometric.

7. The three numbers $n - 2$, n and $n + 3$ are the first three terms of a geometric sequence. Find the value of n and hence write down the first four terms of the sequence.

8. The third term of a geometric sequence is -63 and the fourth term is 189. Find
   (i) the values of a and r
   (ii) an expression for T_n.

9. The first term of a geometric sequence is 16 and the fifth term is 9. What is the value of the seventh term?

10. The product of the first three terms of a geometric sequence is 27 and their sum is 13. Find the first four terms of the sequence.

11. The nth term, T_n, of a geometric sequence is $T_n = 3 \times 2^{n-1}$. Write down the first five terms of the sequence in their simplest form.

12. Given $T_n = 8\left(\frac{3}{4}\right)^n$, write out the first four terms of the sequence.

13. Write out the first four terms of the sequence defined by $T_n = (-1)^{n+1} \times \dfrac{5}{2^{n-4}}$.

14. If each of the following are the first three terms of a geometric sequence, find one or two possible values of x and hence write down possible sequence(s) for each.

    (i) $x - 3, x$ and $3x + 4$ (ii) $x + 1, x + 4$ and $3x + 2$

    (iii) $x - 2, x$ and $x + 3$ (iv) $x - 6, 2x$ and x^2.

15. Show that the sequence whose nth term is $T_n = 2 \times 3^n$ is a geometric sequence.

> To show that a sequence is geometric, we must show that $\dfrac{T_{n+1}}{T_n} = $ a constant (r).

16. Investigate if the sequence $T_n = 3 \times n^2$ is geometric.

17. Find the number of terms in each of the following geometric sequences:

    (i) $5, 15, 45, \ldots\ldots 3645$ (ii) $48, 6, ¾, \ldots\ldots \dfrac{3}{2048}$

18. A rubber orb is dropped from a height of 27 m on to a concrete floor. Each time it hits the concrete, it bounces back to $\frac{2}{3}$ of the original height. Find

    (i) the height of each of the first four bounces

    (ii) a formula for the height of the nth bounce

    (iii) the height of the 12th bounce using the formula found in (ii).

19. The value of a sum of money on deposit at 3% per annum compound interest is given by $A = €4000\,(1.03)^t$ where t is the number of years of the investment. Find

    (i) the amount of money on deposit

    (ii) the value of the investment at the end of each of the first four years

    (iii) the value of the investment at the end of the 10th year

    (iv) the number of years, correct to the nearest year, needed for the investment to double in value.

20. The value, A, of an investment is given by $A = P(1 + i)^t$ where P is the sum on deposit, t the number of years and i the rate of interest, expressed as a decimal.

    Given that over a 10 year period €2500 on deposit amounted to €3047, calculate the rate of interest (correct to 1 place of decimals).

Section 4.5 Geometric series

When the terms of a geometric sequence are added, a **geometric series** is created.

For example, $2 + 6 + 18 + 54 + \ldots\ldots$ is a geometric series.

To find the sum of a geometric series, we use the following procedure:

$$S_n = a + ar + ar^2 + \ldots\ldots ar^{n-3} + ar^{n-2} + ar^{n-1}$$

$$\Rightarrow r.S_n = \quad ar + ar^2 + \ldots\ldots ar^{n-3} + ar^{n-2} + ar^{n-1} + ar^n \quad \text{… multiplying each term by } r$$

Subtracting: $\quad S_n - rS_n = \quad a - ar^n$

$$\therefore \quad S_n(1 - r) = a(1 - r^n)$$

$$\therefore \quad S_n = \frac{a(1 - r^n)}{1 - r}$$

The sum to n terms of a geometric sequence,

$$S_n = \frac{a(1 - r^n)}{1 - r}, \quad \text{where } a \text{ is the first term and } r \text{ is the common ratio.}$$

Example 1

Find T_5 and S_5 of each of the following:

(i) $1 + 3 + 9 + \ldots$ (ii) $1 + \frac{1}{4} + \frac{1}{16} + \ldots$

(i) $a = 1$
$\left. \begin{array}{l} \end{array} \right\}$
$r = \frac{3}{1} = 3$

$T_n = ar^{n-1}$
$T_n = 1.3^{n-1}$
$= 3^{n-1}$
$\therefore \quad T_5 = 3^{5-1}$
$= 3^4$
$= 81$

$S_n = \frac{a(1 - r^n)}{1 - r}$
$= \frac{1(1 - 3^n)}{1 - 3}$
$= \frac{1 - 3^n}{-2}$
$S_n = \frac{3^n - 1}{2}$
$\therefore \quad S_5 = \frac{3^5 - 1}{2} = 121$

(ii) $a = 1$
$\left. \begin{array}{l} \end{array} \right\}$
$r = \frac{\frac{1}{4}}{1} = \frac{1}{4}$

$T_n = ar^{n-1}$
$= 1.\left(\frac{1}{4}\right)^{n-1}$
$T_n = \frac{1}{4^{n-1}}$
$\therefore \quad T_5 = \frac{1}{4^{5-1}}$
$T_5 = \frac{1}{4^4}$
$= \frac{1}{256}$

$S_n = \frac{a(1 - r^n)}{1 - r}$
$= \frac{1\left(1 - \left(\frac{1}{4}\right)^n\right)}{1 - \frac{1}{4}}$
$= \frac{1 - \frac{1}{4^n}}{\frac{3}{4}}$
$S_n = \frac{4}{3}\left(1 - \frac{1}{4^n}\right)$
$\therefore \quad S_5 = \frac{4}{3}\left(1 - \frac{1}{4^5}\right) = \frac{341}{256}$

Example 2

In a geometric series, $T_3 = 32$ and $T_6 = 4$; find a and r and hence find S_8, the sum of the first eight terms.

$T_n = ar^{n-1}$
$T_3 = ar^{3-1} = ar^2 = 32$
$T_6 = ar^{6-1} = ar^5 = 4$

Dividing these equations, we get $\frac{\cancel{a}r^2}{\cancel{a}r^5} = \frac{32}{4}$

$\frac{1}{r^3} = 8$

$r^3 = \frac{1}{8}$

$r = \sqrt[3]{\frac{1}{8}} = \frac{1}{2}$

If $r = \frac{1}{2}$, then $a\left(\frac{1}{2}\right)^2 = 32$

$$a\left(\frac{1}{4}\right) = 32$$

$$a = 128.$$

$$\therefore \quad S_n = \frac{a(1 - r^n)}{1 - r}$$

$$= \frac{128\left(1 - \left(\frac{1}{2}\right)^n\right)}{1 - \frac{1}{2}}$$

$$S_n = 256\left(1 - \frac{1}{2^n}\right)$$

$$S_8 = 256\left(1 - \frac{1}{2^8}\right)$$

$$= 255$$

It is very important to understand the effect the value of r has on the sum of a geometric series. Consider three geometric sequences – A, B and C – where A has a common ratio of $r = 2$, B has a common ratio of $r = 1$, and C has a common ratio of $r = \frac{1}{2}$.

Starting with a first term value of 1, we get:

Sequence	r	T_1	T_2	T_3	T_4	T_5	T_6	.....	T_{100}
A	2	1	2	4	8	16	32		6.3×10^{29}
B	1	1	1	1	1	1	1		1
C	$\frac{1}{2}$	1	$\frac{1}{2}$	$\frac{1}{4}$	$\frac{1}{8}$	$\frac{1}{16}$	$\frac{1}{32}$		1.6×10^{-30}

$\Rightarrow$

Series	r	S_1	S_2	S_3	S_4	S_5	S_6	.....	S_{100}
A	2	1	3	7	15	31	63		1.3×10^{30}
B	1	1	2	3	4	5	6		100
C	$\frac{1}{2}$	1	1.5	1.75	1.875	1.9375	1.96875		2

If $|r| > 1$, the values of T_n and S_n, as n gets bigger, increase very rapidly.

If $|r| = 1$, then the sequence behaves like an arithmetic sequence with a constant amount added each term.

If $|r| < 1$, then the value of S_n is said to have a "limiting value".

In series C above, the sum S_n approaches the value 2.

By taking a sufficiently large value of n, we can make S_n as near to 2 as we wish, that is, we can make $2 - S_n$ as small as we wish.

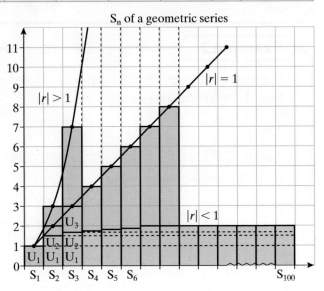

S_n of a geometric series

We say that S_n approaches **a limiting value of 2** as n approaches infinity.

This is written as: $S_n \to 2$ as $n \to \infty$ or $\lim_{n \to \infty} S_n = 2$.

In words, we say that "the limit of the partial sum S_n, as n tends to infinity, is 2."

Now consider the formula for the sum to n terms of a geometric series if $|r| < 1$.

$$S_n = \frac{a(1 - r^n)}{1 - r}$$

When $|r| < 1$, r^n will approximate to zero for large values of n, i.e. $r^n \to 0$ as $n \to \infty$.

Thus, $S_n = \dfrac{a(1 - r^n)}{1 - r}$ becomes $S_n = \dfrac{a(1 - 0)}{1 - r}$

$$\therefore \quad S_n = \frac{a}{1 - r} \quad \text{as} \quad n \to \infty.$$

or $\lim_{n \to \infty} S_n = \dfrac{a}{1 - r}$

> For a geometric series with $|r| < 1$,
> $$\lim_{n \to \infty} S_n = \frac{a}{1 - r}.$$

Example 3

Find the sum to infinity of the geometric series $16 + 12 + 9 + \ldots$

$\left. \begin{array}{l} a = 16 \\ r = \frac{12}{16} = \frac{3}{4} \end{array} \right\}$ $\Rightarrow$ $\lim_{n \to \infty} S_n = \dfrac{a}{1 - r}$

$$= \frac{16}{1 - \frac{3}{4}} = 64$$

Recurring decimals

Recurring decimals can be expressed as a sum to infinity of a geometric sequence, where the common ratio $r < 1$.

$$\overset{\times \frac{1}{10} \quad \times \frac{1}{10} \quad \times \frac{1}{10}}{}$$

For example, $0.\dot{3} = 0.3333\ldots = \dfrac{3}{10} + \dfrac{3}{10^2} + \dfrac{3}{10^3} + \dfrac{3}{10^4} + \ldots$

where $a = 0.3$ and $r = \dfrac{1}{10}$.

Similarly,

$0.2\dot{3}\dot{5} = 0.2353535\ldots = 0.2 + [0.035 + 0.00035 + \ldots]$

$$= 0.2 + \frac{35}{1000} + \frac{35}{100000} + \ldots$$

$$= 0.2 + \text{an infinite geometric series}$$

where $a = \dfrac{35}{1000}$ and $r = \dfrac{1}{100}$.

Write the recurring decimal $0.\dot{2}\dot{3}$ as a fraction in the form $\frac{a}{b}$, $a, b, \in N$.

$$0.\dot{2}\dot{3} = 0.232323 \ldots = 0.23 + 0.0023 + 0.000023 + \ldots$$

$$= \frac{23}{100} + \frac{23}{10000} + \frac{23}{1000000} + \ldots$$

$$\Rightarrow \quad a = \frac{23}{100} \quad \text{and} \quad r = \frac{23}{10000} \div \frac{23}{100} = \frac{1}{100}$$

$$\Rightarrow \quad \lim_{n \to \infty} S_n = \frac{a}{1-r} = \frac{\frac{23}{100}}{1 - \frac{1}{100}} = \frac{23}{100} \times \frac{100}{99} = \frac{23}{99}$$

$$\left[\text{Note:} \quad \lim_{n \to \infty} S_n \text{ is often written as } S_\infty. \text{ Thus, } S_\infty = \frac{23}{99} \right]$$

Note: If we let $x = 0.232323 \ldots$,

then $100x = 23.232323 \ldots$

$\Rightarrow \quad 99x = 23 \ldots$ subtracting both lines

$\therefore \quad x = \frac{23}{99}$

Exercise 4.5

1. Find the sum of the first 10 terms of the series $2 + 6 + 18 + 54 + \ldots$

2. Find the number of terms, n, in the following series:
   $1024 + 512 + 256 + \ldots 32$. Hence find the sum of the series.

3. Find S_8 of the series $1 + 2 + 4 + 8 + \ldots$

4. Find S_{10} of the series $32 + 16 + 8 + \ldots$

5. Find S_6 of the series $4 - 12 + 36 - 108 + \ldots$

6. Find the number of terms in the series $729 - 243 + 81 - \ldots - \frac{1}{3}$.
   Hence find the sum of the series.

7. Write out the first three terms of the series $\sum_{r=1}^{6} 4^r$ and hence find the sum of the series.

8. Evaluate $\sum_{r=1}^{8} 2 \times 3^r$.

9. Find the sum of $\sum_{r=1}^{10} 6 \times \left(\frac{1}{2}\right)^r$ correct to three places of decimals.

10. Write each of the following recurring decimals as an infinite geometric series.
    Hence express each as a decimal in the form $\frac{a}{b}$, $a, b \in N$.

    (i) $0.\dot{7}$ (ii) $0.\dot{3}\dot{5}$ (iii) $0.2\dot{3}$ (iv) $0.3\dot{7}0$ (v) $0.16\dot{2}$ (vi) $0.3\dot{2}\dot{1}$

11. Find S_n, the sum to n terms, of $1 + \frac{1}{2} + \left(\frac{1}{2}\right)^2 + \left(\frac{1}{2}\right)^3 + \ldots + \left(\frac{1}{2}\right)^{n-1}$ and hence find S_∞, the sum to infinity of the series.

Find the least value of n such that $S_\infty - S_n < 0.001$.

Section 4.6 Number patterns – Revisited

Linear, Quadratic and Cubic patterns

In our study of algebra, we discovered that we can identify patterns in certain number sequences by calculating differences.

The sequence $-4, 0, 4, 8, 12, \ldots$ has a first difference of $+4$ creating a formula for $T_n = 4n + a$, where $n = 1, 2, 3, \ldots$ etc.

Sequence		-4	0	4	8	12
1st difference			$+4$	$+4$	$+4$	$+4$

Therefore, if $n = 1$, then $T_1 = 4(1) + a = -4$
$$\Rightarrow \quad a = -8$$

$\therefore$ A constant first difference gives rise to an arithmetic (**linear**) pattern, $T_n = 4n - 8$.

As the following table indicates, the sequence $7, 17, 31, 49, 71, \ldots$ does not have a constant first difference.

Sequence		7	17	31	49	71
1st difference			10	14	18	22
2nd difference				4	4	4

A constant second difference indicates a **quadratic** (n^2) pattern, $\boldsymbol{an^2 + bn + c}$.

Consider $T_n = an^2 + bn + c$ for all values of $n \geqslant 1$.
The following table evaluates the first and second differences in terms of a, b and c.

T_1	T_2	T_3	T_4	T_5	
$a + b + c$	$4a + 2b + c$	$9a + 3b + c$	$16a + 4b + c$	$25a + 5b + c$	
	$3a + b + c$	$5a + b + c$	$7a + b + c$	$9a + b + c$	1st difference
		$2a$	$2a$	$2a$	2nd difference

From this table we can see that the second difference of a quadratic pattern of numbers is always $2a$, twice the coefficient of n^2.

$\therefore$ if the second difference is $+4 \Rightarrow 2a = 4$
$$a = 2$$

$\therefore$ $T_n = 2n^2 + bn + c$ for $n = 1, 2, 3$, etc.

To find b and c, we use simultaneous equations as follows.

$T_n = 2n^2 + bn + c$ for $n = 1, 2, 3$, etc.

Let $n = 1$, $T_1 = 2(1)^2 + b(1) + c = 7$
$$\Rightarrow \quad b + c = 5$$

Let $n = 2$, $T_2 = 2(2)^2 + b(2) + c = 17$
$$\Rightarrow \quad 2b + c = 9$$
$$\underline{\quad\quad b + c = 5}$$
$$\therefore \quad b = 4$$

If $\;b = 4$, then $4 + c = 5$,

$$\Rightarrow\quad c = 1$$

$\therefore\quad T_n = 2n^2 + 4n + 1\;$ for $\;n = 1, 2, 3,$ etc.

The method of finite differences can be used to study patterns of numbers with higher powers.

If the third difference is constant we have a **cubic pattern**, $T_n = an^3 + bn^2 + cn + d$ etc.

linear

quadratic

cubic

	Pattern	To find a
1st difference constant	$T_n = an + b$	$a = $ 1st difference
2nd difference constant	$T_n = an^2 + bn + c$	$2a = $ 2nd difference
3rd difference constant	$T_n = an^3 + bn^2 + cn + d$	$6a = $ 3rd difference

Example 1

Express the nth term of the number pattern $-1, 13, 51, 125, 247, \ldots.$ as a cubic polynomial.

Since the 3rd difference is constant, the number pattern has a cubic part and $6a = $ third difference.

$$\Rightarrow\quad a = \tfrac{1}{6} \times 12 = 2$$

Sequence		-1		13		51		125		247
1st difference			14		38		74		122	
2nd difference				24		36		48		
3rd difference					12		12			

$\therefore\quad T_n = 2n^3 + bn^2 + cn + d\;$ for $\;n \geqslant 1$

$T_1 = 2 + b + c + d = -1$

$\qquad\Rightarrow\quad b + c + d = -3$

$T_2 = 2(2)^3 + b(2)^2 + c(2) + d = 13$

$\qquad\qquad\Rightarrow\quad 4b + 2c + d = -3$

$T_3 = 2(3)^3 + b(3)^2 + c(3) + d = 51$

$\qquad\qquad\Rightarrow\quad 9b + 3c + d = -3$

Solving the equations:

1. $b + c + d = -3$

2. $4b + 2c + d = -3$

3. $9b + 3c + d = -3$

we get $\;b = 0, c = 0, d = -3$

$\therefore\quad T_n = 2n^3 - 3\;$ for $\;n \geqslant 1.$

Example 2

A mosaic arrangement is constructed on a floor as shown.
Find the number of tiles needed for the 30th pattern.

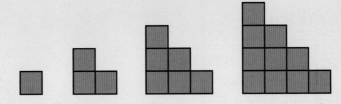

The number of tiles required forms the pattern 1, 3, 6, 10, ...

Checking differences, we find a constant 2nd difference.

Therefore, a quadratic pattern –
$T_n = an^2 + bn + c$ – exists.

Sequence	1	3	6	10
1st difference		2	3	4
2nd difference			1	1

And $2a = 1 \Rightarrow a = \frac{1}{2}$

$\therefore \quad T_n = \frac{1}{2}n^2 + bn + c$

$T_1 = \frac{1}{2}(1)^2 + b(1) + c = 1$

$\Rightarrow \quad b + c = \frac{1}{2}$

$T_2 = \frac{1}{2}(2)^2 + b(2) + c = 3$

$\Rightarrow \quad 2b + c = 1$

Solving these equations, we find
$b = \frac{1}{2}, c = 0$

$\therefore \quad T_n = \frac{1}{2}n^2 + \frac{1}{2}n$, for $n \geqslant 1$

$\therefore \quad T_{30} = \frac{1}{2}(30)^2 + \frac{1}{2}(30) = 465$.

In summary, when a process is examined and a number pattern identified, we can create a formula for successive elements under such headings as (i) Arithmetic (Linear) (ii) Quadratic (iii) Cubic (iv) Geometric (Exponential) by identifying the link between elements of the pattern.

Exercise 4.6

1. Using the method of differences, find the nth term, T_n, for each of the following number patterns:

   (i) 5, 9, 13, 17, 21, ...   (ii) 1, 4, 7, 10, 13, ...   (iii) 11, 16, 21, 26, 31, ...

2. Find a formula for T_n, the nth term, of the following number patterns:

   (i) 2, 1, 0, −1, −2, ...   (ii) 0, −2, −4, −6, −8, ...   (iii) −6, −4, −2, 0, 2, ...

3. If each square in this pattern measures 5 mm × 5 mm, find

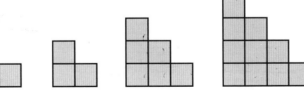

   (i) the area   (ii) the perimeter   of the 28th pattern.

4. If each triangle has an area of 1 cm², convert this triangular pattern into a number pattern. Hence find,

   (i) the area of the 30th part of the design
   (ii) which part would have an area of 441 cm².

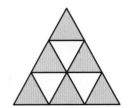

163

5. If this pattern of triangles continues, find

    (i) the area of the 100th triangle
    (ii) which triangle has an area of 240 cm².

 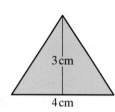 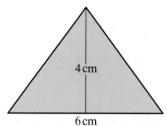

6. Each of the following number patterns can be written in the form $an^3 + bn^2 + cn + d$. Find the values of $a, b, c,$ and d in each case:

    (i) 6, 27, 74, 159, 294
    (ii) 3, −1, −1, 9, 35
    (iii) −1, 2, 17, 50, 107

7. Form a rule for determining the number of bright tiles in each of the following patterns. Determine the number of bright and dark tiles needed for the 24th pattern of each.

    (a)

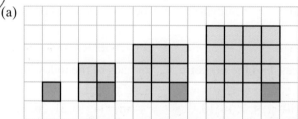

    (b)

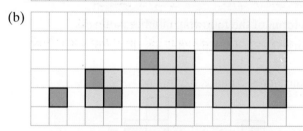

    (c)

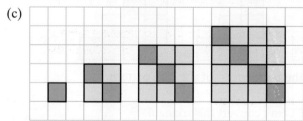

8. Write a formula for the nth term of each of the following number sequences.

    (i) 7, 16, 31, 52, 79, ...
    (ii) 1, 0, −3, −8, −15, ...
    (iii) −1, 14, 53, 128, 251, ...
    (iv) −2, 2, 6, 10, 14, ...
    (v) 4, 31, 98, 223, 424, ...

Revision Exercise 4 (Core)

1. Find the first four terms of these sequences given the nth term in each case:

   (i) $T_n = 3n + 4$

   (ii) $T_n = 6n - 1$

   (iii) $T_n = 2^{n-1}$

   (iv) $T_n = (n + 3)(n + 4)$

   (v) $T_n = n^3 + 1$

2. The third term of an arithmetic sequence is 71 and the seventh term is 55.
   Find the first term and the common difference.

3. In a geometric series, the first term is 12 and the sum to infinity is 36.
   Find the common ratio.

4. Find the common ratio in each of the following geometric progressions and hence write an expression for T_n, the nth term.

   (i) $-2,\ 4,\ -8,\ ...$

   (ii) $1,\ \frac{1}{2},\ \frac{1}{4},\ ...$

   (iii) $2,\ -6,\ 18,\ ...$

5. Using matchsticks, a series of cubes are made and joined as cuboids, as shown in the diagram.

   (i) Determine the number of matchsticks needed for the nth cuboid.

   (ii) Determine the maximum number of cubes in the cuboid if there are 2006 matchsticks left for the construction.

6. The second term of a geometric sequence is 21.
   The third term is -63.
   Find   (i) the common ratio   (ii) the first term.

7. €2000 is invested in a savings scheme which offers 2.5% compound interest.
   Explain how the expression $A = €2000(1.025)^5$ represents the value of the investment after 5 years.

8. Find the sum of the first 200 natural numbers.

9. The fifth term of an arithmetic sequence is twice the second term.
   The two terms also differ by 9.
   Find the sum of the first 10 terms of the sequence.

10. Evaluate $\displaystyle\sum_{r=3}^{16} (2r + 1)$.

Revision Exercise 4 (Advanced)

1. A set of mirrors is arranged, as shown in the diagram. A lamp of 2000 lumens shines its light so that it reflects continuously from consecutive mirrors.
    (**Note:** A lumen is a measure of brightness)

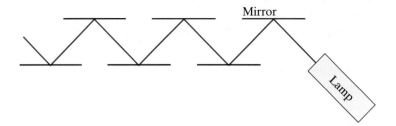

Mirror

Lamp

Each mirror reflects $\frac{3}{5}$ of the light that hits it.

(i) Find the intensity of the light reflecting from the 10th mirror.

(ii) Write an equation representing the intensity of the light reflecting from the nth mirror.

(iii) After how many reflections (mirrors) will the intensity be reduced to $\frac{1}{10}$ of its original value?

2. The value of a sum of money, €P, on deposit for t years is given by
    $A = P(1 + i)^t$, where i is the interest rate over the saving period.

    (i) Show that the time taken for the initial investment to double in value for any investment depends only on the interest rate i and not on the sum invested. Hence find an expression, in terms of i, the interest rate, for the time taken for an investment to double in value.

    (ii) Hence calculate the time taken for a sum of money to double in value if invested at an interest rate of
       (a) 2%   (b) 5%   (c) 10%.

3. A ball is dropped from a height of 10 m and bounces back up to 6m and then to 3.6 m and so on, as shown in the diagram. Copy the graph and add in the next five heights of the ball from the ground.

    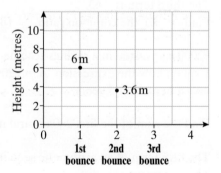

    (i) Write down a series of numbers representing the total distance travelled by the ball.

    (ii) Describe what type of series is generated.

    (iii) Find the total distance travelled by the ball.

    (iv) How is the size of the ball accounted for in this problem?

4. (i) Write an equation for the *nth* term of the sequence 3, 6, 12, 24, 48 ...

(ii) Use logs to find the first term of this sequence to exceed one million.

5. A rich auntie is pleased to see you take up the game of chess. To encourage you, she says that she will put 1 cent on the first square of the board and tells you that she will double the amount for each week that you continue to learn the game.

How much money, in euros, will your aunt owe you by the end of

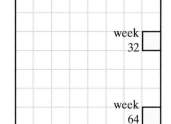

(i) week 32

(ii) week 64 ?

6. An arithmetic sequence has three consecutive terms with a sum of 33 and a product of 935. Find these terms.

7. The value of a car depreciates by 13% per year. If the car is bought new for €30 000,

(i) find a formula linking the value $€V$ of the car with its age a

(ii) find the value of the car after five years

(iii) find the year in which the car is worth less than €6000.

8. A sequence of numbers is given by the formula $T_n = 3\left(\frac{2}{3}\right)^n - 1$, where n is a positive integer.

(i) Find T_1, T_2, T_3 of this sequence.

(ii) Show that $T_{n+1} = 2\left(\frac{2}{3}\right)^n - 1$.

(iii) If $3T_{n+1} - 2T_n = k$, find k if $k \in \mathbb{Z}$.

(iv) Show that $\displaystyle\sum_{n=1}^{15} \left[3\left(\frac{2}{3}\right)^n - 1\right] = -9.014$ correct to 4 significant figures.

9. Given that S_n is the sum to n terms of a series,

(i) show that $T_n = S_n - S_{n-1}$, where T_n is the *nth* term of the series

(ii) if $S_n = 3n^2 + n$, find an expression for T_n

(iii) obtain an expression, in terms of n, for $\displaystyle\sum_{r=1}^{n}(T_r)^2$, given that $\Sigma n = \frac{n}{2}(n+1)$ and $\Sigma n^2 = \frac{n}{6}(n+1)(2n+1)$.

10. Express $\log_4 x$ in terms of $\log_2 x$ in its simplest form.

Hence show that $\log_2 x$, $\log_4 x$ and $\log_{16} x$ are three consecutive terms of a geometric series and state the value of the common ratio.

If the sum to infinity of the geometric series is $k \log_2 x$, find the value of k.

(See Chapter 7 for the rules for logs.)

Revision Exercise 4 (Extended-Response Questions)

1. A cubic sequence can be represented by the nth term $T_n = an^3 + bn^2 + cn + d$, where $a, b, c \in R$ and $a \neq 0$.
   (i) Complete the following Table 1 in terms of a, b, and c.

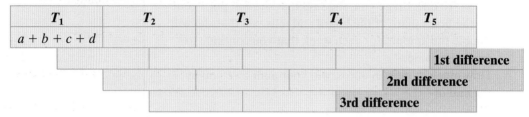

T_1	T_2	T_3	T_4	T_5
$a + b + c + d$				

Table 1

   (ii) Based on this table, copy and complete the following statement:
   The third difference for all cubic sequences is always ....
   (iii) Compete the following two statements about quadratic sequences:
   (a) The second difference for all quadratic sequences is always ....
   (b) The first difference, $T_2 - T_1$, for all quadratic sequences is always ....
   (iv) Complete Table 2 for the sequence 5, 12, 25, 44, ...

T_1	T_2	T_3	T_4
5	12	25	44

Table 2

   (v) Use your expressions for first and second differences in (iii) to find a, b and c.
   (vi) Hence evaluate T_{20}.

2. A ball is dropped from an initial height of 40 m onto a concrete floor.
   On the tenth bounce, it rises 1 m up from the floor.

   (i) Write an expression for the height of the ball after n bounces.
   (ii) What percentage of the height from which it fell does the ball bounce back up each time?
   (iii) Find the heights of the ball after each of its first 5 bounces and hence complete the table:

Bounce	1st	2nd	3rd	4th	5th
Height					

   (iv) Draw a graph representing the height of the ball after each bounce.
   (v) Estimate from your sketch the number of bounces needed before the bounce does not exceed 2 m.
   (vi) Using the expression in part (i), calculate the minimum number of bounces needed for the ball to stay under 2 m.
   (vii) According to the expression in part (i) and the graph in part (iv), the ball could go on bouncing forever. Explain why this does not actually happen.

3. Ronan is in his Leaving Certificate year.
   At the end of fifth-year, his parents gave him €20 a week pocket money.
   To encourage him to work harder in sixth-year, they proposed two types of "pocket money schemes" for Ronan.

   Scheme 1: €20 in week one. €22 in week two … and so on, increasing by €2 each week.

   Scheme 2: €20 in week one. €21 in week two … and so on, increasing by a constant factor of $\frac{21}{20}$ each week.

   (i) Find separately the total amount in euro he would receive in week n for Scheme 1 and Scheme 2, leaving each answer in its simplest form.
   (ii) Assuming that a school year consists of 36 "five-day" weeks, which scheme do you think Ronan should choose? Justify your answer.
   (iii) Ronan is interested in saving for a new games console which costs €400.
   If he spends just €1.50 per school day and saves the rest of his pocket money, which is the earliest week he will be able to buy the games console?
   Assume that he has chosen Scheme 1 above for his pocket money.

4. A liquid is kept in a barrel. At the start of the year 2010, 160 litres of liquid is poured into the barrel. If 15% of the volume of the liquid is lost by evaporation during the year,

   (i) evaluate the amount of liquid in the barrel at the end of the year
   (ii) show that the amount of liquid in the barrel at the end of 2020 is approximately 31.5 litres.

   At the start of each year, starting in 2010, a new barrel is filled with 160 litres of liquid. This process is continued for twenty years until 2030.

   (iii) Calculate the total amount of liquid in the barrels after evaporation at the end of the year 2030.

5. A company bought a new graphics machine for €15 000 at the start of 2005.
   Each year the value of the machine decreases by 20% of its value at the start of the year.

   (i) Show that the value of the machine at the start of 2007 was €9,600.
   (ii) When the value of the machine falls below €500, the company plans to replace it. Find the year in which the machine will need to be replaced.
   (iii) To plan for the replacement, the company pays €1000 at the start of each year into a savings account. The interest rate on the account is 5% per annum. If the first payment is made when the machine was first bought, and the last payment made at the start of the year in which the machine is to be replaced, using your answer to part (ii), find the value of the account when the machine is replaced.
   (iv) If the amount saved is to fully cover the total cost of a new machine, calculate the upper limit on the average annual inflation rate over the period of the investment.

5 Financial Maths

Key words

future value   present value   compound interest   depreciation   annuity

instalment savings   instalment payments   loans   mortgage

Geometric series are very important in the world of economics where we meet such terms as (i) Compound Interest   (ii) Future Value   (iii) Present Value   (iv) Pensions   (v) Annuity (vi) Mortgage repayments   (vii) Instalment savings, etc.

Section 5.1 Compound interest

When the interest earned by a sum of money on deposit in a bank is not withdrawn, it is added to the **principal** for the second year.

The interest grows year by year and is said to be *compounded*.

At a rate of 5% per annum, the increase in the interest earned by €10 000 can be seen year-on-year from the table.

Year	Principal	Interest
One	€10 000	€500
Two	€10 500	€525
Three	€11 025	€551
Four	€11 576	€579
Five	€12 155	€608
	€12 763	

If the interest is withdrawn and not reinvested each year, a total of 5 × €500 = €2500 is earned.

Compounding the interest, a total of €2763 is earned.

Generally, if i (per cent, expressed as a decimal) is the interest rate, then $i \times P$ is the interest earned, where €P is the principal or investment at the beginning of the year.

At the start of the second year, there is $P + iP = \mathbf{P(1 + }i\mathbf{)^1}$ on deposit in the bank.

The change in the principal, year-by-year, can be seen from the following table:

Year (end)	Principal	Interest
	$\mathbf{P}$	$i \times P$
one	$P + iP = \mathbf{P(1 + }i\mathbf{)^1}$	$i \times P(1 + i)$
two	$P(1+ i) + iP(1 + i) = P(1+ i)(1 + i) = \mathbf{P(1 + }i\mathbf{)^2}$	$i \times P(1 + i)^2$
three	$P(1 + i)^2 + iP(1 + i)^2 = P(1 + i)^2(1 + i) = \mathbf{P(1 + }i\mathbf{)^3}$	
year t	$= \mathbf{P(1 + }i\mathbf{)^t}$	

At the end of year t, there is $€P(1 + i)^t$ on deposit.

For example, the interest on €10 000, invested for 5 years at 5% compounded annually, amounts to €10 000 $(1 + 0.05)^5 = €12,763$.

> **APR** ("Annual Percentage Rate") is the "true" annual rate of interest charged for borrowing money.
>
> **AER** ("Annual Equivalent Rate") is the rate of interest paid on **investments**.

1. Future value

If the interest is fixed for a period of time t, then the principal $€P$ added to the compound interest is called the **future value** of $€P$.

> The future value of a sum of money $€P$, invested now at i% for t years, is
> $$\text{Future value (F)} = €P(1 + i)^t$$
> $$\text{Interest earned} = €P(1 + i)^t - €P$$

Example 1

Find the future value of €5000 invested at 4% (AER) per annum, compounded annually, for 6 years. Find also the interest earned over the period.

Future value $= €P(1 + i)^t = €5000\ (1 + 0.04)^6 = €6326.60$

Interest earned $= €6326.60 - €5000 = €1326.60$

Example 2

An investment bond offers a return of 15% if invested for 4 years. Calculate the AER (annual equivalent rate) for this bond, correct to two places of decimals.

A return of 15% after 4 years means that the amount (future value) is 1.15 times the sum invested, $€P$.

$\therefore \quad €P(1 + i)^4 = €P(1.15)$

$\therefore \quad (1 + i)^4 = 1.15$

$(1 + i) = 1.15^{\frac{1}{4}} = 1.03555$ ... taking the fourth root of both sides

$\therefore \quad i(\text{annual equivalent rate}) = .03555 = 3.555\%$

$\qquad\qquad\qquad\qquad\qquad\quad = 3.56\%$

It is now common practice to have interest "added monthly" to a savings account. In this case a monthly interest rate is applied that is equivalent to the annual rate.

If r is the monthly rate and $i = 5\%$ is the annual equivalent rate (AER), then for 12 payments

$$(1 + r)^{12} = (1 + i) = (1 + 0.05) = 1.05$$
$$\therefore \quad (1 + r) = (1.05)^{\frac{1}{12}} = 1.004074$$
$$\therefore \quad r = 1.004074 - 1 = 0.004074 = 0.4074\%$$

$$\therefore \quad 5\% \text{ per year is equivalent to } 0.4074\% \text{ per month.}$$

Note: i is always expressed as a decimal, e.g. $5\% = 0.05$

> To calculate monthly interest rates, $r\%$:
> $$(1 + r)^{12} = (1 + i) \qquad r\% \text{ per month}, \quad i\% \text{ per year}$$

Example 3

€5000 is invested at 4% AER. If the interest is added monthly, find the future value of this investment after (i) $3\frac{1}{2}$ years (ii) 5 years 2 months.

The monthly effective rate r is found by solving the equation $(1 + r)^{12} = 1.04$.

$$\therefore \quad (1 + r) = 1.04^{\frac{1}{12}} = 1.003274$$
$$\therefore \quad r = 0.003274 = 0.3274\% \text{ per month.}$$

The future value after
(i) $3\frac{1}{2}$ years $= 3\frac{1}{2} \times 12 = 42$ months
$$\Rightarrow F = 5000(1.003274)^{42} = €5735.77$$

(ii) 5 years 2 months $= 62$ months
$$\Rightarrow F = 5000(1.003274)^{62} = €6123.26.$$

2. Present value

To find the present value of €10 000 due in three years time, we must calculate what sum of money, invested at $i\%$ (e.g. $5\% = 0.05$) compounded annually, would have a future value of €10 000.

Future value = Present value $\times (1 + i)^t$

$$\Rightarrow \text{Present value} = \frac{\text{Future value}}{(1 + i)^t}$$

$$\text{Present value} = \frac{\text{Future value}}{(1 + i)^t}$$

$$\Rightarrow \text{Present value} = \frac{10\,000}{(1.05)^3} = €8638.38$$

Therefore, at an annual equivalent rate of 5%, the present value of €10 000 (in 3 years time) is €8638.38.

Example 4

The local GAA club runs a draw.
You win first prize and you are offered

> When calculating present value, the rate $i\%$ is often referred to as the "*discount rate*".

(a) €15 000 now **or**
(b) €18 000 in four years time.

Which prize should you choose
to have the greatest value? Assume a discount rate of 4%.

The present value of €18 000 based on a discount rate of 4% is

$$\text{Present value} = \frac{\text{Future value}}{(1 + i)^t} = \frac{18\,000}{(1.04)^3} = €15\,386.48$$

Therefore, the best value prize, based on a discount rate of 4%, is
option (b) €18 000 in four years time.

Summary

Future value: $F = P(1 + i)^t$	Present value: $P = \dfrac{F}{(1 + i)^t}$

Example 5

In how many years would €5000 increase in value to €6500 if invested at
an AER of 3.5%?

Method 1 (Trial and error)

$$F = P(1 + i)^t$$
$$\therefore \quad €6500 = €5000\,(1.035)^t$$

Try $t = 4 \Rightarrow €5000\,(1.035)^4 = €5737.62 < €6500$ ...... $t = 4$ is too small
Try $t = 8 \Rightarrow €5000\,(1.035)^8 = €6584.05 > €6500$ ...... $t = 8$ is too big
Try $t = 7 \Rightarrow €5000\,(1.035)^7 = €6361.40 < €6500$ ...... $t = 7$ is too small
Try $t = 7.5 \Rightarrow €5000\,(1.035)^{7.5} = €6471.76 < €6500$ ...... $t = 7.5$ is too small
Try $t = 7.75 \Rightarrow €5000\,(1.035)^{7.75} = €6527.36 > €6500$ ...... $t = 7.75$ is too big
Try $t = 7.6 \Rightarrow €5000\,(1.035)^{7.6} = €6494.07 < €6500$ ...... $t = 7.6$ is too small
Try $t = 7.65 \Rightarrow €5000\,(1.035)^{7.65} = €6505.25 > €6500$ ...... $t = 7.65$ is too big
Try $t = 7.63 \Rightarrow €5000\,(1.035)^{7.63} = €6500.77 > €6500$ ...... $t = 7.63$ is too big
Try $t = 7.625 \Rightarrow €5000\,(1.035)^{7.625} = €6499.65 < €6500$ ...... $t = 7.625$ is too small

Answer $t = 7.63$ years, correct to 2 places of decimals.

Method 2 (Logs)
(see chapter 7)

$$F = P(1 + i)^t$$
$$\therefore \; €6500 = €5000\,(1.035)^t$$

$\Rightarrow \quad (1.035)^t = \dfrac{€6500}{€5000} = 1.3$

$\Rightarrow \quad ln(1.035)^t = ln\,1.3 \;\; \dots \text{taking the log of both sides}$

$\Rightarrow \quad t\,ln(1.035) = ln\,1.3 \;\; \dots \, lnA^n = n\,lnA$

$\Rightarrow \quad t = \dfrac{ln1.3}{ln(1.035)} = 7.63 \text{ years}$

Exercise 5.1

1. Find the future value, correct to 2 places of decimals, of €3000 invested for 10 years at an annual equivalent rate (AER) of 3%.

2. Given an AER of 2.5%, find the future value, correct to 2 places of decimals, of €5000 invested for 8 years. What interest would be paid on this investment?

3. Given $(1 + r)^{12} = (1 + i)$, where r is the interest rate per month and i the interest rate per year, find r in terms of i.

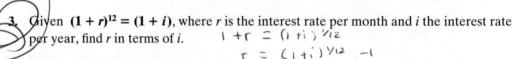
$1 + r = (1 + i)^{1/12}$
$r = (1+i)^{1/12} - 1$

4. What monthly rate of interest, correct to 2 places of decimals, is equivalent to an annual rate of (i) 6% (ii) 2.5% (iii) 4% ?

5. Sean invested €4500 for five years in EUROBANK.
His investment amounted to €5607.82 at the end of its term.
Find the AER that applied to his investment.

6. Sandra wins €15 000 in a draw and invests it in a credit union where the AER is 3.5%.

   Copy and complete this chart, showing how the value of her money changes over the five years of the investment.

Year	Principal	Interest
One	€15 000	
Two		
Three		
Four		
Five		

7. Kamil asks for interest to be added half-yearly to his account.
If the bank offers an AER of 4%, find, correct to four significant figures, the equivalent half-yearly rate.

8. Find the future value of €6500 invested for 6 years 4 months if the monthly equivalent rate is 1.932%.

9. €12 000 is invested at an AER of 3.5%.
   Find the value of the investment after
   (i) 5 years 3 months   (ii) 8 years 2 months   (iii) 10 years 6 months.

10. If a bank offers a discount rate of 4.2%, find the present value of €10 000 due to be paid in 10 years time.

11. Jonathan is 12 years old. When he is 21, he is due to inherit €25 000.
    What is the present value of his inheritance assuming a discount rate of 4.5%?

12. €50000 is invested in a bank offering an AER of 3.5%.
    How long will it take this investment to double in value?

13. I plan to borrow €175 000 to buy a house.
    If the bank charges an AER of 4.5%, what would this loan amount to in 20 years, assuming no repayments?

14. Using (a) trial and error and (b) logs, find how many years it will take €1130 to have a future value of €3000 if invested at 5% per annum compound interest.

15. The formula $(1 + r)^{12} = (1 + i)$, where r is the interest rate per month and i the interest rate per annum, is used to calculate the effective monthly interest rate.
    (i) If 6% interest is offered per year, calculate the effective monthly rate correct to four places of decimals.
    (ii) If r was simply calculated by dividing the yearly interest by 12, calculate using both methods, the difference in future values of €10 000 in 3 years at 6% per annum, if the interest is compounded monthly.
    (iii) What is the minimum number of places of decimals that need to be taken in calculating r before a difference is noted in future values?

16. Anna invests €15 000 at an AER of 3%. After two years, she withdraws €2000 but leaves the remainder of her investment for a further three years.
    What is the value of her investment at the end of this period?

Section 5.2 Depreciation

In the previous section, money lodged into a savings account appreciated in value. The future value was greater than the present value.

Depreciation occurs when the future value of an asset is less than the present value. Cars, computers and household appliances generally depreciate in value over time. Houses in Ireland appreciated in value up to 2007 but have since greatly depreciated in value relative to this "peak" value. Two types of depreciation can be considered.

1. **Straight line depreciation** occurs when the value of an object reduces by a constant amount each year.
   For example, take a car costing €20 000 that loses 10% of its original value each year. This car loses €2000 in value each year and so the car has no value after 10 years.

2. **Reducing balance depreciation** occurs when the value of an object reduces by a fixed percentage of its value each year.

Consider a car costing €20 000 that loses 10% of its value each year on a reducing balance.

The value of the car after 10 years = €20 000 $(1 - 0.1)^{10}$ = €6973.57.

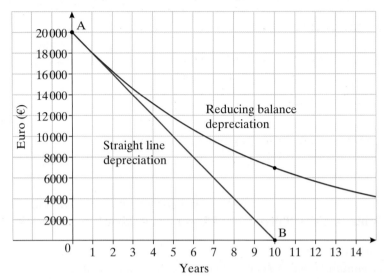

(**Note:** Our course emphasises the reducing balance method for calculating depreciation.)

Similar to compound interest when $F = P(1 + i)^t$, the future value of an item based on a reducing balance is given by the formula $\mathbf{F = P(1 - i)^t}$.

Depreciation: $F = P(1 - i)^t$

F = future value
i = the percentage depreciation of €P per year
t = number of years
P = initial value

Example 1

A company buys a new machine priced at €35 000.
The machine depreciates by 20% on a reducing balance basis each year.

(i) What will the value of the machine be in 4 years time?
(ii) By how much has the machine depreciated in value during this time?

(i) Future value: $F = P(1 - i)^t$ = €35 000 × $(1 - 0.2)^4$
$\qquad\qquad\qquad\qquad\qquad$ = €35 000 × $(0.8)^4$ = €14 336.

(ii) Depreciation = €35 000 − €14 336 = €20 664.

Example 2

A garage has a petrol stock of 100 000 litres.
If the manager estimates (a) that he will sell 4000 litres a day
(b) that he will sell 5% of his stock per day,
calculate the difference in his estimates after 20 days.

After 20 days: $4000 \times 20 = 80\,000$ litres sold
$\Rightarrow \quad 100\,000 - 80\,000 = 20\,000$ litres left.

After 20 days the future (depleted) stock, $F = P(1 - i)^t$
$$= 100\,000\,(1 - 0.05)^{20} = 35\,849 \text{ litres}$$

Therefore the difference in his estimates is 15 849 litres.

Exercise 5.2

(In the following exercise, depreciation is used on a reducing balance basis unless otherwise stated.)

1. How much will a car, costing €30 000, be worth in
    (i) five years   (ii) ten years time   based on a depreciation of 15% per annum?

2. A new television costs €1400. Assuming a depreciation rate of 8% per month, find the value of the television after 15 months.

3. A car costing €44 000 depreciates in value by 20% in the first year, and by 15% per year on a reducing balance basis for each subsequent year.
    Find the value of the car after   (i) 3 years   (ii) 6 years.

4. A company buys a machine costing €140 000.
    In order to facilitate its replacement, the company invests €25 000 in a bank offering a return of 3.5% per annum compound interest.
    If the machine depreciates at a rate of 20% per annum, find
    (a) (i) the value of the machine in 4 years time
         (ii) the value of their savings investment in 4 years time.
    (b) If inflation over the 4 years averages 2% per annum, find
         (i) the cost of buying a new machine in 4 years time
         (ii) how much money the company will need to add to their savings in order to replace the machine, taking the second-hand value of the machine in 4 years time into account.

    (**Note:** Inflation is a rise in the *general level of prices* of goods and services in an economy.)

5. A company asset reduces in value from €175 000 to €73 187.09, at a depreciation rate of 16% per annum over t years.
    (i) By trial and error, estimate the value of t.
    (ii) Using logs, find the value of t.

6. A creamery has a stock of 60 000 kg of dried milk powder at the end of January 2004. If the stock is reduced at a rate of 15% per month, find the dried milk stock, to the nearest kg, at the beginning of April 2005.

7. A farmer buys a tractor for €180 000.
   He assumes that the tractor will have a trade-in value of €80 000 in 10 years time.
   (i) Calculate the rate of depreciation per annum, correct to one place of decimals, based on these figures.
   (ii) At this rate, when will the value of the tractor fall below €60 000?

8. A computer is bought for €2500.
   Compare the trade-in value of the computer after 4 years based on
   (a) a net loss in value of €550 per year or   (b) a loss of 35% per year.

9. A computer system is bought for €23 500. It depreciates at a rate of 28% per annum.
   Find the value of the computer after
   (i) 2 years   (ii) 5 years   (iii) 7 years.

10. An air-conditioning system cost €8000. A straight line depreciation and a reducing balance curve for this system are shown below.

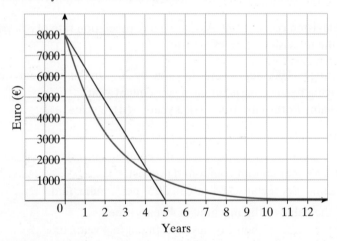

   (i) Using the graph, estimate the rate of depreciation.
       (Let the value after 20 years be €1.)
   (ii) Explain why the reducing balance curve can never have a zero value.
   (iii) Find the slope of the straight line representing depreciation.
   (iv) Estimate the point of intersection of the two graphs.
   (v) After 5 years, what is the value of the system on a reducing balance basis?
   (vi) In your opinion, which method of depreciation gives a more realistic value for the system? Explain your answer.

Section 5.3 Instalment savings (annuities) —————

1. Instalment saving

If a constant amount of money is saved each month for 3 years in total, then each instalment earns different (compound) interest, since it is invested for a different length of time. The first instalment is in the bank for 3 years = 36 months ; the last instalment is in the bank for only one month.

Let €P be invested at the beginning of each month for 3 years at a monthly rate of $i\%$.

The first payment has a value of $P(1 + i)^{36}$ after 36 months.
The second payment has a value of $P(1 + i)^{35}$ after 35 months, etc ...

The total value of the investment is the sum of these 36 individual amounts.
This sum is calculated as follows:

$$P(1 + i)^{36} + P(1 + i)^{35} + P(1 + i)^{34} + \ldots\ldots P(1 + i)^2 + P(1 + i)^1.$$

If we reverse the order, we get

$$P(1 + i)^1 + P(1 + i)^2 + P(1 + i)^3 \ldots\ldots + P(1 + i)^{35} + P(1 + i)^{36}$$

which is the sum of the geometric series where

the first term, $a = P(1 + i)^1$
the common ratio, $r = (1 + i)$
the number of terms, $n = 36$

Using the formula for the sum of n terms of a geometric sequence, $S_n = \dfrac{a(1 - r^n)}{(1 - r)}$, we get

$$\text{future value} = \frac{P(1 + i)[1 - (1 + i)^{36}]}{1 - (1 + i)} = \frac{P(1 + i)[1 - (1 + i)^{36}]}{-i}$$

$$= \frac{P(1 + i)[(1 + i)^{36} - 1]}{i}$$

Future value, F, of instalment savings over t instalments:

$$F = €P(1 + i)^1 + €P(1 + i)^2 + €P(1 + i)^3 + \ldots €P(1 + i)^t = \frac{€P(1 + i)[(1 + i)^t - 1]}{i}$$

$€P$ = the amount saved at the start of each month/year
t = the number of payments (months/years)
i = the interest rate, expressed as a decimal

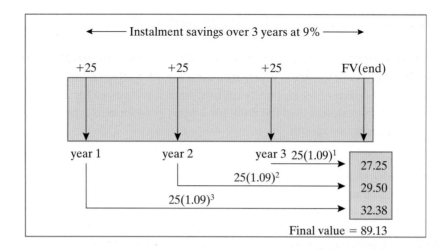

For example, if I save €25 every year for 3 years, the accumulated total (future value) of my savings would be €89.13.

Example 1

Catríona saves €400 every three months for five years at an effective quarterly rate of 0.9%.
(i) Represent her savings by a geometric series
(ii) Find the value of her investment at the end of the period.

$$i = 0.9\% = 0.009$$
$$5 \text{ years} = (5 \times 4) \text{ quarters} = 20 \text{ payments}$$

(i) Catríona's savings are represented by
$$400(1.009) + 400(1.009)^2 + 400(1.009)^3 + \ldots + 400(1.009)^{20}$$

(ii) $a = 400(1.009)$ $\left.\begin{array}{l} \\ r = (1 + i) = 1.009 \\ n = 20 \end{array}\right\}$ $S_n = \dfrac{a(1 - r^n)}{(1 - r)}$ $a = \text{first term}$

$$S_n = \frac{400(1.009)[1 - (1.009)^{20}]}{1 - 1.009}$$

$$= €8800.89$$

Note: In all calculations, the rate "i" is converted from a percentage to a decimal.
E.g. $i = 5\% = 0.05$.

Example 2

Find the sum of money, €P, that needs to be saved per month to cover the cost of a €1500 holiday in 18 months time. The interest rate on offer is 0.4% per month.

The future value (FV) needed = €1500

$$F = €P(1 + i) + €P(1 + i)^2 \ldots\ldots = \frac{€P(1 + i)[(1 + i)^n - 1]}{i}$$

$\left.\begin{array}{l} i = 0.4\% \\ n = 18 \end{array}\right\}$ $i = 0.004 \Rightarrow 1 + i = 1.009$

$\therefore$ FV $= €1500 = €P(1.004) + €P(1.004)^2 \ldots\ldots €P(1.004)^{18}$

$\therefore$ $€1500 = \dfrac{€P(1.004)[(1.004)^{18} - 1]}{0.004} = \dfrac{€P \times 0.0748}{0.004} = €P \times 18.70$

$\therefore$ P $= €1500 \div 18.7$

$\qquad = €80.21$ per month

2. Pensions

Similar to instalment savings, we can calculate the sum of money needed to be invested now to guarantee a **fixed pension** payable over a number of years.

For example, if I want a pension of €P per year for the next 20 years, I will need to calculate the present value of each of the payments, €P, I will receive.

The total of these "present value" amounts is the sum of money that needs to be invested.

The sum of €P, paid to you at the end of the first year, has a present value now of $\dfrac{€P}{(1 + i)}$.

The sum of €P, paid at the end of the second year, has a present value now of $\dfrac{€P}{(1 + i)^2}$.

The sum to be invested is obtained by summing all these amounts.

$$\frac{€P}{(1 + i)} + \frac{€P}{(1 + i)^2} + \frac{€P}{(1 + i)^3} + \ldots + \frac{€P}{(1 + i)^{20}}$$

This is the sum of a geometric series containing 20 terms, where $\left\{\begin{array}{l} a = \dfrac{€P}{(1 + i)} \\ r = \dfrac{1}{(1 + i)} \\ n = 20 \end{array}\right.$

$$\therefore \quad S_n = \frac{a(1 - r^n)}{(1 - r)} = \frac{P}{(1 + i)} \times \frac{\left(1 - \left(\dfrac{1}{1 + i}\right)^{20}\right)}{\left(1 - \left(\dfrac{1}{1 + i}\right)\right)}$$

The present value of a pension fund is given by

$$PV = \frac{€P}{(1+i)} + \frac{€P}{(1+i)^2} + \frac{€P}{(1+i)^3} + \ldots\ldots \frac{€P}{(1+i)^n} = \frac{P}{(1+i)} \times \frac{\left(1 - \left(\frac{1}{1+i}\right)^n\right)}{\left(1 - \left(\frac{1}{1+i}\right)\right)}$$

$€P$ = yearly pension
n = number of years (lifetime of pension)
i = fixed rate of interest over the term of the pension

Note: Most pensions operate on a guaranteed rate of interest.

However, some may depend on market performance and gain or lose compared to the fixed (guaranteed) rate.

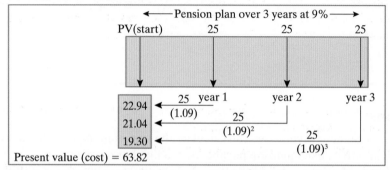

That is, if I want a pension of €25 every year for 3 years, I need to invest €63.82 now.

Example 3

What amount of money is needed now to provide a pension of €25 000 a year for 20 years, assuming an AER of 4%?

$$i = 4\% = 0.04 \quad \Rightarrow \quad 1 + i = 1.04$$

The amount required, or present value (P) of this pension, is represented by the geometric series:

$$P = \frac{25\,000}{1.04} + \frac{25\,000}{(1.04)^2} + \frac{25\,000}{(1.04)^3} + \ldots\ldots \frac{25\,000}{(1.04)^{20}}$$

$$\left. \begin{array}{l} a = \dfrac{€25\,000}{(1.04)} \\[3mm] n = 20 \\[3mm] r = \dfrac{1}{1+i} = \dfrac{1}{1.04} \end{array} \right\} \quad S_n = \frac{a(1 - r^n)}{(1 - r)} = \frac{25\,000}{(1.04)} \times \frac{\left(1 - \left(\frac{1}{1.04}\right)^{20}\right)}{\left(1 - \left(\frac{1}{1.04}\right)\right)}$$

$$= €339\,758.16$$

Thus, a pension fund of €339 758.16 invested now will provide 20 yearly payments of €25 000.

Summary

The future value of	The present value (cost) of
n payments of €P at $i\%$	n payments of €P at $i\%$
Future value $= P(1 + i)\left(\dfrac{1 - (1 + i)^n}{1 - (1 + i)}\right)$	Present value $= \left(\dfrac{P}{1 + i}\right)\left[\dfrac{1 - \left(\dfrac{1}{1 + i}\right)^n}{1 - \left(\dfrac{1}{1 + i}\right)}\right]$
$= P(1 + i)\left(\dfrac{(1 + i)^n - 1}{i}\right)$	$= \dfrac{P}{(1 + i)^n}\left(\dfrac{(1 + i)^n - 1}{i}\right)$

Note: Although most questions on instalment savings and pensions can be answered by using the appropriate formula, it is good practice to set up the geometric series underpinning each question. It is important to identify the first term, the common ratio and the number of terms in the series for each particular question.

Example 4

Calculate the future value of an instalment savings plan based on saving €600 at the **start** of each year @ 4% per annum for 5 years.

(i) Calculate the present value of these payments.
(ii) Hence show that if the present value was put on deposit at the same rate for the same length of time, it would have the same future value.

Savings plan: $FV = 600(1.04) + 600(1.04)^2 + 600(1.04)^3 + 600(1.04)^4 + 600(1.04)^5$

$$= €600(1.04)\left(\frac{(1.04)^5 - 1}{0.04}\right) = €3\,379.79 \text{ (at the end of 5 years)}$$

(i) Present value $(PV) = €600 + \dfrac{€600}{(1.04)^1} + \dfrac{€600}{(1.04)^2} + \dfrac{€600}{(1.04)^3} + \dfrac{€600}{(1.04)^4}$

$$= €600 \times \frac{\left(1 - \left(\frac{1}{1.04}\right)^5\right)}{\left(1 - \left(\frac{1}{1.04}\right)\right)} = \frac{600}{(1.04)^4}\left(\frac{(1.04)^5 - 1}{0.04}\right)$$

$$= €2777.94 \text{ (at the start of the 5 years)}$$

(ii) If €2777.94 is invested @ 4% for 5 years its future value is €2777.94(1.04)^5 = €3379.79.

ICT: Using a graphics calculator or computer software, a comparison between instalment savings and the future value (amount) of a sum of money left on deposit can easily be made.

Saving €600 per year @ 4%: $\quad$ FV$(y) = 600*(1.04)(1.04^x - 1)/(0.04)$

€2778 on deposit @ 4%: $\quad\quad$ FV$(y) = 2778(1.04)^x \quad\quad$ y: the FV in euro

$\quad\quad\quad\quad\quad\quad\quad\quad\quad\quad\quad\quad\quad\quad\quad\quad\quad\quad\quad\quad\quad\quad x$: the number of years

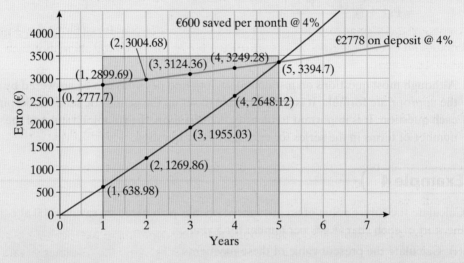

Exercise 5.3

1. Calculate the future value of 36 monthly instalments of €20.00 at an interest rate of 0.5% per month. What is the total interest earned on these savings?

2. Marie has saved €30.00 per month since her 18th birthday.
   If her bank has guaranteed her an interest rate of 4% per annum, find

   (i) the equivalent monthly rate of interest, correct to two places of decimals
   (ii) the value of her savings on her 21st birthday.

3. A special savings account offers an AER of 4% per annum. If I invest €2000 per year in this account, how much will my investment be worth in 5 years time?

4. Show that the future value of a series of n payments of €P, earning an interest rate of i% per annum, can be written as:

$$\text{Future value} = P(1 + i)\left(\frac{(1 + i)^n - 1}{i}\right)$$

5. Show that the present value of a series of n payments of €P, earning an interest rate of i% per annum, can be written as:

$$\text{Present value} = \frac{P}{(1 + i)^n}\left(\frac{(1 + i)^n - 1}{i}\right)$$

6. Anne received a cheque in the post for €6523.33 after saving for 5 years with her bank in a scheme offering 9% per annum. If she invested €A per annum,
    (i) write down a geometric series representing the value of her investment over the 5 years
    (ii) find the value of A.

7. Use the future value formula to find the final value if €200 is invested every month for 2 years. The interest rate is 9% per annum, compounded monthly.

8. George wants to make regular payments into an account that pays 8.5% per annum compound interest in order to have €10 000 after 7 years. Find the amount of each annual payment.

9. Ella wants to have €5000 in 3 years time.
    She invests in an annuity that pays 7.2% per annum, compounded quarterly.
    How much does she need to deposit each quarter to achieve her target of €5000?

10. Prove that the present value of an annuity (instalments paid at the beginning of each period) is given by:
    Future value (calculated at the end of each period) $\div (1 + i)^n$.

11. Show how the present value of an annuity involving depositing €3000 per year in an account for 6 years can be written as a geometric series, given that the interest rate is 8% per annum.
    (i)   Calculate the present value.
    (ii) Calculate the future value of the annuity.
    (iii) If the present value of the annuity in (i) was put on deposit as a single investment at 8% per annum, show that it will amount to the same future value of the annuity after 6 years.

Section 5.4 Loans – Mortgages

If we wish to calculate the repayments needed for a car loan or a mortgage on a house, we use the same procedure for finding the present value as was used in the previous section.

The sum of the present values of each repayment over the given period of time must be equal to the value of the car loan or mortgage.

$$\text{€ Mortgage} = \frac{\text{€ Payment}}{1 + i} + \frac{\text{€ Payment}}{(1 + i)^2} + \frac{\text{€ Payment}}{(1 + i)^3} + \dots \cdot \frac{\text{€ Payment}}{(1 + i)^n}$$

$$= \left(\frac{\text{€ Payment}}{1 + i}\right) \left[\frac{1 - \left(\frac{1}{1 + i}\right)^n}{1 - \left(\frac{1}{1 + i}\right)}\right]$$

$$\text{Mortgage} = \left(\frac{\text{€ Payment}}{1+i}\right)\left[\frac{1-\left(\frac{1}{1+i}\right)^n}{1-\left(\frac{1}{1+i}\right)}\right] = \left(\frac{\text{€ Payment}}{1+i}\right)\left[\frac{\frac{(1+i)^n-1}{(1+i)^n}}{\left(\frac{i}{1+i}\right)}\right]$$

$$= \left(\frac{\text{€ Payment}}{i}\right)\left[\frac{(1+i)^n-1}{(1+i)^n}\right]$$

$$\therefore \quad \text{€ Payment} = \frac{\text{€ Mortgage }(i)(1+i)^n}{(1+i)^n-1}$$

(formulae and tables, p.31)

i = the effective monthly rate of interest (expressed as a decimal)
n = the number of payments (years/months)
€M = the amount of the mortgage or loan
€P = the repayment per month

Example 1

Calculate the size of the monthly repayments needed for a car loan of €10 000 if the loan is to be repaid over a 5-year term at an effective monthly rate of 0.72%.

$i = 0.72\% = 0.0072 \quad \Rightarrow \quad 1+i = 1.0072$

$n = 5 \times 12 = 60$ repayments

$$\therefore \quad \text{€ Repayment} = \frac{\text{€ Loan }(i)(1+i)^n}{(1+i)^n-1} = \frac{\text{€}10\,000(0.0072)(1.0072)^{60}}{(1.0072)^{60}-1}$$

$$= \text{€}206 \quad \ldots \text{ correct to the nearest euro}$$

Note: When using the mortgage/loan formula, each (re)payment is paid at the end of each accounting period, i.e. at the end of a month or at the end of a year.

Example 2

Find the monthly repayments required for a mortgage of €150 000, based on an annual rate of 4.5% over 20 years.

We first find the effective monthly rate:

$(1+r)^{12} = (1+i)$, where $r\%$ = rate per month and $i\%$ = rate per year.

$\Rightarrow (1+r)^{12} = 1.045$

$\Rightarrow (1+r) = (1.045)^{\frac{1}{12}} = 1.00367$

$\Rightarrow r = 0.00367$ per month $= 0.367\%$ per month

$n = 20 \times 12 = 240$ payments

$$\therefore \text{€ Payment} = \frac{\text{€ Mortgage }(i)(1+i)^n}{(1+i)^n-1} = \frac{\text{€}150\,000\,(0.00367)(1.00367)^{240}}{(1.00367)^{240}-1} = \text{€}941.22$$

Therefore the monthly repayment is €941.22.

Exercise 5.4

1. Calculate the monthly repayments required for a mortgage of €200 000, paid over a 30-year period at an annual interest rate of 6%.

2. Alice wants to take out a 20-year mortgage.
   The average interest rate over the lifetime of the mortgage is 8% per annum.
   Alice can afford repayments of €850 per month.
   What is the largest mortgage she can afford?
   Give your answer to the nearest €100.

3. What is the monthly payment, correct to the nearest euro, on a mortgage of €75 000, assuming an interest rate of 8%, for
   (a) 20 years   (b) 25 years   (c) 30 years?
   How much interest is paid under each option?

4. Your local car dealer offers you two different payment plans to buy a €15 000 car.

   Plan A: A 10% discount on the price of the car and a loan on the balance at an annual rate of 9% for 5 years.

   Plan B: No discount but a loan for the total price €15 000 at an annual rate of 3% for 5 years.

   Which plan should you opt for?

5. A woman has saved €250 000 to fund a pension and she now plans to retire.
   She wishes to draw down equal annual instalments from these savings for the next 25 years.
   Assuming a 5% interest rate, calculate the value of each yearly instalment.

6. Two people want to buy your house. The first person offers you €200 000 now.
   The second person offers you 25 annual payments of €15 000 each.
   Assuming you can get an annual rate of 5% on your money, which offer should you accept?

7. Malcolm needs €400 per month, for 3 years, while he studies at college.
   What amount of money do his parents need to invest, at 6.6% p.a. compounded monthly, to provide the money that Malcolm needs?

Revision Exercise 5 (Core)

1. A woman invests €1000 each year at 8% per annum, compound interest.
   Find the value of her investment after 5 years.

2. €300 is invested each month for eight years.
   Find the total value of the investment after eight years, assuming a constant rate of 6% per annum.

3. A car loan of €20 000 is to be repaid in 25 equal instalments.
   If the effective interest rate is 2%, calculate the amount of each instalment, correct
   to the nearest euro.

4. Silvia is planning an overseas trip lasting 3 years and she estimates that she will
   need €600 per month for expenses.
   How much money does she need to have saved to fund this trip?
   Assume an average rate of interest of 4% per annum over the period of the trip.

5. A credit card company offers clients an introductory interest rate on outstanding
   balances of 1.25% per month, and a regular rate of 2.5% per month after 1 year.
   Find the equivalent interest rates (AER) per annum.

6. John makes savings of €200 a month for 5 months at an effective monthly
   rate of 0.75%.
   Express these savings as a geometric series.
   Write down the first term, the common ratio and an expression for the sum of
   the five terms.

7. Use the future value formula to find what €1600 would amount to if invested each
   year for 5 years at 6 % p.a. compound interest.

8. An annuity involves saving €3000 per year at 7.3% p.a. for 8 years.
   (i) Use the present value formula to calculate the single amount of money which
       could be invested at the same rate and for the same amount of time to give the
       same final amount.
   (ii) Using the compound interest (future value) formula, find the final amount of
        the investment.
   (iii) Using the future value annuity formula, check that the annuity gives the same
         final amount.

Revision Exercise 5 (Advanced)

1. Your company has an expected pension liability of €500 000 in 10 years time.
   (i) What amount of money would you now require to cover this expected liability.
       Assume an annual rate of 9%.
   (ii) How much would you need to set aside at the end of each year for the next
        10 years to cover the liability (assume the same rate applies)?

2. Which is the better result at the end of 20 years?
   (i) An investment of €100 000 at 12% per annum compounded monthly **or**
   (ii) €1000 invested monthly at 12% per annum compounded monthly.

3. The graphs of two different bank accounts, C and D, are shown below.
The interest rate applying to each account is the same.
Use the data in the graphs to calculate the rate of interest applying to both accounts.
Describe the difference between the accounts.
Calculate the value of account C after 5 years.

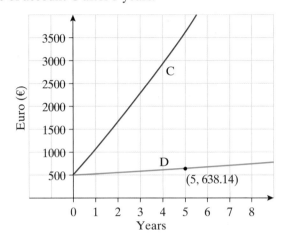

4. A bank offers you a rate of 10% on a 20-year mortgage to be paid in monthly repayments.
If the most you can afford to pay in monthly repayments is €700, find the value of the biggest mortgage you can afford.

5. Assume that you are going to retire in 25 years time.
You want a mortgage of €100 000 now to extend and renovate your house but want to have it paid in full before you retire. The maximum repayment per month your budget will allow is €800. Using iteration (trial and error), what is the rate of interest you need from your bank to have the loan repaid in 300 monthly payments (i.e. 25 years)?

6. A ten-year pension fund of €127 953 is to be drawn down at the rate of €15 000 per year.

If a 3% annual rate applies to the fund, copy and complete this chart which indicates the value of the fund at the start of each year.

Year	Pension fund	Interest	Payment
One	€127 953	€3838.59	€15 000
Two	€116 791.59	€3503.75	€15 000
Three	€105 295.38		€15 000
Four			€15 000
Five			€15 000
Six			€15 000
Seven			€15 000
Eight			€15 000
Nine			€15 000
Ten			€15 000

Revision Exercise 5 (Extended-Response Questions)

1. Assume that the APR charged by a bank is 5%, compounded annually.
    Copy and complete the following charts which compare the principal still owing
    after the repayments of
    (i) €6000   (ii) €12 000   per year on a principal loan of €100 000.
    Calculate the amount still owing after 10 years using each re-payment scheme.

Year	Principal	Interest	Payment		Year	Principal	Interest	Payment
One	100 000	5000	6000		One	100 000	5000	12 000
Two	99 000	4950	6000		Two	93 000	4650	12 000
Three	97 950		6000		Three	85 650		12 000
Four			6000		Four			12 000
Five			6000		Five			12 000
Six			6000		Six			12 000
Seven		4659.9	6000		Seven			12 000
Eight			6000		Eight		2150.3	12 000
Nine			6000		Nine			12 000
Ten			6000		Ten			12 000

2. You are 35 years-old today and you are planning for your retirement needs.
    You expect to retire at the age of 65 years and actuarial studies suggest that you will
    live to be a 100 year-old.
    You want to move to a country location when you retire.
    You estimate that it will cost you €300 000 to move (on your 65th birthday) and
    your living expenses will be €20 000 a year, starting at the end of the first year
    after retirement.
    Assume an average annual rate of 4% over the lifetime of the plan, including retirement.

    (i)   How much will you need to have saved on your retirement to afford this plan?
    (ii) You have €40 000 in savings now.
          If you can invest this money (tax-free) at 5% per year, how much money do you
          need to save each year in order to afford your retirement plan?
    (iii) If you have no savings and could not start saving for another 5 years, how much
          would you then have to set aside each year to afford this plan assuming $i = 5\%$?

3. You want to take out a building society mortgage of €100 000 advertised at a
    rate of 9% p.a..
    However, you can only afford €800 per month repayments.

    (i)   Write an equation for the repayments of a mortgage, explaining each term
          in the equation.
    (ii) Calculate the monthly interest rate equivalent to 9% p.a..
    (iii) Calculate the number of payments needed to clear the mortgage.
    (iv) How long would you need to clear this mortgage in full?

4. Richard and Natalie take out a loan of €150 000 over 30 years at 8.25% p.a. interest, compounding monthly. Their repayments are fixed at €1127 per month.
   (i) Using a spreadsheet similar to the one below, calculate the amount of the loan remaining after 5 years.

	A	B	C	D	E
1	Mortgage	Interest	Payment	Balance	
2	150000	994	1127	149867.2	
3	149867.2	993.32	1127	149733.5	
4	149733.5	992.43	1127	149599	
5	149599	991.54	1127	149463.5	
6	149463.5	990.64	1127	149327.1	
7					

(Note: By highlighting row 3 and by clicking and dragging the bottom right-hand cross, the balance on the account can be seen month-by-month.)
   (ii) After how many payments will this loan be cleared?
        Give your answer correct to the nearest month.
   After 5 years of repaying the loan, they make a lump-sum payment of €40 000.
   (iii) How long will it take to repay the loan after this payment?

5. A lottery game in the USA offers a first prize with an advertised jackpot of $21.5 million. This prize is to be given in 26 annual instalments each of $A, with the first instalment given immediately.

   The value of the payment is guaranteed to increase by 4% each year.
   (i) Write down, in terms of A, the amount of each of the first four payments.
   (ii) Hence write down a geometric series representing the jackpot of $21.5 million.
   (iii) Find, correct to the nearest dollar, the value of $A.
   (iv) Using your value for A and your answer to (i), complete a chart of the first four payments.

Payment number	1	2	3	4
Actual amount		$504 607		$545 783

   (v) A cash-value option exists whereby the winner receives now the present value of each of the payments.
       The interest rate used for the cash option is 4.78%.
       Using the chart in (iv), complete the following table:

Payment number	1	2	3	4
Present value	$485 199		$478 002	

   (vi) Write down, in terms of n, an expression for the present value of the nth annual payment.
   (vii) Find the total sum of the present values, i.e., the prize money payable under the cash-value option.
   (viii) This jackpot was won recently and the winner received $7.9 million as the cash-value option after tax.
        Using your answer to (vii), find the percentage of tax charged on her winnings.
        (Adapted from SEC Leaving Certificate 2011.)

Length − Area − Volume

Key words

polygon   area   perimeter   diagonal   trapezium   cyclic quadrilateral

arc   sector   radian   quadrilateral

Section 6.1 Revision

In the following table, we revise key properties of 2-dimensional shapes already encountered in your study of mathematics.

Shape	Diagram	Properties
Square		› all sides have the same length › all angles are 90° › perimeter = $4x$ › area = x^2 › diagonal = $\sqrt{2}x$ › diagonals perpendicularly bisect each other
Rectangle		› opposite sides have the same length › all angles are 90° › perimeter = $2(x + y)$ › area = xy › diagonal = $\sqrt{x^2 + y^2}$ › diagonals have the same length › diagonals bisect each other
Parallelogram		› opposite sides have the same length › opposite angles are equal › perimeter = $2(x + y)$ › area = $yh = yx \sin \theta$ › diagonals bisect each other

Triangle	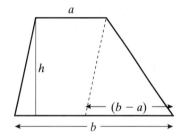	> perimeter $= x + y + z$
		 > area $= \frac{1}{2}x.h = \frac{1}{2}x.z.\sin\theta$
		 > $\dfrac{y}{\sin\theta} = \dfrac{z}{\sin\alpha}$
		 > types include isosceles, equilateral, scalene, right-angled
		 > $\alpha + \beta + \theta = 180°$
		 > special right-angled triangles with sides
		     • $3, 4, 5$ ...... $(36.9°, 53.1°, 90°)$
		     • $1, \sqrt{3}, 2,$ ...... $(30°, 60°, 90°)$
		     • $1, 1, \sqrt{2}$ ...... $(45°, 45°, 90°)$

1. Trapezium

A **trapezium** is a quadrilateral which has one pair of parallel sides.

The area of a trapezium $= ah_{\text{parallelogram}} + \frac{1}{2}(b - a)\,h_{\text{triangle}}$

$$= ah + \tfrac{1}{2}bh - \tfrac{1}{2}ah$$

$$= \tfrac{1}{2}ah + \tfrac{1}{2}bh \;=\; \left(\dfrac{a + b}{2}\right)h$$

$=$ half the sum of the lengths of the parallel sides times the height.

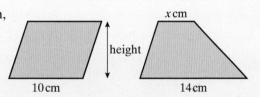

Example 1

If a parallelogram has a base of 10 cm, and a trapezium of the same area and height has a base of 14 cm, find x, the length of the other parallel side of the trapezium.

Area of parallelogram $=$ Base $\times$ perpendicular height $(h) = 10h$

Area of trapezium $= \frac{1}{2}(x + 14) \times$ perpendicular height $(h) = \frac{1}{2}(x + 14)h$

$\therefore \quad 10h = \tfrac{1}{2}(x + 14)h$

$\Rightarrow \quad 20 = x + 14$

$\Rightarrow \quad x = 6 \quad \Rightarrow \quad$ the other parallel side $= 6$ cm

POLYGONS

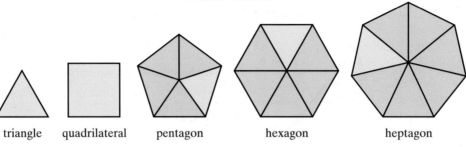

| triangle | quadrilateral | pentagon | hexagon | heptagon |

2. Polygons

A **polygon** is a plane (2-dimensional) shape with straight edges.

Regular polygons are symmetrical, with a base triangle repeated in polygons with more than 4 sides. The interior angles of regular polygons are:

Triangle = 60°, Quadrilateral = 90°, Pentagon= 108°, Hexagon = 120°, Heptagon = 128.6°

Example 2

The area of the regular pentagon shown here is 600 cm². Calculate the length of one side, x, of the pentagon.

Since the total angle at the centre of the pentagon = 360°,

$\therefore$ each angle at the centre $= \dfrac{360°}{5} = 72°$.

Each triangle is congruent and has equal base angles $= \dfrac{(180 - 72)°}{2} = 54°$

Each triangle has an area of $\left(\dfrac{600}{5}\right)$ cm² = 120 cm².

$\text{Tan } 54° = \dfrac{h}{\frac{x}{2}} \;\Rightarrow\; h = \dfrac{x}{2} \tan 54°$

The area of the triangle $= \dfrac{1}{2} \times \text{base} \times h = \dfrac{1}{2} \times x \times h = 120$ cm²

$$= \dfrac{1}{2} \times x \times \dfrac{x}{2} \tan 54° = 120 \text{ cm}^2$$

$\Rightarrow\; x^2 = \dfrac{480}{\tan 54°} = 348.74 \;\Rightarrow\; x = 18.675 = 18.7 \text{ cm}$

Exercise 6.1

1. A parallelogram is drawn inside a rectangle as shown.
   Using the measurements given, find
   (i) the fraction, in terms of a, of the rectangle's area that is taken up by the parallelogram
   (ii) the value of a required so that the area of the parallelogram $= \frac{4}{5}$ the area of the rectangle.

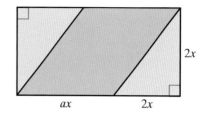

2. Calculate, in terms of x,
   (i) the area of the darker section of the rectangle
   (ii) the area of the lighter section of the rectangle
   (iii) "the ratio of these areas."

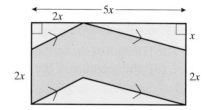

3. If the height of a triangle is 5 cm less than the length of its base, and if the area of the triangle is 52 cm², find the length of the base and also the height of the triangle.

4. Given that the hypotenuse of a right-angled triangle is 41 cm, and the sum of the other two sides of the triangle is 49 cm, find the lengths of these two sides.

5. A rectangular wooden frame is built to lay a concrete foundation for a patio.
   To support the frame while the concrete is being poured, steel cables are fixed diagonally across the rectangle and protrude out of the frame by 50 cm.
   If the perimeter of the frame is 14 m, and the length of the frame is one metre longer than its width, find the length of steel cable required.

6. In a scalene triangle, the smallest angle is two thirds the size of the middle angle, and the middle angle is three sevenths the size of the largest angle. Find the measure of all three angles.

7. E is the midpoint of [DC].
   Draw the image of the trapezium ABCD rotated by 180° about the point E.
   (i) What shape is made by the image and the original trapezium?
   (ii) What is the area of this composite shape?
   (iii) Explain how this proves the formula for the area of a trapezium.

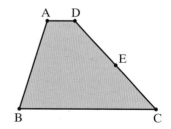

8. Three times the width of a certain rectangle exceeds twice its length by 3 cm, and four times its length is 12cm more than its perimeter.
   Find the dimensions of the rectangle.

9. Peter has three narrow rods of lengths p, q, and r, where $|p| > |q| > |r|$.
He wants to make a trapezium shape with two right angles as shown. The dotted line completes the trapezium.
Draw the three possible arrangements of rods.
Given the inequality above, find which arrangement has the greatest area.
(Note: if $a > b$, then $ac > bc$, given $c > 0$)

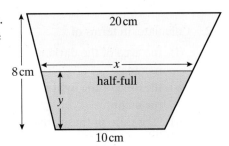

10. A drawing of the cross-section of a skip is shown. The skip company wants to draw a line along the side of the skip indicating half-full.
Using the dimensions given, find the

    (i) length of the line x and
    (ii) the height, y, of the line above the base.

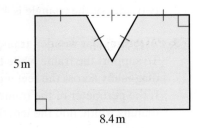

11. (i) The area of an equilateral triangle is $173\,cm^2$. Find the length of one side.

    (ii) The length of one side of an equilateral triangle is $10.75\,cm$.
    Find the perpendicular height of the triangle and hence find the area of the triangle.
    Verify your answer by using the triangle area formula $\frac{1}{2}ab\sin C$.

12. Find the area of this figure in square metres, correct to 3 decimal places.

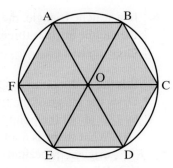

13. A regular hexagon is circumscribed by a circle of radius $5\,cm$. Find

    (i) the size of the angle EOD
    (ii) the size of the angle ODE
    (iii) the area of the hexagon ABCDEFA.

14. A composite design of regular polygons is shown.

    (i) Find the sizes of the angles α, β, θ
    (ii) If the square has a side of $4\,cm$, find the area of this composite shape correct to one place of decimals.

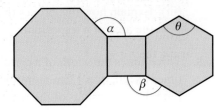

15. Using the measurements given, find the area of this trapezium.
(Diagram not to scale.)

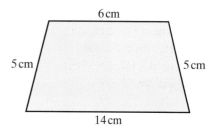

16. (i) Show that the area of $\triangle ABD : \triangle CBD = |AD| : |DC|$.
(ii) ABCD below is a trapezium. Prove that Area c = Area d.
(iii) Hence show that the area of the trapezium $ABCD = a + b + 2\sqrt{ab}$.

ICT: Using suitable computer software, similar trapeziums can be drawn with diagonals as shown.
This area formula can then be verified by using the software to calculate the separate areas.

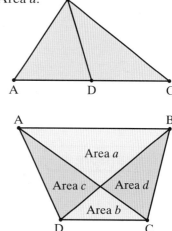

Section 6.2 Sectors of circles

1. Revision of circles and sectors of circles

Circle/ Disc	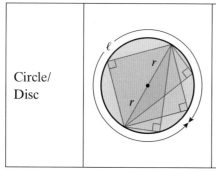	• perimeter (circumference) $= \ell$; since $\dfrac{\ell}{2r} = \pi$ $\qquad\qquad\qquad\qquad \Rightarrow \ell = 2\pi r$ • area $= \pi r^2$ • a cyclic quadrilateral is a quadrilateral inscribed in a circle • every triangle inscribed in a semicircle is a right-angled triangle • **360° $= 2\pi$ radians**

2. Arc of a circle

In the chapter on trigonometry, the length of an arc, the area of a sector, and radian measure were introduced. The length of an arc of a circle is found using the ratios

$$\frac{\ell}{2\pi r} = \frac{\theta\,(\text{degrees})}{360} = \frac{\theta\,(\text{radians})}{2\pi}$$

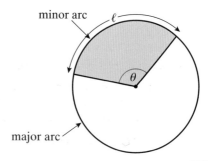

$$\therefore \text{ Length of arc } (l) = 2\pi r \frac{\theta\,(\text{degrees})}{360} = 2\pi r \frac{\theta\,(\text{radians})}{2\pi}$$

$$= r\theta \ (\theta \text{ in radians})$$

3. Area of a sector

Similarly, the area of a sector of a circle is found using the ratios

$$\frac{A}{\pi r^2} = \frac{\theta\,(\text{degrees})}{360} = \frac{\theta\,(\text{radians})}{2\pi}$$

$$\therefore \text{ Area of sector } (A) = \pi r^2 \frac{\theta\,(\text{degrees})}{360} = \pi r^2 \frac{\theta\,(\text{radians})}{2\pi} = \tfrac{1}{2}r^2\theta \ (\theta \text{ in radians})$$

Example 1

A flowerbed in the shape of a section of a sector of a circle is placed in the centre of a rectangular lawn, as shown in the diagram. Calculate

(i) the length of edging needed for the flowerbed

(ii) the area of grass in the garden.

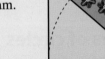

Correct each answer to one place of decimals.

(i) length of large arc $\text{IH} = 2\pi r \dfrac{\theta(\text{degrees})}{360} = \left(\dfrac{90}{360}2\pi 8\right)\text{m} = 4\pi\,\text{m}$

length of small arc $\text{JK} = \left(\dfrac{90}{360}2\pi 3\right)\text{m}$

$= \dfrac{3\pi}{2}\text{m}$

Total perimeter =

$4\pi + \dfrac{3\pi}{2} + (2 \times 5) = \left(\dfrac{11\pi}{2} + 10\right)\text{m}$

$= 27.3\,\text{m}$

.... edging needed

(ii) The area of the sector (flowerbed portion) =
Area of large sector − Area of small sector

$$= \left(\frac{90}{360}\right)\pi 8^2\,\text{m}^2 - \left(\frac{90}{360}\right)\pi 3^2\,\text{m}^2 = \left(\frac{90}{360}\right)55\pi\,\text{m}^2 = 43.197\,\text{m}^2$$

Area of rectangle $= (8 \times 16)\,\text{m}^2 = 128\,\text{m}^2$

$\therefore$ The area of grass $= (128 - 43.197)\,\text{m}^2 = 84.8\,\text{m}^2$

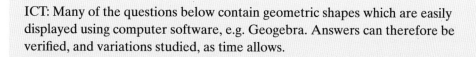

> ### Example 2
>
> A minor arc CD of a circle, centre O and radius 20 cm, subtends an angle
> x radians at O. The major arc CD of the circle subtends an angle $5x$ radians at O.
> Find, in terms of π, the length of the minor arc.
>
> The minor arc CD $= r\theta = 20x$.
>
> The major arc CD $= r\theta = 20 \times 5x = 100x$.
>
> The major arc $= 2 \times \pi \times r -$ the minor arc ... circumference $= 2\pi r$
>
> $\therefore$ $100x = 2 \times \pi \times 20 - 20x$
>
> $\therefore$ $120x = 40\pi$
>
> $\therefore$ $x = \dfrac{\pi}{3}$ $\Rightarrow$ the minor arc CD $= 20x = \dfrac{20\pi}{3}$ cm.
>
> (Note: This is an exact measurement. An approximate answer is obtained when
> we substitute a value for π.)

ICT: Many of the questions below contain geometric shapes which are easily
displayed using computer software, e.g. Geogebra. Answers can therefore be
verified, and variations studied, as time allows.

Exercise 6.2

1. A drawing of a curved flower bed is shown.
   The scale in the drawing is 1 cm : 1 m.
   Calculate, correct to 1 place of decimals,

   (i) the perimeter of the bed

   (ii) the area of the bed.

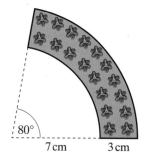

2. Find:

   (i) the total area, correct to the nearest cm²

   (ii) the total perimeter enclosed by this composite figure,
   correct to the nearest cm.

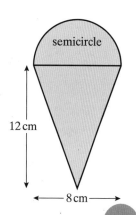

3. Write a formula for each of the following shaded areas.

(a)

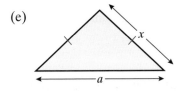

(b)

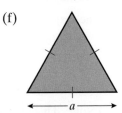

(c)

(d)

(e)

(f)

4. Write a formula for the radius of the sector of a circle in terms of the perimeter P of the sector and the angle θ radians subtended at the centre.

5. The points R and S lie on the circumference of a circle with centre O and radius 8.5 cm. The point T lies on the major arc RS.
Given that $|\angle RTS| = 0.4$ radians, calculate the length of the minor arc RS.

6. A square is inscribed inside a circle of radius r. Find

   (i) the area of the square BCDE
   (ii) the shaded area in terms of r.

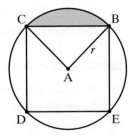

7. A farmer has 80 metres of fencing to make a circular chicken coop.
Find the radius and the area of the coop to a suitable degree of accuracy.
Explain why the radius cannot be measured with complete accuracy.

8. (i) A circle is shown with both an inscribed and a circumscribed square.

   Find the ratio of the area of the inner square to the area of the outer square.

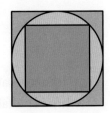

   (ii) An equilateral triangle is shown with both an inscribed and a circumscribed circle.

   Calculate the ratio of the area of the circumcircle to the area of the incircle.

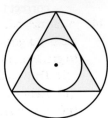

9. A circle of circumference 12 cm is inscribed in a
   square which in turn is inscribed in an outer circle.
   This outer circle touches the parallel sides of a
   trapezium as shown.
   Find the area of the trapezium, giving your answer in the
   form $\dfrac{a\sqrt{b}}{\pi}$.

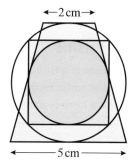

10. The shaded portion of the semicircle is to be cut
    from a large sheet of metal.
    (i) Write down in radians the measure of the
        angle AOB.
    (ii) Find the **exact** length of the perimeter of
         the shaded portion.
    (iii) Find the area of the shaded portion and
    (iv) hence find the area of the non-shaded segment.

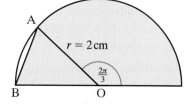

11. Derive a formula in terms of r and θ radians for the
    area of the minor segment under the chord BC.
    Hence, find the ratio of the area of the major
    segment to the area of the minor segment
    subtended by an angle of $\dfrac{\pi}{2}$ radians.

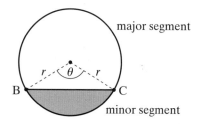

12. Five discs fit exactly into a rectangular frame of width 20 cm.
    Find the area of the remaining space in the frame.

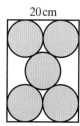

13. If the area of a sector of a circle is 48 cm², and its perimeter is 28 cm, find the length
    of the radius.

14. A farmer has a shed measuring 4 m by 5 m in the centre of a large field of grass.
    He ties a goat to one corner of this shed, and using a rope measuring 8 m, allows him
    to graze on the grass.
    (i) Draw a diagram showing the grazing area.
    (ii) Indicate on the diagram the different sectors of circles represented by this area.
    (iii) Calculate this total grazing area correct to the nearest m².

201

Section 6.3 3-Dimensional objects _____

1. Prisms

A **prism** is a three-dimensional figure that
has the same cross-section all along its length.
Shown here is a standard triangular prism.

The volume $= (A \times l)\, m^3$

The external surface area $= [2A + 3(l \times b)]\, m^2$

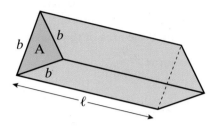

A rubbish skip is also a prism where the base is in the
shape of a trapezium.

Given that the width and perpendicular height of this
skip are both 1.8 m,

the volume $V = \text{Area}_{\text{trapezium}} \times 1.8\, m^3$

$$= \left(\frac{3.5 + 2.3}{2}\right) \times 1.8 \times 1.8\, m^3$$

$$= 9.369\, m^3 = 9.4\, m^3.$$

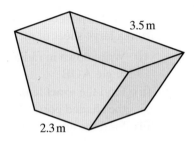

3.5 m

2.3 m

The surface area of a prism is best obtained by expanding the net of the prism.

The slant height is $\sqrt{0.6^2 + 1.8^2} = 1.9\, m$

The area of each end (E) $= (1.8 \times 1.9)\, m^2$

This skip has an external surface area of:

$$\text{Area} = 2\left(\frac{3.5 + 2.3}{2}\right) \times 1.8 + 1.8 \times 2.3 + 2(1.8 \times 1.9)$$

$$= 21.42\, m^2$$

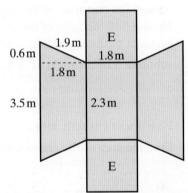

1.9 m   E
0.6 m   1.8 m
1.8 m
3.5 m   2.3 m
E

2. Revision of Cylinder, Cone and Sphere

Shape	Diagram	Properties
Cylinder	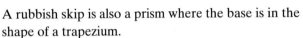	Volume $= \pi r^2 \times h$ Surface Area $= 2 \times \pi r^2 + 2\pi r \times h$ Net of cylinder: $2\pi r$ h r

Cone		Volume = $\frac{1}{3}\pi r^2 \times h$ Surface Area = $\pi r^2 + \pi rl$ Net of cone: Note: (i) In a **right circular cone**, the apex is directly over the centre of the base. Hence, $l^2 = r^2 + h^2$. (ii) The arc length of the sector (s) = circumference of the base ($2\pi r$).
Sphere		Volume$_{\text{sphere}} = \frac{4}{3}\pi r^3$ Volume$_{\text{hemisphere}} = \frac{2}{3}\pi r^3$ Surface area of sphere = $4\pi r^2$ Surface area of hemisphere = $3\pi r^2$
Pyramid		Volume = $\frac{1}{3}a^2 \times h$ Surface Area = $a^2 + 4(\frac{1}{2}al) = a^2 + 2al$ $l^2 = h^2 + \frac{a^2}{4}$ Net of pyramid:

Note: Both a prism and a pyramid can have many differently-shaped (polygonal) bases.

Generally, (i) the volume of a **prism** = (area of the base) $\times h$

(ii) the volume of a **pyramid** = $\frac{1}{3}$(area of the base) $\times h$

3. Degrees of accuracy

When a measurement is made to a given degree of accuracy, an *error* on the measurement is created. If x is the measurement, the real measurement could be in the range $x \pm \Delta x$.

E.g. If a length is measured as 10.3 cm, corrected to one place of decimals, this implies a minimum possible length of 10.25 cm and a maximum possible length of 10.34 cm.

If the measurement is area or volume, each dimension will have a similar range.

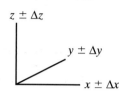

Example 1

Find the volume of the truncated cone shown (a frustum) correct to 1 place of decimals.

By drawing the cross-section through the centre of the truncated cone, we can see that by subtracting the smaller cone on the top from the larger cone, the remainder is the volume of the frustrum.

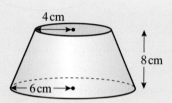

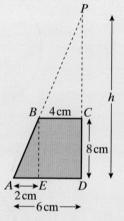

From similar triangles we have,

$$\frac{h - 8}{4} = \frac{h}{6} \Rightarrow 6h - 48 = 4h$$

$$2h = 48$$

$$h = 24.$$

Volume of larger cone $= \frac{1}{3}\pi r^2 h = \frac{1}{3}\pi \times 6^2 \times 24 = 288\pi$

The height of the smaller cone $|PC| = h - 8 = 16$ cm

$\therefore$ Volume of smaller cone $= \frac{1}{3}\pi r^2 h = \frac{1}{3}\pi \times 4^2 \times 16 = \frac{256}{3}\pi$

$\therefore$ Volume of frustum $= 288\pi - \frac{256}{3}\pi = \frac{608}{3}\pi = 636.7$ cm^3

Example 2

A company makes ball bearings (spheres) for a machine with a diameter of 12 mm. They claim that they are produced to an accuracy of ± 0.02 mm. Find the largest and smallest ball bearing volumes produced.

Find the percentage error on   (i) the diameter   (ii) the volume.

$\text{Diameter} = 12\,\text{mm} \Rightarrow \text{Diameter}_{max} = 12.02\,\text{mm}, \ \text{Diameter}_{min} = 11.98\,\text{mm}$

$\text{Volume} = \frac{4}{3}\pi r^3 \Rightarrow \text{Volume max} = \frac{4}{3}\pi(6.01)^3 = 909.310\,\text{mm}^3$

$\Rightarrow \text{Volume min} = \frac{4}{3}\pi(5.99)^3 = 900.262\,\text{mm}^3$

(i) % error on the diameter $= \frac{0.02}{12} \times 100\% = \pm0.167\%$

(ii) Volume $= \frac{4}{3}\pi(6)^3 = 904.779\,\text{mm}^3$

$\Rightarrow$ % error on the volume $= \dfrac{909.310 - 904.779}{904.779} \times 100\% = \pm0.5\%$

Exercise 6.3

1. Examine each of the following shapes closely and
   (i) by drawing a suitable net of each, calculate the total area correct to one place of decimals
   (ii) find the volume of each shape correct to one place of decimals.

   (a)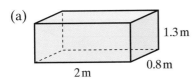
   1.3 m
   0.8 m
   2 m

   (b)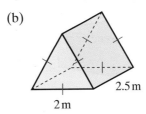
   2.5 m
   2 m

   (c)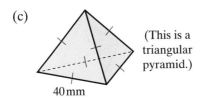
   (This is a triangular pyramid.)
   40 mm

   (d)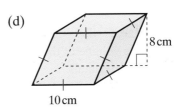
   8 cm
   10 cm

   (e)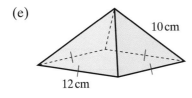
   10 cm
   12 cm

   (f)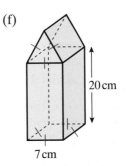
   20 cm
   7 cm

2. In a woodwork class, the students were asked to list in order from largest to smallest, the (i) volume (ii) **total** surface area of each of the following solid 3-dimensional objects, each answer given correct to the nearest whole number.
Make two separate lists for (i) the areas (ii) the volumes, each arranged in descending order.

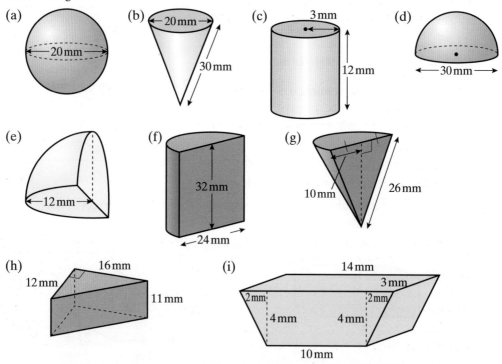

3. This model of a skip is used by a recycling company.

(i) Find the volume of the skip, correct to two places of decimals.

(ii) The company offers a 'volume pick-up' at 80 per m³ or a 'weight pick-up' at 30 per 100 kg, assuming a full skip weighs 1.3 tonnes. Which option represents the best "value for money" for the customer?

(iii) Write an equation for the volume of the skip in terms of *a, h, w* and *θ*.

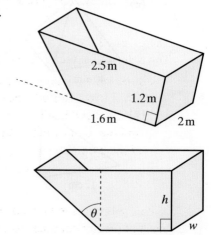

(iv) The recycling company wants to redesign the skip with a new angle *θ* = 45°. If the width, height and overall volume must remain the same in order to fit on the truck, find, correct to one place of decimals, the new dimensions of the top and the bottom of the skip.

4. The net of a 3D figure is shown in the diagram. Both triangles are isosceles and congruent.

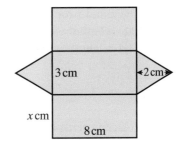

(i) Calculate the length of the side x cm.

(ii) Draw a sketch of the 3D figure and name it.

(iii) Calculate its volume.

(iv) Design a trapezoidal prism with the same volume.

5. (i) A student in a woodwork class is asked to fashion the largest sphere possible from the cube opposite. What volume of wood must be chipped away?

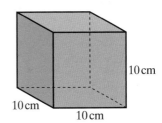

(ii) The student is then asked to calculate the volume of the smallest sphere that can enclose the cube fully.

6. A water tank, in the shape of a cuboid(rectangular solid), is full of water. Water is drained from the tank at a rate of 8 litres per minute.
The dimensions of the tank are given to the nearest 10 cm. The rate at which the water is drained from the tank is given to the nearest 0.5 litres per minute.
Calculate, correct to the nearest minute,

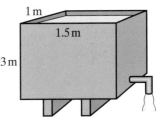

(i) the shortest time possible to drain the tank

(ii) the longest time possible to drain the tank.

7. The pyramid shown opposite has a rectangular base. The point X is directly above the midpoint of the base.

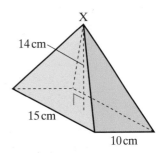

(i) Find the volume of the pyramid.

(ii) Draw two different possible nets of the pyramid and hence (using one of them) find the total external surface area of the pyramid.

8. A steel support is to be made from a rectangular block of metal 4 cm thick, as shown. If a quarter-circle is removed, calculate the total surface area and the total volume of the support.

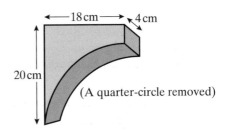

(A quarter-circle removed)

9. If x, y, and z represent lengths, and π and a are numbers with no dimensions, state whether each of the following formulae represents
    (i) a length   (ii) an area   (iii) a volume or (iv) a combination of these
    (a) $\pi x^2 + \pi y^2 + \pi z^2$ (b) $ax + \pi y$ (c) axz (d) $a\pi y$
    (e) $axy + \pi az$ (f) $ax + xy$ (g) $axyz$ (h) $x^2y + y^2z + z^2x$

10. If A represents area, V represents volume, and x, y, z are lengths, which of these formulae are consistent, and which are inconsistent, in terms of dimensions? Explain your answers.

    (i) $Ax = z^3$ (ii) $x = \dfrac{V}{Ay}$ (iii) $V = xy + z$ (iv) $A = x^2 + y^2 + z^2$

    (v) $V = A(x + y + z)$ (vi) $A = \dfrac{V}{x} + y$ (vii) $x = y + z$

11. The formula for the volume of a pyramid is
    $$V = \tfrac{1}{3}(\text{base area}) \times \text{perpendicular height}.$$

    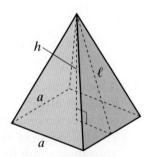

    (i) For the square-based pyramid opposite, find the volume in terms of a and h.
    Find the volume of a pyramid if the length of the base is 6 cm and the height is 7 cm.

    (ii) Another square-based pyramid has a base length of 5 cm and a volume of 100 cm³.
    Find its perpendicular height.
    Hence, and by drawing its net, find the total surface area.

    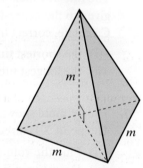

    (iii) The pyramid shown opposite has been cut from a square-based pyramid. Find its volume in terms of m. Describe this pyramid. Draw its net and find its total surface area in terms of m.

12. (i) A solid sphere just fits into a cubical box, as shown. If the edge of the box is 14 cm in length, and taking $\pi = \frac{22}{7}$, find
    (a) the volume of the box in cm³
    (b) the volume of the sphere in cm³
    (c) the percentage of space not occupied by the sphere.
    Give your answer correct to the nearest integer.

    (ii) The same solid sphere fits exactly inside a cylinder.
    Determine if the percentage of unoccupied space in the cylinder is greater or less than the space unoccupied in the cubical box.

13. Find, correct to 1 place of decimals, the volume of this rubber stopper.

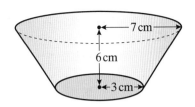

Section 6.4 Trapezoidal rule for calculating area _____

To calculate the areas of shapes with irregular boundaries, e.g. fields, lakes, etc., surveyors have usually divided the area into a series of parallel strips, each in the shape of a trapezium; a quadrilateral with two of the four sides parallel to each other.

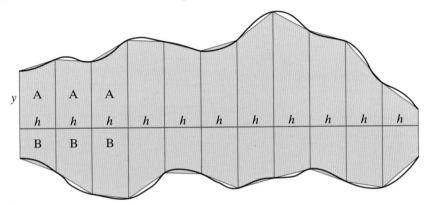

A straight line is drawn across the centre of the area, dividing it into a series of two different areas, A and B.

The area of each section, above and below the line, can be calculated separately using the formula for the area of a trapezium and then added together.

Along the line and at equal intervals of h, perpendicular lines are drawn up to the boundary. These ordinates (offsets) – y_1, y_2, y_3, etc – are the parallel sides of the trapezium.

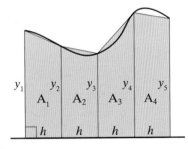

Using the area formula for a trapezium, $\frac{a+b}{2} \times h$, we get

$A_1 = \frac{y_1 + y_2}{2} \times h$. Similarly, $A_2 = \frac{y_2 + y_3}{2} \times h$, and so on.

Therefore, the total area $A = A_1 + A_2 + A_3 + A_4$.

$$= \left(\frac{y_1 + y_2}{2} \times h\right) + \left(\frac{y_2 + y_3}{2} \times h\right) + \left(\frac{y_3 + y_4}{2} \times h\right) + \left(\frac{y_4 + y_5}{2} \times h\right)$$

$$= \frac{h}{2}(y_1 + y_2 + y_2 + y_3 + y_3 + y_4 + y_4 + y_5)$$

$$= \frac{h}{2}\left[y_1 + 2(y_2 + y_3 + y_4) + y_5\right]$$

In words, $\text{Area} \approx \dfrac{\text{interval width}}{2}\left[\text{first height} + \text{last height} + 2(\text{remaining heights})\right]$

When n strips are made, the Trapezoidal formula becomes

$$\text{Area} \approx \frac{h}{2}\left[y_1 + y_n + 2(y_2 + y_3 + y_4 + \dots y_{n-1})\right]$$

Note 1: Because the top of each trapezium does not match the boundary at all points, the area obtained by this formula is only approximate.
Its accuracy depends on the gap width h; the smaller the gap width, the greater the accuracy.

Note 2: If offsets are measured from the same points above and below the line, then the area $(A + B)$ can be obtained using

$$\text{Area} \approx \frac{h}{2}\left[y_1 + y_7 + 2(y_2 + y_3 + y_4 + y_5 + y_6)\right]$$

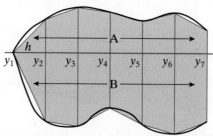

Example 1

Using the measurements provided, find the area of this shape given $h = 1$ unit.

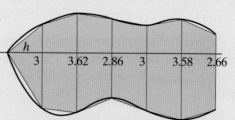

$y_1 = 0$, $y_2 = 3$, $y_3 = 3.62$, $y_4 = 2.86$, $y_5 = 3$, $y_6 = 3.58$, $y_7 = 2.66$.

$\text{Area} \approx \dfrac{h}{2}\left[y_1 + y_7 + 2(y_2 + y_3 + y_4 + y_5 + y_6)\right]$

$= \frac{1}{2}\left[0 + 2.66 + 2(3 + 3.62 + 2.86 + 3 + 3.58)\right] = 17.390$ sq. units

Example 2

The circle shown has equation $x^2 + y^2 = 25$.

(i) Find y in terms of x.

(ii) Hence complete this table.

x	0	1	2	3	4	5
y						

(iii) Use the table to estimate the area of the quarter-circle using intervals of $h = 1$ unit.

(iv) Complete the table below using intervals of $h = 0.5$ unit.

x	0	0.5	1	1.5	2	2.5	3	3.5	4	4.5	5
y											

(v) Compare both answers with the answer obtained from the area of a disc formula (correct to 3 places of decimals). What conclusion can be drawn?

(i) $x^2 + y^2 = 25 \Rightarrow y^2 = 25 - x^2$

$\Rightarrow y = \sqrt{25 - x^2}$

(ii)

x	0	1	2	3	4	5
y	5	$\sqrt{24}$	$\sqrt{21}$	4	3	0

(iii) $\therefore$ Area $\approx \frac{1}{2}\left[5 + 0 + 2(\sqrt{24} + \sqrt{21} + 4 + 3)\right] = 18.982$ sq. units

x	0	0.5	1	1.5	2	2.5	3	3.5	4	4.5	5
y	5	4.975	4.899	4.77	4.583	4.33	4	3.571	3	2.179	0

(iv) $\therefore$ Area $\approx \frac{0.5}{2}\left[5 + 0 + 2(4.975 + 4.899 + 4.77 + 4.584 + 4.33 + 4 + 3.571 + 3 + 2.179)\right] = 19.404$ sq. units

Area of $\frac{1}{4}$ disc $= \frac{1}{4}\pi r^2 = \frac{1}{4}\pi 5^2 = 19.635$ sq. units

(v) As h gets smaller, the answer approximates more closely to the disc formula answer. We also note that both the approximations are smaller than the true answer, as would be expected from the shape of the graph.

Note: If there are 5 strips, there are 6 ordinates.
If there are 10 strips, there are 11 ordinates.
If there are n strips, there are $n + 1$ ordinates.

Exercise 6.4

1. A farmer wants to find the area of one
   of his fields which is shaped as shown.
   He uses a map which has a scale of
   1000 : 1. He divides the map of the
   field in two, using a horizontal line,
   and then draws perpendicular offsets
   at 10 mm intervals. By measuring the
   lengths of the offsets, use the trapezoidal
   rule to estimate the area of A + B.
   Give your answer in hectares, correct to 2 places of decimals.

   (Note: One hectare = $10\,000\,\text{m}^2$)

   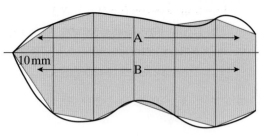

2. If $h = 1\,\text{cm}$ and the lengths of the offsets
   are as shown, find the area of this map.

   (i) If the area of the map is $17.23\,\text{cm}^2$,
       find the percentage error in using
       the trapezoidal rule and $h = 1\,\text{cm}$.

   (ii) By taking new measurements with
        $h = \frac{1}{2}\,\text{cm}$, find a second estimate of
        the area.

   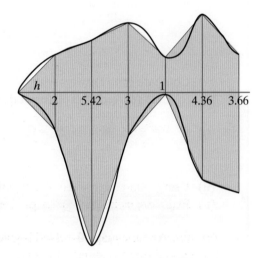

3. Using the trapezoidal rule, and an interval
   value of (i) $h = 1\,\text{cm}$ and (ii) $h = 0.5\,\text{cm}$,
   estimate the area under the curve
   $$y = 3x - (0.5)x^2.$$

   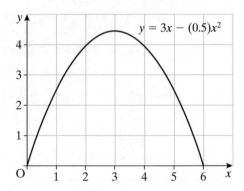

4. Copy these axes and use them to plot the function $y = \sqrt{x}$ for $0 \leqslant x \leqslant 2$.

Using four trapezoids, approximate the area under the curve for $0 \leqslant x \leqslant 2$.

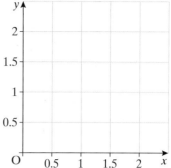

5.

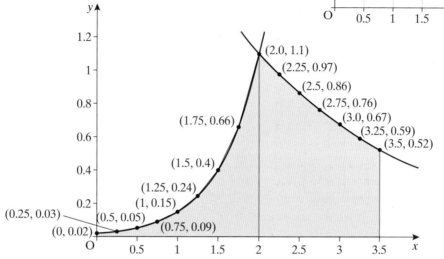

(i) Using an interval width of 0.25, find the ratio of the coloured areas under the curve.
(ii) Estimate, using trial and error, the maximum value of x so that both areas are equal.

6. An outline of the map of Ireland is given. If the scale used is $1\,\text{cm} = 20\,\text{km}$, use the trapezoidal rule to estimate the area of the island of Ireland.
Offsets are taken every 3 cm.

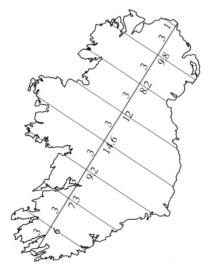

213

Revision Exercise 6 (Core)

1. The diagram shows a square, a diagonal and a line joining a vertex to the midpoint of a side.
   What is the ratio of the area P to the area Q?

   (ICT: Check your answer by drawing this figure with a computer graphics program, e.g. Geogebra)

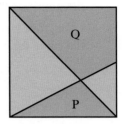

2. Find the total surface area and the volume of each of the following composite figures.
   Correct your answers to the nearest whole number.

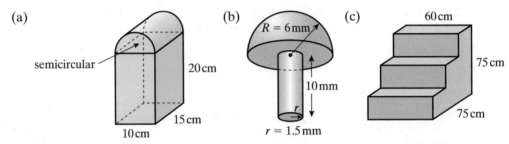

   (a) semicircular 20 cm 15 cm 10 cm

   (b) $R = 6$ mm 10 mm $r = 1.5$ mm

   (c) 60 cm 75 cm 75 cm

3. A circle of radius 5 cm has a centre O and a minor arc [CB] of length 6.4 cm, as indicated.

   (i) Calculate, in radians, the size of the acute angle COB.
   (ii) Calculate the area of the minor sector COB.
   (iii) Calculate the ratio of
        minor sector : major sector in the form $1 : p$,
        giving p correct to 3 significant figures.

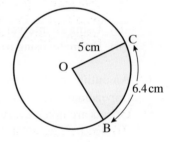

4. Determine the capacity of a swimming pool with the dimensions given.
   If the water mains can supply water at a rate of 10 litre per minute, how long would it take to fill the pool?

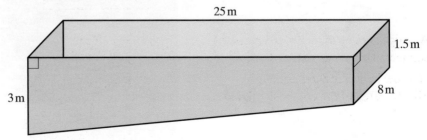

5. Find the value of x in each of the following circles.

(i)

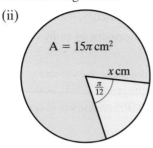

1.2 rads

$A = 12\,\text{cm}^2$ $x\,\text{cm}$

(ii)

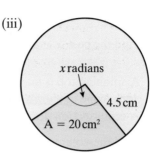

$A = 15\pi\,\text{cm}^2$

$x\,\text{cm}$

$\frac{\pi}{12}$

(iii)

x radians

4.5 cm

$A = 20\,\text{cm}^2$

6. The net of a cone is shown in the diagram. Use this diagram to show that the curved surface area of a cone can be written as $A = \pi.r.\ell$, where r is the radius of the circular base and ℓ is the slant height of the cone. (Note: s is the length of the minor arc.)

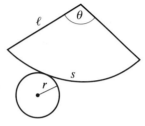

7. The graph of the function $y = (1 + 2x^2)^{0.3}$ is as shown.

(i) By using the rectangle OPRQ and the triangle KPR, estimate the area under the graph for $0 < x < 5$.

(ii) Using the trapezoidal rule, and the offsets as indicated, find a second estimate for the area.

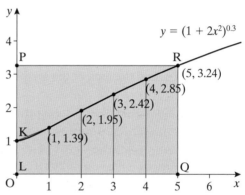

$y = (1 + 2x^2)^{0.3}$

(5, 3.24)

(4, 2.85)

(3, 2.42)

(2, 1.95)

(1, 1.39)

8. Find

(i) the perimeter and

(ii) the area of this composite figure, leaving your answers in surd form.

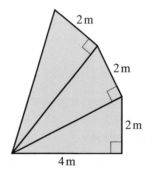

2 m

2 m

2 m

4 m

9. A badge is to be made from a series of connected circles as shown. Find

(i) the length of the perimeter

(ii) the area of the composite figure.

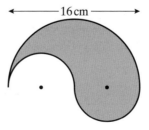

16 cm

10. The cost of manufacturing a hemispherical glass dome is given by

  Cost = $(5200 + 35A)$ where A is the surface area in square metres.

  Find the cost of making a hemisphere of radius 10 m.

11. A spinning top is made from a cube, a cylinder
  and a cone as shown in this diagram.
  A cross-section drawing with dimensions is given.

  Find the volume of the spinning top
  correct to 1 place of decimals.

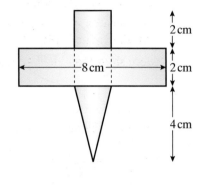

Revision Exercise 6 (Advanced)

1. The figure shows the minor sector BCE of a circle of
  centre E and radius r cm. The perimeter of the sector
  is 100 cm and the area of the sector is A cm².

  (i) Show that $A = (50r - r^2)$ cm².
  (ii) Given that r can vary, find (by completing the square)
   the value of r for which A is a maximum and show
   that A is a maximum.
  (iii) Find the value of $\angle$CEB for this maximum area.

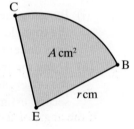

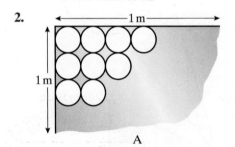

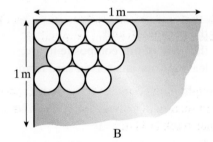

Circular holes, of radius 1 cm, are to be cut out of a sheet of metal. The sheet of metal
  measures 1 m × 1 m. Two methods, A or B, could be used, as shown above.

  (i) Calculate the number of holes possible with each method.
  (ii) Calculate the percentage waste from each piece of metal.

3. In this diagram, the area of the shaded triangle PNQ is three times the area of the segment created by the chord [OQ].

Find, in terms of r and θ,

   (i) the area of $\triangle$PQO

   (ii) the area of the segment formed by [OQ]

   (iii) the area of $\triangle$PQN.

Hence show that $3\theta - 4\sin\theta = 0$.

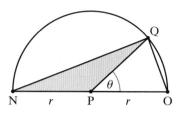

4. Find the total surface area and the volume of the metal in each of the following objects, correct to the nearest whole number.

(a)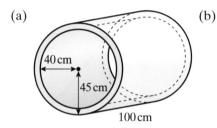

(b)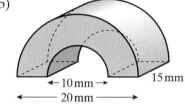

(c)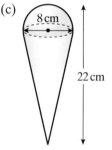

5. The outline of a design for a wind ornament is as shown. A circular wire holds a sector of a circle.

If the angle of the minor sector is $\dfrac{2\pi}{3}$ radians,

find the area (i) of the minor sector

           (ii) of the minor segment.

Show that if $\theta = 1.895$ radians, the area of the sector is bisected by the dotted horizontal line.

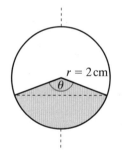

6. A straight path connects two points C and D on a curved section of railway track. The radius of the circular track is 44 m.

   (i) Show that the angle COD is 1.84 radians.

   (ii) Calculate the length of the railway track shown.

   (iii) Calculate the shortest distance from O to the path.

   (iv) Calculate the area bound by the path and the railway track.

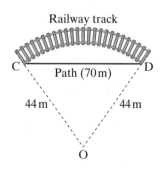

7. Show that the area of the minor segment is $\frac{1}{2}r^2(\theta - \sin\theta)$.

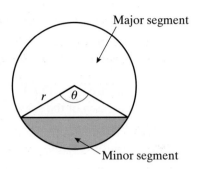

(i) Given that the area of the major segment is 23.32 cm² when $\theta = 2$ radians, find r, correct to one place of decimals.

(ii) If this diagram represents the cross-section of a bowl containing water, find the surface area of the water. (Take $\theta = 2$ radians.)

8. The motion of a courier van is represented by a speed/time graph as shown.

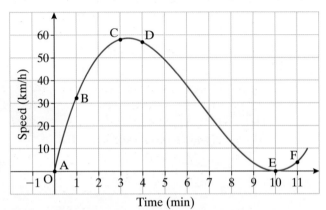

(i) Comment on the differences in the motion of the courier between points A to B, C to D and E to F.

(ii) What quantity is obtained when speed is multiplied by time?

(iii) Using the trapezoidal rule and readings from the graph, estimate the total distance travelled by the courier in 10 min.

9. A regular tetrahedron has four faces, each of which is an equilateral triangle.

One such tetrahedron is placed in a cylinder with one face flat against the bottom. If the length of one edge of the tetrahedron is $2a$, show that the volume of the smallest possible cylindrical container into which it

will fit is $\dfrac{8\sqrt{6}}{9}\pi a^3$.

(Adapted from 2011 SEC sample paper.)

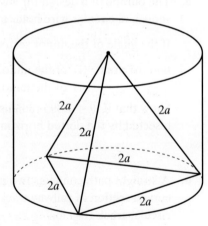

10. Find the area of the shaded trapezium. Note: the sides are not drawn to scale.

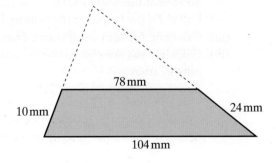

Revision Exercise 6 (Extended-Response Questions)

1. A piece of wire of length 4 m is bent into the shape
   of a sector of a circle of radius r metres and angle θ radians.
   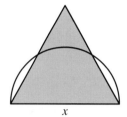
   (i) State, in terms of θ and r,
       (a) the length of the arc
       (b) the area A of the sector.
   (ii) Hence, show that $A = 2r - r^2$.
   (iii) By completing the square, rewrite this equation in the form $A = q - (r - p)^2$.
   (iv) Draw a graph of A against r, $0 \leqslant r \leqslant 3$. Write down the maximum point on the
        graph and hence find the maximum value of r which will make the area
        a maximum.
   (v) Deduce the corresponding value of θ.

2. (i) Groups of students were asked to compare the areas
      of an equilateral triangle and a semicircle, where the
      base of the equilateral triangle had the same measurement
      as the diameter of the semicircle.
      Group one said that they had the same area.
      Group two said that the triangle was larger by 10.18%.
      Group three said that there was a 9.24% difference.
      Investigate the claims of each group.
   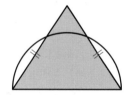

   (ii) The groups were then asked to calculate the size of
        the base angles of an isosceles triangle which
        had exactly the same area as the semicircle, and again
        where the base was the same size as the diameter of
        the semicircle.
        What size angle should they have come up with?
   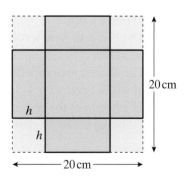

   (iii) If the equal areas are rotated about a line vertically through the apex of the
         triangle, a cone and a hemisphere are created. Investigate if the volumes are
         the same.

3. A diagram of the net of a drawer is given.
   When constructed, the drawer has the shape of an
   open-topped cuboid.
   (i) Find, in terms of h, an expression for
       the area of a square base.
   (ii) For what value of h would the drawer
        be an open-topped cube?
   (iii) Find an expression for the volume of
         the drawer in terms of h.
         Sketch a graph of the volume as a function
         of h from $h = 0$ cm to $h = 14$ cm.
   (iv) Use your graph to estimate the value of h
        that maximises the volume of the drawer.

(v) You need a drawer with a volume of 500 cm³.
    Estimate from your graph the three different values of *h* that would create
    a volume of 500 cm³.

(vi) Explain why all values of *h* are not physically possible.

4. A programmer wants to make a program to estimate
   the area of a circle using the trapezoidal rule.
   In his initial investigation he draws a semicircle
   of radius 10 cm. He then divides the diameter into
   8 equal intervals.

   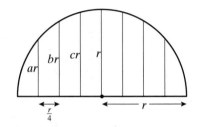

   (i) Construct a semicircle of radius 10 cm and by
       measuring the length of each offset, estimate the
       area of the semicircle using the trapezoidal rule.

   (ii) Find the percentage error in this method by comparing with the true area of $\frac{1}{2}\pi r^2$.

   (iii) Using his construction, the programmer calculated the length of each offset in
         terms of *r*.
         Using the diagram above, calculate the values for *a, b,* and *c*, correct to a
         reasonable degree of accuracy.

   (iv) The programmer derived the approximate area as

$$\text{Area} = \frac{r^2}{4}(2a + 2b + 2c + 1).$$

   Show clearly how this formula was derived.

   (v) Using your calculated values for *a, b* and *c* in the programmer's equation, find
       a formula for the area of a semicircle of radius *r* cm.

   (vi) Using this formula, estimate the areas of semicircles of radii 5 cm,
        10 cm, and 15 cm.

   (vii) Comment on the accuracy of the programmer's formula.

5. A large sheet of cardboard
   22 cm × 31 cm is to be used
   to make a box.
   The box is to have a volume
   of 500 cm³.
   The shaded areas are flaps
   of width 1 cm.
   The height of the box is *h* cm
   as shown in the diagram.

   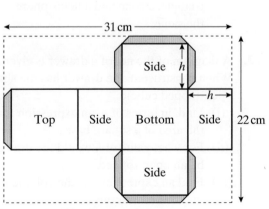

   Write, in terms of *h,* the

   (i) (a) length   (b) width   (c) height of the box.
   (ii) Write an expression for the capacity of the box in terms of *h*.
   (iii) Find the value of *h* for the box if it is to have a square base.
   (iv) Show that this value of *h* gives the required capacity.

(v) Find, correct to 1 place of decimals, the other value of h that gives a capacity of 500 cm³.

(vi) A graph of the capacity as a function of h is drawn. Indicate on this graph your answers to parts (iv) and (v).

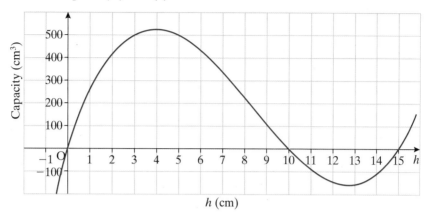

h (cm)

(vii) Is it possible to increase the capacity of the box by 10% using the same size piece of cardboard? Explain.

(Adapted from SEC, Project Maths sample paper, 2012)

Algebra 3

Key words

inequality   quadratic inequality   rational inequality   modulus

modular equations   modular inequalities   direct proof   proof by contradiction

absolute value   abstract inequalities   indices   base number

exponential growth   exponential decay   logarithm   proof by induction

Section 7.1 Revision

The inequality symbols $>$, $\geqslant$, $<$, $\leqslant$ are needed when solving problems in which a range of possible values satisfy the given conditions.

$>$	greater than
$\geqslant$	greater than or equal to
$<$	less than
$\leqslant$	less than or equal to

e.g. If $3x - 4 > 5$,

$\qquad\quad 3x > 9$,

$\qquad$ and $x > 3$, which means that **all values of x**

$\qquad\qquad$ greater than 3 satisfy $3x - 4 > 5$.

An expression such as $3x - 4 > 5$ is called an **inequality**.

Basic rules of inequalities

Adding or subtracting a constant, a	$x > y$	$x \pm a > y \pm a$
Multiplying or dividing by a **positive** number, $a > 0$	$x > y$	$ax > ay$ $\dfrac{x}{a} > \dfrac{y}{a}$

When multiplying or dividing by a negative number, the inequality symbol is **reversed**.

E.g. $5 > 2$; if both sides are multiplied by (-1), we get $5 \times (-1) < 2 \times (-1)$, i.e. $-5 < -2$.

Multiplying or dividing by a **negative** number, $a < 0$	$x > y$	$ax < ay$ $\dfrac{x}{a} < \dfrac{y}{a}$

Also,

Combining inequalities	$\begin{array}{c} x > y \\ y > z \end{array}$	$x > z$
	$\begin{array}{c} x > y > 0 \\ a > b > 0 \end{array}$	$ax > by$

Graphical construction

If a graph of the function is given or is easily constructed, this provides an extra technique in helping to understand and solve inequalities.

If $f(x) = (x + 3)(x - 1)(x - 4) \geqslant 0$,

then the points $x = -3, x = 1$ and $x = 4$ are the critical points in determining the solution set.

The set of values of x for which

$$f(x) = (x + 3)(x - 1)(x - 4) \geqslant 5$$

can also be estimated.

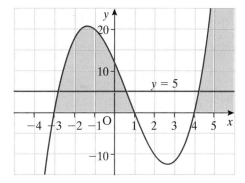

Note:

(i) When solving inequalities, the solution is often restricted to specific number systems, i.e. $\in N, \in Z, \in R$, and the resulting range of numbers plotted on the number line.
e.g. $5x - 1 > 14, x \in N$.

(ii) An inequality creates an ordered pair (a, b);
If $a > b$, then if the order is reversed (b, a), the inequality is also reversed, i.e. $b < a$.

Example 1

Solve the inequality $3x + 7 \geqslant x + 2, x \in Z$, and plot the solution on a number line.

$3x + 7 \geqslant x + 2$
$2x + 7 \geqslant 2$ ... subtracting x from both sides
$2x \geqslant -5$ ... subtracting 7 from both sides
$x \geqslant \dfrac{-5}{2}, x \in Z.$

(All integer values greater than or equal to $-2\frac{1}{2}$ will satisfy the original inequality.)

```
  +----+----+----+----•----•----•----•----•----•----•----•---->
  -5   -4   -3   -2   -1    0    1    2    3    4    5    6
```

Example 2

Solve the inequality $\frac{1}{6}(x - 1) \geqslant \frac{1}{3}(x - 4), x \in R$.

Graph your solution on a number line.

$\frac{1}{6}(x - 1) \geq \frac{1}{3}(x - 4)$

$\Rightarrow x - 1 \geq 2x - 8$ ... multiplying both sides by 6

$\quad \Rightarrow -x \geq -7$ ... adding 1 and subtracting $2x$ from both sides

$\quad\quad \Rightarrow x \leq 7$ ... multiplying both sides by (-1) and reversing the inequality sign.

(**Note:** A closed circle on 7 indicates that 7 is included in the range.)

Example 3

Solve the inequality $-9 < 3 - 4x \leq 1, x \in R$.

Graph your solution on the number line.

$-9 < 3 - 4x \leq 1$

$\Rightarrow -12 < -4x \leq -2$ ... subtracting 3 from each part of the inequality

$\quad \Rightarrow 3 > x \geq \frac{1}{2}$ ... dividing each part of the inequality by -4 and reversing

$\quad\quad\quad$ the inequality symbol

$\quad\quad \Rightarrow \frac{1}{2} \leq x < 3$ ... reversing the order

(**Note:** An open circle on 3 indicates that it is not to be included.)

Example 4

(i) Find the solution set $A, \{x \mid 7 \leq 10 - 3x, x \in R\}$.

(ii) Find the solution set $B, \{x \mid 2 > \frac{4}{3} - 2x, x \in R\}$.

(iii) Find the set $A \cap B$ and graph the solution on the number line.

$A: 7 \leq 10 - 3x$ $\qquad\qquad$ $B: 2 > \frac{4}{3} - 2x$

$\quad 3x \leq 3$ $\qquad\qquad\qquad\quad$ $2x > \frac{4}{3} - 2$

$\quad\ x \leq 1$ $\qquad\qquad\qquad\quad\ $ $2x > \frac{-2}{3}$

$\qquad\qquad\qquad\qquad\qquad\qquad x > \frac{-1}{3}$

$\therefore\ A \cap B$ is the set of values $\frac{-1}{3} < x \leq 1$.

Exercise 7.1

1. Graph on a number line the set of values of $x \in N$ for which

    (i) $3x - 5 > x + 3$ (ii) $6x - 5 \leqslant 2x - 1$ (iii) $1 - 3x > 10$.

2. Solve each of the following inequalities and plot the solution set on a number line.

    (i) $\frac{x}{2} + 2 < 7, x \in N$ (ii) $\frac{1}{6}(x - 1) \geqslant \frac{1}{3}(x - 4), x \in Z$

    (iii) $\frac{4 - x}{2} > \frac{2 - x}{3}, x \in R$

3. Plot the solution of each of the following inequalities on a number line, $x \in R$.

    (i) $12x - 3(x - 3) < 45$ (ii) $x(x - 4) \geqslant x^2 + 2$ (iii) $x - 2(5 + 2x) < 11$

4. Plot on a number line the set of values of $x \in R$ for which

    (i) $-2 \leqslant x + 1 \leqslant 3$ (ii) $13 > 1 - 3x \geqslant 7$ (iii) $3 \geqslant 4x + 1 > -1$.

5. Solve each of the following inequalities, $x \in R$.

    (i) $3 > \frac{3}{5}(x - 2) > 0$ (ii) $-4 \leqslant \frac{2}{5}(1 - 3x) \leqslant 1$ (iii) $3 \leqslant 2 - \frac{x}{7} < 4$

6. Find the set of values for which $3(x - 2) > x - 4$ and $4x + 12 > 2x + 17, x \in R$, and plot your answers on a number line.

7.   (i) Find the solution set A of $2x - 5 < x - 1, x \in R$.
    (ii) Find the solution set B of $7(x + 1) > 23 - x, x \in R$.
    (iii) Plot the solution set $A \cap B$ on a number line.

8.   (i) Find the solution set C of $2x - 3 > 2, x \in R$.
    (ii) Find the solution set D of $3(x + 2) < 12 + x, x \in R$.
    (iii) Plot the solution set $C \cap D$ on a number line.

9.   (i) Find the solution set E of $15 - x < 2(11 - x), x \in Z$.
    (ii) Find the solution set F of $5(3x - 1) > 12x + 19, x \in Z$.
    (iii) Find the set of values $E \cap F$.

10. (i) Find the set of values G for which $3x + 8 \leqslant 20, x \in N$.
    (ii) Find the set of values H for which $2(3x - 7) \geqslant x + 6, x \in N$.
    (iii) Find the set of values $G \cap H$.

11. A 38 m rope is used to form a rectangular area on a sports day. If the width of the rectangle has to be at least 2 m long, and the length has to be exactly 1 m longer than its width, find the maximum dimensions of the rectangle.

12. If $a < n < b$, and $100 < 2^n < 200$,
    find the values of a and b, where $a, b \in R$ and n where $n \in N$.

13. Give one example to show that if $a > b > 0$ and $n > 0 \Rightarrow a^n > b^n$.
Now give an example to show that if $a > b > 0$ and $n < 0 \Rightarrow a^n < b^n$.

Write an equivalent set of conclusions for these:
    If $a < b < 0$ and $n > 0 \ldots$,
    but if $a < b < 0$ and $n < 0 \ldots$

14. Find x if $x \in Z$ and $Z = \{5 - 3x < -10\} \cap \{4x + 6 < 32\}$.

Section 7.2 Quadratic and rational inequalities _____

1. Quadratic inequalities

$ax^2 + bx + c \geqslant 0$ is an example of a quadratic inequality.

To solve a quadratic inequality of the form $ax^2 + bx + c \geqslant 0$ (or $\leqslant 0$), proceed as follows:

1. Solve $ax^2 + bx + c = 0$ to find the (real) roots of the quadratic equation.
2. Draw a rough sketch of the graph using these roots.
    (i) If $a > 0$, the graph is $\cup$-shaped.
    (ii) If $a < 0$, the graph is $\cap$-shaped.
3. Use the graph to find the set of values of x that satisfies the inequality.

Example 1

Solve the inequality $x^2 - 2x - 8 \leqslant 0$.

Step 1. Solve $x^2 - 2x - 8 = 0$.
$$\Rightarrow x^2 - 2x - 8 = (x + 2)(x - 4) = 0$$
$$\Rightarrow x = -2 \text{ or } x = 4$$

Step 2. Since $a = +1$, i.e. > 0, $\therefore$ a $\cup$-shaped graph.

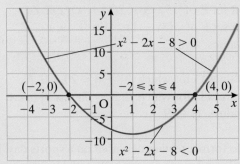

Step 3. The solution of the inequality is the set of values of x that produces the points of the graph that are on or below the x-axis, i.e. $x^2 - 2x - 8 \leqslant 0$. The solution is $-2 \leqslant x \leqslant 4$.

Questions involving values for which the roots of an equation are real,
i.e. $b^2 - 4ac \geqslant 0$, result in quadratic inequalities as shown in the following example.

Example 2

Find the range of values of k for which the
equation $x^2 + (k - 4)x + (k - 1) = 0$
has real roots.

Condition for real roots: $b^2 - 4ac \geqslant 0$.

$a = 1, b = (k - 4), c = (k - 1)$

$\Rightarrow b^2 - 4ac = (k - 4)^2 - 4(1)(k - 1)$
$\qquad = k^2 - 8k + 16 - 4k + 4$
$\qquad = k^2 - 12k + 20$

$b^2 - 4ac \geqslant 0 \Rightarrow k^2 - 12k + 20 \geqslant 0$.

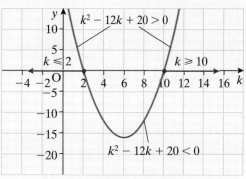

(i) Solving $k^2 - 12k + 20 = 0$;

$\Rightarrow (k - 2)(k - 10) = 0$

$\Rightarrow k = 2$ and $k = 10$ are the roots.

(ii) Sketch the graph; $a = +1$, i.e. >0,

$\therefore$ a $\cup$-shaped graph.

The solution of the inequality is the set of values of k that produces points on a
graph that are on or above the k-axis, i.e. $k^2 - 12k + 20 \geqslant 0$.

The solution is $k \leqslant 2$ and $k \geqslant 10$.

2. Rational inequalities

$f(x) = \dfrac{3x - 2}{x + 1}$ is a *rational function* as the denominator and numerator are
both polynomials in x.

$\dfrac{3x - 2}{x + 1} \geqslant 2$ is a *rational inequality*.

Since we do not know if $(x + 1)$ is positive or negative, we cannot simply multiply
both sides by $(x + 1)$ when solving for x as the inequality symbol would have to be
reversed if $(x + 1)$ was negative.

However, if we multiply both sides by $(x + 1)^2$, we can retain the same inequality
sign since $(x + 1)^2$ is always positive.

$\Rightarrow \dfrac{3x - 2}{x + 1} \times (x + 1)^2 \geqslant 2 \times (x + 1)^2$

$\Rightarrow (3x - 2)(x + 1) \geqslant 2(x^2 + 2x + 1)$

$\Rightarrow 3x^2 + x - 2 \geqslant 2x^2 + 4x + 2$

$\Rightarrow x^2 - 3x - 4 \geqslant 0$, creating a quadratic inequality (with the same solution set)
from the rational inequality.

Example 3

Find the range of values of x for which $\dfrac{2x+1}{x+2} < \dfrac{1}{2}$.

Since $\dfrac{2x+1}{x+2} < \dfrac{1}{2}$,

multiply both sides by $(x+2)^2$.
$[(x+2)^2$ is always positive for all values of x.]

$\Rightarrow \dfrac{2x+1}{x+2} \times (x+2)^2 < \dfrac{1}{2} \times (x+2)^2$

$\Rightarrow (2x+1)(x+2) < \dfrac{1}{2}(x^2+4x+4)$

$\Rightarrow 2x^2+5x+2 < \dfrac{1}{2}(x^2+4x+4)$

$\Rightarrow 4x^2+10x+4 < x^2+4x+4$

$\Rightarrow 3x^2+6x < 0$

$\Rightarrow x^2+2x < 0.$

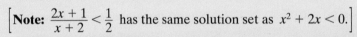

$\left[\textbf{Note: } \dfrac{2x+1}{x+2} < \dfrac{1}{2} \text{ has the same solution set as } x^2+2x < 0.\right]$

(i) Solving the equation $x^2+2x=0$;
$\Rightarrow (x)(x+2)=0$
$\Rightarrow x=0$ and $x=-2$ are the roots.

(ii) Sketch the graph; $a=+1$, i.e. >0,
$\therefore$ a $\cup$-shaped graph.

$\Rightarrow$ The solution of the inequality is the set values of x that produces points on the graph that are below the x-axis (i.e. $x^2+2x < 0$).

The solution is $-2 < x < 0$.

Exercise 7.2

In each of the following questions, $x \in R$ unless otherwise stated.

1. Solve each of the following quadratic inequalities:
   (i) $x^2 - x - 6 \geqslant 0$
   (ii) $x^2 + 3x - 10 \leqslant 0$
   (iii) $2x^2 - 5x + 2 < 0.$

2. Solve each of the following inequalities for x:
   (i) $6 - x - x^2 \geqslant 0$
   (ii) $12 - 5x - 2x^2 > 0$
   (iii) $-2x^2 - 7x \geqslant 0.$

3. Find the set of values of x for which
   (i) $6x^2 - x > 15$
   (ii) $16 - x^2 \leqslant 0$
   (iii) $2(x^2 - 6) \geqslant 5x.$

4. Find the set of values of x for which $(4-x)(1-x) < x + 11.$

5. If $x^2 - 6x + 2 \leqslant 0$, show that $3 - \sqrt{7} \leqslant x \leqslant 3 + \sqrt{7}.$

6. Find the range of values of k for which $x^2 + (k + 1)x + 1 = 0$ has real roots.

7. Find the range of values of k for which the equation $kx^2 + 4x + 3 + k = 0$ has real roots.

8. Find the range of values of p for which the quadratic equation $px^2 + (p + 3)x + p = 0$ has real roots.
If $x = -2$ is a root of the equation, find the value of p.

9. Solve each of the following rational inequalities for x.

(i) $\dfrac{x + 3}{x + 2} < 2, x \neq -2$
(ii) $\dfrac{x + 5}{x - 3} > 1, x \neq 3$
(iii) $\dfrac{2x - 1}{x + 3} > 3, x \neq -3$

10. Find the range of values of x for which

(i) $\dfrac{3x + 4}{x - 5} > 2, x \neq 5$
(ii) $\dfrac{1 - 2x}{4x + 2} > 2, x \neq \dfrac{-1}{2}$
(iii) $\dfrac{3 + 4x}{5x - 1} > 3, x \neq \dfrac{1}{5}$

11. Find the set of values of x for which each of the following inequalities is true.

(i) $\dfrac{x}{2x - 3} \leqslant 1, x \neq \dfrac{3}{2}$
(ii) $\dfrac{2x - 4}{x - 1} < 1, x \neq 1$
(iii) $\dfrac{x - 5}{x - 1} \leqslant 3, x \neq 1$

12. Solve these equations.

(i) $\dfrac{2x - 7}{x + 3} < 1, x \neq -3$
(ii) $\dfrac{2x - 3}{x - 5} < \dfrac{3}{2}, x \neq 5$
(iii) $\dfrac{x + 2}{x - 1} \leqslant 3, x \neq 1$

13. Examine the graphs of $y = 2x^2 + 4x$ and $y = x^2 - x - 6$ and estimate the range of values of x for which

$$2x^2 + 4x > x^2 - x - 6.$$

By simplifying the quadratic inequality, find the range of values of x for which $2x^2 + 4x > x^2 - x - 6, x \in R$.

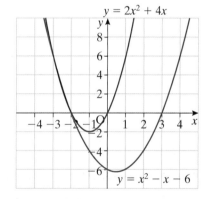

ICT: Study the functions in **Q13.** using graphics software. Enlarge the scale on the x-axis and focus particularly on the domain $-3 < x < -2$.

14. Show that $x^2 + x + 1 > 0$ for all values of x.

15. The path of a ball is given by the expression $f(t) = -11 + 13t - 2t^2$, where t represents time.
Find the range of values of t that satisfies each of the following inequalities.
(i) $f(t) \leqslant 4$
(ii) $f(t) \geqslant 7$, and hence deduce the set of values of t that satisfies
(iii) $4 < f(t) < 7$.

16. Examine the graphs of the following quadratic functions.

Find, as accurately as the graph allows, the range of values of x that satisfies each of the following inequalities.

    (i) $f(x) > 0$
    (ii) $g(x) \le 8$
    (iii) $f(x) \le g(x)$
    (iv) $g(x) > 0$

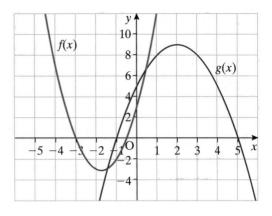

17. The width of a rectangle is to be 3 m shorter than its length. If the ratio of the length to the width is to be less than 5, find the range of possible dimensions for

    (i) the length of the rectangle
    (ii) the width of the rectangle.

18. The graphs of $x^2 - 2px + p + 6$ are shown for $p = 1.5, 2, 2.5$.

Find the range of values of p for which the graphs are always positive, for all real values of x.

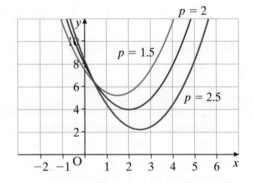

19. Find the range of values of x for which

    (i) the perimeter of this rectangle is less than 50 m
    (ii) the area of this rectangle is greater than 12 m^2
    (iii) the perimeter of this rectangle is less than 50 m and the area is greater than 12 m^2.

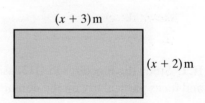

20. Find the range of values of $x, x \in Z$, so that the perimeter of this triangle is between 8 m and 12 m long.

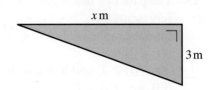

Section 7.3 Modulus

1. Modular equations

The modulus of a number is a measure of its size or magnitude and is written as $|x|$.

> If $|x| = a$, then
> $x = +a$ or $-a$
> and $|x|^2 = a^2$.

$|3| = 3, |-4| = 4, |15.5| = 15.5, |-6.2| = 6.2 \ldots$ in other words, for all $x \in R$, $|x|$ is the positive value of the number.

Conversely, if $|x| = 6$, then $x = +6$ or -6.
And therefore, $|x|^2 = 36$.

Geometrically, the modulus function multiplies any negative part of the graph by (-1).
Compare the following graphs:

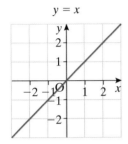

$y = x$

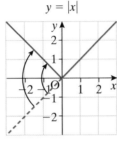

$y = |x|$

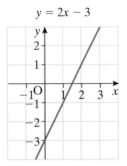

$y = 2x - 3$

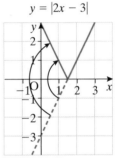

$y = |2x - 3|$

The graph of $f(x) = |x|$ is found from the graph of $f(x) = x$ by reflecting, in the x-axis, that part of the graph for which $f(x) < 0$.

Example 1

Sketch the graph of $f(x) = |3x + 5|$ and hence solve the equation $|3x + 5| = 2$
(i) geometrically and (ii) algebraically.

(i) Geometrically:
   Given $f(x) = 3x + 5$.
   At $x = 0$, $f(x) = 5 \Rightarrow (0, 5)$ is the $f(x)$ intercept.

   At $f(x) = 0; 0 = 3x + 5 \Rightarrow x = \dfrac{-5}{3} \Rightarrow \left(\dfrac{-5}{3}, 0\right)$ is the x-axis intercept.

   $f(x) = 3x + 5$ is the line passing through $(0, 5)$ and $\left(\dfrac{-5}{3}, 0\right)$.

Reflecting the negative region of the graph in the x-axis creates the graph of $f(x) = |3x + 5|$.

The x-coordinates of the intersection points of $f(x) = |3x + 5|$ and $f(x) = 2$ give the solution to the equation $|3x + 5| = 2$.

The x-coordinates are $x = -1$ and $x \cong -2.3$.

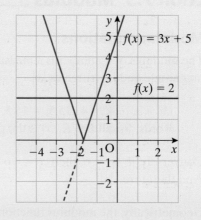

(ii) Algebraically:

Method 1

Since $|3x + 5| = 2$,

$$\Rightarrow 3x + 5 = +2 \qquad \therefore x = -1$$
$$\text{or } 3x + 5 = -2 \qquad \therefore x = \frac{-7}{3}$$

The solution is $x = \dfrac{-7}{3}$ or $x = -1$

Method 2

$$|3x + 5| = 2$$
$$\Rightarrow (3x + 5)^2 = (2)^2$$
$$\Rightarrow 9x^2 + 30x + 25 = 4$$
$$\Rightarrow 9x^2 + 30x + 21 = 0$$
$$\Rightarrow 3x^2 + 10x + 7 = 0$$
$$\Rightarrow (3x + 7)(x + 1) = 0$$
$$\Rightarrow \text{The solution is } \left(-\tfrac{7}{3}, -1\right)$$

Note 1: The method of "squaring both sides" of a modular equation is useful when the modulus sign appears on both sides of the equation, e.g. $|3x + 5| = |x - 2|$.

Note 2: Getting the modulus of an expression is sometimes referred to as getting the **absolute value** of the expression.

2. Modular inequalities

If $|x| < 1$, then the value of x must lie between $+1$ and -1, i.e. $-1 < x < +1$.

If $|x| > 1$, then the value of x must lie outside this range, i.e. $x > 1$ or $x < -1$.

Example 2

Sketch the graph of $f(x) = |2x - 5|$ and hence solve the inequality

$$|2x - 5| < 3.$$

$f(x) = 2x - 5$ is drawn first by using two points on the line, e.g. $(2.5, 0)$ and $(4, 3)$.

$f(x) = |2x - 5|$ is then drawn by reflecting the negative portion of the graph in the x-axis as before.

Drawing the line $f(x) = 3$ on the same axes, the red segment represents where $|2x - 5| < 3$.

The x-values that create that portion of the graph are $1 < x < 4$.

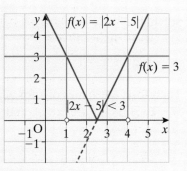

Note : If $|2x - 5| = 3$, then $2x - 5 = 3$ or $2x - 5 = -3$.

If $|2x - 5| < 3$, then $-3 < 2x - 5 < 3$.

$$\therefore \quad 2 < 2x < 8 \quad \text{... adding 5 to each part of the inequality}$$

$$1 < x < 4 \quad \text{... dividing each part of the inequality by 2}$$

This produces the same solution set as above.

Example 3

Draw a graph of $f(x) = |x + 3|$ and $f(x) = |3x - 7|$.
Solve the inequality $|x + 3| < |3x - 7|$ algebraically and indicate graphically the solution set.

$$|x + 3| < |3x - 7|$$
$$\Rightarrow (x + 3)^2 < (3x - 7)^2$$
$$\Rightarrow x^2 + 6x + 9 < 9x^2 - 42x + 49$$
$$\Rightarrow -8x^2 + 48x - 40 < 0$$
$$\Rightarrow x^2 - 6x + 5 > 0.$$

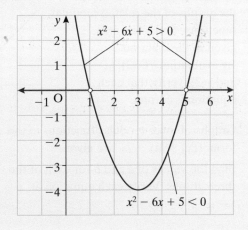

Solving $x^2 - 6x + 5 = 0$,

$$(x - 5)(x - 1) = 0$$

$$\Rightarrow x = 5 \text{ or } x = 1$$

Therefore, the values of x for which
$x^2 - 6x + 5 > 0$ are $x < 1$ and $x > 5$.

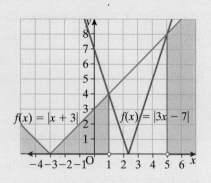

Exercise 7.3

1. Solve each of the following inequalities for $x \in R$.

   (i) $|x + 3| = 1$ (ii) $|x - 2| = 4$ (iii) $|2x - 1| = 5$

   (iv) $|3x - 2| = x$ (v) $2|x - 3| = 2$ (vi) $|x - 5| = |x + 1|$

2. Copy and complete the following table and hence sketch a graph of $f(x) = |3x - 2|$.

x	-3	-2	-1	0	1	2	3
$f(x) = \|3x - 2\|$							

   Use your graph to solve the equation $|3x - 2| = 5$.

3. Write an equation for each of
   the graphs of the related modular
   functions, $f(x), g(x), h(x)$,
   given in the diagram.
   By evaluating $f(-2), h(-5)$
   and $g(2)$, verify that each
   equation is correct.

   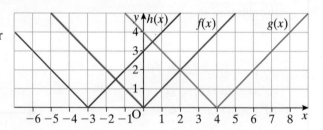

4. Graphs of three modular functions in the
   form $f(x) = |ax + b|$ are given.

   Find the values of a and b for each of the
   three graphs. Verify each equation at $x = -2$.

   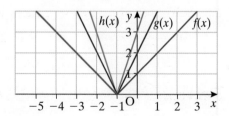

5. On the same set of axes, sketch the graphs of the functions

   $$f : x \rightarrow |x - 2| \text{ and } g : x \rightarrow |x - 6|.$$

   Hence solve the equation $|x - 2| = |x - 6|$.

   Verify your answer algebraically.

6. Solve each of the following inequalities for $x \in R$.

   (i) $|x - 6| < 2$ (ii) $|x + 2| \leqslant 4$ (iii) $|2x - 1| \geqslant 5$

   (iv) $|2x - 1| \geqslant 11$ (v) $|3x + 5| < 4$ (vi) $|x - 4| < 3$

7. Solve the following inequalities, $x \in R$.

   (i) $|2x - 1| \geqslant 7$ (ii) $|3x + 4| \leqslant |x + 2|$ (iii) $2|x - 1| \leqslant |x + 3|$

8. On the same set of axes, sketch the graphs of the functions

$$f(x) = |x| - 4 \text{ and } g(x) = \tfrac{1}{2}x.$$

Hence solve the inequality $|x| - 4 \leqslant \tfrac{1}{2}x$.

9. Sketch the graph of the function $f(x) = |\tfrac{1}{4}x + 3|$ and hence find the solution to the inequality $|\tfrac{1}{4}x + 3| \geqslant 3$.

10. Solve the inequality $|1 + 2x| < |x + 2|$ for $x \in R$.

11. For what real values of $x \in R$ is $\left|\dfrac{1}{1 + 2x}\right| = 1, x \neq -\dfrac{1}{2}$?

Hence solve the inequality $\left|\dfrac{1}{1 + 2x}\right| < 1$.

12. Use the graphs of the functions $f(x) = |x + 1|$, $g(x) = |3x - 6|$ and $h(x) = 3$ to estimate the range of values of x that satisfies each of the following inequalities.

   (i) $f(x) < h(x)$
   (ii) $h(x) < f(x)$
   (iii) $g(x) < f(x)$
   (iv) $g(x) < h(x) < f(x)$
   (v) $g(x) < f(x) < h(x)$
   (vi) $f(x) > h(x) > g(x)$
   (vii) $f(x) > g(x) > h(x)$

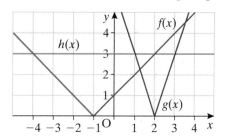

13. Solve each of the following for $x \in R$.

   (i) $\dfrac{x}{2x - 1} < -2$ (ii) $|x - 3| = 2|x - 1|$ (iii) $|x - 1| - |2x + 1| > 0$

Section 7.4 Mathematical proof

In mathematics, we use deductive reasoning to prove that a statement is *always* true.

The statement, when proved true, then becomes a theorem.
e.g. De Moivre's theorem, Pythagoras' theorem, etc.

The different methods of proof include direct proofs, proofs by contradiction and proofs by induction (see Section 7.12).

1. Direct proof

Direct proof uses axioms, definitions and other proven theorems to verify the new statement.

Example 1

Prove that the sum of two even integers x and y is always even.

Proof:

Since x is even, we can write it as $x = 2a$, where $a \in Z$.

Also since y is even, $y = 2b$, where $b \in Z$.

Therefore, $x + y = 2a + 2b = 2(a + b)$.

Since $x + y$ has a factor of $2 \Rightarrow x + y$ must be even.

$\therefore$ The sum of two even integers is always even.

2. Proof by contradiction

In a proof by contradiction, we show that if we claim some statement to be true, then a logical contradiction occurs which proves that the original statement must be false.

Example 2

Prove that $\sqrt{2}$ is irrational.

Proof: Assume $\sqrt{2}$ is a rational number.

$\therefore$ $\sqrt{2}$ can be written as $\frac{a}{b} : a, b \in Z$ and $b \neq 0$, and a and b have no common factor.

$\therefore$ $2 = \dfrac{a^2}{b^2}$ ... squaring both sides

$\therefore$ $a^2 = 2b^2$

$\therefore$ a^2 is even since it is equal to $2 \times (b^2)$ .... any integer multiplied by 2 is even

$\therefore$ a is even

$\therefore$ a can be written as $a = 2c$ ... since a is divisible by 2

$\therefore$ $a^2 = 4c^2 = 2b^2$

$\therefore$ $2c^2 = b^2$

$\therefore$ b is also even

$\therefore$ a and b have a common factor of 2 which contradicts our assumption.

$\therefore$ $\sqrt{2}$ is not a rational number.

$\therefore$ $\sqrt{2}$ is an irrational number, i.e. it cannot be written as $\frac{a}{b}$ with no common factors.

Exercise 7.4

1. Prove by contradiction that there are no positive integer solutions to $x^2 - y^2 = 1$. (Hint: Assume that x and y are both positive integers and use the difference of two squares.)

2. Prove by contradiction that if a is a rational number and b an irrational number, then $a + b$ is an irrational number.

3. Prove by contradiction that there are no positive integer solutions to $x^2 - y^2 = 10$. (Hint: Assume that x and y are both positive integers and use the difference of two squares.)

4. Prove that if a divides b, and b divides c, then a divides c.

5. Prove that if a divides b, and a divides c, then a divides $(b + c)$.

6. If a and b are real numbers, prove that $a^2 + b^2 \geqslant 2ab$. (Abstract inequality proof.)

7. Prove that the sum of two rational numbers is a rational number.

8. Prove that the sum of two odd numbers is always even.

Section 7.5 Proofs of abstract inequalities

If $a > 0$ and $b > 0$, then $\dfrac{a}{b} + \dfrac{b}{a} \geqslant 2$ is an example of an **abstract inequality** (see Example 2).

To prove that an inequality statement is true, we will use two important facts:

   (i) (Any real number)$^2 \geqslant 0$
   (ii) $-$(Any real number)$^2 \leqslant 0$.

If both sides of an inequality are squared, the inequality sign is retained only if both sides of the inequality are positive.

For example, $4 > 3 \Rightarrow 4^2 > 3^2$, i.e. $16 > 9$.

However, if one or both sides are negative, then this does not hold.

E.g. $\quad 2 > -3 \not\Rightarrow 2^2 > (-3)^2$,
$\qquad\qquad$ i.e. $4 \not> 9$.

> If a and b are real numbers, then
> $$a^2 \geqslant 0 \ \text{ and } \ b^2 \geqslant 0$$
> $$(a + b)^2 \geqslant 0$$
> $$(a - b)^2 \geqslant 0$$
> $$-(a + b)^2 \leqslant 0$$
> $$-(a - b)^2 \leqslant 0$$

To prove an abstract inequality;

1. Write down the statement you are asked to prove.
2. Use the rules of inequalities to adapt the inequality until …
3. you arrive at an inequality that is obviously true.

237

Example 1

Prove that $a^2 + b^2 \geqslant 2ab$ for all $a, b \in R$.

If: $a^2 + b^2 \geqslant 2ab$,

then $a^2 - 2ab + b^2 \geqslant 0$ ... subtracting $2ab$ from both sides.

$\therefore (a - b)^2 \geqslant 0$ ... factorising the left-hand side.

which is always true. $\therefore a^2 + b^2 \geqslant 2ab$.

Example 2

If $a > 0$ and $b > 0$, prove that $\dfrac{a}{b} + \dfrac{b}{a} \geqslant 2$.

If: $\dfrac{a}{b} + \dfrac{b}{a} \geqslant 2$,

then $a^2 + b^2 \geqslant 2ab$ ... multiply each term by the common denominator ab.

$\therefore a^2 - 2ab + b^2 \geqslant 0$

$\therefore (a - b)^2 \geqslant 0$ ... which is always true.

$\therefore \dfrac{a}{b} + \dfrac{b}{a} \geqslant 2$.

Example 3

Show that $x^2 + 4x + 6 > 0$ (i.e. is positive) for all $x \in R$.

If: $x^2 + 4x + 6 > 0$,

then $x^2 + 4x + 4 - 4 + 6 > 0$ ... adding and subtracting $\left(\dfrac{4}{2}\right)^2$ to complete the square.

$\Rightarrow (x + 2)^2 - 4 + 6 > 0$ ... completing the square.

$\Rightarrow (x + 2)^2 + 2 > 0$ ... which is true for all values of x, since $(x + 2)^2 > 0$ for all values of x.

$\therefore x^2 + 4x + 6 > 0$ for all $x \in R$.

Example 4

Show for all real numbers $a, b > 0$ that $(a + b)\left(\dfrac{1}{a} + \dfrac{1}{b}\right) \geq 4$.

If: $(a + b)\left(\dfrac{1}{a} + \dfrac{1}{b}\right) \geq 4$,

then $(a + b)\left(\dfrac{a + b}{ab}\right) \geq 4$ ... using the common denominator ab to add the fractions.

$\therefore \quad \dfrac{(a + b)^2}{ab} \geq 4$ ... simplifying.

$\therefore \quad (a + b)^2 \geq 4ab$ ... multiplying both sides by ab.

$\therefore \quad a^2 + 2ab + b^2 \geq 4ab$ ... expanding the left-hand side.

$\therefore \quad a^2 - 2ab + b^2 \geq 0$ ... subtracting $4ab$ from both sides.

$\therefore \quad (a - b)^2 \geq 0$ ... which is true for all $a, b \in R$.

$\therefore \quad (a + b)\left(\dfrac{1}{a} + \dfrac{1}{b}\right) \geq 4$.

Exercise 7.5

1. Prove that (i) $a^2 + 2ab + b^2 \geq 0$ (ii) $a^2 + 2ab + 2b^2 \geq 0$ for all $a, b \in R$.

2. Prove that $(a + b)^2 \geq 4ab$ for all $a, b \in R$.

3. Prove that $-(a^2 + 2ab + b^2) \leq 0$ for all $a, b \in R$.

4. If $a > 0$ and $b > 0$, show that

    (i) $a + \dfrac{1}{a} \geq 2$ (ii) $\dfrac{1}{a} + \dfrac{1}{b} \geq \dfrac{2}{a + b}$.

5. Prove that $a^2 - 6a + 9 + b^2 \geq 0$ for all real values of a and b.

6. Prove that for all real values of x,

    (i) $x^2 + 6x + 9 \geq 0$ (ii) $x^2 - 10x + 25 \geq 0$ (iii) $x^2 + 4x + 6 > 0$

    (iv) $x^2 - 6x + 10 > 0$ (v) $4x^2 + 12x + 11 > 0$ (vi) $4x^2 - 4x + 2 > 0$.

7. Show that (i) $-x^2 + 10x - 25 \leq 0$ (ii) $-x^2 - 4x - 7 \leq 0$ for all $x \in R$.

8. Prove that for all real numbers p and q,

    (i) $p^2 + 4q^2 \geq 4pq$ (ii) $(p + q)^2 \leq 2(p^2 + q^2)$.

9. Factorise $a^3 + b^3$.

    Hence prove that $a^3 + b^3 > a^2b + ab^2$ for all real $a > 0$ and $b > 0$.

10. Given that $a^2 + b^2 \geq 2ab$, deduce an expression for (i) $a^2 + c^2$ and (ii) $b^2 + c^2$.
    Use these results to prove that
    $$a^2 + b^2 + c^2 \geq ab + bc + ca \text{ for all real values of } a, b \text{ and } c.$$

11. If $p > 0$ and $q > 0$ and $p \neq q$, prove that $\dfrac{p + q}{2} > \sqrt{pq}$.

12. Show that $(ax + by)^2 \leq (a^2 + b^2)(x^2 + y^2)$ for all $a, b, x, y \in R$.

13. Prove that $a^4 + b^4 \geq 2a^2b^2$ for all $a, b \in R$.

14. If a and b are positive numbers, show that
    $$(a + 2b)\left(\frac{1}{a} + \frac{1}{2b}\right) \geq 4.$$

15. Show that for all real a, $\dfrac{a}{(a + 1)^2} < \dfrac{1}{4}, a \neq -1$.

16. (i) Express $a^4 - b^4$ as the product of three factors.
    (ii) Factorise $a^5 - a^4b - ab^4 + b^5$.
    (iii) Use the results from (i) and (ii) to show that $a^5 + b^5 > a^4b + ab^4$, where a and b are positive unequal real numbers.

17. If $a^2 + b^2 = 1$ and $c^2 + d^2 = 1$, show that $ab + cd \leq 1$.
    (Hint: Use the result that $a^2 + b^2 \geq 2ab$.)

18. Prove that $\sqrt{ab} > \dfrac{2ab}{a + b}$ if a and b are positive and unequal.

19. Prove that $a + \dfrac{9}{a + 2} \geq 4$, where $a + 2 > 0$.

20. If a, b, c, d are positive numbers and $\dfrac{a}{b} > \dfrac{c}{d}$, prove that $\dfrac{a + c}{b + d} > \dfrac{c}{d}$.

21. Explain why $(a^3 - b^3)(a - b)$ is always positive for $a > b$.
    Hence prove that $a^4 + b^4 \geq a^3b + ab^3$ for all $a, b \in R$ and $a > b$.

Section 7.6 Indices

When a number is multiplied by itself many times, we use the index form to represent the product.
$4 \times 4 \times 4 \times 4 \times 4 = 4^5$, i.e. 4 to the power of 5.

In this case, 5 is the **index** (plural indices) and 4 is the **base number**.

Revision of the rules of indices.

	Example	Rule
1.	$6^3 \times 6^4 = 6^7$	$a^m . a^n = a^{m+n}$
2.	$\frac{4^5}{4^2} = 4^3$, also $\frac{4^5}{4^7} = 4^{-2}$	$\frac{a^m}{a^n} = a^{m-n}$
3.	$(2^4)^3 = 2^{12}$	$(a^m)^n = a^{m.n}$
4.	$3^0 = 5^0 = 9^0 = (-3)^0 = \left(\frac{1}{4}\right)^0 = 1$	$a^0 = 1$
5.	$3^{-1} = \frac{1}{3}$, $3^{-4} = \frac{1}{3^4}$	$a^{-n} = \frac{1}{a^n}$
6.	$7^{\frac{1}{2}} = \sqrt[2]{7}$, $5^{\frac{1}{3}} = \sqrt[3]{5}$	$a^{\frac{1}{n}} = \sqrt[n]{a}$
7.	$8^{\frac{2}{3}} = \left(8^{\frac{1}{3}}\right)^2$ or $(8^2)^{\frac{1}{3}}$	$a^{\frac{m}{n}} = \sqrt[n]{a^m} = (\sqrt[n]{a})^m$
8.	$(2 \times 5)^2 = 2^2 \times 5^2$	$(a.b)^n = a^n.b^n$
	$\left(\frac{5}{6}\right)^4 = \frac{5^4}{6^4}$	$\left(\frac{a}{b}\right)^n = \frac{a^n}{b^n}$

Each of these rules can be verified by expanding the powers and simplifying, e.g.

$(2^4)^3 = 2^4 \times 2^4 \times 2^4 = 2^{12} = 4096$

Note: $\sqrt{x} = \sqrt[2]{x} = x^{\frac{1}{2}} =$ the square root of x.

$\sqrt[3]{x} = x^{\frac{1}{3}} =$ the cube root of x.

$\sqrt[4]{x} = x^{\frac{1}{4}} =$ the fourth root of x … etc.

Note: $25^{\frac{3}{2}} = \left(25^{\frac{1}{2}}\right)^3 = (5)^3 = 125$ (most often, it is easier to get the root first and then raise to the power.)

Example 1

Evaluate each of the following.

(i) $27^{\frac{1}{3}}$ (ii) $36^{\frac{3}{2}}$ (iii) $64^{-\frac{2}{3}}$ (iv) $\left(\frac{27}{125}\right)^{-\frac{2}{3}}$

(i) $27^{\frac{1}{3}} = \sqrt[3]{27} = 3$ … (i.e. 3 multiplied by itself three times equals 27)

(ii) $36^{\frac{3}{2}} = \left(36^{\frac{1}{2}}\right)^3 = (\sqrt{36})^3 = 6^3 = 216$

(iii) $64^{-\frac{2}{3}} = \frac{1}{64^{\frac{2}{3}}} = \frac{1}{\left(64^{\frac{1}{3}}\right)^2} = \frac{1}{(4)^2} = \frac{1}{16}$

(iv) $\left(\frac{27}{125}\right)^{-\frac{2}{3}} = \left(\frac{125}{27}\right)^{\frac{2}{3}} = \left[\left(\frac{125}{27}\right)^{\frac{1}{3}}\right]^2 = \left(\frac{5}{3}\right)^2 = \frac{25}{9}$

Numerical expressions containing complex fractions with indices can be simplified and evaluated with a calculator.

Since the procedure on each calculator may be slightly different, it is important to gain practice on your calculator, particularly when dealing with fractional powers.

However, it is most important to understand the rules of indices and to be able to apply them to general problems containing unknowns.

Example 2

Simplify each of the following. (i) $\left(\dfrac{x^2 y^{-3}}{x^{-4} y^5}\right)^{\frac{1}{2}}$ (ii) $\dfrac{\sqrt{a^3}}{\sqrt[4]{a} \times \sqrt[3]{a^2}}$

(i) $\left(\dfrac{x^2 y^{-3}}{x^{-4} y^5}\right)^{\frac{1}{2}} = (x^6 y^{-8})^{\frac{1}{2}} = (x^6)^{\frac{1}{2}} (y^{-8})^{\frac{1}{2}} = x^3 y^{-4} = \dfrac{x^3}{y^4}$

(ii) $\dfrac{\sqrt{a^3}}{\sqrt[4]{a} \times \sqrt[3]{a^2}} = \dfrac{a^{\frac{3}{2}}}{a^{\frac{1}{4}} \times a^{\frac{2}{3}}} = \dfrac{a^{\frac{3}{2}}}{a^{\frac{3+8}{12}}} = \dfrac{a^{\frac{3}{2}}}{a^{\frac{11}{12}}} = a^{\frac{3}{2} - \frac{11}{12}} = a^{\frac{7}{12}}$

Example 3

Show that $\dfrac{5^{n+1} - 4.5^n}{5^{n-2} + 5^n} = \dfrac{25}{26}$.

$\dfrac{5^{n+1} - 4.5^n}{5^{n-2} + 5^n} = \dfrac{5^n . 5^1 - 4.5^n}{5^n . 5^{-2} + 5^n} = \dfrac{5.5^n - 4.5^n}{\dfrac{5^n}{25} + 5^n} = \dfrac{5^n}{\dfrac{5^n + 25.5^n}{25}} = \dfrac{5^n}{\dfrac{26.5^n}{25}} = \dfrac{25}{26}$

Exercise 7.6

1. Simplify each of the following:

   (i) $a^2 \times a^3$ (ii) $x . x . x^2$ (iii) $2x^3 \times 3x^3$ (iv) $\dfrac{x^5}{x^2}$ (v) $\dfrac{x^4}{x^5}$

   (vi) a^0 (vii) $\sqrt[3]{27}$ (viii) $(a^3)^2$ (ix) $\dfrac{(x^3)^2}{x^3}$ (x) $(3ab)^2$

2. Express each of the following as a rational number:

   (i) $\sqrt[3]{64}$ (ii) 3^{-2} (iii) $\dfrac{1}{2^{-3}}$ (iv) $\dfrac{2^{-2}}{3^{-2}}$ (v) $\dfrac{1}{4^{-\frac{1}{2}}}$

3. Express as rational numbers,

    (i) $8^{\frac{2}{3}}$ (ii) $16^{\frac{3}{4}}$ (iii) $27^{\frac{2}{3}}$ (iv) $81^{\frac{3}{4}}$ (v) $125^{\frac{2}{3}}$.

4. Simplify each of these:

    (i) $\left(\dfrac{2}{3}\right)^{-2}$ (ii) $\left(\dfrac{4}{9}\right)^{-\frac{1}{2}}$ (iii) $\left(\dfrac{9}{25}\right)^{-\frac{3}{2}}$ (iv) $\left(\dfrac{27}{125}\right)^{-\frac{2}{3}}$ (v) $\left(3\dfrac{3}{8}\right)^{\frac{1}{3}}$

5. Express $\dfrac{4^2 \times 16^{\frac{1}{2}}}{64^{\frac{2}{3}} \times 4^3}$ in the form 4^n, $n \in Z$.

6. Find the value of the rational number p for which $\dfrac{3^{\frac{1}{4}} \times 3 \times 3^{\frac{1}{6}}}{\sqrt{3}} = 3^p$.

7. Simplify each of the following, writing your answers with positive indices.

    (i) $\dfrac{(xy^2)^3 \times (x^2y)^{-2}}{xy}$ (ii) $\left(\dfrac{p^2q}{p^{-1}q^3}\right)^4$ (iii) $a^{\frac{1}{4}} \times a^{-\frac{5}{4}}$

    (iv) $\left(\dfrac{y^{-2}}{y^{-3}}\right)^{\frac{2}{3}}$ (v) $\dfrac{(a\sqrt{b})^{-3}}{\sqrt{a^3b}}$ (vi) $\dfrac{\sqrt[4]{x^7}}{\sqrt{x^3}}$

8. Simplify each of these

    (i) $\dfrac{x^{\frac{1}{2}} + x^{-\frac{1}{2}}}{x^{\frac{1}{2}}}$ (ii) $\left(x + x^{\frac{1}{2}}\right)\left(x - x^{\frac{1}{2}}\right)$ (iii) $\dfrac{\sqrt{x} + \sqrt{x^3}}{\sqrt{x}}$

9. By multiplying the numerator and denominator by $(x - 1)^{\frac{1}{2}}$, simplify

    $$\dfrac{(x - 1)^{\frac{1}{2}} + (x - 1)^{-\frac{1}{2}}}{(x - 1)^{\frac{1}{2}}}.$$

10. The expression $\sqrt{3^{2n+1}} \times \sqrt[3]{3^{-3n}}$ can be written in the form 3^k; find k.

11. The keys on a piano are tuned so that each key (white and black) produces a note that has a frequency of $2^{\left(\frac{1}{12}\right)}$ times that of the previous note. If the A key (2 keys below middle C) is tuned to a frequency of 220 Hz, find, correct to the nearest whole number, the frequency (in Hz) of middle C.

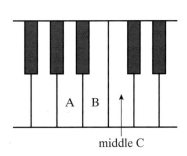

middle C

12. The surface area of a sphere is given by

    $A = 4\pi r^2$ and its volume V by $\frac{4}{3}\pi r^3$, where r is the radius of the sphere.

    Show that if we have two spheres of radii r_1 and r_2 respectively, then the ratio of the surface areas can be written as $\dfrac{A_1}{A_2} = \left(\dfrac{V_1}{V_2}\right)^{\frac{2}{3}}$.

If two such spheres have volumes $162\,\text{cm}^3$ and $384\,\text{cm}^3$ respectively, find the ratio of their

areas, expressing your answer in the form $\frac{a}{b}$, where $a, b \in N$.

13. Given $f(n) = 3^n$, find expressions for   (i) $f(n + 3)$ (ii) $f(n + 1)$.

    Hence find the value of k such that $f(n + 3) - f(n + 1) = kf(n)$, where $k \in N$.

14. Given $f(n) = 3^{n-1}$, find the value of k such that $f(n + 3) + f(n) = kf(n)$, where $k \in N$.

Section 7.7 Exponential equations

    $y = 3^x$ is an example of an exponential function.
    $3^x = 27$ is an example of an **exponential equation**.

As in the last section, 3 is the **base number** and x is the **index** (power) or **exponent.**

When solving exponential equations, it is important to identify the base number (usually a prime number) that is common to all the individual terms of the equation.

E.g. $3^x = 27$; 3 is the base number for both sides. ... $(3^x = 3^3)$

    $25^x = 125$; 5 is the base number. ... $(5^x = 5^3)$

Example 1

Solve these equations.   (i) $\dfrac{1}{8^x} = 16^{\frac{1}{3}}$ (ii) $27^{x-3} = 3 \times 9^{x-2}$

(i) $\dfrac{1}{8^x} = 16^{\frac{1}{3}}$ (the base number is 2)

    $\dfrac{1}{(2^3)^x} = (2^4)^{\frac{1}{3}}$

    $2^{-3x} = 2^{\frac{4}{3}} \;\Rightarrow\; -3x = \dfrac{4}{3}$

                        $\Rightarrow x = -\dfrac{4}{9}$

(ii) $27^{x-3} = 3 \times 9^{x-2}$
    (the base number is 3)

      $(3^3)^{x-3} = 3 \times (3^2)^{x-2}$

      $\Rightarrow 3^{3x-9} = 3^1 \times 3^{2x-4}$

      $\Rightarrow 3^{3x-9} = 3^{2x-3}$

      $\Rightarrow 3x - 9 = 2x - 3$

         $\Rightarrow x = 6$

By using a suitable **change of variable,** an exponential equation can be transformed into a quadratic equation and then solved.

Note: If $2^x = y$,

       $\Rightarrow 3.2^x = 3y$

       $\Rightarrow 2^{2x} = (2^x)^2 = y^2$

       $\Rightarrow 2^{x+2} = 2^x.2^2 = 4y$

Example 2

If $y = 3^x$, express 3^{2x} in terms of y.

Hence solve the equation $3^{2x} - 4.3^x + 3 = 0$.

(i) $3^{2x} = (3^x)^2 = y^2$

(ii) Given $3^{2x} - 4.3^x + 3 = 0$.

$\Rightarrow y^2 - 4y + 3 = 0$ ... using the substitution $3^x = y$ and $3^{2x} = y^2$

$\Rightarrow (y - 1)(y - 3) = 0$

$\Rightarrow y = 1$ or $y = 3$ ... are the solutions of the new quadratic equation

$\Rightarrow 3^x = 1$ or $3^x = 3$ ... re-substituting to find values of x

$\Rightarrow 3^x = 3^0$ or $3^x = 3^1$ ... using the base number 3

$\therefore$ $x = 0$ or $x = 1$ are the solutions.

Exercise 7.7

1. Find the value of x in each of these equations:

   (i) $2^x = 32$ (ii) $16^x = 64$ (iii) $25^x = 125$ (iv) $3^x = \frac{1}{27}$

2. Solve each of these index (exponential) equations.

   (i) $9^x = \frac{1}{27}$ (ii) $4^x = \frac{1}{32}$ (iii) $4^{x-1} = 2^{x+1}$ (iv) $\frac{1}{9^x} = 27$

3. Find the value of x in each of these equations:

   (i) $2^x = \frac{\sqrt{2}}{2}$ (ii) $25^x = \frac{125}{\sqrt{5}}$ (iii) $\frac{1}{8^x} = \sqrt{2}$ (iv) $7^x = \frac{1}{\sqrt[3]{7}}$

4. Write $\sqrt{32}$ as a power of 2 and hence solve the equation $16^{x-1} = 2\sqrt{32}$.

5. If $27^x = 9$ and $2^{x-y} = 64$, find the values of x and y.

6. Express   (i) 2^{x+2} and   (ii) $2^x + 2^x$ in the form $k2^x$, where $k \in N$.

   Hence solve for c in the equation $2^x + 2^x = 2^{x+2}(c - 2)$.

7. By letting $3^x = y$, solve the equation $3^{2x} - 12(3^x) + 27 = 0$.

8. Solve the equation $2^{2x} - 3(2^x) - 4 = 0$ and verify your answer by substitution.

9. Solve each of these equations: (i) $2^{2x} - 9(2^x) + 8 = 0$ (ii) $3^{2x} - 10(3^x) + 9 = 0$

10. If $y = 2^x$, write   (i) 2^{2x} (ii) 2^{2x+1} and   (iii) 2^{x+3} in terms of y.

    Hence solve the equation $2^{2x+1} - 2^{x+3} - 2^x + 4 = 0$.

11. By using the substitution $y = 3^x$, find the two values of x such that $3.3^x + 3^{-x} = 4$ and verify each solution by substitution into the original exponential equation.

12. Solve the equation $2(4^x) + 4^{-x} = 3$.

13. Solve the equation $3^x - 28 + 27(3^{-x}) = 0$.

14. By letting $2^x = y$, solve the equation $2^{x+1} + 2(2^{-x}) - 5 = 0$.

15. Solve the exponential equation $3^x + 81(3^{-x}) - 30 = 0$.

Section 7.8 Exponential functions

Exponential functions such as $f(x) = a^x$ are used in modelling many physical occurrences. These include:

  (i) the growth of a biological cell
 (ii) changes in population, e.g. algae growth on stagnant water
(iii) compounded interest and depreciation
 (iv) radioactive decay
  (v) the rate at which a body loses heat (Newton's law of cooling).

> **ICT:** Functions of the form $y = a^x$, $a =$ constant, can be studied graphically. Remember, when using a keyboard, to use the "^" button to raise a power (exponent), i.e. $y = 2 \wedge x$.
> Proper use of brackets is essential, i.e. $y = 2 \wedge (2x) = 2^{2x}$.

All of the graphs associated with exponential functions have a characteristic shape and are easily identified. From this diagram we can see that graphs of the form $f(x) = a^x$, where $a > 0$ and $a \neq 1$, have the following properties;

1. At $x = 0$, $f(0) = a^0 = 1$.
  $\Rightarrow (0, 1)$ is a point on all graphs.

2. At $x = 1$, $f(1) = a^1 = a$.
  $\Rightarrow (1, a)$ is a point on all graphs.

3. At $x = -1$, $f(-1) = a^{-1} = \dfrac{1}{a}$.
  $\Rightarrow \left(-1, \dfrac{1}{a}\right)$ is a point on all graphs.

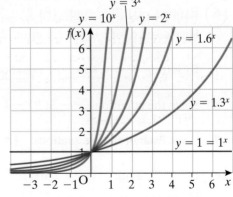

4. They are defined for all real values of x.

5. The x-axis is a horizontal asymptote to all the curves $\Rightarrow f(x) = a^x$ is always positive.

6. If $a > 1$, all of the curves increase as x increases. As a increases, the curves rise more steeply.

7. If $0 < a < 1$, then the curve $f(x) = a^x$ reflects in the y-axis, producing a set of curves that decrease rapidly as x increases.

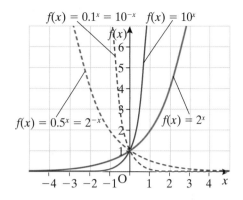

Note: If $a = \left(\frac{1}{2}\right) = 2^{-1}$

$\Rightarrow f(x) = \left(\frac{1}{2}\right)^x = (2^{-1})^x = 2^{-x}$

Note: The general formula for an increasing exponential function is $f(x) = A a^x$, where A is the value at the start, i.e. when $x = 0$.

Exponential functions $f(x) = A.a^x$

Increasing exponential functions $a > 1$.

Decreasing exponential functions $0 < a < 1$.

$(0, A)$ is the y-axis intercept.

Decreasing functions can be written in the form

$$f(x) = A.a^{-x}$$

Example 1

A bacterial colony doubles every hour. If 10 bacteria cells were present at the start of an experiment, (i) complete the following table (ii) draw a graph of the number of bacteria present up to 5 hours.

Time in hours	0	1	2	3	4	5
Number of bacteria						

(iii) By how many would the population increase in the 6th hour?

(iv) What percentage increase in the population occurred in the 6th hour by comparison to the first hour?

(v) Write an expression for the size of the population (N) after t hours.

(i) Time in hours	0	1	2	3	4	5
Number of bacteria	10	20	40	80	160	320

(ii)

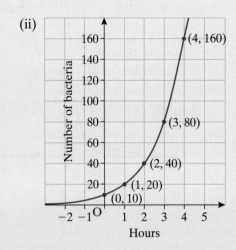

Hours

(iii) At $t = 5$ hours, there are 320 bacteria.
At $t = 6$ hours, there are 640 bacteria.
$\Rightarrow$ an increase of 320 bacteria.

(iv) Percentage increase
$$= \left(\frac{320}{10}\right) \times \frac{100}{1} \%$$
$$= 3200\%$$

(v) After t hours, $N = A.a^t$.
At $t = 0, N = 10 = A.a^0$.
$\Rightarrow 10 = A$.
At $t = 1, N = 10.a^1 = 20$.
$\Rightarrow a = 2$.
$\therefore N = 10.2^t$.

Example 2

The graphs of two exponential functions, $y = Aa^x$, are given in this diagram. Find the values of A and a for each graph.

(i) $f(x) = Aa^x$
$f(0) = 1, \therefore Aa^0 = 1 \Rightarrow A = 1$.
$f(1) = 2, \therefore a^1 = 2 \Rightarrow a = 2$
[$\therefore f(x)$ is an increasing function]
$\therefore f(x) = 2^x$

(ii) $h(x) = Aa^x$
$f(0) = 4, \therefore Aa^0 = 4 \Rightarrow A = 4$.
$f(1) = 2, \therefore 4a^1 = 2 \Rightarrow a = \frac{2}{4} = \frac{1}{2}$.
[$\therefore f(x)$ is a decreasing function]
$h(x) = 4\left(\frac{1}{2}\right)^x = 4.2^{-x}$

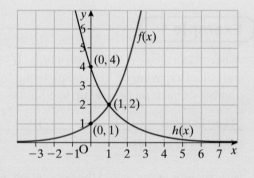

During earthquakes, the amplitude of the earth's movement is a measure of the intensity of the quake.

If M is the *magnitude* (size) of the quake on the Richter scale, and A is the *amplitude* of the ground movements, then the intensity of the earthquake is given by the exponential formula $A = 10^M$, and the *energy* released by an earthquake of magnitude M is $E \cong 10^{1.5M + 4.8}$ joules.

Example 3

Given that the intensity of an earthquake is represented by the formula $A = 10^M$, and the energy released during a quake by the formula $E \cong 10^{1.5M + 4.8}$, where A is the amplitude and M is the magnitude on the Richter scale, compare (i) the intensity (ii) the energy of an earthquake of magnitude 6.1 on the Richter scale with a quake of magnitude 4.7.

(i) $M_1 = 6.1 \Rightarrow A_1 = 10^{6.1}$
    $M_2 = 4.7 \Rightarrow A_2 = 10^{4.7}$

$\Rightarrow \dfrac{A_1}{A_2} = \dfrac{10^{6.1}}{10^{4.7}} = 10^{1.4} \cong 25$

$A_1 \cong 25A_2$

(ii) $E_1 \cong 10^{1.5M + 4.8} = 10^{1.5 \times 6.1 + 4.8} = 10^{13.95}$
    $E_2 \cong 10^{1.5M + 4.8} = 10^{1.5 \times 4.7 + 4.8} = 10^{11.85}$

$\Rightarrow \dfrac{E_1}{E_2} = \dfrac{10^{13.95}}{10^{11.85}} = 10^{2.1} \cong 126$

$E_1 \cong 126E_2$

Exercise 7.8

1. Match each of the following exponential functions with one of the graphs.

    (i) $y = 2^x$
    (ii) $y = (0.1)^x$
    (iii) $y = 10^x$
    (iv) $y = (0.5)2^x$

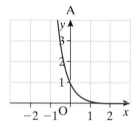

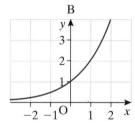
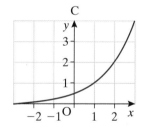
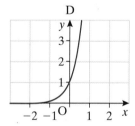

2. An entomologist monitoring a grasshopper plague notices that the area affected by the grasshoppers is given by $A(n) = 1000 \times 2^{0.2n}$ hectares, where n is the number of weeks that have elapsed after the initial observation. Find

    (i) the area originally affected
    (ii) the affected area after (a) 10 weeks (b) 12 weeks.
    (iii) Draw a graph of $A(n)$ against n for $0 \leqslant n \leqslant 10$.
    (iv) From the graph or otherwise, calculate the "doubling time" for the colony.

3. State whether each of the following graphs is increasing or decreasing.

    (i) $y = \left(\frac{1}{4}\right)^x$
    (ii) $y = (0.8)^x$
    (iii) $y = 4 \times 2^x$
    (iv) $y = 3 \times 4^{-x}$

4. What is the y-intercept of each of the following curves?

    (i) $y = (0.6)2^x$ (ii) $y = 3.2^{-x}$ (iii) $y = 8.2^x$ (iv) $y = 6.4^{-x}$

5. For each of the following, use one set of axes to sketch the graphs $(-2 \leqslant x \leqslant 4)$.

    (i) $y = 2^x$ and $y = 3^x$ (ii) $y = 2^{-x}$ and $y = 3^{-x}$ (iii) $y = 3.2^x$ and $y = 2.3^{-x}$
    (iv) For what values of x is $2^x > 3^x$?
    (v) For what values of x is $2^x < 3^x$?
    (vi) For what value(s) of x is $2^x = 3^x$?
    (vii) For what values of x is $\left(\frac{1}{2}\right)^x > \left(\frac{1}{3}\right)^x$?

6. The number of days, D, that yoghurt stays fresh, if stored at the temperature $T°C$, is
$$D = 18(0.72)^T.$$

    (i) Is this an example of exponential growth or decay? Explain your answer.
    (ii) For how many days will the yoghurt stay fresh if stored at
        (a) $5°C$ (b) $2°C$ (c) $0°C$?
    (iii) Estimate the temperature required to keep the yoghurt fresh for at least 5 days.

7. Carbon-14, the radioactive element of carbon, decays according to the formula
$P = 100(0.99988)^n$, where P is the percentage of the original mass of Carbon-14 that remains after n years.

    (a) Find the percentage of Carbon-14 that remains after (i) 200 years (ii) 500 years.
    (b) Estimate (using trial and error) how long it will take the Carbon-14 sample to decay to half its original mass. Give your answer correct to the nearest 10 years.
    (c) A bone containing 79% of its original Carbon-14 was discovered in a bog in County Offaly. Estimate its age.

8. A science researcher monitoring a mosquito plague notices that the area affected by the mosquitoes is given by $A(n) = 1000 \times 2^{0.2n}$ hectares, where n is the number of weeks after the initial observation.

    (i) Find the original area affected.
    (ii) Find the area affected after (a) 5 weeks (b) 10 weeks (c) 12 weeks.
    (iii) Using the answers to (i) and (ii), draw a graph of $A(n)$ against n.

9. The pulse rate, $P(t)$, of a runner, t-minutes after he finishes training, is given by
$$P(t) = 90 \times 3^{-0.25t} + 50.$$

    (i) Sketch the graph of $P(t)$ using the values of $t = 0, 2, 4, 6, 8, 10$ min.
    (ii) Find the pulse rate immediately after finishing training.
    (iii) How long did it take for his pulse rate to drop to
        (a) 70 beats per minute   (b) 55 beats per minute?
    (iv) What is the runner's normal pulse rate? Explain your answer.

10. The energy released by an earthquake is given by $E \cong 10^{1.5M + 4.8}$ where A is the amplitude and M is the magnitude on the Richter scale.
How many times greater is the energy released by an earthquake of magnitude 7 compared to an earthquake of magnitude 5?

11. Celina invests €5000 in a fixed-term account paying 0.55% per month compound interest. If €A is the amount of money after t months, find the amount after

   (i) 1 month   (ii) 2 months   (iii) 3 months   (iv) t months.

12. In an experiment involving a population of flies, the model $P(t) = 40b^t$ was established for the population $P(t)$ after t days from the beginning of the experiment, $t \geqslant 0$.

   (i) How many flies were there initially?
   (ii) After 1 day, there were 48 flies. Find the value of b and interpret it.
   (iii) Sketch a graph of $P(t)$ versus t for $0 \leqslant t \leqslant 5$.

Section 7.9 Logarithmic function _____

The **logarithm** is a function that focuses on the index (or exponent) of a number.

If $y = 2^5$, then $y = 32$ is easily calculated.
However, if $200 = 2^x$, it is not as easy to find the index x that gives the number 200.
To find x, we use logarithms (**logs** for short).

Consider the result $32 = 2^5$; using log notation, $\mathbf{\log_2 32 = 5.}$
This is read as "the log of 32 to the base 2 is 5",
i.e., **5 is the index (power)** to which the base number 2 must be raised to get 32.

Similarly, $10^2 = 100$ can be rewritten using logs as $\log_{10} 100 = 2$
(the log of 100 in the base 10 is 2),
i.e., **2 is the index (power)** to which the base number 10 must be raised to get 100.

Thus, the equations $2^3 = 8$ and $\log_2 8 = 3$ are **identical and interchangeable**.

Index form	Log form
$32 = 2^5$	$\log_2 32 = 5$
$100 = 10^2$	$\log_{10} 100 = 2$
$200 = 2^x$	$\log_2 200 = x$

The **logarithm** of a number is the **power** to which the base number must be raised to get that number.

$a^x = y$ is equivalent to $\log_a y = x$

From this definition of a log, it is clear that

(i) $\log_5 25 = 2$ (ii) $\log_3 27 = 3$ (iii) $\log_2 16 = 4$ (iv) $\log_3 81 = 4$,

i.e. to what power must 5 be raised, to get 25 ...? Answer $= 2$ ... etc.

If the log or base is not a whole number, proceed as follows.

251

Example 1

Evaluate (i) $\log_9 27$ (ii) $\log_{\frac{1}{3}} 9$ (iii) $\log_{\sqrt{2}} 8$.

(i) Let $\log_9 27 = x$.

$$\Rightarrow 9^x = 27$$
$$\Rightarrow (3^2)^x = 3^3$$
$$\Rightarrow 2x = 3$$
$$\Rightarrow x = \tfrac{3}{2}$$

(ii) Let $\log_{\frac{1}{3}} 9 = x$.

$$\Rightarrow \left(\tfrac{1}{3}\right)^x = 9$$
$$\Rightarrow (3^{-1})^x = 3^2$$
$$\Rightarrow -x = 2$$
$$\Rightarrow x = -2$$

(iii) Let $\log_{\sqrt{2}} 8 = x$.

$$\Rightarrow (\sqrt{2})^x = 8$$
$$\Rightarrow \left(2^{\frac{1}{2}}\right)^x = 2^3$$
$$\Rightarrow \tfrac{x}{2} = 3$$
$$\Rightarrow x = 6$$

1. The laws of logarithms

When the rules of indices are expressed in logarithm form, we produce the very important laws of logarithms.

These laws enable us to solve many complex equations.

Using your calculator, verify each of the following.

1. $\log_{10} 4 + \log_{10} 3 = \log_{10} 12 = 1.0792$

2. $\log_{10} 8 - \log_{10} 6 = \log_{10}\left(\tfrac{8}{6}\right) = 0.1249$

3. $\log_{10} 8^3 = 3\log_{10} 8 = 2.7093$

4. $\log_{10} 10 = 1$

5. $\log_{10} 1 = 0$

The Laws of Logarithms

1. $\log_a xy = \log_a x + \log_a y$

2. $\log_a\left(\dfrac{x}{y}\right) = \log_a x - \log_a y$

3. $\log_a x^n = n\log_a x$

4. $\log_a a = 1$

5. $\log_a 1 = 0$

6. $\log_a x = \dfrac{\log_b x}{\log_b a}$

The rules of logs apply to any base, however, the two most widely-used bases in logs are the base 10 and the base e (2.718).

Base ten logs, e.g. **$\log_{10} 1000$,** are used for calculation purposes and are referred to as **common logs**.

Base e (= 2.718), e.g. **$\log_e 1000$**, is used when dealing with naturally-occurring events, e.g. earthquakes, growth of colonies etc., and hence are called **natural logs** and are written **$\log_e x = \ln x$**.

Example 2

Without using a calculator, simplify the following number:

$$2\log_{10}3 + \log_{10}16 - 2\log_{10}\left(\frac{6}{5}\right)$$

$$
\begin{aligned}
2\log_{10}3 + \log_{10}16 - 2\log_{10}\left(\frac{6}{5}\right) &= \log_{10}3^2 + \log_{10}16 - \log_{10}\left(\frac{6}{5}\right)^2 \\
&= \log_{10}\left(3^2 \times 16\right) - \log_{10}\left(\frac{36}{25}\right) \\
&= \log_{10}\frac{9 \times 16}{\left(\frac{36}{25}\right)} \\
&= \log_{10}100 = 2
\end{aligned}
$$

Example 3

Without using a calculator, simplify the following number:

$$\log_2 128 + \log_3 45 - \log_3 5$$

$$\log_2 128 + \log_3 45 - \log_3 5 = \log_2 128 + \log_3\left(\frac{45}{5}\right) = \log_2 128 + \log_3 9$$

(Since the bases are different, these logs cannot be added!)

Let $\log_2 128 = x \Rightarrow 128 = 2^x$

$\qquad\qquad\qquad\qquad 2^7 = 2^x$

$\qquad\qquad\qquad\qquad\quad 7 = x$

also, let $\log_3 9 = y \Rightarrow 9 = 3^y$

$\qquad\qquad\qquad\qquad\quad 3^2 = 3^y$

$\qquad\qquad\qquad\qquad\quad 2 = y$

$\therefore \quad \log_2 128 + \log_3 9 = 7 + 2 = 9$

Example 4

Evaluate the following number correct to two significant figures:

$$\log_8 11 - \log_6 4$$

$$\log_8 11 = \frac{\log_{10}11}{\log_{10}8} \quad \ldots \log_a x = \frac{\log_b x}{\log_b a} \qquad\qquad \text{also,} \quad \log_6 4 = \frac{\log_{10}4}{\log_{10}6}$$

$$= \frac{1.041}{0.903} = 1.153 \qquad\qquad\qquad\qquad\qquad = \frac{0.602}{0.778} = 0.774$$

$$\therefore \quad \log_8 11 - \log_6 4 = 1.153 - 0.774 = 0.38$$

Note: For all bases,

(i) if $\log_e(e)^k = x$ also (ii) if $a^{(\log_a n)} = x$

$\Rightarrow k\log_e(e) = x$ $\Rightarrow \log_a a^{(\log_a n)} = \log_a x$ ... taking the log of both sides.

but $\log_e(e) = 1$ $\therefore \log_a n . \log_a a = \log_a x$

$\Rightarrow k = x$

> The log of a number to its own base is 1.

$\therefore \log_a n . 1 = \log_a x$

$\Rightarrow n = x$

> If e is a positive integer, $e \geqslant 2$, $k > 0$ (i) $\log_e(e)^k = k$ and (ii) $e^{(\log_e k)} = k$

2. Solving logarithmic equations

- When solving log equations, always check that each term has the same base. If this is not the case, *the change of base rule* must first be used to change to a common base.

- If no base is given, the equation holds true for all bases.

- If $\log_a b = \log_a c$, then $b = c$.

- If $\log_a b = k$, then $b = a^k$.

- Check all solutions to make sure they do not produce logs of negative numbers as these are not defined. (See page 257.)

Example 5

Solve the equation $2\log_3 x - \log_3(18 - x) = 1$.

$2\log_3 x - \log_3(18 - x) = 1$

$\Rightarrow \log_3 x^2 - \log_3(18 - x) = 1$

$\Rightarrow \log_3\left(\dfrac{x^2}{18 - x}\right) = 1$

$\Rightarrow \left(\dfrac{x^2}{18 - x}\right) = 3^1 = 3$

$\Rightarrow x^2 = 54 - 3x$

$\Rightarrow x^2 + 3x - 54 = 0$

$\Rightarrow (x - 6)(x + 9) = 0$

$\Rightarrow x = 6$ or $x = -9$.

If $x = -9$, the equation becomes

$2\log_3(-9) - \log_3(18 + 9) = 1$.

Since the $\log_3(-9)$ is undefined, $x = -9$ is rejected as an answer.

$\Rightarrow x = 6$.

Example 6

Solve the equation $\log_3 x + 3\log_x 3 = 4$.

This equation contains logs with different bases.
Therefore, we need to change base 3 to base x (or vice versa).

$$\log_3 x = \frac{\log_x x}{\log_x 3} = \frac{1}{\log_x 3} \quad \text{because} \quad \log_x x = 1$$

$$\therefore \quad \log_3 x + 3\log_x 3 = 4 \quad \Rightarrow \quad \frac{1}{\log_x 3} + 3\log_x 3 = 4$$

Using the substitution $\log_x 3 = y$,

$\dfrac{1}{y} + 3y = 4$

$\Rightarrow 1 + 3y^2 = 4y$

$3y^2 - 4y + 1 = 0$

$(3y - 1)(y - 1) = 0$

$\therefore \quad y = 1$ or $y = \frac{1}{3}$

$\therefore \quad \log_x 3 = 1 \Rightarrow 3 = x^1$

$\Rightarrow 3 = x$

or $\log_x 3 = \frac{1}{3} \Rightarrow 3 = x^{\frac{1}{3}}$

$\Rightarrow 3^3 = x$

$\Rightarrow 27 = x$

$\therefore \quad x = 3$ or 27 (both solutions give positive logs and thus are acceptable).

> **Note:** This result can be verified by repeating the procedure using the base 3 instead of the base x: $\log_x 3 = \dfrac{\log_3 3}{\log_3 x} = \dfrac{1}{\log_3 x}$.

Exercise 7.9

1. Write down the value of each of these:
   (i) $\log_2 4$ (ii) $\log_3 81$ (iii) $\log_{10} 1000$ (iv) $\log_2 64$

2. Find the value of each of the following:
   (i) $\log_8 16$ (ii) $\log_9 27$ (iii) $\log_{16} 32$ (iv) $\log_{\frac{1}{2}} 8$ (v) $\log_{\frac{1}{3}} 81$

3. Change each of the following to index form and solve for x.
   (i) $\log_{\frac{1}{3}} 27 = x$ (ii) $\log_{\sqrt{2}} 4 = x$ (iii) $\log_8 x = 2$ (iv) $\log_{64} x = \frac{1}{2}$

4. Solve each of the following equations:
   (i) $\log_2 x = -1$ (ii) $\log_3 \sqrt{27} = x$ (iii) $\log_x 2 = 2$ (iv) $\log_2(0.5) = x$

5. Simplify each of the following, expressing your answers without logs.
   (i) $\log_4 2 + \log_4 32$ (ii) $\log_6 9 + \log_6 8 - \log_6 2$ (iii) $\log_6 4 + 2\log_6 3$

6. Write each of the following in the form $\log_a x$ and then simplify:
   (i) $\log_3 2 + 2\log_3 3 - \log_3 18$ (ii) $\log_8 72 - \log_8\left(\dfrac{9}{8}\right)$

255

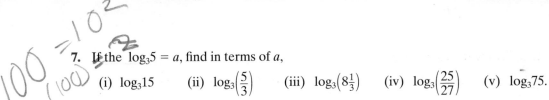

7. If the $\log_3 5 = a$, find in terms of a,

  (i) $\log_3 15$ (ii) $\log_3\left(\dfrac{5}{3}\right)$ (iii) $\log_3\left(8\frac{1}{3}\right)$ (iv) $\log_3\left(\dfrac{25}{27}\right)$ (v) $\log_3 75$.

8. Use common logarithms (i.e. logarithms to the base 10) to find, correct to three significant figures, the value of x in each of the following:

  (i) $200 = 2^x$ (ii) $5^x = 500$ (iii) $3^{x+1} = 25$ (iv) $5^{2x+3} = 51$

9. Let $y = 2^{x-1} + 3$.
   (i) Express x in terms of y using common logarithms.
   (ii) Hence find, correct to 4 decimal places, the value of x for which $y = 8$.

10. If $\log_{10} x = 1 + a$ and $\log_{10} y = 1 - a$, show that $xy = 100$.

11. If $p = \log_a\left(\dfrac{21}{4}\right)$, $q = \log_a\left(\dfrac{7}{3}\right)$ and $r = \log_a\left(\dfrac{7}{2}\right)$, show that $p + q = 2r$.

12. If $\log_a x = 4$ and $\log_a y = 5$, find the exact values of:

  (i) $\log_a x^2 y$ (ii) $\log_a axy$ (iii) $\log_a \dfrac{\sqrt{x}}{y}$

13. Use the change of base law to show that $\log_{25} x = \frac{1}{2}\log_5 x$.

14. Using a calculator, evaluate each of the following logs correct to three significant figures:
  (i) $\log_{10} 4$ (ii) $\log_{10} 27$ (iii) $\log_{10} 356$ (iv) $\log_{10} 5600$
  (v) $\log_{10} 29\,000$ (vi) $\log_{10} 350\,000$ (vii) $\log_{10} 3\,870\,000$.

15. If the $\log_{10} x = 3.123$, and using the results of Q14, find the max and min values of x without using your calculator.

16. By converting to the base 10, find, correct to three significant figures, the value of $\log_3 15 - \log_2 5$.

17. Use the change of base rule to evaluate (i) $\log_{27} 81$ (ii) $\log_{32} 8$.

18. Show that $\log_b a = \dfrac{1}{\log_a b}$.

19. If $x > 0$ and $x \neq 1$, show that $\dfrac{1}{\log_2 x} + \dfrac{1}{\log_3 x} + \dfrac{1}{\log_5 x} = \dfrac{1}{\log_{30} x}$.

20. If $\log_r p = \log_r 2 + 3\log_r q$, use the laws of logarithms to express p in terms of q.

21. If $\log_3 a + \log_9 a = \frac{3}{4}$, $a > 0$, find the exact value of a.

22. Find the value of $3\ln 41.5 - \ln 250$, correct to three significant figures.

Solve the following log equations:

23. $\log_2(x - 2) + \log_2 x = 3$

24. $\log_{10}(x^2 + 6) - \log_{10}(x^2 - 1) = 1$

25. $\log 2x - \log(x - 7) = \log 3$

26. $\log(2x + 3) + \log(x - 2) = 2\log x$

27. $\log_{10}(17 - 3x) + \log_{10} x = 1$

28. $\log_{10}(x^2 - 4x - 11) = 0.$

29. Given that $2\log_2 x = y$ and $\log_2(2x) = y + 4$, find the value of x.

30. If $\log_6 x + \log_6 y = 1$, $x, y > 0$, show that $x = \dfrac{6}{y}$.

Hence solve the simultaneous equations $\log_6 x + \log_6 y = 1$
$$5x + y = 17.$$

31. Use the change of base rule to solve each of the following equations:

(i) $4\log_x 2 - \log_2 x - 3 = 0$

(ii) $2\log_4 x + 1 = \log_x 4.$

Section 7.10 The graph of $y = \log_a(x)$

Using computer software, the graphs of $\log_{10}(x)$, $\log_e(x)$ [i.e. $\ln(x)$] and $\log_2(x)$ are drawn in the domain $0 \leqslant x \leqslant 10$.

Comparing the graphs, we conclude that $y = \log_a(x)$ has the following properties:

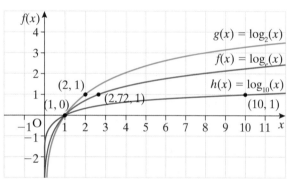

1. $\log_{(\text{any base})} 1 = 0$.
2. $\log_2 2 = \log_e e = \log_{10} 10 = 1$.
3. All graphs of log functions are increasing.
4. $y = \log_a(x)$ is defined for $x > 0$ **only**.
5. $y = \log_a(0)$ is not defined.
6. The y-axis is a vertical asymptote to all curves.

Comparing $\log_a(x)$ with $y = a^x$

If we let $a = 2$; comparing $y = 2^x$ and $y = \log_2(x)$, we have

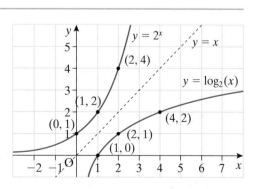

x	$y = 2^x$	x	$y = \log_2 x$
0	$y = 2^0 = 1$	1	$y = \log_2 1 = 0$
1	$y = 2^1 = 2$	2	$y = \log_2 2 = 1$
2	$y = 2^2 = 4$	4	$y = \log_2 4 = 2$
3	$y = 2^3 = 8$	8	$y = \log_2 8 = 3$
4	$y = 2^4 = 16$	16	$y = \log_2 16 = 4$

The points $(0, 1), (1, 2), (2, 4), (3, 8), (4, 16), \ldots$ are on the curve $y = 2^x$.

The points $(1, 0), (2, 1), (4, 2), (8, 3), (16, 4), \ldots$ are on the curve $y = \log_2(x)$.

$\therefore$ $y = \log_2(x)$ is the inverse function of $y = 2^x$.

Also, $y = \log_{10}x$ is the inverse function of $y = 10^x$.

The graphs of $y = 2^x$ and $y = \log_2(x)$ reflect in the line $x = y$.

Exercise 7.10

1. Using your knowledge of indices, explain properties 1, 2 and 5 on the previous page.

2. Using a graphics calculator or computer software, plot $y = 10^x$ and $y = \log_{10}x$ on the same axes and find the axis of symmetry.
   From your graph, estimate correct to one place of decimals, the value of $y = 10^{1.5}$ by enlarging the scale on the y-axis.

3. Consider the function $y = \log_3 x$.
   (i) Complete the following table.

x	$\frac{1}{9}$		1	3	
$y = \log_3 x$	-1			2	

   (ii) Using the values in this table, sketch the graph of $y = \log_3 x$.
   (iii) Estimate the value of $\log_3 2.5$ from your graph.
   (iv) Using the change of base rule, $\log_3 x = \dfrac{\log_{10}x}{\log_{10}3}$, find the value of $y = \log_3 2.5$.

4. On the same axes, sketch the graphs of
   (i) $y = 5^x, 0 \leqslant x \leqslant 2$ (ii) $y = \log_5 x, 0 \leqslant x \leqslant 25$
   (iii) What is the relationship between the two graphs?

5. On the same axes, sketch the graphs of
   (i) $y = \log_2 x$ at $x = 1, 2, 4, 8$.
   (ii) $y = \log_2 2x$ at $x = 1, 2, 4, 8$.
   (iii) $y = \log_2(x - 2)$ at $x = 3, 4, 10$.

6. On the same axes, sketch the graphs of $y = \log_{10}x$, $y = \log_{10}\dfrac{x}{2}$ and $y = \log_{10}(x + 2)$.

7. Given $y = 3^{x+2} - 5$,
   (i) express x in terms of y using common logarithms.
   (ii) If $y = 30$, find correct to 3 places of decimals, the value of x.

8. Copy this graph of the function $y = \log_{10}x$ into your copybook (or using a computer) and use it to draw rough sketches of the following functions:
   (i) $y = \log_{10}x + 2$ (ii) $y = \log_{10}(x + 2)$
   (iii) $y = \log_{10}x - 2$ (iv) $y = 2\log_{10}x$
   (v) $y = -\log_{10}x$

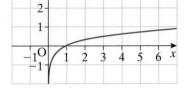

9. Copy this graph of the function $y = \log_{10} x$ into your copybook and use it to draw rough sketches of the following functions:

    (i) $y = \log_{10}(2x)$

    (ii) $y = \log_{10}\left(\dfrac{x}{2}\right)$

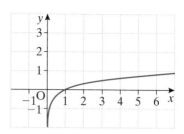

10. Copy this graph of the function $y = 2^x$ into your copybook and use it to draw rough sketches of the following functions:

    (i) $y = 2^x + 1$

    (ii) $y = 1 - 2^x$

    (iii) $y = 2^{x+1}$

    (iv) $y = \left(\dfrac{1}{2}\right).2^x$

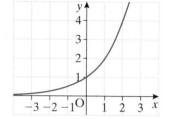

Section 7.11 Problem-solving with exponential and log functions

As stated already, exponential and log functions are used to model a wide variety of problems.

The loudness of sounds, the acidity of a solution and the intensity of earthquakes on the Richter scale are some examples, among many, of their application.

Example 1

The acidity of a substance is determined by the ion concentration formula $pH = -\log[H^+]$, where a pH of 7 is defined as neutral, <7 acidic, >7 alkaline. Determine the acidity of each of the following substances.

(a) Apple juice with a $[H^+]$ ion concentration of 0.0003.
(b) Ammonia with a $[H^+]$ ion concentration of 1.3×10^{-9}.

(a) $[H^+] = 0.0003 \Rightarrow pH = -\log[H^+]$
$$= -\log[0.0003]$$
$$= 3.52 \quad \therefore \quad \text{the apple juice is acidic}$$

(b) $[H^+] = 1.3 \times 10^{-9} \Rightarrow pH = -\log[H^+]$
$$= -\log[1.3 \times 10^{-9}]$$
$$= 8.87 \quad \therefore \quad \text{the ammonia solution is alkaline}$$

Example 2

The loudness of a sound of intensity I is given by the formula $dB = 10 \log\left(\dfrac{I}{I_o}\right)$,

where dB is measured in decibels and I_o is the threshold intensity of hearing $(I_o = 1 \times 10^{-12}\,Wm^{-2})$.

(a) Find the loudness (in decibels) of a sound at the threshold of hearing.

(b) Given that prolonged exposure to sounds over 85 decibels can cause hearing damage, and that a gunshot from a .22 rifle has an intensity of $I = 2.5 \times 10^{13}\,I_o$, should you wear ear protection when firing this gun?

(a) Threshold of hearing $= 1 \times 10^{-12}\,Wm^{-2}$

$$dB = 10 \log\left(\frac{I}{I_o}\right) = 10 \log\left(\frac{1 \times 10^{-12}}{1 \times 10^{-12}}\right) = 10 \log 1 = 0\,dB, \text{ i.e. no loudness.}$$

(b) $I = 2.5 \times 10^{13}\,I_o$

$$dB = 10 \log\left(\frac{I}{I_o}\right) = 10 \log\frac{2.5 \times 10^{13}\,I_o}{I_o} = 10 \log 2.5 \times 10^{13} = 134\,dB.$$

Yes, since the loudness is well above 85 dB, you should wear ear protection.

Compound interest (increasing value)

The future value, €A, of a sum of money, €P, invested at a rate of $i\%$ compound interest for t years, is given by the formula $A = P(1 + i)^t$. It is often required that we calculate the time, t (the index), for a particular investment to mature. This can be done by using logs as follows;

If $\qquad A = P(1 + i)^t,$

$\Rightarrow \qquad \dfrac{A}{P} = (1 + i)^t$ ... dividing both sides by P

$\Rightarrow \quad \ln\left(\dfrac{A}{P}\right) = \ln(1 + i)^t$ ... taking the natural log of both sides

$\Rightarrow \quad \ln\left(\dfrac{A}{P}\right) = t.\ln(1 + i)$ ... $\ln B^n = n.\ln B$

$\Rightarrow \dfrac{\ln\left(\dfrac{A}{P}\right)}{\ln(1 + i)} = t.$

Example 3

How long would it take €5000 to increase in value to €6000, if invested in a credit union at a yearly compound interest rate of 2%?

Since $A = P(1 + i)^t$, where €P is invested for t years at $i\%$,

$A =$ €6000 $\qquad P =$ €5000 $\qquad i = 2\% = 0.02 \qquad \therefore \quad 1 + i = 1.02$

$\Rightarrow$ €6000 = €5000 $(1.02)^t$

$\dfrac{6000}{5000} = (1.02)^t$

$1.2 = (1.02)^t$

$\ln 1.2 = \ln(1.02)^t$ ... taking the natural log of both sides

$\ln 1.2 = t . \ln 1.02$

$\dfrac{\ln 1.2}{\ln 1.02} = t$

9.21 years $= t \cong$ 9 years and 77 days

Depreciation (reducing value)

If a quantity reduces by a fixed amount over a given term (e.g. per annum), the same equation can be adapted to track the reducing value over time.

The present population P then becomes $P = P_0(1 - i)^t$ where P_0 was the initial population.

For example, if the population of red squirrels is reducing at a rate of 5% per year, then $P = P_0(1 - 0.05)^t = P_0(0.95)^t$ is the number of red squirrels after "t" years.

Example 4

The population of red squirrels in a given region was estimated to be 5000 at the start of 2003. Assuming a rate of decrease of 5% per year, estimate the size of the population in 2013.

Since $P = P_0(1 - i)^t$ and $i = 5\% = 0.05$,

and given that $P_0 = 5000$ and $t = 10$ years,

$\therefore \quad P = 5000(1 - 0.05)^{10} = 5000(0.95)^{10} = 2994$ squirrels

Doubling time

The **doubling time** is the time required for a quantity to double in size or value.

If a quantity is growing exponentially, then the number (or value) present at time t can be expressed by $y = A.e^{bt}$, where A is the amount or value at the start (i.e. $t = 0$) and b is a growth constant, specific to a particular organism.

261

If this quantity doubles in size, then there are 2A present.

$\therefore$ $2A = Ae^{bT}$, where T is the time taken to produce 2A, i.e. the doubling time.

$\therefore$ $2 = e^{bT}$

$\therefore$ $\ln 2 = \ln e^{bT} = bT \ln e = bT$

$\Rightarrow$ $\dfrac{\ln 2}{b} = T$, the doubling time.

> $\ln x^n = n.\ln x$
>
> and $\ln e = 1$

Example 5

A certain type of bacteria is growing exponentially, where $y = A\,e^{bt}$ is the number of bacteria present after t (hours) and b is the growth constant. Under certain conditions, the bacteria doubles in population every 6.5 hours. If at the start of the experiment under these conditions there are 100 bacteria present, find (i) the growth constant b (ii) how many bacteria will be present after 2 days.

Since $y = A\,e^{bt}$, then $200 = 100e^{6.5b}$ … since 100 doubles to 200 in 6.5 hours

$\qquad \therefore \quad 2 = e^{6.5b}$

$\qquad \therefore \quad \ln 2 = \ln e^{6.5b} = 6.5b \ln e = 6.5b.$

(i) The growth constant $b = \dfrac{\ln 2}{6.5} = 0.1066$ per hour.

(ii) Two days = 48 hours

The number present after 48 hours $= 100\,e^{0.1066 \times 48}$

$\qquad\qquad\qquad\qquad\qquad\qquad = 16\,680$ bacteria.

Exercise 7.11

1. Anne invests €5000 in a fixed-term account paying 0.6% per month compound interest. Find
   (i) the money in Anne's account after
       (a) 1 month   (b) 2 months   (c) 3 months
   (ii) a formula for the amount Anne has saved after t-months
   (iii) the minimum time for which Anne needs to invest her money if she wants to double her money.

2. A biologist puts 100 bacteria into a controlled environment at the start of an experiment.
   Six hours later, she returns and counts 450 bacteria in the colony.
   Assuming exponential growth of the form $y = A\,e^{bt}$ where b is the growth constant, find a value for b, correct to two decimal places.

3. Milk for a baby, which was heated up to 45°C, is left to cool. The temperature T°C of the milk, after t minutes left cooling, is given by the rule $T = 15 + 30 \times 10^{-0.02t}$.

(i) Verify that the initial temperature was 45°C.

(ii) If the milk is to be given to a baby when it has cooled to 35°C, find how long it has to be left to cool to reach this temperature.

(iii) Use this rule to find the room temperature, explaining your answer.

4. The loudness L (measured in dB) of a sound is given by the formula $L = 10 \log_{10}\left(\frac{I}{I_o}\right)$,

where I_o is the threshold of hearing $(1 \times 10^{-12}\,\text{Wm}^{-2})$ and I the intensity of the sound.

(i) If thunder can have a range of loudness between $100-110$ dB, what is the corresponding range of intensities in Wm^{-2}?

(ii) The threshold of pain is generally assumed to be $10\,\text{Wm}^{-2}$. Find in dB the loudness of a sound that starts to cause pain.

Watts per m^2 = Wm^{-2}

5. The amplitude of an earthquake is given by $A = 10^M$, where M is the magnitude (size) of the quake on the Richter scale. The energy released by the earthquake is $E \cong 10^{1.5M + 4.8}$ joules. Using the rules of logs, find a and b such that $E = 10^a A^b$, $a, b \in Q$.

6. The consumer price index (CPI) measures the cost of goods and services on a yearly basis. Assuming that a commodity was valued at €100 in 2000, and that the CPI has been rising exponentially at 4.5% since that year, find

(i) the value of that commodity in €, t years after 2000

(ii) the predicted cost of that commodity in 2010.

(iii) Using the same predicted rate of increase, what was the value of that commodity in 1995?

7. During the early stages of development, the weight W kg of a certain mammal, t months after birth, is given by the formula $W = 0.6 \times 1.15^t$.

(i) What was the weight of the mammal at birth?

(ii) State the growth constant per month as a percentage.

(iii) How long does it take this mammal to double its weight?

8. The decay of Polonium-210, a radioactive substance, is given by the formula $M = M_0 e^{-kt}$, where M_0 is the mass at the start,

M is the mass after t days,

k is a decay constant specific to Polonium.

If $M = 10$ g when $t = 0$, and $M = 5$ g when $t = 140$ days, find

(i) the value of M_0 and k

(ii) the mass of Polonium after 70 days

(iii) after how many days there will be 2 g of Polonium left.

Section 7.12 Proofs by induction _____

Many theorems in mathematics are proven true using the method of mathematical induction.

To prove a statement true by induction, we follow clearly-defined steps.

(i) The statement is proven true for some fixed value, usually $n = 1$ or $n = 2$.
(ii) The statement is then assumed true for values up to $n = k$.
(iii) Based on this assumption, we must show that the statement is true for $n = k + 1$.
(iv) In conclusion, a "rolling proof" is formed:
    a. Since it was true for $n = 1$,
    b. it is now true for $n = 1 + 1 = 2$.
    c. Since it is true for $n = 2$, it is true for $n = 2 + 1 = 3$, etc.
    d. It is therefore true for all values of n.

Example 1

Prove that **for all values of n**, $1 + 2 + 3 + 4 + \ldots n = \dfrac{n}{2}(n + 1)$.

Proof:

(i) Prove the statement true for $n = 1$.

$$\Rightarrow 1 = \tfrac{1}{2}(1 + 1) = \tfrac{1}{2}(2) = 1, \text{ which is true.}$$

(ii) Assume true for $n = k$.

$$\Rightarrow 1 + 2 + 3 + 4 + \ldots k = \frac{k}{2}(k + 1).$$

(iii) Based on this assumption, we must show that the statement is true for $n = k + 1$.

$$1 + 2 + 3 + 4 + \ldots k + (k + 1) = \frac{k}{2}(k + 1) + (k + 1) \quad \ldots \text{ adding } (k + 1) \text{ to both sides.}$$

$$= (k + 1)\left(\frac{k}{2} + 1\right) \quad \ldots \text{ factorising } (k + 1) \text{ from RHS.}$$

$$= (k + 1)\left(\frac{k + 2}{2}\right) \quad \ldots \text{ getting a common denominator.}$$

$$= \left(\frac{k + 1}{2}\right)(k + 2) \quad \ldots \text{ re-arranging the denominator.}$$

$$= \left(\frac{k + 1}{2}\right)[(k + 1) + 1]$$

$\therefore$ It is true for $n = k + 1$.

(iv) But since it is true for $n = 1$, it now must be true for $n = 1 + 1 = 2$.
And if it is true for $n = 2$, it is true for $n = 2 + 1 = 3, \ldots$ etc.

(v) Therefore, it is true for all values of n.

Note 1: Although we could prove this statement true for many discrete values of n, the important feature of this method of proof is that it proves the statement true **for all values of n**.

Note 2: Mathematical induction is not a means of discovering a result, but when we have a result that seems to be true, this method provides us with a rigorous proof.

Note 3: Proof by induction can be applied to several different categories of results including;

    (i) Results involving **series of numbers**   e.g. $1 + 2 + 3 + 4 + \dots n = \frac{n}{2}(n + 1)$.

    (ii) Results involving **factors of expressions**   e.g. $10^n - 7^n$ is divisible by 3.

    (iii) Results involving **inequalities**   e.g. $3^n > 3n + 1$, for $n \geqslant 2$.

Example 2

Prove that for all values of $n \in N$, $3 + 3^2 + 3^3 + 3^4 + 3^5 + \dots 3^n = \frac{3}{2}(3^n - 1)$.

Proof:

(i) Prove the statement true for $n = 1$.

$$3^1 = \tfrac{3}{2}(3^1 - 1) = \tfrac{3}{2}(2) = 3 \text{ ... which is true.}$$

(ii) Assume true for $n = k$.

$$3 + 3^2 + 3^3 + 3^4 + 3^5 + \dots 3^k = \tfrac{3}{2}(3^k - 1).$$

(iii) Based on this assumption, we must now show that the statement is true for $n = k + 1$.

$$3 + 3^2 + 3^3 + 3^4 + 3^5 + \dots 3^k + \mathbf{3^{k+1}} = \tfrac{3}{2}(3^k - 1) + \mathbf{3^{k+1}}. \text{ ... adding } 3^{k+1}$$
$$\text{to both sides.}$$

$$= \tfrac{3}{2}(3^k - 1) + 3^k.3^1$$

$$= 3\left(\frac{(3^k - 1)}{2} + 3^k\right) \text{ ... factorising 3.}$$

$$= 3\left(\frac{3^k - 1 + 2.3^k}{2}\right) \text{ ... common}$$
$$\text{denominator.}$$

$$= \tfrac{3}{2}(3.3^k - 1) \text{ ... rearranging.}$$

$$= \tfrac{3}{2}(3^{k+1} - 1)$$

$\therefore$ It is true for $n = k + 1$.

(iv) But since it is true for $n = 1$, it now must be true for $n = 1 + 1 = 2$.

And if it is true for $n = 2$, it is true for $n = 2 + 1 = 3$, ... etc.

(v) Therefore, it is true for all values of n.

Example 3

Prove by induction that $\dfrac{1}{1.2} + \dfrac{1}{2.3} + \dfrac{1}{3.4} + \ldots \dfrac{1}{n(n+1)} = \dfrac{n}{n+1}, n \in N$.

Proof:

(i) Prove the statement true for $n = 1$.

$$\frac{1}{1(1+1)} = \frac{1}{1+1} = \frac{1}{2} \ldots \text{ which is true.}$$

(ii) Assume true for $n = k$.

$$\frac{1}{1.2} + \frac{1}{2.3} + \frac{1}{3.4} + \ldots \frac{1}{k(k+1)} = \frac{k}{k+1}, k \in N.$$

(iii) Based on this assumption, we must now show that the statement is true for $n = k + 1$.

$$\frac{1}{1.2} + \frac{1}{2.3} + \frac{1}{3.4} + \ldots \frac{1}{k(k+1)} + \frac{1}{(k+1)(k+2)} = \frac{k}{k+1} + \frac{1}{(k+1)(k+2)}$$

$$= \frac{k(k+2) + 1}{(k+1)(k+2)}$$

$$= \frac{k^2 + 2k + 1}{(k+1)(k+2)}$$

$$= \frac{(k+1)(k+1)}{(k+1)(k+2)} = \frac{(k+1)}{(k+1)+1}$$

∴ It is true for $n = k + 1$.

(iv) But since it is true for $n = 1$, it now must be true for $n = 1 + 1 = 2$.
And if it is true for $n = 2$, it is true for $n = 2 + 1 = 3, \ldots$ etc.

(v) Therefore, it is true for all values of n.

Exercise 7.12(A)

In each of the following questions, prove the results by mathematical induction for all positive integer values of n.

1. $2 + 4 + 6 + 8 + \ldots 2n = \displaystyle\sum_{n=1}^{n} 2n = n(n+1)$.

2. $1 + 4 + 7 + 10 + \ldots (3n - 2) = \dfrac{n}{2}(3n - 1)$.

3. $1.2 + 2.3 + 3.4 + 4.5 + \ldots n(n+1) = \displaystyle\sum_{n=1}^{n} n(n+1) = \dfrac{n}{3}(n+1)(n+2)$.

4. $\dfrac{1}{2.3} + \dfrac{1}{3.4} + \dfrac{1}{4.5} + \dfrac{1}{5.6} + \ldots \dfrac{1}{(n+1)(n+2)} = \dfrac{n}{2(n+2)}$.

5. $\dfrac{1}{4.5} + \dfrac{1}{5.6} + \dfrac{1}{6.7} + \dfrac{1}{7.8} + \ldots \dfrac{1}{(n+3)(n+4)} = \displaystyle\sum_{n=1}^{n} \dfrac{1}{(n+3)(n+4)} = \dfrac{n}{4(n+4)}$.

6. $1^3 + 2^3 + 3^3 + 4^3 + \ldots n^3 = \displaystyle\sum_{n=1}^{n} n^3 = \dfrac{n^2}{4}(n+1)^2.$

7. $\displaystyle\sum_{n=1}^{n} n(n+2) = \dfrac{n(n+1)(2n+7)}{6}.$

8. $x + x^2 + x^3 + x^4 + \ldots x^n = \dfrac{x(x^n - 1)}{x - 1}, x \neq 1.$

Divisibility proofs

Example 4

Prove that for all $n \in N$, 3 is a factor of $4^n - 1$.

Proof:

(i) Prove the statement true for $n = 1$.

$\qquad$ 3 is a factor of $4^1 - 1 = 3$ ... true.

(ii) Assume true for $n = k$.

$\qquad \Rightarrow$ 3 is a factor of $4^k - 1, k \in N$.

(iii) Based on this assumption, we must now show that the statement is true for $n = k + 1$.

$\qquad$ Is 3 a factor of $4^{k+1} - 1$?

$$\begin{aligned}
&= 4^k.4^1 - 1 \\
&= 4^k.(3 + 1) - 1 \\
&= 3.4^k + 1.4^k - 1 \\
&= 3.4^k + (4^k - 1).
\end{aligned}$$

Since 3.4^k is divisible by 3 and $(4^k - 1)$ is assumed divisible by 3,

$\qquad \therefore \quad 3.4^k + (4^k - 1)$ is divisible by 3.

$\qquad \therefore \quad$ It is true for $n = k + 1$.

(iv) But since it is true for $n = 1$, it now must be true for $n = 1 + 1 = 2$.

And if it is true for $n = 2$, it is true for $n = 2 + 1 = 3$, ... etc.

(v) Therefore, it is true for all values of n.

Example 5

Prove by induction that $8^n - 7n + 6$ is divisible by 7 for all $n \in N$.

Proof:

(i) Prove the statement true for $n = 1$.

   7 is a factor of $8^1 - 7.1 + 6 = 7$ ... which is true.

(ii) Assume true for $n = k$.

   $\Rightarrow$ 7 is a factor of $8^k - 7k + 6, k \in N$.

(iii) Based on this assumption, we must now show that the statement is true for $n = k + 1$.

   Is 7 a factor of $8^{k+1} - 7(k + 1) + 6$?
   $$= 8^k.8^1 - 7k - 7 + 6$$
   $$= 8^k.(7 + 1) - 7k - 7 + 6$$
   $$= 7.8^k + 1.8^k - 7k - 7 + 6$$
   $$= 7.8^k + (8^k - 7k + 6) - 7$$

   Since 7.8^k is divisible by 7, $(8^k - 7k + 6)$ is assumed divisible by 7 and -7 is divisible by 7,

   $\therefore \quad 8^{k+1} - 7(k + 1) + 6$ is divisible by 7.

   $\therefore \quad$ It is true for $n = k + 1$.

(iv) But since it is true for $n = 1$, it now must be true for $n = 1 + 1 = 2$.

   And if it is true for $n = 2$, it is true for $n = 2 + 1 = 3$, ... etc.

(v) Therefore, it is true for all values of n.

Example 6

Show that $n(n + 1)(n + 2)$ is divisible by 3 for $n \in N$.

Proof:

(i) Prove the statement true for $n = 1$.

   3 is a factor of $n(n + 1)(n + 2) = 1(1 + 1)(1 + 2)$
   $$= 6. \text{ ... which is true.}$$

(ii) Assume true for $n = k$.

   $\Rightarrow$ 3 is a factor of $k(k + 1)(k + 2), k \in N$.

(iii) Based on this assumption, we must now show that the statement is true for $n = k + 1$.

Is 3 a factor of $(k + 1)(k + 1 + 1)(k + 1 + 2)$?

$$= (k + 1)(k + 2)[k + 3]$$
$$= (k + 1)(k + 2)k + (k + 1)(k + 2)3$$
$$= k(k + 1)(k + 2) + 3(k + 1)(k + 2)$$

Since 3 is assumed a factor of $k(k + 1)(k + 2)$, and 3 is a factor of $3(k + 1)(k + 2)$,

∴ $(k + 1)(k + 2)(k + 3)$ is divisible by 3.

∴ It is true for $n = k + 1$.

(iv) But since it is true for $n = 1$, it now must be true for $n = 1 + 1 = 2$. And if it is true for $n = 2$, it is true for $n = 2 + 1 = 3, \ldots$ etc.

(v) Therefore, it is true for all values of n.

Exercise 7.12(B)

Prove by induction that

1. $6^n - 1$ is divisible by 5 for $n \in N$.

2. $5^n - 1$ is divisible by 4 for $n \in N$.

3. $9^n - 5^n$ is divisible by 4 for $n \in N$.

4. $3^{2n} - 1$ is divisible by 8 for $n \in N$.

5. $7^n - 2^n$ is divisible by 5 for $n \in N$.

6. $7^{2n + 1} + 1$ is divisible by 8 for $n \in N$.

7. $2^{3n - 1} + 3$ is divisible by 7 for $n \in N$.

8. $5^n - 4n + 3$ is divisible by 4 for $n \in N$.

9. $7^n + 4^n + 1$ is divisible by 6 for $n \in N$.

10. $n(n + 1)(2n + 1)$ is divisible by 3 for $n \in N$.

11. $n^3 - n$ is divisible by 3 for $n \in N$.

12. $13^n - 6^{n - 2}$ is divisible by 7 for $n \geqslant 2,\ n \in N$.

Inequality proofs

When dealing with inequalities we noted two important deductions, namely

   (i) If $a > b$, then $a - b > 0$

   (ii) (any real number $)^2 > 0$.

Example 7

Prove by induction that $2^n > n^2$ for $n \geqslant 5, n \in N$.

Proof:

  (i) Prove the statement true for $n = 5$.

$$2^5 > 5^2$$
$$32 > 25 \;\; \text{... which is true.}$$

 (ii) Assume true for $n = k, k \geqslant 5$.

$$\Rightarrow 2^k > k^2, k \in N \text{ and } k \geqslant 5.$$

(iii) Based on this assumption, we must now show that the statement is true for $n = k + 1$.

$$\text{Is} \quad 2^{k+1} > (k + 1)^2 \;?$$
$$\text{Since } 2^k > k^2 \text{ (assumed)}$$
$$\therefore \quad 2^k . 2 > 2k^2$$
$$\therefore \quad 2^{k+1} > 2k^2$$

$\therefore$ we need to prove that $2k^2 > (k + 1)^2$.

$$2k^2 > k^2 + 2k + 1$$
$$k^2 - 2k - 1 > 0$$
$$k^2 - 2k + \mathbf{1} - \mathbf{1} - 1 > 0 \;\; \text{... completing the square by adding and}$$
$$\left(k^2 - 2k + 1\right) - 2 > 0 \quad \text{subtracting half the coefficient of } k \text{ squared.}$$
$$(k - 1)^2 - 2 > 0 \text{ which is true for } k \geqslant 5.$$

$$\therefore \quad 2^{k+1} > 2k^2 > (k + 1)^2$$

$\therefore$ It is true for $n = k + 1$.

(iv) But since it is true for $n = 5$, it now must be true for $n = 5 + 1 = 6$. And if it is true for $n = 6$, it is true for $n = 6 + 1 = 7, \ldots$ etc.

 (v) Therefore, it is true for all values of $n \geqslant 5, n \in N$.

Example 8

Prove by induction that $n! > 2^n, n \geqslant 4, n \in N$.

Proof:

  (i) Prove the statement true for $n = 4$.

$$4! > 2^4$$
$$24 > 16 \;\; \text{... which is true.}$$

(ii) Assume true for $n = k, k \geqslant 4$.

$\Rightarrow k! > 2^k, k \in N$ and $k \geqslant 4$.

(iii) Based on this assumption, we must now show that the statement is true for $n = k + 1$.

Is $(k + 1)! > 2^{k+1}$?

Is $(k + 1)k! > 2^k . 2$? ... $(k + 1)k! = (k + 1)!$

Since $k! > 2^k$ (assumed),

∴ $(k + 1)k! > (k + 1)2^k$

∴ we need to prove that $(k + 1)2^k > 2^k . 2$

$(k + 1)2^k > 2.2^k$ which is obviously true if $k > 1$.

∴ $(k + 1)! > 2^{k+1}$

∴ It is true for $n = k + 1$.

(iv) But since it is true for $n = 4$, it now must be true for $n = 4 + 1 = 5$. And if it is true for $n = 5$, it is true for $n = 5 + 1 = 6, ...$ etc.

(v) Therefore, it is true for all values of $n \geqslant 4, n \in N$.

Example 9

Prove that $(1 + x)^n \geqslant 1 + nx$ for $n \geqslant 1, n \in N, x \in R$.

Proof:

(i) Prove the statement true for $n = 1$.

$\Rightarrow (1 + x)^1 \geqslant 1 + 1.x$ ... which is true.

(ii) Assume true for $n = k, k \geqslant 1$.

$(1 + x)^k \geqslant 1 + kx, k \in N$ and $k \geqslant 1$.

(iii) Based on this assumption, we must now show that the statement is true for $n = k + 1$.

Is $(1 + x)^{k+1} \geqslant 1 + (k + 1)x$?

Is $(1 + x)^k(1 + x) \geqslant 1 + kx + x$?

Since $(1 + x)^k \geqslant 1 + kx$ ... (assumed).

∴ $(1 + x)^k(1 + x) \geqslant (1 + kx)(1 + x)$

∴ we need to prove that $(1 + kx)(1 + x) \geqslant 1 + kx + x$

$1 + x + kx + kx^2 \geqslant 1 + kx + x.$

$\Rightarrow kx^2 \geqslant 0$ which is true for $k \geqslant 1$ and $x \in R$.

∴ It is true for $n = k + 1$.

(iv) But since it is true for $n = 1$, it now must be true for $n = 1 + 1 = 2$. And if it is true for $n = 2$, it is true for $n = 2 + 1 = 3, ...$ etc.

(v) Therefore, it is true for all values of $n \geqslant 1, n \in N$.

Exercise 7.12(C)

Prove by induction each of the following statements:

1. $2^n > 2n + 1$ for $n \geqslant 3, n \in N$.

2. $3^n > n^2$ for $n \geqslant 2, n \in N$.

3. $3^n > 2n + 2$ for $n \geqslant 2, n \in N$.

4. $n! > 2^{n-1}$ for $n \geqslant 3, n \in N$.

5. $(n + 1)! > 2^n$ for $n \geqslant 2, n \in N$.

6. $(1 + 2x)^n \geqslant 1 + 2nx$ for $x > 0, n \in N$.

7. $(1 + ax)^n \geqslant 1 + anx$ for $a > 0, x > 0, n \in N$.

Revision Exercise 7 (Core)

1. Find the values of x that satisfy the following inequality:

$$-1 \leqslant \frac{2x + 4}{3} \leqslant 2 , x \in R.$$

2. (a) Using the log and 10^x keys on your calculator, evaluate each of the following:
   (i) $10^{3.5}$ (ii) $\log_{10} 4.5$ (iii) 10^{3t}, where $t = 0.04$ (iv) $\log 5n$, where $n = 100$.
   (b) Using the *ln* and e^x keys on the calculator, evaluate
   (i) $e^{3.4}$ (ii) $\ln 589$ (iii) $e^{-0.02t - 4}$,where $t = 40$ (iv) $\ln\left(\frac{10}{k}\right)$, where $k = 3.7$.

3. An exponential function is defined by $f(x) = 3 \times 4^x$. Find
   (i) the value of a if $(a, 6)$ lies on $f(x)$
   (ii) the value of b if $\left(\frac{-1}{2}, b\right)$ lies on $f(x)$.

4. Solve the equation $|x - 8| = 3$.

5. Solve each of the following:
   (i) $5^{2n} \times 25^{2n-1} = 625$ (ii) $27^{n-2} = 9^{3n+2}$

6. A graph of the exponential curve $y = a2^x + b$ is shown in the diagram.
   (i) Write down two equations in terms of a and b.
   (ii) Solve the simultaneous equations to find the values of a and b.

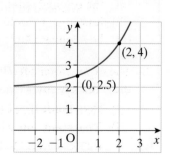

7. The graphs of the log functions
   (i) $\ln(x)$
   (ii) $\ln(x + 1)$
   (iii) $\ln(x) + 1$
   are shown in this diagram. Identify each curve,
   giving a reason for your answers.

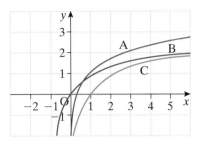

8. Solve the equation $\ln(x - 1) + \ln(x + 2) = \ln(6x - 8)$.

9. $y = Ae^{bt}$. Given that $y = 6$ when $t = 1$, and $y = 8$ when $t = 2$, find the values of A and b.

10. Find the values of a and b if the graph of $y = a\log_2(x - b)$ passes through the points $(5, 2)$ and $(7, 4)$.

11. Solve $32^{x-1} = 28$ for x, correct to two places of decimals.

12. Prove by induction that
$$3 + 6 + 9 + 12 + \ldots 3n = \frac{3n}{2}(n + 1), \text{ for all positive integer values.}$$

13. Prove by induction that
$$8^n + 6 \text{ is divisible by 7 for } n \in N.$$

14. Prove by induction that
$$n^2 > 4n + 3 \text{ for } n \geqslant 5, n \in N.$$

Revision Exercise 7 (Advanced)

1. Find the range of values of x that satisfies
$$3x + 4 < x^2 - 6 < 9 - 2x.$$

2. The mass M of a radioactive material remaining after t years is given by the formula
$$M = 30 \times 2^{-0.001t} \text{ grams. Find}$$
   (i) the original mass
   (ii) how long it would take for the material to decay to 10 grams
   (iii) how long it would take to decay to the "safe level" of 1% of its original mass.

3. The exponential curve $I = I_0 \times 10^{0.1S}$ measures the loudness of sounds compared to the threshold intensity of hearing I_0, where S is the perceived loudness (in decibels).
   (i) How many times louder than the threshold intensity is a sound of 30 decibels?
   (ii) How many times louder is a sound of 28 dB than a sound of 15 dB, give your answer correct to the nearest integer?

4. By choosing a suitable base, solve the following equation for x.

$$\log_5 x - 1 = 6\log_x 5$$

5. Solve $0.7^x \geqslant 0.3$ for x, giving your answer correct to 3 significant figures.

6. Using the same axes, draw a sketch of each of the following in the domain $-3 \leqslant x \leqslant 3$.

   (i) $f(x) = |x|$
   (ii) $g(x) = |x| + 2$
   (iii) $h(x) = |x + 2|$.
   (iv) Find the values of x that satisfy $f(x) \cap h(x)$.
   (v) For what values of x is $g(x) > h(x)$?

7. Sketch the graph of $y = \ln(x - 3)$.

   Express x in terms of y and hence sketch the image of $y = \ln(x - 3)$ in the line $y = x$.

8. Sketch the graph of the function $f(x) = |\frac{1}{4}x + 3|$ and hence find the solution to the inequality $|\frac{1}{4}x + 3| \geqslant 3$.

9. Simplify $\dfrac{x^{\frac{3}{2}} - x^{\frac{-1}{2}}}{x^{\frac{1}{2}} - x^{\frac{-1}{2}}}$.

10. Prove by induction that

$$\frac{1}{(1 + r)^n} \leqslant \frac{1}{1 + nr} \text{ for } r > 0 \text{ and } n \in N.$$

11. Prove that $\dfrac{4x}{(x + 1)^2} \leqslant 1$ for all $x \in R, x \neq -1$.

12. Given that k is real, find the set of values of k for which the roots of the quadratic equation $(1 + 2k)x^2 - 10x + (k - 2) = 0$

   (i) are real
   (ii) have a sum which is greater than 5.

13. Prove by induction that

$$1 + 2.2 + 3.2^2 + 4.2^3 + \ldots n.2^{n-1} = (n - 1)2^n + 1.$$

14. If for all integers n, $u_n = (n - 20)2^n$, write an expression for u_{n+1}, u_{n+2}. Hence verify that $u_{n+2} - 4u_{n+1} + 4u_n = 0$.

15. Solve the following simultaneous equations for $x, y \geqslant 0$.

$$2 \log y = \log 2 + \log x \quad \text{and} \quad 2^y = 4^x$$

16. The population of a city grows according to the law $P = 40\,000\,(1.03)^n$, where n is the time in years and P is the population size.

(i) What type of function is this?

(ii) Estimate the size of the population in 12 years time.

(iii) What was the initial population of the city before the city started growing?

(iv) Determine when the population will have doubled (to the nearest half-year).

17. The population of a town was 8000 at the beginning of the year 2000 and 15 000 at the end of the year 2007. Assuming that the growth was exponential,

(i) write an expression for the growth of the population, defining each of the terms used

(ii) find the population at the end of the year 2009.

(iii) In what year will the population be double that of the year 2007?

Revision Exercise 7 (Extended-Response Questions)

1. The manufacturer of a facial cream *SPOTLESS* claims that the population of bacteria which create spots will be halved within five days of using their cream.

During a trial in his laboratory, Professor Snape finds that the number of bacteria N in the population is given by the formula $N = 5000e^{-0.15t}$, where t is time, measured in days.

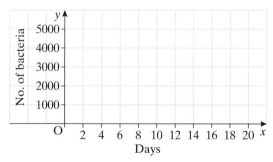

(i) Using this formula, test the claim that the bacteria population will halve in five days.

(ii) According to Professor Snape's equation, what will the level of bacteria be after 10 days?

(iii) How many bacteria are present at the beginning of the trial?

(iv) After how many days will the population reduce to 100?

(v) Copy this grid and sketch a graph of the number of bacteria in the population over a 20-day trial.

2.

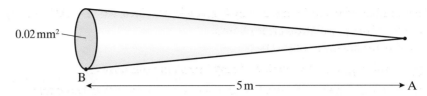

The diagram shows a conical glass fibre.

The circular cross-sectional area at the end B is 0.02 mm².

The cross-sectional area reduces along the length from B to A by a factor of $(0.92)^{\left(\frac{1}{10}\right)}$ per metre length of the fibre.

The total length of the fibre is 5.0m.

(i) Write down a rule for the cross-sectional area of the fibre at a distance x m from B.

(ii) What is the cross-sectional area of the fibre at a point one-third of its length from B?

(iii) The strength of the fibre increases from B to A.

At a distance x m from B, the strength of the fibre is given by the formula

$$S = (0.92)^{10-3x}.$$

If the weight that the fibre will support at each point before breaking is given by Weight = Strength × Cross-sectional area, write down an expression, in terms of x, for the weight the fibre will support at a distance x m from B.

(iv) A piece of glass fibre is needed to carry weights of up to $0.02 \times (0.92)^{2.5}$ units. How much of the 5 m could be used for this purpose?

3. A trans-european train developed a fault in the lighting systems in two carriages A and B. Before the fault, the light intensity in carriage A was **I** units and in carriage B was 0.66**I** units.

At each station at which the train stopped, the light intensity in carriage A decreased by 17% and in carriage B by 11%.

(i) Write down exponential expressions for the expected light intensity in each carriage after n station-stops.

(ii) At some time after the initial fault, the light intensity in both carriages was the same. At how many stations did the train stop before this occurred?

4. There are approximately ten times as many red squirrels as grey squirrels in a particular region.

If the population of red squirrels is reducing at a rate of 5% per year, and the grey squirrel population is increasing at a rate of 11% per year,

(i) write an expression for the size of the population of grey squirrels after t years

(ii) write an expression for the size of the population of red squirrels after t years.

(iii) After how many years, correct to 1 place of decimals, will the populations of both species be equal (assuming the present increase/decrease rates continue)?

(iv) Find how many years it will take (again, assuming the present increase/decrease rates continue) before the proportions of the squirrel populations will be reversed.

(v) Using the same axes, draw exponential graphs indicating your answers to (i), (ii), (iii), (iv) above. [Take $t = 0, 5, 10, 15, \ldots$, years.]

5. The number of bacteria in a colony is given by the formula $n = A(1 - e^{-bt})$, where n is the size of the population after t hours.
    A and b are positive constants.

   (i) Is this a graph of growth or decay? Explain your answer.

   (ii) If $t = 2$ when $n = 10\,000$, and $t = 4$ when $n = 15\,000$, show that
       $$2e^{-4b} - 3e^{-2b} + 1 = 0.$$

   (iii) Using the substitution $a = e^{-2b}$, show that
       $$2a^2 - 3a + 1 = 0.$$

   (iv) Solve this equation for a.

   (v) Find the exact value of b.

   (vi) Find the exact value of A.

   (vii) Sketch the graph of n against t.

   (viii) After how many hours is the population of the bacteria $18\,000$?

Answers

Chapter 1: Algebra 1

Exercise 1.1

1. (i) 3 (ii) -9 (iii) 5
2. (i) 2 (ii) 3 (iii) 4
3. (i) $\frac{3}{2}$ is not an integer
    (ii) $-4x^{-1}$, -1 is not a positive power
4. (i) $8x^2 - 4x - 2$ (ii) $4x^3 + 2x^2 - 6x$
    (iii) $7x^2 - 5x$ (iv) $9x^2 - 9x - 19$
5. (i) $22x^3 - 19x^2$ (ii) $9x^4 - 26x^3$
    (iii) $7x^4 - 5x^3 + 5x^2$ (iv) $15x^3 - 31x^2 + 3x$
6. (i) $2x^2 + 13x + 20$ (ii) $2x^2 - x - 6$
    (iii) $3x^2 + 7x - 6$ (iv) $12x^2 - 11x + 2$
    (v) $6x^2 + 13x - 5$ (vi) $8x^2 - 22x - 6$
    (vii) $x^2 - 4$ (viii) $4x^2 - 25$
    (ix) $a^2x^2 - b^2y^2$
7. (i) $x^2 + 4x + 4$ (ii) $x^2 - 6x + 9$
    (iii) $x^2 + 10x + 25$ (iv) $a^2 + 2ab + b^2$
    (v) $x^2 - 2xy + y^2$ (vi) $a^2 + 4ab + 4b^2$
    (vii) $9x^2 - 6xy + y^2$ (viii) $x^2 - 10xy + 25y^2$
    (ix) $4x^2 + 12xy + 9y^2$
8. (i) $x^2 + x + \frac{1}{4}$ (ii) $8x^2 - 4x + \frac{1}{2}$
    (iii) $-x^2 + 2x - 1$
9. (i) No (ii) No (iii) Yes.
    Parts (i) and (ii) cannot be expressed in the form $(ax + b)^2$
10. $p = 4$ **11.** $t = 20$ **12.** $s = 16$
13. (i) $x^3 + 4x^2 + 10x + 12$
    (ii) $2x^3 - 5x^2 - 13x + 4$
    (iii) $2x^3 - 3x^2 - 5x + 6$
    (iv) $6x^3 - 16x^2 + 14x - 4$
14. Proof
15. Proof
16. 14
17. $2x^3 - x^2 - 25x - 12$
18. $2x^4 - 10x^3 + 9x^2 + 5x - 2$
19. -47
20. (i) $x + 2$ (ii) $x + 2$
    (iii) $x^2 - 2x$ (iv) $3x - 2y$
21. (i) $2x + 3y - 1$ (ii) $2x^2 - 3x + 4$
22. (i) $4a$ (ii) $4ab$ (iii) $2yz$ (iv) $\frac{y}{x}$
23. (i) $x + 3$ (ii) $2x + 4$ (iii) $2x + 3$
24. (i) $x^2 - 7x + 12$ (ii) $x^2 - 1$
    (iii) $x^2 - 1$ (iv) $4x^2 + 5x - 6$
    (v) $x^2 - 5x + 3$ (vi) $2x^2 + 3x + 6$
25. (i) $x - 2$ (ii) $x - 3$
    (iii) $3x - 1$ (iv) $x + 2$
26. (i) $x^2 + 2x + 4$ (ii) $4x^2 + 6xy + 9y^2$

Exercise 1.2

1. (i) $x^2 + 4x$ (ii) $4x + 8$
2. (i) $2x + 2$ (ii) $10x + 2$
3. (a) $2x^3 + 5x^2 + 3x$
    (b) $8x^2 + 15x + 6$
    (c) (i) $390\,\text{cm}^3$ (ii) $281\,\text{cm}^2$
4. (a) -4 (b) -8 (c) -14
    (d) $54a^3 - 9a^2 - 15a - 4$
5. (a) 6 (b) 46 (c) 7.75
    (d) $\frac{a^2}{16} - \frac{3a}{4} + 6$
6. (a) $2x^2 + xy - 3y^2$ (b) $6x + 4y$
7. (a) $2x^3 - 10x^2$ (b) $18x^2 - 50x$
8. (i) Number of diagonals in a 4-sided polygon (2)
    (ii) Number of diagonals in a 5-sided polygon (2),
    (5), (9)
    A triangle has no diagonal
9. $a^2 - 3a - 8$
10. (i) $4t^2 + 6t + 6$ (2) (ii) $t^4 - 3t^2 + 6$ (4)
    (iii) $t^2 - 7t + 16$ (2)
11. (i) $1372\pi\,\text{cm}^3$ (ii) $\frac{1}{3}\pi r^3$ (iii) $\frac{4}{3}\pi h^3$
12. $36, 28, 4x + 7$
13. $\frac{40}{\pi^2}\,\text{m}$
14. $3\,\text{m}$
15. (i) 10 (ii) 15 (iii) 45; 17

Exercise 1.3

1. $5x(x - 2)$
2. $6b(a - 2c)$
3. $3x(x - 2y)$
4. $2x^2(y - 3z)$
5. $2a(a^2 - 2a + 4)$
6. $5xy(y - 4x)$
7. $2ab(a - 2b + 6c)$
8. $3xy(x - 3y + 5z)$
9. $2\pi r(2r + 3h)$
10. $(3a - 4)(2b - c)$
11. $(x - 9)(x + 3)$
12. $(c - 2d)(2c + 1)$
13. $(2x + y)(4a - 3b)$
14. $(y - 3b)(7y + 2a)$
15. $(2x - 3y)(3y - 4z)$
16. $(2x - 3y)(3x - 2a)$
17. $(x - y)(x + y)(3a - 4b)$
18. $(a - b)(a + b)$
19. $(x - 2y)(x + 2y)$
20. $(3x - y)(3x + y)$
21. $(4x - 5y)(4x + 5y)$

22. $(6x - 5)(6x + 5)$
23. $(1 - 6x)(1 + 6x)$
24. $(7a - 2b)(7a + 2b)$
25. $(xy - 1)(xy + 1)$
26. $(2ab - 4c)(2ab + 4c)$
27. $3(x - 3y)(x + 3y)$
28. $5(3 - x)(3 + x)$
29. $5(3a - 2)(3a + 2)$
30. $(2x + y - 2)(2x + y + 2)$
31. $(3a - 2b - 3)(3a - 2b + 3)$
32. $(a - b)(a + b)(a^2 + b^2)$
33. $(x + 2)(x + 7)$
34. $(2x + 1)(x + 3)$
35. $(2x + 7)(x + 2)$
36. $(x - 2)(x - 7)$
37. $(x - 4)(x - 7)$
38. $(2x - 1)(x - 3)$
39. $(3x - 5)(x - 4)$
40. $(7x - 4)(x - 2)$
41. $(2x + 3)(x - 5)$
42. $(3x - 4)(x + 5)$
43. $(4x - 5)(3x + 1)$
44. $(3x + 5)(2x - 3)$
45. $(3x - 2)(x + 5)$
46. $(3x - 1)(2x - 3)$
47. $(9x - 4)(4x + 1)$
48. $(5x + 2)(3x - 4)$
49. $(3y - 5)(2y + 7)$
50. $(4x - y)(3x + 5y)$
51. (i) $(x + 2\sqrt{3})(x + \sqrt{3})$
    (ii) $(x + 3\sqrt{5})(x - \sqrt{5})$
    (iii) $(2x + \sqrt{2})(x - 3\sqrt{2})$
52. (i) $(a + b)(a^2 - ab + b^2)$
    (ii) $(a - b)(a^2 + ab + b^2)$
    (iii) $(2x + y)(4x^2 - 2xy + y^2)$
53. (i) $(3x - y)(9x^2 + 3xy + y^2)$
    (ii) $(x - 4)(x^2 + 4x + 16)$
    (iii) $(2x - 3y)(4x^2 + 6xy + 9y^2)$
54. (i) $(2 + 3k)(4 - 6k + 9k^2)$
    (ii) $(4 - 5a)(16 + 20a + 25a^2)$
    (iii) $(3a + 4b)(9a^2 - 12ab + 16b^2)$
55. (i) $(a - 2bc)(a^2 + 2abc + 4b^2c^2)$
    (ii) $5(x + 2y)(x^2 - 2xy + 4y^2)$
    (iii) $(x + y - z)((x + y)^2 + z(x + y) + z^2)$

Exercise 1.4

1. (i) $\dfrac{3}{y^2}$ (ii) $\dfrac{a}{2b}$ (iii) x

   (iv) $\dfrac{7 + 2y}{7}$ (v) $\dfrac{x}{3 + 2a}$

2. (a) $\dfrac{26x}{15}$ (b) $\dfrac{x}{10}$

(c) $\dfrac{2x + 9}{12}$ (d) $\dfrac{13x + 1}{20}$

(e) $\dfrac{-(x + 6)}{6}$ (f) $\dfrac{3x + 5}{12}$

(g) $\dfrac{17x + 11}{20}$ (h) 0

(i) $\dfrac{11x + 4}{20}$ (j) $\dfrac{8}{15x}$

(k) $\dfrac{1}{8x}$ (l) $\dfrac{2x + 3}{x(x + 3)}$

(m) $\dfrac{5x + 14}{(x + 2)(x + 4)}$ (n) $\dfrac{7x - 8}{(x - 2)(2x - 1)}$

(o) $\dfrac{17 - x}{(3x - 1)(x + 3)}$ (p) $\dfrac{13x + 13}{(2x - 7)(5x + 2)}$

(q) $\dfrac{13 - 3x}{4(3x - 5)}$ (r) $\dfrac{-x - 7}{(2x - 1)(x - 2)}$

(s) $\dfrac{x^2 + y^2}{x^2 - y^2}$ (t) $\dfrac{4x + 9y - 2}{3xy}$

(u) $\dfrac{x - 7}{x(x - 1)}$

3. (i) $\dfrac{z - 2}{z - 5}$ (ii) $\dfrac{y + 2}{y - 5}$

   (iii) $\dfrac{t + 4}{t - 2}$ (iv) $\dfrac{2}{(x + 2)(x - 2)}$

   (v) $\dfrac{a - 8}{(a + 3)(a - 3)}$ (vi) $\dfrac{2x + 1}{(x + 2)(x - 2)}$

4. (i) $\dfrac{-4}{(2x + 1)}$ (ii) $\dfrac{-1}{2x + 1}$

5. (i) $\dfrac{-x - 4}{(x + 3)(x - 3)(x + 2)}$

   (ii) $\dfrac{x + 5}{(x + 1)(x - 1)(x + 2)}$

   (iii) $\dfrac{5}{(3x + 4)(3x - 4)(2x + 1)}$

   (iv) $\dfrac{1}{xy}$

6. (i) 5 (ii) 4 (iii) $x - 1$

7. (i) $\dfrac{1 + x}{1 - x}$ (ii) $\dfrac{1 + 2x}{x}$ (iii) xy

8. (i) $\dfrac{8y - 3}{4}$ (ii) $\dfrac{2x - 1}{2x}$

   (iii) $\dfrac{3x^2 + 1}{2x}$ (iv) $\dfrac{4y + 1}{2}$

9. (i) $\dfrac{6z - 2}{6z - 3}$ (ii) $\dfrac{8x + 2}{4x + 1}$

   (iii) $\dfrac{6z^2 - 3}{6z^2 - 2}$ (iv) $\dfrac{x^2 + x - 1}{x^2 - 1}$

10. (i) $\dfrac{x - 2}{x}$ (ii) $\dfrac{1}{x^2}$ (iii) $x + 2$

11. (i) $\dfrac{2b}{9 - b}$ (ii) $\dfrac{x^2}{x^2 - 3}$ (iii) $\dfrac{3y - 1}{3y + 1}$

12. Proof (constant $= 3$)

Exercise 1.5

1. $a = 6, b = -1, c = -12$
2. $p = 13, q = -10$
3. $a = 3, b = 7$
4. $a = 2, b = -10$
5. $p = 2, q = \frac{5}{4}, r = \frac{23}{8}$
6. $a = 3, b = 9$
7. $m = 9, n = 2$
8. (i) $a, b, c, d = 1, 10, 31, 30$
   (ii) $p, q, r = 5, 33, 52$
9. $p = 2, q = -5$
10. $a = 7.5, b = 37.75, c = 4.5$
11. $p = -12, q = 48$
12. $a = -3, b = 1$
13. $b = 4, c = 3$
14. $a = \frac{-2c}{5}$
15. $pq = 8$
16. Proof
17. $A = -\frac{1}{2}, B = \frac{1}{2}$
18. $C = -\frac{1}{5}, D = \frac{1}{5}$
19. $A = \frac{1}{3}, B = -\frac{1}{3}$
20. $a = -27, b = 54$
21. $p = -12, q = 16$
22. $c = 3, d = -4; (x - 2)(x + 2)(x + 3)$
23. 5
24. $a = 9 - p^2, b = 9p, p = 8, 1$
25. Proof
26. Proof
27. Proof
28. $2x - 1$
29. $A = 2, B = -1, C = -1$

Exercise 1.6

1. (i) $x = \dfrac{4 + 2y}{3}$ (ii) $x = \dfrac{4c + b}{2}$

   (iii) $x = \dfrac{y + 8}{10}$ (iv) $x = \dfrac{2y + 15}{5}$

   (v) $x = 9y + 6$ (vi) $x = \dfrac{yz}{y - z}$

2. (i) $x = \dfrac{y + 1}{6}$ (ii) $x = \dfrac{y - 3z}{2}$

   (iii) $x = \dfrac{a}{b + c}$

3. (a) $r = \sqrt{\dfrac{V}{\pi h}}$ (b) $r = \dfrac{A}{2\pi h}$ (c) Proof

4. (a) πr^2 (b) $4r^2$

   (c) $r^2(4 - \pi)$ (d) $\dfrac{r^2}{4}(16 - \pi)$

5. (i) $v = \dfrac{c(f^1 - f)}{f^1}$ (ii) $c = \dfrac{f^1 v}{f^1 - f}$

6. (i) $l = \dfrac{T^2 g}{4\pi^2}$ (ii) $l = 2.3\,\text{m}$

7. (i) $a = \dfrac{b(x + y)}{x - y}$ (ii) $a = \dfrac{b}{2}$

8. (i) $v = \dfrac{3u - 4y}{3}$ (ii) $v = \dfrac{2s - ut}{t}$

9. (i) $i = 100\sqrt[3]{\dfrac{A}{P}} - 100$ (ii) 2.0%

10. (i) $c = \dfrac{a - b}{ad^2}$ (ii) $c = \dfrac{b - 1}{b - 2}$

11. (i) $h = \sqrt{225 - r^2}$ (ii) $h = 10\sqrt{2}$
    (iii) $h = 13\,\text{cm}$

12. (i) $L = 300 - 2W$
    (ii) $A = W(300 - 2W)$
    (iii) $W = 50, L = 200$ or $W = 100, L = 100$

Exercise 1.7

1. (a) Linear   (b) Linear
   (c) Quadratic   (d) Quadratic
   (e) Quadratic   (f) Quadratic
   (g) Quadratic   (h) Linear
   (i) Quadratic   (j) Quadratic
2. (a) $4x^2 - 1$ (b) $4 - x^2$
3. (i) $5x + 2$ (ii) $4x - 6$ (iii) $3 - x$
   (iv) $-2 - 5x$ (v) $\frac{x}{2} + 3$ (vi) $-1 + \frac{x}{5}$
4. $2x + 5$
5. $2x + 5$
6. (a) $3x; 45$ (b) $4x; 60$ (c) $2x + 1; 31$
7. $70 + 35x; 125 + 24x; 5$ months
8. $f(t) = 2t^2 + t + 4$; in the 16th hour

Exercise 1.8

1. (i) x^2 is not of degree 1
   (ii) $(x - 1)^{-1}$ is not of degree 1
   (iii) $y^2 = 3x + 4 \Rightarrow y = \sqrt{3x + 4}$;
   not of degree 1
2. (i) 7 (ii) 3 (iii) -3
3. (i) 2 (ii) 2 (iii) -1 (iv) 2.5
4. (i) 2 (ii) 11 (iii) 7
5. (i) 2 (ii) 12 (iii) 3
6. (i) 3 (ii) 9 (iii) -5 (iv) 1.5
7. (i) 2.5 (ii) -2

Exercise 1.9

1. (i) $(4, 2)$ (ii) $(2, 5)$ (iii) $(3, 1)$
2. (i) $(3, -2)$ (ii) $(2, 5)$ (iii) $(3, 2\frac{1}{2})$
3. $(10, 5)$
4. $(10, 7)$
5. (i) $(x, y, z) = (2, 3, 1)$
   (ii) $(x, y, z) = (2, -3, 1)$
   (iii) $(x, y, z) = (5, 0, 1)$
6. (i) $(a, b, c) = (1, 4, 2)$
   (ii) $(x, y, z) = (2, 3, -1)$
   (iii) $(x, y, z) = (3, 1, -2)$
7. $(x, y, z) = (-1, 2.5, -0.5)$
8. $(a, b, c) = (1, -1, 2)$

9. $(a, b, c) = (2, 5, -6)$
10. $32\,000$
11. 17 years, 15 years
12. $y = \frac{1}{2}x + 4$
13. $N_1 = 88, N_2 = 22$
14. $a = 1, b = -1$
15. $c = \frac{4}{5}, d = -\frac{4}{5}$
16. 25 litres
17. $x = 15, y = 11$
18. $a = 0.5, u = -1.5$
19. $(4, 26), (8, 13)$
20. $(a, b, c) = (3, -2, 1)$
21. (i) $(x, y, z) = (3, 4, 1)$
    (ii) $(x, y, z) = (6, 4, -3)$
22. $(a, b, c) = (-2, -2, 1)$

Revision Exercise 1 (Core)

1. (i) $\dfrac{1}{3m^6n^7}$ (ii) $\dfrac{3x + 1}{5 + 4x}$ (iii) $\dfrac{1}{2x - 8}$

2. (i) $(x, y) = (-2, 2)$
   (ii) $(x, y) = \left(\frac{6}{5}, \frac{17}{5}\right), (-2, 3)$

3. $x^2 + 2x - 1$
4. $3x^3 + 6x^2 + 3x + 33$
5. (i) $(0, 3, -3)$ (ii) $\frac{1}{2}, 2$
6. 5
7. (i) $a = 11, b = 6$ (ii) $a = 2, b = 3$
8. $(x - 3)(x^2 + 3x + 9)$
9. $(p, q, r) = (2, 3, -13)$
10. $(x, y, z) = (2, -1, 4)$
11. $6b^2 + 2$

12. (i) $3n^2$ (ii) $5n^2$ (iii) $\dfrac{n^2}{2}$

13. $n^2 + 3n + 2; 10\,302$
14. $l = 21\,\text{cm}, w = 15\,\text{cm}$

15. (i) $r = \dfrac{2uv}{u + v}$ (ii) $m = \dfrac{v}{u}$

Revision Exercise 1 (Advanced)

1. $\dfrac{n(n + 1)}{2}; 1225$

2. $0.5\,\text{m}^3$
3. (i) $x + y = 8.4, 0.6x + 0.4y = 0.5(x + y)$
   (ii) $4.2\,\text{kg}$
4. Proof
5. $-\frac{1}{2}$
6. (i) $7.5\,l$ (ii) $2.5\,l$
7. (i) $a = 0.3; b = 0.28$ (ii) $3.57\,\text{m/sec}$

Revision Exercise 1 (Extended Response Questions)

1. (a) (i) 436   (ii) 112   (iii) 0.7956
   (b) €58 358
2. (ii) $x + 1.5y = 26$
   (iii) 14 standard, 8 deluxe

3. (i) $h = \dfrac{40}{x^2}$ (ii) Proof
   (iii)
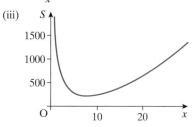
   (iv) $x = 4, h = 2.5\,\text{cm}$ or $x = 2.9, h = 4.76\,\text{cm}$
4. (i) $C(x) = 3500 + 10.5x$
   (ii) $I(x) = 0.5x$
   (iii)
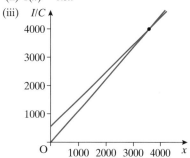
   (iv) 3500
   (v) Profit
   (vi) 5500 games
5. (a) €110.40
   (b) 12 blue, 84 white
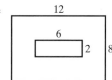
6. (i) $C = 40x + 30\,000$
   (ii) €45
   (iii) 5000
   (iv) $R = 80x$
   (v)
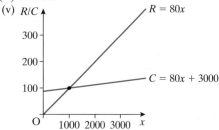
   (vi) 751
   (vii) $P = 40x - 30\,000$

7.

Number in queue	(a)	(b)
4	2	1
5	3	2
6	2	3
7	3	4
8	4	2
9	3	3
10	4	4
11	5	5
12	4	3
13	5	4
14	6	5
15	5	6
70	(24)	(19)

Chapter 2: Algebra 2

Exercise 2.1

1. (a) (i) $-5, 4$ (ii) $3, 4$ (iii) $-1, 5$

(b) (i) $-3, 5$ (ii) $-5, \frac{3}{2}$ (iii) $-\frac{2}{3}, 5$

(c) (i) $-\frac{2}{5}, 3$ (ii) $-\frac{5}{3}, \frac{4}{3}$ (iii) $-\frac{5}{4}, \frac{3}{2}$

(d) (i) ± 3 (ii) $0, \frac{10}{3}$ (iii) $0, \frac{8}{5}$

(e) (i) $-5, \frac{3}{2}$ (ii) $-\frac{5}{3}, 2$ (iii) $-2, 1$

(f) (i) $-5, \pm 4$ (ii) $3, \pm 1$

(g) (i) $-\frac{4}{3}, \pm 2$ (ii) $-4, -3, 5$

2. (a) (i) $-0.7, 2.7$ (ii) $-3.6, 0.6$ (iii) $0.6, 2.4$

(b) (i) $0.6, 5.4$ (ii) $0.1, 2.5$ (iii) $-2.9, 0.9$

3. (a) (i) $\dfrac{-2 \pm \sqrt{19}}{3}$ (ii) $\dfrac{6 \pm \sqrt{46}}{2}$

(iii) $\dfrac{3 + 2\sqrt{2}}{2}$

(b) (i) $-2 \pm 2\sqrt{3}$ (ii) $\dfrac{-2 \pm \sqrt{14}}{5}$

(iii) $\dfrac{1 \pm \sqrt{5}}{2}$

4. (a) (i) $2, 3$ (ii) $\frac{2}{3}, 2$ (iii) $-2, 3$

(b) (i) $\dfrac{9 \pm \sqrt{57}}{6}$ (ii) $0, 7$

(iii) $\frac{3}{2}$

5. (a) (i) $\pm\sqrt{2}, \pm\sqrt{5}$ (ii) $\dfrac{-5 \pm \sqrt{17}}{2}$

(iii) $\pm\sqrt{1 \pm \sqrt{3}}$ (iv) $\dfrac{11 \pm \sqrt{41}}{4}$

(b) (i) $-\frac{3}{2}, 4$ (ii) $1, 2$

(c) $1, 2, 4$

(d) $-1, -\frac{1}{2}, \frac{5}{2}, 5$

6. $-\dfrac{\sqrt{3}}{2}, \sqrt{3}$

7. (a) $-4.2, 1.2$ (b) $-2.3, 1.3$

(c) $-9.5, -0.5$ (d) $-1.6 \leqslant x \leqslant 0.6$

(e) $-1.6, 0.6$ (f) $-3, 1$

(g) $-3.6, 0.6$ (h) $-4.2 \leqslant x \leqslant -0.8$

8. Graph does not intercept the x-axis

9. (a) 21 units   (b) 25 units

10. (a) $-0.5, 2$ (b) -0.8

(c) $-0.5, 2.4$

11. (i) 1   (ii) 4

Only one solution is real in each case

12. (i) $-\sqrt{7}, 2\sqrt{7}$ (ii) $-3\sqrt{5}, -\dfrac{\sqrt{5}}{2}$

Exercise 2.2

1. (i) Curve f (ii) Curve h (iii) Curve g

(iv) 1. Curve f has roots $= 1.5$ and 4.5

2. Curve h has roots $= 3$

3. Curve g has no real roots

2. $A = \left(\dfrac{-b - b\sqrt{b^2 - 4ac}}{2a}, 0\right)$

$B = \left(\dfrac{-b + b\sqrt{b^2 - 4ac}}{2a}, 0\right)$

3. (i) $-39 < 0$ ∴ No real roots

(ii) $17 > 0$ ∴ Roots are real and different

(iii) $16 > 0$ ∴ Roots are real and different

(iv) $-8 < 0$ ∴ No real roots

(v) 0 ∴ Roots are real and equal

(vi) 0 ∴ Roots are real and equal

4. $k < -12$ or $k > 12$

5. (i) $k = 25$ (ii) $k = \pm 12$

(iii) $k = 0, 3$

6. $k = -\frac{1}{3}, 1$

10. $k = -\frac{1}{12}$

12. $a = \dfrac{b^2}{4}; -\dfrac{2}{b}$

Exercise 2.3

1. $x = -3, y = 9$ or $x = 1, y = 1$

2. $x = -2, y = -1$ or $x = 1, y = 2$

3. $x = -1, y = 4$ or $x = \frac{1}{2}, y = 1$

4. $x = 1, y = 0$ or $x = 4, y = -3$

5. $x = 3, y = 4$ or $x = 4, y = 3$

6. $x = 2, y = 3$

7. $x = 2, y = 2$ or $x = 5, y = 11$

8. $x = 3, y = 1$

9. $x = 2, y = 0$ or $x = 0, y = 1$

10. $x = -2, y = -2$ or $x = 1, y = 4$

11. $x = 1, y = 1$ or $x = \frac{7}{2}, y = -4$

12. $x = 0, y = 3$ or $x = -2, y = 1$

13. $t = 2, s = 3$ or $t = -\frac{4}{3}, s = -\frac{11}{3}$

14. $t = -7, s = -5$ or $t = 1, s = -1$

15. $t = 2, s = 1$ or $t = 11, s = 7$

Exercise 2.4

1. $-6, -5$ or $5, 6$

2. $-6, -4$ or $4, 6$

3. (i) $2x + 2y = 62; xy = 198$

(ii) Length $= 22\,\text{m}$, width $= 9\,\text{m}$

4. Sides are 3, 4, 5 and perimeter = 12 units
5. $t = 2.68$ or $t = 9.32$
6. $x = -3$ or $x = 5$
7. 0.25 seconds or 1.25 seconds
8. 12 cm
9. $-1, 1$ or 7, 9
10. 9 cm
11. Length = 10 m, width = 6 m
12. $-1, 0, 1$ or 7, 8, 9
13. Width = 2 m
14. Length = 24 m, width = 10 m
15. 9.35 m
16. $t = 3, s = 5$
Negative values are not valid
17. $(-2.2, 2.4); (6.2, -0.4)$
$k > 10$

Exercise 2.5

1. (a) (i) -9 (ii) 4
   (b) (i) 2 (ii) -5
   (c) (i) 7 (ii) 2
   (d) (i) 9 (ii) -3
   (e) (i) $\frac{7}{2}$ (ii) $\frac{1}{2}$
   (f) (i) $-\frac{1}{7}$ (ii) $-\frac{1}{7}$
   (g) (i) $-\frac{10}{3}$ (ii) $-\frac{2}{3}$
   (h) (i) -2 (ii) $\frac{1}{5}$
   (i) (i) -2 (ii) -3
   (j) (i) $\frac{3}{4}$ (ii) $\frac{5}{4}$

2. (a) $x^2 + 3x - 1 = 0$
   (b) $x^2 - 6x - 4 = 0$
   (c) $x^2 - 7x - 5 = 0$
   (d) $3x^2 + 2x - 7 = 0$
   (e) $2x^2 + 5x - 4 = 0$
   (f) $2x^2 + 3x - 10 = 0$
   (g) $12x^2 + 3x - 4 = 0$
   (h) $6x^2 + 10x + 3 = 0$

3. (i) $x^2 - 10x + 24 = 0$
   (ii) $x^2 + x - 6 = 0$
   (iii) $x^2 + 6x + 5 = 0$
   (iv) $x^2 - (4 + \sqrt{5})x + 4\sqrt{5} = 0$
   (v) $x^2 - 4ax + 3a^2 = 0$
   (vi) $25x^2 - 25x + 6 = 0$
   (vii) $b^2x^2 - 5bx + 6 = 0$
   (viii) $10x^2 - 31x + 15 = 0$

Exercise 2.6

1. (i) 196 (ii) 9 (iii) $\frac{25}{4}$
2. (i) $(x - 4)^2 - 19$ (ii) $(x - 1)^2 - 6$
   (iii) $(x - 1)^2$
3. (i) $(x + 2)^2 - 10$ (ii) $(x + \frac{9}{2})^2 - \frac{65}{4}$
   (iii) $(x - \frac{7}{2})^2 - \frac{61}{4}$
4. (i) $(-1, -7)$ (ii) $(1, -4)$
   (iii) $(-\frac{1}{2}, 2)$

5. $k > 9$
6. $2(x - 3)^2 - 11$
8. (i) $(-1, -5), (2, -1), (4, 1)$
   (ii) (a) $y = (x + 1)^2 - 5$
       (b) $y = x^2 + 2x - 4$
       (a) $y = (x - 2)^2 - 1$
       (b) $y = x^2 - 4x + 3$
       (a) $y = (x - 4)^2 + 1$
       (b) $y = x^2 - 8x + 17$
9. (i) 3 (ii) -2 (iii) $\frac{1}{3}$
10. Maximum point = (3, 9)
    Greatest height = 9 units
11. (i) $C; y = (x - 3)^2 - 1$
    (ii) $B; y = (x - 3)^2$
    (iii) $A; y = (x - 3)^2 + 1$
12. Curve $C: y = 16 - (x - 2)^2 \Rightarrow p = 16, a = 1, q = 2$
    Curve $D: y = 4 - (x - 2)^2 \Rightarrow p = 4, a = 1, q = 2$
13. $f(x) = -\frac{1}{2}x^2 + 1\frac{1}{2}x + 9$ or
    $f(x) = 9 - \frac{1}{2}(x - 1\frac{1}{2})^2$
14. $f(x) = x^2 + 2x + 4$ or $f(x) = (x + 1)^2 + 3$
15. (i) $f(x) = 4 - (0.1)(x - 6)^2$
    (ii) $(6 - 2\sqrt{10}, 0)$ and $(6 + 2\sqrt{10}, 0)$
    (iii) $4\sqrt{10}$

Exercise 2.7

1. (i) $2\sqrt{2}$ (ii) $3\sqrt{3}$ (iii) $3\sqrt{5}$
   (iv) $10\sqrt{2}$ (v) $9\sqrt{2}$
2. (i) $5\sqrt{2}$ (ii) $5\sqrt{2}$ (iii) $7\sqrt{2}$
   (iv) $5\sqrt{3}$ (v) $9\sqrt{2}$ (vi) $7\sqrt{5}$
3. (i) $\frac{\sqrt{3}}{3}$ (ii) $\frac{\sqrt{2}}{2}$ (iii) $\frac{\sqrt{2}}{5}$
   (iv) $2\sqrt{2}$ (v) $\frac{\sqrt{2}}{2}$
4. (i) $4\sqrt{6}$ (ii) 30 (iii) $6 + 2\sqrt{3}$
   (iv) 22 (v) 2 (vi) $a^2 - 4b$
5. (i) $\sqrt{5} - 1$ (ii) $\frac{12(3 + \sqrt{2})}{7}$
   (iii) $-9 + 4\sqrt{5}$ (iv) $\frac{\sqrt{2}}{2}$
6. (i) 2 (ii) 4
7. (i) 7 (ii) $-12 - 2\sqrt{5}$
8. (i) $4\sqrt{2}$ (ii) $\sqrt{6}$
   (iii) $\frac{13}{2}$ (iv) $\frac{19 + 8\sqrt{3}}{13}$
10. $5(2 - \sqrt{3})$
11. $\sqrt{2}$

Exercise 2.8

1. $\sqrt{2(x^2 + 4)}$ m
2. (a) $\sqrt{14}$ km
   (b) (i) $2(4 - \sqrt{14})$ km
       (ii) 12 seconds

3. $(8 + 2\sqrt{6})$ km

5. $\dfrac{-9 - 5\sqrt{3}}{6}$

6. (i) $2\sqrt{a}$ (ii) $\dfrac{2}{\sqrt{a}}$; 2

7. (i) $x = 4$ (ii) $x = 5$
(iii) $x = 9$ (iv) $x = 2, 3$
(v) $x = 2$ (vi) $x = -2, 8$

8. (i) $x = 4$ (ii) $x = \frac{2}{9}, 2$
(iii) $x = 9$ (iv) $x = 2, 6$

9. $a + \dfrac{1}{a} + 1$

10. $a = 2, b = 5$

11. (i) $\sqrt{2x^2 + 8}$
(ii) $\sqrt{3x^2 + 8}$; $x = 4$ m

Exercise 2.9

5. True
7. True
8. $k = 8$
9. $p = 11$
10. $(x - 1)(x + 2)$
11. $(x - 2)(x - 3)$
12. (i) $(x - 1)(x - 4)(x + 1)$
(ii) $(x - 1)(x - 3)(x - 4)$
(iii) $(x - 2)(x + 3)(x + 5)$
(iv) $(x - 1)(x + 1)(3x - 4)$
(v) $(x + 1)(x - 3)(2x + 1)$
(vi) $(x - 2)^2(2x + 5)$
13. $(x + 2)(x + 5)(2x - 1)$
14. $a = 2; (x - 1)(x + 1)$
15. $(x - 2)(x - 3)(x + 4); x = 2, 3, -4$
16. $-4, -2$
17. (i) $-1, 1, 4$ (ii) $-1, -4, 3$
(iii) $-1, 1, \frac{4}{3}$ (iv) $-1, -2, 3$
18. $a = 7, b = 2; (2x - 1); -1, -3, \frac{1}{2}$
19. $k = -8; (x - 2)(x + 6)$
20. $a = 3, b = -30; (2x + 5)$
21. $a = -5, b = 19; -1, 3, -\frac{2}{5}$
22. (i) $\left(\dfrac{b + c}{a}\right)^{\frac{1}{3}}$ (ii) $\left(\dfrac{c}{a}\right)^{\frac{1}{3}} - b$

Exercise 2.10

1. (i) $f(x) = x^3 - 3x^2 - x + 3$
(ii) $f(x) = x^3 + x^2 - 10x + 8$
2. (i) $f(x) = x^3 + x^2 - 6x$
$g(x) = 3x^3 + 3x^2 - 18x$
(ii) $f(x) = -x^3 + 6x^2 - 11x + 6$
$g(x) = -2x^3 + 12x^2 - 22x + 12$
3. $a = 6, b = 3, c = -15, d = 6$
4. $a = 0, b = -7, c = -6$
5. (i) $f(x) = x^3 + 2$
(ii) $g(x) = x^3$
(iii) $h(x) = 2x^3$
$A = (2^{\frac{1}{3}}, 4)$

6. $f(2) = 16, f(5) = -5$
7. $f(0) = 6$
$f(\frac{1}{2}) = 3\frac{3}{8}$
$f(2) = -4$
8. (i) $f(x) = -1(x + 1)(x - 1)(x - 2)^2$
(ii) $a = -1, b = 4, c = -3, d = -4, e = 4$
9. (i) $a = -2$
(ii) $f(x) = (x + 2)^2(x - 1)^2$
$g(x) = -\frac{1}{2}(x + 2)^2(x - 1)^2$
10. (i) $x^3 - 6x^2 + 3x + 10 = 0$
(ii) $x^3 + 4x^2 + 3x = 0$
(iii) $4x^3 - 5x^2 - 23x + 6 = 0$
(iv) $2x^3 - 13x^2 + 22x - 8 = 0$
11. (i) $f(x) = 2x^3 - 17x^2 + 27x + 18$
(ii) $f(x) = -4x^3 - 8x^2 + 37x + 20$
12. $a = -\frac{1}{3}, b = -18$
13. (i) $-1, 0, 2$
(ii) $-1\frac{1}{4}, 0, 2\frac{1}{4}$
(iii) $-1.3, 0, 2.3$
14. (i) $V = x(x - 1)(x + 1)$
(ii) $x = 3$ cm
15. $V = \dfrac{\pi}{4}h^3 = ah^3$
$a = 0.79$
$V = 1051.49$ cm^3
$d = 6.5$ cm
16. $x = 4.8$ (from graph); $x = 4.84$ (algebra);
$x = 3.6$

Revision Exercise 2 (Core)

1. $x = 1, 5; t = -2, -1, 3, 6$
2. $x = 1 \pm \sqrt{13}$
3. $p > 1$
5. $a = -21, b = 8$
6. (i) One of $2, -3, 5$
(ii) $(x - 2)(x + 3)(x - 5)$
(iii) Roots are $2, -3, 5$
7. (i) Real roots
(ii) Imaginary roots
(iii) Imaginary roots
8. $y^2 - 12y + 27 = 0; x = 1, 2$

Revision Exercise 2 (Advanced)

1. $2(x - 1)^2 - 7$
(i) $1 \pm \sqrt{\frac{7}{2}}$
(ii) $(1, -7)$
2. $11 - 4\sqrt{6}$
3. $\dfrac{\sqrt{35} + 5}{25}$
4. 7
5. (i) t has a value slightly less than 1
(ii) $t = 0.90$ (iii) 0.49%
6. $p = -\frac{1}{2} \pm \dfrac{\sqrt{1 + 4n^2\sigma^2}}{2}$

7.

	$k < 0$	$0 < k < \frac{1}{4}$	$k > \frac{1}{4}$
k	*Negative*	*Positive*	*Positive*
$4k$	*Negative*	*Positive*	*Positive*
$4k - 1$	*Negative*	*Negative*	*Positive*
$k(4k - 1)$	*Positive*	*Negative*	*Positive*

$0 < k < \frac{1}{4}$

9. $B(-\sqrt{2}, 1 - 5\sqrt{2})$ $A(\sqrt{2}, 1 + 5\sqrt{2})$
10. $k \leqslant -3$ or $k \geqslant 0$
11. -6
12. $(2, -7), \left(-\frac{13}{5}, \frac{34}{5}\right)$
13. Length $= 18$ m, width $= 6$ m
14. $y \leqslant -4$ or $y \geqslant 0$
15. $y = -2x^2 - x + 5$
16. (iii) $f(0) = -6, f(1) = 0, f(2) = 0, f(3) = 0, f(3) = 0, f(4) = 6$

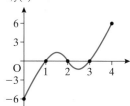

17. (i) $2, 5$
(ii) $f(x) = p(x - 2)(x - 5)^2$
(iii) $a = 2, b = -24, c = 90, d = -100$
(iv) $f(x) = -2x^3 + 24x^2 - 90x + 100$
(v) $f(x) = -2x^3 - 24x^2 - 90x - 100$

Revision Exercise 2 (Extended Response Questions)

1. (i) $a = 0.0002$
(ii) 10 hours
(iii) Because a is so small, the effect of at^3 is not noticed until it is near 10
2. (i) $6x^2 + 7xy + 2y^2$
(ii) $k = 7$
(iii) $x = \frac{1}{2}$ m
$3.5y + 2y^2 = 1$
$\Rightarrow y = \frac{1}{4}$ m
3. (a) $V = x(96 - 4x)(48 - 2x) = 8x(24 - x)^2$
(b) (i) $0 < x < 24$
(ii) Maximum volume occurs at A
No volume exists at B and C
(iii) Maximum $= 16\,400$ cm³; $x = 8$ cm
(iv) $15\,680$ cm³   (v) $14\,440$ cm³
(vi) 9720 cm³
(c) $a = 4, b = 24, c = 48$
4. (ii) Roots $= 0, 40$

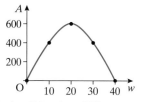

(iii) $A = 600 - (w - 20)^2$
Maximum area $= 600$ m²
(iv) $w = 20$ m
(v) width $= 20$ m, length $= 15$ m
5. (a) (i) 1 second or 3 seconds
(ii) 4.5 seconds
(b) 4.45 seconds
(c) $h = 6 - (t - 2)^2; (p, q) = (2, 6)$
6.

No. of price hikes	Price per rental	Number of rentals	Total income (I)
	€12	36	€432
1 price hike	€12.5	34	€425
2 price hikes	€13	32	€416
3 price hikes	€13.5	30	€405
x price hikes	$12 + 0.5x$	$36 - 2x$	$(12 + 0.5x) \times (36 - 2x)$

(i) $I = (12 + 0.5x)(36 - 2x) = 432 - 6x - x^2$
(ii) $441 - (x + 3)^2$
(iii) €441
(iv) Reduce rental price
7. (a) $A = xy + \frac{\pi}{2}x^2$
(b) (i) $y = 100 - \pi x$
(ii) $A = 100x - \frac{\pi}{2}x^2$
(iii) $0 \leqslant x \leqslant \frac{100}{\pi}$
(c) 12.4 m
(d) (i) $\frac{x^2}{50}\left(100 - \frac{\pi}{2}x\right)$
(ii) 247.6 m²
(iii) 18.8 m
8. (a) $A\left(\frac{3 - \sqrt{33}}{2}, 3 - \sqrt{33}\right),$
$B\left(\frac{3 + \sqrt{33}}{2}, 3 + \sqrt{33}\right)$
(b) $d = 6 + 3x - x^2$
(c)

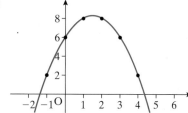

(d) $y = 8\frac{1}{4} - (x - 1\frac{1}{2})^2$

(e) $(1\frac{1}{2}, 8\frac{1}{4})$

(f) $0 \le d \le 8\frac{1}{4}$

9. (iii)

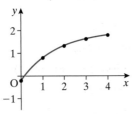

(iv) $(\frac{1}{4}, \frac{1}{4})$

(v) (a) $k < 0$ (b) $k = 0$ (c) $k > 0$

Chapter 3: Complex Numbers

Exercise 3.1

1. (i) $3\sqrt{2}$ (ii) $2\sqrt{3}$ (iii) $3\sqrt{5}$ (iv) $2\sqrt{7}$
2. (i) $8\sqrt{2}$ (ii) $11\sqrt{3}$
3. (i) $Z\backslash N = \{-3, -5\}$
   (ii) $Q\backslash Z = \{\frac{2}{3}, -\frac{7}{8}\}$
   (iii) $R\backslash Q = \{\sqrt{2}, \pi\}$
4. (i) Z is the set of positive and negative whole numbers including zero.
   (ii) $Q\backslash Z$ is the set of rational numbers (fractions) that cannot be simplified to an integer
   (iii) $Q\backslash N$ is the set of rational numbers (fractions) that cannot be simplified to an natural number
   (iv) $R\backslash Z$ is the set of all real numbers except integers
   (v) $R\backslash Q$ is the set of all real numbers except rational numbers, i.e. irrational numbers
5. (i) $3\sqrt{5}$ (ii) $-\sqrt{2}$ (iii) $11\sqrt{2}$ (iv) $-3\sqrt{3}$
6. Constructions
7. $3\sqrt{2}$, construction
8. $2\sqrt{3}$, construction
9. Construction
10. $9\sqrt{5}$
11. $\sqrt{3}, \pi, e, \sqrt[5]{2}$
12. $\sqrt{2}, \sqrt{3}, 2, \sqrt{5}, \sqrt{6}, \sqrt{7}, \sqrt{8}$; Length of c is rational.
13. $4\sqrt{2}, 2(\sqrt{6} - \sqrt{2})$
14. (i) $x = -1$
    (ii) Any value of x for which $3 - x$ is a perfect square

Exercise 3.2

1. (i) $2i$ (ii) $6i$ (iii) $3\sqrt{3}i$ (iv) $2\sqrt{5}i$
2. (i) $\pm 3i$ (ii) $\pm 2\sqrt{3}i$
3. (i) $8 + i$ (ii) $10 - 6i$ (iii) $3 + 0i$
   (iv) $-5 + 5i$ (v) $0 + 3i$ (vi) $3 - 2i$
4. (i) $1 + 2i$ (ii) $1 - 9i$ (iii) $5 - 10i$
   (iv) $2 - 4i$ (v) $3 - 10i$ (vi) $-7 + 5i$

5. (i) $0 + 13i$ (ii) $17 - 17i$ (iii) $5 - 31i$
   (iv) $25 + 0i$ (v) $26 - 0i$ (vi) $5 - 12i$
6. (i) $6 + 12i$ (ii) $7 - 3i$ (iii) $7 + 7i$
   (iv) $-9 + 3i$ (v) $10 + 10i$ (vi) $10 - 10i$
   (vii) $2 + 4i$ (viii) $2 + 16i$
7. (i) $1 + 4i, 1 - 4i$ (ii) $2 + 3i, 2 - 3i$
   (iii) $5 + i, 5 - i$ (iv) $4 + 6i, 4 - 6i$
8. $2 + \frac{\sqrt{2}}{2}i, 2 - \frac{\sqrt{2}}{2}i$
9. $i^3 = -i, i^4 = 1, i^5 = i, i^6 = -1$
   Since $i^4 = i^8 = i^{12} = \ldots 1$, divide power of i by 4 and find the remainder,
   i.e. $i^{29} = i^{4.7+1} = (i^4)^7 i^1 = i^1$
10. (i) -1 (ii) $-i$ (iii) $-i$
    (iv) i (v) 1
11. (i) -2 (ii) 0
12. (i) i (ii) -24 (iii) $8i$
13. $3i$

Exercise 3.3

1. (i) $3 - 4i$ (ii) $2 + 6i$
   (iii) $-5 + 2i$ (iv) $-8 - 3i$
2. (i) $2 - 5i$ (ii) $-3 + 4i$
   (iii) $1 - 7i$ (iv) $-5 - i$
3. (i) $\frac{5}{17} + \frac{14}{17}i$ (ii) $\frac{23}{26} + \frac{11}{26}i$
   (iii) $1 - 2i$ (iv) $\frac{4}{13} - \frac{19}{13}i$
4. (i) $40 + 0i$ (ii) $4 + 0i$
   (iii) $0 + 12i$ (iv) $-32 + 24i$
5. (i) $\frac{15}{17} + \frac{25}{17}i$ (ii) $-\frac{9}{4} - \frac{7}{4}i$
   (iii) $\frac{12}{5} - \frac{6}{5}i$ (iv) $3 + 2i$
   (v) $\frac{3}{10} - \frac{11}{10}i$ (vi) $\frac{43}{85} - \frac{49}{85}i$
6. (i) $x = 4, y = -2$ (ii) $x = 8, y = -1$
   (iii) $\frac{13}{5} + \frac{9}{5}i$ (iv) $x = -5, y = -12$
7. (i) $a = -11, b = 22$ (ii) $a = -10, b = -5$
8. $x = \frac{2}{3}, y = 1$
9. $p = -1, q = -2$
10. $2 + i, -2 - i$
11. $x = 3, y = -1$ and $x = -3, y = 1$
12. (i) $2 - 4i, -2 + 4i$ (ii) $1 + 4i, -1 - 4i$
    (iii) $5 - 4i, -5 + 4i$
13. (i) $1 + 2i$ (ii) $13 + 13i$

Exercise 3.4

1. Plot
2. (iii) $2 - i$ (iv) $-4 - 3i$
   (v) $-2 + 4i$ (vi) $6 - 2i$
   (vii) $-11 + 2i$ (viii) $-\frac{1}{5} - \frac{2}{5}i$
3. (i) 10 (ii) $6 + 0i$
   (iii) $\frac{3}{10} + \frac{1}{10}i$ (iv) $10 + 10i$
4. (c) Vertices join up to form a parallelogram
5. Adding z to each, translates each point
6. (i) $-2 + 3i$ (ii) $-3 - 2i$ (iii) $2 - 3i$

7. (i) $\sqrt{29}$ (ii) $2\sqrt{5}$ (iii) $2\sqrt{5}$ (iv) $\sqrt{10}$

8. $-2 + 5i, -2 - 5i, 5 + 2i$

9. (i) $\sqrt{\frac{10}{13}}$ (ii) $10\sqrt{2}$ (iii) $\frac{\sqrt{34}}{34}$

10. True

11. $\frac{7}{2} + \frac{1}{2}i$

12. $2\sqrt{5}, 4\sqrt{5}, 6\sqrt{5}$, yes

13. Yes

14. (i) $s = \pm 6$ (ii) $t = \pm 4\sqrt{21}$

15. $\frac{1}{\sqrt{2}}$

16. Circle, centre $(1, 0)$, radius $= 1$

17. z_1 and z_2 must be both real or both imaginary numbers or $z_2 = az_1$, i.e. z_2 and z_1 must be on the same line from the origin

Exercise 3.5

1. Plot

2. Collinear points

3. (i) Translation $-3 - 4i$
(ii) Plot
(iii) Rotation of (i^2) followed by a translation $(+3)$

4. Plot

5. $z_2 = 2 + 6i, z_3 = -6 + 2i$

6. (i) $a = 3$
(ii) $b = i$
(iii) $c = i^2 = -1$

7. Plot

8. (i) Translation of the plane
(ii) Stretching by a factor of k
(iii) Stretching and rotating

9. Plot

10. (i) Stretching by a factor of 3
(ii) Contracting by a factor of $\frac{1}{2}$

Exercise 3.6

1. $-2 - 4i$

2. (i) $1 \pm 4i$ (ii) $-2 \pm \sqrt{3}i$

3. (i) $z^2 - 2z + 10 = 0$ (ii) $z^2 + 4z + 5 = 0$
(iii) $z^2 - 8z + 20 = 0$ (iv) $z^2 + 25 = 0$

4. Proof

5. $-2 - 2i, 1$

6. $2 - 3i, \frac{1}{2}$

7. Coefficients are not real

8. $a = 5, b = 6$

9. $a = 1, b = 1$. Roots are $1, -\frac{1}{2} \pm \frac{\sqrt{3}}{2}i$

10. $z^2 + 4z + 5 = 0, 3, -2 \pm i$

11. $z^2 + 6z + 13 = 0: z^3 + 4z^2 + z - 26 = 0$

12. $z^3 - 2z - 4 = 0$

13. $\alpha = -\frac{1}{2} + \frac{\sqrt{3}}{2}i, \beta = -\frac{1}{2} - \frac{\sqrt{3}}{2}i$

Exercise 3.7

1. (i) $0 + 4i$ (ii) $-\sqrt{3} + i$
(iii) $-1 + i$ (iv) $1 + \sqrt{3}i$

2. (i) $2\sqrt{2}, \frac{\pi}{4}$ (ii) $3, -\frac{\pi}{2}$
(iii) $4, 0°$ (iv) $2, \frac{5\pi}{6}$

3. (i) $\sqrt{2}\left(\cos\frac{\pi}{4} + i\sin\frac{\pi}{4}\right)$
(ii) $2\left(\cos\frac{\pi}{6} + i\sin\frac{\pi}{6}\right)$
(iii) $\sqrt{6}(\cos 144.7° + i\sin 144.7°)$
(iv) $\sqrt{6}(\cos(-144.7°) + i\sin(-144.7°))$
(v) $4\left(\cos\frac{\pi}{2} + i\sin\frac{\pi}{2}\right)$
(vi) $5(\cos\pi + i\sin\pi)$
(vii) $3\left(\cos\left(-\frac{\pi}{2}\right) + i\sin\left(-\frac{\pi}{2}\right)\right)$
(viii) $1\left(\cos\left(-\frac{\pi}{3}\right) + i\sin\left(-\frac{\pi}{3}\right)\right)$

4. (i) $4\left(\cos\frac{2\pi}{3} + i\sin\frac{2\pi}{3}\right)$
(ii) $1\left(\cos\frac{\pi}{6} + i\sin\frac{\pi}{6}\right)$

5. (i) $-\sqrt{3} + i$ (ii) $-1 - \sqrt{3}i$
(iii) $\sqrt{3} - i$
(i) $\frac{\pi}{3}$ (ii) $\frac{5\pi}{6}$ (iii) $\frac{4\pi}{3}$
(iv) $\frac{11\pi}{6}$, rotation of $90°$

6. (i) $2\left(\cos\frac{\pi}{2} + i\sin\frac{\pi}{2}\right)$
(ii) $2\sqrt{3}\left(\cos\left(-\frac{5\pi}{6}\right) + i\sin\left(-\frac{5\pi}{6}\right)\right)$
(iii) $\sqrt{2}\left(\cos\left(-\frac{3\pi}{4}\right) + i\sin\left(-\frac{3\pi}{4}\right)\right)$

7. $\sqrt{2}\left(\cos\frac{\pi}{4} + i\sin\frac{\pi}{4}\right)$,
$\sqrt{2}\left(\cos\left(-\frac{\pi}{4}\right) + i\sin\left(-\frac{\pi}{4}\right)\right)$

8. $t = -8$

Exercise 3.8

1. (i) $8(\cos\pi + i\sin\pi)$
(ii) $2\left(\cos\frac{\pi}{2} + i\sin\frac{\pi}{2}\right)$

2. $4\left(\cos\frac{2\pi}{3} + i\sin\frac{2\pi}{3}\right)$

3. (i) $3, \frac{\pi}{2}$ (ii) $4, \frac{\pi}{3}$
(iii) $12, \frac{5\pi}{6}$ (iv) $\frac{3}{4}, \frac{\pi}{6}$

4. $12\left(\cos\frac{\pi}{2} + i\sin\frac{\pi}{2}\right)$

5. $\frac{3}{2}\left(\cos\frac{\pi}{2} + i\sin\frac{\pi}{2}\right)$

6. $2 + 2\sqrt{3}i$

7. $\cos \pi + i \sin \pi$

8. (a) $8(\cos \pi + i \sin \pi)$

 (b) $16\cos\left(\left(-\frac{2\pi}{3}\right) + i \sin\left(-\frac{2\pi}{3}\right)\right)$

 $\equiv 16\cos\left(\frac{4\pi}{3}\right) + i \sin\left(\frac{4\pi}{3}\right)$

9. (i) $\frac{1}{3}(\cos(\pi) - i \sin(\pi))$

 (ii) $-\frac{1}{3} + 0i$

10. $4\left(\cos\frac{2\pi}{3} + i \sin\frac{2\pi}{3}\right)$

 (a) $z^2 = 16\left(\cos\left(\frac{4\pi}{3}\right) + i \sin\left(\frac{4\pi}{3}\right)\right)$

 $= 16\left(\cos\left(-\frac{2\pi}{3}\right) + i \sin\left(-\frac{2\pi}{3}\right)\right)$

 $= -8 - 8\sqrt{3}i$

 (b) $z^3 = 64(\cos(2\pi) + i \sin(2\pi)) = 64 + 0i$

11. Proof

12. $\frac{1}{\sqrt{2}} + \frac{1}{\sqrt{2}}i$

13. Proof

Exercise 3.9

1. (i) $0 + i$ (ii) $-\frac{\sqrt{3}}{2} - \frac{1}{2}i$

 (iii) $-\frac{1}{2} + \frac{\sqrt{3}}{2}i$ (iv) $1 + 0i$

 (iv) $1 + 0i$ (v) $0 + i$

 (vi) $1 + 0i$ (vii) $0 - i$

 (viii) $0 - i$

2. $-2, -2\sqrt{3}i$

3. $0 + 243i$

4. (i) $\cos\frac{2\pi}{3} + i \sin\frac{2\pi}{3}$

 (ii) $\cos\frac{8\pi}{3} + i \sin\frac{8\pi}{3}, -\frac{1}{2} - \frac{\sqrt{3}}{2}i$

5. (i) $2\left(\cos\frac{\pi}{6} + i \sin\frac{\pi}{6}\right)$

 (ii) $3\left(\cos\frac{2\pi}{3} + i \sin\frac{2\pi}{3}\right)$

 (iii) $2\left(\cos\left(-\frac{\pi}{6}\right) + i \sin\left(-\frac{\pi}{6}\right)\right)$

 (iv) $3\left(\cos\left(-\frac{2\pi}{3}\right) + i \sin\left(-\frac{2\pi}{3}\right)\right)$

 (v) $6\left(\cos\frac{5\pi}{6} + i \sin\frac{5\pi}{6}\right)$

 (vi) $\frac{2}{3}\left(\cos\left(-\frac{\pi}{2}\right) + i \sin\left(-\frac{\pi}{2}\right)\right)$

6. (i) $-4 + 0i$ (ii) $-8 + 0i$ (iii) $-64 + 0i$

7. -4

8. $4\sqrt{2}\left(\cos\left(-\frac{\pi}{4}\right) + i \sin\left(-\frac{\pi}{4}\right)\right); -\frac{1}{256} + \frac{1}{256}i$

9. (i) $-1728 + 0i$ (ii) 4096

10. $\cos\left(-\frac{\pi}{6}\right) + i \sin\left(-\frac{\pi}{6}\right); -1$

Exercise 3.10

1. (i) $-1 - 0i$ (ii) $+1 + 0i$
 (iii) $-1 + 0i$ (iv) $1 + 0i$

2. (i) $\sin 2\theta = 2 \sin \theta \cos \theta$
 (ii) $\cos 3\theta = 4 \cos^3 \theta - 3 \cos \theta$

3. Proof

4. $2, -1 + \sqrt{3}i, -1 - \sqrt{3}i$

5. $-2, 1 + \sqrt{3}i, 1 - \sqrt{3}i$

6. $4\left(\cos\frac{\pi}{3} + i \sin\frac{\pi}{3}\right); \sqrt{3} + i, -\sqrt{3} - i$

7. (a) $(\cos 2n\pi + i \sin 2n\pi), 1, -\frac{1}{2} + \frac{\sqrt{3}}{2}i,$

 $-\frac{1}{2} - \frac{\sqrt{3}}{2}i$

8. $-3i, \frac{3\sqrt{3}}{2} + \frac{3}{2}i, -\frac{3\sqrt{3}}{2} + \frac{3}{2}i$

9. (i) $\frac{\sqrt{3}}{\sqrt{2}} + \frac{1}{2}i, -\frac{\sqrt{3}}{\sqrt{2}} - \frac{1}{2}i$

 (ii) $\sqrt{3} - i, -\sqrt{3} + i$

 (iii) $\sqrt{2} + \sqrt{2}i, -\sqrt{2} - \sqrt{2}i$

10. $\cos\left(\frac{2n\pi}{5}\right) + i \sin\left(\frac{2n\pi}{5}\right),$

 $n \in \{0, 1, 2, 3, 4\}$. Proof

Revision Exercise 3 (Core)

1. $2\sqrt{5}$

2. $x = 5, y = 4$

3. $z = -1 + 0i$ or $z = -3 + 0i$

4. $24 + 10i$, proof

5. (i) $-2 - 2\sqrt{3}i$ (ii) $p = 2$

6. $\sqrt{2}\left(\cos\frac{\pi}{4} + i \sin\frac{\pi}{4}\right); z^4 = -4 + 0i$

7. $2\left(\cos\frac{2\pi}{3} + i \sin\frac{2\pi}{3}\right)$

8. $2 - 3i$

9. Yes

10. $1 - 3i$

11. i

12. $f(z) = z^2 - (1 + 7i)z - 14 + 5i$

13. (i) $1 - 2i$ (ii) $3 + 3i$ (iii) $-2 - 5i$

14. (i) Rotation of $(-90°)$ and stretching by a factor of $1\frac{1}{2}$

 (ii) Translation $(4 - i)$

 (iii) If $z = x + iy, z_1 = -1\frac{1}{2}i$

 (iv) $z_3 = (4 - i)$

Revision Exercise 3 (Advanced)

1. $x = \frac{4}{5}, y = \frac{3}{5}$

2. $2 - 3i, \frac{1}{2}$

3. $2\left(\cos\frac{\pi}{6} + i \sin\frac{\pi}{6}\right); 2^{10}(\sqrt{3} - i)$

4. $p = -5 - 4i, q = 1 + 7i$

5. $w_2 = -\frac{1}{2} - \frac{\sqrt{3}}{2} i$. Proof

6. $\bar{p} = 2\left(\cos \frac{\pi}{3} - i \sin \frac{\pi}{3}\right), \bar{p}p = 4$

7. $-\frac{7}{2} + \frac{1}{2}i$

8. $k = -\frac{1}{3}$

9. i

10. $2 + i$

11. $-\frac{1}{2} - \frac{\sqrt{3}}{2} i$

12. $p = 30, 1 + 3i, -3$

13. $x = 3, y = -1$ and $x = -3, y = 1$

14. $t = +\sqrt{2}, -\sqrt{2}; \sqrt{2}i, -\sqrt{2}i, 1 + 2i, 1 - 2i$

15. $2 - 3i, 2 + i$

16. $p = 4, q = -1$ or $p = -4, q = 1; z = -1$
    or $z = \frac{1}{2} - \frac{5}{2}i$

Revision Exercise 3 (Extended Response Questions)

1. (i) $pq = 6\sqrt{3} - 6i$
   (ii) $|p| = 3, |q| = 4, |pq| = 12, |p + q| = 5$

2. (i) $-\frac{1}{2} + \frac{\sqrt{3}}{2}i$

   (iii) $1\left(\cos \frac{2\pi}{3} + i \sin \frac{2\pi}{3}\right)$

   (iv) Proof

3. (i) $p - 3q + (3p + q)i$
   (ii) Proof
   (iii) $p = 4, q = -2$

4. (i) 3   (ii) $\frac{5\pi}{12}$ (iii) 9

   (iv) 1   (v) $\frac{\pi}{3}$ (vi) $\frac{\pi}{2}$

   (a) True   (b) True

5. $z^2 = 2 + 2\sqrt{3}i, z^4 = -8 + 8\sqrt{3}i, z^6 = -64$
   (iii) Rotation and a stretching (rotation of 60°)

6. $1\left(\cos\left(-\frac{\pi}{6}\right) + i \sin\left(-\frac{\pi}{6}\right)\right); -1$

7. $0, z_1, z_2$ must be collinear points

8. (i) $ac - bd = 1, ad + bc = 0$

   (ii) $b = \frac{-d}{c^2 + d^2}, a = \frac{c}{c^2 + d^2}$

   (iii) Proof
   (v) Proof

9. Proof

10. (a) (i) $2\left(\cos \frac{2\pi}{3} + i \sin \frac{2\pi}{3}\right)$

    (ii) $z = \left(\frac{\sqrt{2}}{2} + i\frac{\sqrt{6}}{2}\right), \left(-\frac{\sqrt{2}}{2} - i\frac{\sqrt{6}}{2}\right)$

(b) (i)

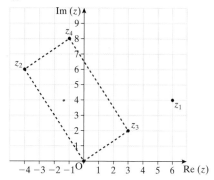

(ii) $k = \frac{1}{2}$

(iii) $z_3 = kz_1$. This represents a stretch along a line through the origin, i.e. z_3 and z_1 are the only collinear points with the origin

11. (a) (i) $\sqrt{2}\left(\cos\left(-\frac{\pi}{4}\right) + i \sin\left(-\frac{\pi}{4}\right)\right)$

    (ii) $16 - 16i$

(b) (i)

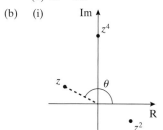

(ii) $\theta = 150° \left(\frac{5\pi}{6}\right)$

(iii) If $|z| > 1$
     then $|z^2| > |z|$
     and $|z^3| > |z^2|$ i.e. the points spiral way from the origin

(c) (i) $z^2 = 2a^2i, z^4 = -4a^4, z^6 = -8a^6i$
    (ii) The points spiral way from the origin and are restricted to the real and imaginary axes

12. (i) $z^k = (\cos k\theta + i \sin k\theta)$
    (ii) Proof

    (iii) $\cos k\theta = \frac{1}{2}(z^k + z^{-k})$,

         $\sin k\theta = \frac{1}{2i} (z^k + z^{-k})$

    (iv) Proof

    (v) $\cos^2\theta \sin^2\theta = \frac{1}{8} - \frac{1}{8}\cos 4\theta, a = \frac{1}{8}, b = -\frac{1}{8}$

Chapter 4: Sequences – Series – Patterns

Exercise 4.1

1. (i) 30, 36, 42   (ii) 27, 32, 37
   (iii) 9.5, 10.7, 11.9   (iv) $-10, -13, -16$
   (v) 38, 51, 66   (vi) 46, 38, 30
   (vii) $-15, -20, -25$ (viii) $-28, -19, -10$
   (ix) 54, 162, 486   (x) 30, 42, 56
   (xi) $-\frac{3}{4}, -1\frac{1}{4}, -1\frac{3}{4}$ (xii) 16, 22, 29
   (xiii) 35, 48, 63   (xiv) $48, -96, 192$
   (xv) $\frac{1}{30}, \frac{1}{42}, \frac{1}{56}$

2. (i) 2, 6, 10, 14   (ii) 4, 9, 16, 25
   (iii) $-1, 0, 3, 8$ (iv) 8, 15, 24, 35
   (v) 0, 7, 26, 63   (vi) $\frac{1}{3}, \frac{2}{4}, \frac{3}{5}, \frac{4}{6}$
   (vii) 2, 4, 8, 16   (viii) $-3, 9, -27, 81$
   (ix) 2, 8, 24, 64

3. (i) 5, 9, 13, 17   (ii) 21 cm

4. (i) 1, 2, 4, 7, 11, 16   (ii) 8

5. $u_1 = 1, u_5 = 17, u_{10} = 37$

6. $u_1 = 4, u_6 = -128, u_{11} = 4096$

7. (i) 5, 9, 13, 17, 21, 25
   (ii) 1, 5, 10, 17, 26, 37
   (iii) 2, 4, 8, 16, 32, 64

8. (i) C   (ii) B   (iii) D   (iv) A

9. (i) $n + 4$ (ii) $2n$ (iii) $3n - 1$
   (iv) n^2 (v) $n^2 + 1$ (vi) $(-1)^n$
   (vii) $4n - 3$ (viii) $\frac{1}{n}$ (ix) $\frac{n+1}{n+2}$
   (x) $(n + 1)(n + 2)$

10. Sequence is formed by adding the previous two terms; 34, 55, 89, 144

11.
             1   5   10   10   5   1
          1   6   15   20   15   6   1
       1   7   21   35   35   21   7   1
    1   8   28   56   70   56   28   8   1

    (i) 1, 2, 3, 4, 5, ... $T_n = n$
    (ii) 1, 3, 6, 10, 15, ... $T_n = \frac{n(n+1)}{2}$
    (iii) 1, 2, 4, 8, 16, ... $T_n = 2^{n-1}$
    (iv) 3, 6, 10, 15, 21, ... $T_n = \frac{(n+1)(n+2)}{2}$

Exercise 4.2

1. (i) $T_n = 5n + 3, T_{22} = 113$
   (ii) $T_n = 20n - 4, T_{22} = 436$
   (iii) $T_n = 13 - 3n, T_{22} = -53$

2. 3, 8, 13, 18

3. (i) 21   (ii) 20   (iii) 32

4. (i) $a = 4, d = 3$
   (ii) 4, 7, 10, 13, 16
   (iii) $T_{20} = 61$

5. (i) 8 red and 22 orange
   (ii) No since $T_n = 3n + 6 \neq 38$

6. $a = 3, d = 2$;   3, 5, 7, 9, 11, 13

7. (i) $k = 4$
   (ii) $p = -2$

8. (i) 12, 20, 28; $T_n = 8n + 4$
   (ii) 124
   (iii) shape 20

9. $d = 4$ a constant $\Rightarrow$ sequence is arithmetic

10. $d = 2n + 3 \therefore$ not constant

11. (i) 8
    (ii) 49
    (iii) $T_n = n^2 + 8$

12. (i) No, since $T_n = 4n + 2 \neq 87$
    (ii) $T_n - T_{n-1}$ is not constant
    (iii) 5 completed levels and 32 left over

13. 9 weeks

Exercise 4.3

1. (i) $S_n = 2n^2 - n; S_{20} = 780$
   (ii) $S_n = 51n - n^2; S_{20} = 620$
   (iii) $S_n = \frac{n^2 + 19n}{20}; S_{20} = 39$
   (iv) $S_n = 2n^2 - 9n; S_{20} = 620$

2. (i) $n = 12, S_{12} = 336$
   (ii) $n = 100, S_{100} = 5050$
   (iii) $n = 20, S_{20} = 460$

3. 7 terms

4. $a = 2, d = -3; S_{10} = -115$

5. 10 weeks

6. (i) 69   (ii) 54   (iii) 5050

7. (i) $\sum_{n=1}^{31} 4n$ (ii) $\sum_{n=1}^{29} \frac{n-21}{2}$
   (iii) $\sum_{n=1}^{401} \frac{n+99}{10}$

8. 3, 7, 11, 15, 19

9. $S_{33} = 1980$

10. (i) 51 rings
    (ii) 101 rings; $S_{20} = 1070$

11. 14 terms; $d = 4$

12. 4950

13. $a = 3.5, d = 0.1; S_{30} = 148.5$

14. 60

Exercise 4.4

1. (i) $r = 3; 243, 729$
   (ii) $r = \frac{1}{3}; \frac{1}{81}, \frac{1}{243}$
   (iii) $r = -2; -16, 32$
   (iv) $r = -1; 1, -1$
   (v) not geometric
   (vi) $r = a; a^5, a^6$
   (vii) $r = 1.1; 1.4641, 1.61051$
   (viii) not geometric
   (ix) not geometric
   (x) $r = 6; 972, 5832$

2. (i) $a = 5, r = 2; T_{11} = 5120$
(ii) $a = 10, r = 2.5; T_7 = 2441.41$
(iii) $a = 1.1, r = 1.1; T_8 = 2.1436$
(iv) $a = 24, r = -0.5; T_{10} = -0.046875 \left(-\frac{3}{64}\right)$

3. $a = 4, r = 3; 4, 12, 36, 108, 324, \ldots$

4. $r = 3$

5. $-16, 4, -1, \frac{1}{4}, -\frac{1}{16}$

6. A and C are geometric
B and D are not geometric

7. $n = 6; 4, 6, 9, 13.5$

8. $a = -7, r = -3; T_n = -7(-3)^{n-1}$

9. 6.75

10. $1, 3, 9, 27$ or $9, 3, 1, \frac{1}{3}$

11. $3, 6, 12, 24, 48$

12. $6, 4\frac{1}{2}, 3\frac{3}{8}, 2\frac{17}{32}$

13. $40, -20, 10, -5$

14. (i) $x = -1\frac{1}{2}; -4\frac{1}{2}, -1\frac{1}{2}, -\frac{1}{2}$ or $x = 4; 1, 4, 16$
(ii) $x = 3\frac{1}{2}; 4\frac{1}{2}, 7\frac{1}{2}, 12\frac{1}{2}$ or $x = -2; -1, 2, -4$
(iii) $x = 6; 4, 6, 9$
(iv) $x = 10; 4, 20, 100$

15. Proof

16. No

17. (i) $n = 7$ (ii) $n = 6$

18. (i) $18, 12, 8, \frac{16}{3}$ (ii) $T_n = 27(\frac{2}{3})^n$
(iii) 0.21 m

19. (i) €4000
(ii) €4120, €4243.6, €4370.91, €4502.04
(iii) €5375.67
(iv) 23 years

20. $r = 2\%$

Exercise 4.5

1. $S_{10} = 59\,048$
2. $n = 6; S_6 = 2016$
3. $S_8 = 255$
4. $S_{10} = 63.94$
5. -728
6. 8 terms; $S_8 = 546\frac{2}{3}$
7. $4, 16, 64; S_6 = 5460$
8. $S_8 = 19\,680$
9. $S_{10} = 5.994$
10. (i) $\frac{7}{9}$ (ii) $\frac{35}{99}$ (iii) $\frac{7}{30}$
(iv) $\frac{10}{27}$ (v) $\frac{161}{990}$ (vi) $\frac{53}{165}$
11. $S_n = 2 - \frac{1}{2^{n-1}}; S_\infty = 2, n = 11$

Exercise 4.6

1. (i) $T_n = 4n + 1$ (ii) $T_n = 3n - 2$
(iii) $T_n = 5n + 6$
2. (i) $T_n = 3 - n$ (ii) $T_n = 2 - 2n$
(iii) $T_n = 2n - 8$
3. (i) $10\,150$ mm^2 (ii) 560 mm
4. (i) 900 cm^2 (ii) 21st design
5. (i) $10\,100$ cm^2 (ii) 15th triangle

6. (i) $T_n = 2n^3 + n^2 + 4n - 1$
(ii) $T_n = n^3 - 4n^2 + n + 5$
(iii) $T_n = n^3 - 4n + 2$

7. (a) $T_n = n^2 - 1$; 575 bright, 1 dark
(b) $T_n = n^2 - 2$; 574 bright, 2 dark
(c) $T_n = n^2 - n$; 552 bright, 24 dark

8. (i) $T_n = 3n^2 + 4$
(ii) $T_n = 2n - n^2$
(iii) $T_n = 2n^3 + n - 4$
(iv) $T_n = 4n - 6$
(v) $T_n = 3n^3 + 2n^2 - 1$

Revision Exercise 4 (Core)

1. (i) $7, 10, 13, 16$ (ii) $5, 11, 17, 23$
(iii) $1, 2, 4, 8$ (iv) $20, 30, 42, 56$
(v) $2, 9, 28, 65$

2. $a = 79, d = -4$

3. $r = \frac{2}{3}$

4. (i) $r = -2; T_n = (-2)^n$
(ii) $r = \frac{1}{2}; T_n = \left(\frac{1}{2}\right)^{n-1}$
(iii) $r = -3; T_n = 2(-3)^{n-1}$

5. (i) $T_n = 8n + 4$ (ii) 250 cubes
6. (i) $r = -3$ (ii) $a = -7$
7. Explanation
8. $19\,900$
9. 195
10. 280

Revision Exercise 4 (Advanced)

1. (i) 12 lumens (ii) $T_n = 2000\left(\frac{3}{5}\right)^n$
(iii) 5th mirror

2. (i) $t = \dfrac{\ln 2}{\ln(1 + i)}$
(ii) (a) 35 years
(b) 14.2 years
(c) 7.3 years

3. (i) $10 + 2(6 + 3.6 + 2.16 + \ldots)$
(ii) Infinite geometric series
(iii) 40 m

4. (i) $T_n = 3(2)^{n-1}$
(ii) 20th term

5. (i) $€2.1 \times 10^7$
(ii) $€9.2 \times 10^{16}$

6. $5, 11, 17$

7. (i) $V = P(1 - i)^a$
(ii) €14\,953
(iii) end of 12th year

8. (i) $1, \frac{1}{3}, -\frac{1}{9}$
(iii) $k = -1$

9. (ii) $T_n = 6n - 2$
(iii) $2n(6n^2 + 3n - 1)$

10. $\frac{1}{2}\log_2 x; r = \frac{1}{2}; k = 2$

Revision Exercise 4 (Extended Response Questions)

1. (i) $T_2 = 4a + 2b + c$; $T_3 = 9a + 3b + c$;
        $T_4 = 16a + 4b + c$
        First difference = $3a + b$; $5a + b$; $7a + b$
        Second difference = $2a$, $2a$
    (ii) (a) $2a$ (a constant)
        (b) $3a + b$
    (iii) First difference = 7, 13, 19
        Second difference = 2
    (iv) $T_n = 3n^2 - 2n + 4$
    (v) $T_{20} = 1164$
2. (i) $T_n = 40(0.69)^n$
    (ii) 69%
    (iii) 27.6, 19.04, 13.14, 9.07, 6.26
    (v) 9 bounces
    (vi) 9 bounces
3. (i) Scheme 1: $S_n = n(n + 19)$
    (ii) Scheme 2: $S_n = 400\left[\left(\frac{21}{20}\right)^n - 1\right]$
    (ii) Scheme 1
    (iii) 16th week
4. (i) 136 litres   (ii) Proof
    (iii) 872 litres
5. (i) Proof   (ii) 2020
    (iii) €22 657   (iv) 2.8%

Chapter 5: Financial Maths

Exercise 5.1

1. €4031.75
2. €6092.01, €1092.01
3. $r = (1 + i)^{\frac{1}{12}} - 1$
4. (i) 0.49%   (ii) 0.21%   (iii) 0.33%
5. 4.5%

6.

Y	P	i
1	15 000	525
2	15 525	543.83
3	16 068.38	562.39
4	16 630.77	582.07
5	17 212.85	602.45

7. 1.98%
8. €27 830.10
9. (i) €14 375.34
    (ii) €15 892.57
    (iii) €17 220.86
10. €6627.09
11. €16 822.61
12. 20.15 years
13. €422 049.95
14. 20.01 years
15. 0.4868%; €56.46; 4
16. €15 203.66

Exercise 5.2

1. (i) €13 311.16   (ii) €5906.23
2. €400.82
3. (i) €25 432   (ii) €15 618.43
4. (i) €57 344   (ii) €28 688.075
    (iii) €151 540.50   (iv) €65 508.43
5. $t = 5$ years
6. 6166 kg
7. (i) 7.8%   (ii) 13.53 years
8. (i) €300   (ii) €446.27
9. (i) €12 182.4   (ii) €4547.06
    (iii) €2357.19
10. (i) 36%   (iii) −1600
    (iv) (4.2, 1300)   (v) €845.66

Exercise 5.3

1. €790.66; €70.66
2. (i) 0.33%   (ii) €1148.55
3. €11 265.95
4. Proof
5. Proof
6. $P(1.09) + P(1.09)^2 + ... P(1.09)^5$; $A = €1000$
7. €5257.31
8. €1017.23
9. €371.49
10. Proof
11. (i) €14 978.13   (ii) €23 768.41

Exercise 5.4

1. €1178.66
2. €103 800
3. €614; €565; €536; €72 394; €94 455; €117 798
4. Plan B
5. €17 738.11
6. The second offer is better
7. €13 068.78

Revision Exercise 5 (Core)

1. €6335.93
2. €36 778.58
3. €1024
4. €20 344.37
5. 16.1%; 34.5%
6. $200 (1.0075) + 200(1.0075)^2 + 200(1.0075)^3 + ...$
    $a = 200(1.0075)$, $r = (1.0075)$
    $$S_5 = 200(1.0075)\left[\frac{1.0075^5 - 1}{0.0075}\right]$$
7. €9560.51
8. (i) €19 000.13   (ii) €33 385.23

Revision Exercise 5 (Advanced)

1. (i) €211 205.4   (ii) €32 910.04
2. €100 000 gives €964 629.32; €1000 gives €919 857.37
3. $i = 5\%$; €3571
4. €74 734
5. $i = 8.75\%$

6.

Pension fund	Interest
127 953	3838.59
116 791.59	3503.75
105 295.38	3158.86
93 454.24	2803.63
81 257.87	2437.74
68 695.61	2060.87
55 756.48	1672.69
42 429.17	1272.88
28 702.01	861.06
14 563.07	436.89

Revision Exercise 5 (Extended Response Questions)

1. €87 422.1; €11 954.75
2. (i) €673 292.26   (ii) €7173.3
   (iii) €13 435.36
3. (i) $€P = \dfrac{€M(i)(1+i)^n}{(1+i)^n - 1}$

   (ii) $i = 0.72\%$ monthly
   (iii) 321
   (iv) 26 years 9 months
4. (i) €140 254.1   (ii) 324 months
   (iii) 135 months
5. (i) $A + A(1.04) + A(1.04)^2 + A(1.04)^3$

   (ii) $S_{26} = A\left(\dfrac{(1.04)^{26} - 1}{1.04 - 1}\right)$

   (iii) €485 199.00
   (iv) Payment 1: €485 199;
      Payment 3: €524 791.00
   (v) Payment 2: €481 587;
      Payment 4: €474 443.85
   (vi) $\dfrac{485\,199(1.04)^n}{(1.0478)^n}$

   (vii) €11 508, 316
   (viii) 31%

Chapter 6: Length – Area – Volume

Exercise 6.1

1. (i) $\dfrac{a}{2+a}$ (ii) $a = 8$

2. (i) $10x^2$ (ii) $5x^2$ (iii) $2:1$
3. Base = 13 cm, height = 8 cm
4. 9 cm, 40 cm
5. 12 m
6. 30°, 45°, 105°
7. (i) Parallelogram
   (ii) $(|AD| + |BC|) \times h$
   (iii) The area of the trapezium is half the
      area of the rectangle:
      Area $= \dfrac{(|AD| + |BC|)}{2} \times h$

8. 15 cm, 21 cm

9. (i)   (ii)

   (iii)   (iii) has the largest area

10. (i) $x = 15.8$ cm
   (ii) $y = 4.65$ cm
11. (i) 19.99 cm
   (ii) $h = 9.31$ cm, area $= 50.04$ cm²: also area
      $= \frac{1}{2}(10.75)(10.75)\sin 60° = 50.04$ cm²
12. 38.605 m²
13. (i) $\angle EOD = 60°$
   (ii) $\angle ODE = 60°$
   (iii) 64.95 cm²
14. (i) $\alpha = 135°$, $\beta = 150°$, $\theta = 120°$
   (ii) 134.8 cm²
15. 30 cm²
16. Proof

Exercise 6.2

1. (i) 29.7 cm   (ii) 35.6 cm²
2. (i) 73 cm²   (ii) 38 cm

3. (a) $\dfrac{\pi r^2}{2}$ (b) $\pi(R^2 - r^2)$

   (c) $(x + 2a)^2 - \pi a^2$ (d) $\dfrac{\pi a^2}{4} + ab$

   (e) $\dfrac{a}{2}\sqrt{x^2 - \dfrac{a^2}{4}}$ (f) $\dfrac{\sqrt{3}a^2}{4}$

4. $r = \dfrac{P}{2 + \theta}$

5. 6.8 cm

6. (i) $2r^2$ (ii) $\dfrac{r^2}{4}(\pi - 2)$

7. Radius $= \dfrac{40}{\pi} \cong 12.73$ m,

   Area $= \dfrac{1600}{\pi} \approx 509.30$ m² because we use an
   approximation for π
8. (i) $1:2$ (ii) $4:1$

9. $\dfrac{42\sqrt{2}}{\pi}$

10. (i) $\dfrac{\pi}{3}$ radians   (ii) $6 + \dfrac{4\pi}{3}$ cm

   (iii) $\dfrac{4\pi}{3} + \sqrt{3}$ cm²   (iv) $\dfrac{2\pi - 3\sqrt{3}}{3}$

11. Area $= \dfrac{r^2}{2}(\theta - \sin\theta)$; $3\pi + 2 : \pi - 2$

12. 153.71 cm²
13. $r = 6$ cm or 8 cm

14. 170 m²

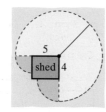

11. (i) 84 cm³   (ii) 12 cm, 148 cm²

    (iii) Volume = $\dfrac{m^3}{6}$, Area = $\dfrac{m^2}{2}(1 + \sqrt{2} + \sqrt{5})$

12. (i) (a) 2744 cm³

       (b) $1437\frac{1}{3}$ cm³

       (c) 48%

    (ii) less, $33\frac{1}{3}$%

13. 496.4 cm³

Exercise 6.3

1. (i) (a) 10.5 m²   (b) 18.5 m²
     (c) 2771.3 cm²   (d) 560 cm²
     (e) 336 cm²   (f) 749.4 cm²
   (ii) (a) 2.1 m³   (b) 4.3 m³
     (c) 7542.3 cm³   (d) 800 cm³
     (e) 254 cm³   (f) 1128.5 cm³

2. (i) *f*: 2427 mm², *d*: 2121 mm², *b\a*: 1257 mm²,
     e: 905 mm², *g*: 805 mm², *h*: 720 mm²,
     c: 283 mm², *i*: 195 mm²
   (ii) *f*: 7238 mm², *d*: 7069 mm², *a*: 4189 mm²,
     b: 2962 mm², *e*: 1810 mm², *g*: 1257 mm²,
     h: 1056 mm², *c*: 339 mm², *i*: 144 mm²

3. (i) 4.92 m³
   (ii) option 2 (€30 per 100 kg): €390
   (iii) $V = \dfrac{h\tan\theta + 2a}{2}.h.w$
   (iv) bottom = 1.5 m, top = 2.7 m

4. (i) *x* = 2.5 cm
   (ii)

, triangular prism

   (iii) 24 cm³
   (iv)

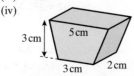

5. (i) 476.4 cm³   (ii) 1481.0 cm³
6. (i) 3 hr 23 min   (ii) 4 hr 46 min
7. (i) 700 cm³
   (ii)

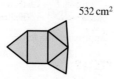

532 cm²

8. Volume = 422 cm³, Area = 484.16 cm²
9. (a) area   (b) length   (c) area
   (d) length (e) area + length (f) length + area
   (g) volume (h) volume
10. (i) consistent   (ii) inconsistent
   (iii) inconsistent   (iv) consistent
   (v) consistent   (vi) inconsistent
   (vii) consistent

Exercise 6.4

1. 0.134 ha
2. 17.61 cm²; (i) 2.3%   (ii) 17.505 cm²
3. (i) 17.5 *u*²   (ii) 17.75 *u*²
4. 1.82 *u*²
5. (i) 1 : 2.14   (ii) 2.75
6. 81 120 km²

Revision Exercise 6 (Core)

1. 2 : 5
2. (a) area = 1464 cm²; volume = 3589 cm³
   (b) area = 434 cm²; volume = 523 cm³
   (c) area = 25 500 cm²; volume = 225 000 cm³
3. (i) 1.28 rad   (ii) 16 cm²   (iii) 1 : 1.391
4. Capacity = 450 m³, 750 hours
5. (i) *x* = $\sqrt{20}$ (ii) *x* = 3.96 cm
   (iii) *x* = 0.99 rads
6. Proof
7. (i) 10.6 *u*²   (ii) 16.73 *u*²
8. (i) $(10 + 2\sqrt{7})$ m   (ii) $(4 + 2\sqrt{5} + 2\sqrt{6})$ m²
9. (i) 16π cm ≈ 50.3 cm
   (ii) 32π cm² ≈ 100.5 cm²
10. €38 186.72
11. 112.7 cm³

Revision Exercise 6 (Advanced)

1. (i) Proof   (ii) *r* = 25
   (iii) θ = 2 radians
2. (i) *A*: 2500 holes; *B*: 2822 holes
   (ii) *A*: 21.46%; *B*: 11.34%
3. (i) Area$_{PQO}$ = $\frac{1}{2}r^2\sin\theta$
   (ii) Area segment = $\frac{1}{2}r^2(\theta - \sin\theta)$
   (iii) Area$_{PQN}$= $\frac{1}{2}r^2(\sin(\pi - \theta))$
4. (d) Surface area = 56 077 cm²;
      volume = 133 518 cm³
   (e) Surface area = 1092 cm²;
      volume = 1767 cm³
   (f) Surface area = 332 cm²;
      volume = 436 cm³
5. (i) 4.189 cm²   (ii) 2.4567 cm²
6. (i) 1.84 rads   (ii) 80.96 m
   (iii) 26.7 m   (iv) 848 m²
7. Proof
   (i) *r* = 3.0 cm   (ii) *A* = 19.95 cm²
8. (i) *A* − *B*: increasing speed (accelerating) nearly
    uniformly

C − D: starts to slow down
E − F: Having stopped starts to move again
(ii) Distance
(iii) 5.47 km
9. Proof
10. 840 mm²

Revision Exercise 6 (Extended Response Questions)

1. (i) (a) $l = r\theta$
(b) $A = \frac{1}{2}r^2\theta$
(ii) $A = 2r - r^2$ ... Proof
(iii) $A = 1 - (r - 1)^2$
(iv)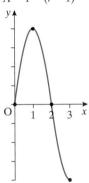

(v) $\theta = 2$ radians
2. (i) Areas are the same ... false
Triangle longer by 10.18% ... true
Difference of 9.24% ... true
(ii) 57.52°
(iii) No
3. (i) $A = 4h^2 - 80h + 400$
(ii) $h = \frac{20}{3}$ cm
(iii) $V = 4h^3 - 80h^2 + 400h$

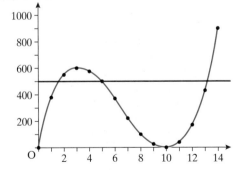

(iv) $h = 3.5$ cm
(v) $h = 2$ cm, 5 cm, 13 cm
(vi) $h > 10 \Rightarrow 20 - 2(10) = 0 \Rightarrow$ no volume
4. (i) $A = 150$ cm²
(ii) 4.8%
(iii) $a = 0.66, b = 0.87, c = 0.96$
(iv) Derivation
(v) $A = \frac{r^2}{4}(5.92) = 1.495r^2$

(vi) $A_5 = 37$ cm², $A_{10} = 149.5$ cm²,
$A_{15} = 336$ cm²
(vii) Since $A = \frac{\pi r^2}{2} = 1.57r^2$, the formula
underestimates the area by 5.78%
5. (i) $l = 15 - h, w = 20 - 2h$, height $= h$
(ii) Volume $= 2h^3 - 50h^2 + 300h$
(iii) $h = 5$ cm
(iv) $V = 500$ cm³
(v) $h = 2.9$ cm
(vi)

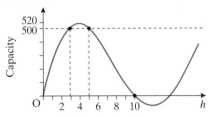

(vii) No, it is not possible, new capacity would be
$500 + 50 = 550$ cm³ and no value of h would
give a capacity of 550 cm³

Chapter 7: Algebra 3

Exercise 7.1

1. (i) $x > 4$ (ii) $x \le 1$ (iii) $x < -3$
2. (i) $x < 10$ (ii) $x \le 7$ (iii) $x < 8$
3. (i) $x < 4$ (ii) $x \le -\frac{1}{2}$ (iii) $x > -7$
4. (i) $-3 \le x \le 2$ (ii) $-4 \le x \le -2$
(iii) $-\frac{1}{2} < x \le \frac{1}{2}$
5. (i) $2 < x < 7$ (ii) $-\frac{1}{2} \le x \le 3\frac{2}{3}$
(iii) $-14 \le x \le -7$
6. $x > 2.5$
7. (i) $x < 4$ (ii) $x > 2$ (iii) $2 < x < 4$
8. (i) $x > 2\frac{1}{2}$ (ii) $x < 3$ (iii) $2\frac{1}{2} < x < 3$
9. (i) $x < 7$ (ii) $x > 8$ (iii) Null set
10. (i) $x \le 4$ (ii) $x \ge 4$ (iii) $x = 4$
11. Length $= 10$ m, width $= 9$ m
12. $a = 6.645, b = 7.645, n = 7$
13. (i) $a^n < b^n$ (ii) $a^n > b^n$
14. $x = 6$

Exercise 7.2

1. (i) $-2 \ge x \ge 3$ (ii) $-5 \le x \le 2$
(iii) $\frac{1}{2} < x < 2$
2. (i) $-3 \le x \le 2$ (ii) $-4 < x < 1\frac{1}{2}$
(iii) $-3\frac{1}{2} \le x \le 0$
3. (i) $-1\frac{1}{2} > x > 1\frac{2}{3}$ (ii) $-4 \ge x \ge 4$
(iii) $-1\frac{1}{2} \ge x \ge 4$
4. $-1 < x < 7$
5. Proof
6. $-3 \ge k \ge 1$

7. $-4 \leqslant k \leqslant 1$

8. $-1 \leqslant p \leqslant 3; p = 2$

9. (i) $-2 > x > -1$ (ii) $x > 3$
  (iii) $-10 < x < -3$

10. (i) $-14 > x > 5$ (ii) $-\frac{1}{2} < x < -\frac{3}{10}$
  (iii) $\frac{1}{5} < x < \frac{6}{11}$

11. (i) $1\frac{1}{2} > x \geqslant 3$ (ii) $1 < x < 3$
  (iii) $-1 \geqslant x > 1$

12. (i) $-3 < x < 10$ (ii) $-9 < x < 5$
  (iii) $1 > x \geqslant 2\frac{1}{2}$

13. $-3 > x > -2$

14. No real roots

15. (i) $1\frac{1}{2} \geqslant t \geqslant 5$ (ii) $2 \leqslant t \leqslant 4.5$
  (iii) $1\frac{1}{2} < t < 2$ and $4.5 < t < 5$

16. (i) $-3 > x > -\frac{1}{2}$ (ii) $1 \geqslant x \geqslant 3$
  (iii) $-1\frac{1}{2} \leqslant x \leqslant 0.5$ (iv) $-1 < x < 5$

17. (i) Length > 3.75 (ii) width > 0.75

18. $-2 < p < 3$

19. (i) $x < 10$
  (ii) $x > 1$
  (iii) $1 < x < 10$

20. $x = 2\,\text{m}$ or $3\,\text{m}$

Exercise 7.3

1. (i) $(-4, -2)$ (ii) $(-2, 6)$ (iii) $(-2, 3)$
  (iv) $(\frac{1}{2}, 1)$ (v) $(2, 4)$ (vi) 2

2. $-1, 2\frac{1}{3}$

3. $f(x) = |x|, g(x) = |x - 4|, h(x) = |x + 3|$,
  $f(-2) = 2, g(2) = 2, h(-5) = 2$

4. $f(x) = |x + 1|, g(x) = |2x + 2|, h(x) = |3x + 3|$

5. 4

6. (i) $4 < x < 8$ (ii) $-6 \leqslant x \leqslant 2$
  (iii) $x \leqslant -2$ or $x \geqslant 3$ (iv) $x \leqslant -5$ or $x \geqslant 6$
  (v) $-3 < x < -\frac{1}{3}$ (vi) $1 < x < 7$

7. (i) $-3 \geqslant x \geqslant 4$ (ii) $-1\frac{1}{2} \leqslant x \leqslant -1$
  (iii) $-\frac{1}{3} \leqslant x \leqslant 5$

8. $-2\frac{2}{3} \leqslant x \leqslant 8$

9. $x \leqslant -24$ or $x \geqslant 0$

10. $-1 < x < 1$

11. $x = -1, 0; -1 > x > 0$

12. (i) $-4 < x < 2$ (ii) $x < -4$ or $x > 2$
  (iii) $1\frac{1}{4} < x < 3\frac{1}{2}$ (iv) $2 < x < 3$
  (v) $1\frac{1}{4} < x < 2$ (vi) $2 < x < 3$
  (vii) $3 < x < 3\frac{1}{2}$

13. (i) $\frac{2}{5} < x < \frac{1}{2}$ (ii) $x = -1, 1\frac{2}{3}$
  (iii) $-2 < x < 0$

Exercise 7.5

1. Proof **2.** Proof **3.** Proof
4. Proof **5.** Proof **6.** Proof

7. Proof **8.** Proof

9. $(a + b)(a^2 - ab + b^2)$; proof

10. Proof **11.** Proof **12.** Proof

13. Proof **14.** Proof **15.** Proof

16. (i) $(a - b)(a + b)(a^2 + b^2)$
  (ii) $(a - b)^2(a + b)(a^2 + b^2)$

17. Proof **18.** Proof **19.** Proof

20. Multiply both sides by $d(b + d)$; then divide both
  sides by bd

21. Proof

Exercise 7.6

1. (i) a^5 (ii) x^4 (iii) $6x^6$ (iv) x^3
  (v) x^{-1} (vi) 1 (vii) 3 (viii) a^6
  (ix) x^3 (x) $9a^2b^2$

2. (i) 4 (ii) $\frac{1}{9}$ (iii) 8
  (iv) $\frac{9}{4}$ (v) 2

3. (i) 4 (ii) 8 (iii) 9
  (iv) 27 (v) 25

4. (i) $\frac{9}{4}$ (ii) $\frac{3}{2}$ (iii) $\frac{125}{27}$
  (iv) $\frac{25}{9}$ (v) $\frac{3}{2}$

5. 4^{-2}

6. $\frac{11}{12}$

7. (i) $\frac{y^3}{x^2}$ (ii) $\frac{p^{12}}{q^8}$ (iii) $\frac{1}{a}$
  (iv) $y^{\frac{2}{3}}$ (v) $\frac{1}{a^{\frac{9}{2}}b^2}$ (vi) $x^{\frac{1}{4}}$

8. (i) $\frac{x + 1}{x}$ (ii) $x^2 - x$ (iii) $1 + x$

9. $\frac{x}{x - 1}$

10. $k = \frac{1}{2}$

11. $262\,\text{Hz}$

12. $\frac{9}{16}$

13. $k = 24$

14. $k = 28$

Exercise 7.7

1. (i) 5 (ii) $\frac{3}{2}$ (iii) $\frac{3}{2}$ (iv) -3

2. (i) $-\frac{3}{2}$ (ii) $-\frac{5}{2}$ (iii) 3 (iv) $-\frac{3}{2}$

3. (i) $-\frac{1}{2}$ (ii) $\frac{5}{4}$ (iii) $-\frac{1}{6}$ (iv) $-\frac{1}{3}$

4. $2^{\frac{5}{2}}; \frac{15}{8}$

5. $x = \frac{2}{3}, y = -\frac{16}{3}$

6. $4.2^x; 2.2^x; c = \frac{5}{2}$

7. $x = 1, 2$

8. $x = 2$

9. (i) $x = 0, 3$ (ii) $x = 0, 2$

10. (i) y^2 (ii) $2y^2$
  (iii) $8y; x = -1, 2$

11. $x = -1, 0$ **12.** $x = -\frac{1}{2}, 0$

13. $x = 0, 3$ **14.** $x = \pm 1$

15. $x = 1, 3$

Exercise 7.8

1. (i) B   (ii) A   (iii) D   (iv) C

2. (i) 1000 ha

     (ii) (a) 4000 ha   (b) 5278 ha

     (iii)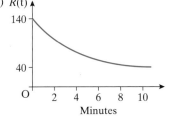

     (iv) 5 weeks

3. (i) decreasing   (ii) decreasing

     (iii) increasing   (iv) decreasing

4. (i) 0.6   (ii) 3   (iii) 8   (iv) 6

5. (iv) $-2 \leqslant x < 0$ (v) $0 < x \leqslant 4$

     (vi) $x = 0$ (vii) $0 < x \leqslant 4$

6. (i) Decay

     (ii) (a) 3 days

         (b) 9 days

         (c) 18 days

     (iii) 3.9°C

7. (a) (i) 97.6%   (ii) 94.2%

     (b) 5780 years

     (c) 1964 years

8. (i) 1000 ha

     (ii) (a) 2000 ha   (b) 4000 ha   (c) 5278 ha

9. (i) $R(t)$

     (ii) 140 beats per minute

     (iii) (a) 5.5 minutes

         (b) 10.5 minutes

     (iv) 50 beats per minute

10. 1000

11. (i) €5027.5   (ii) €5055.15

     (iii) €5082.95   (iv) $5000 (1.0055)^t$

12. (i) 40

     (ii) $b = 1.2; b > 1$ $\therefore$ the number of flies is increasing

Exercise 7.9

1. (i) 2   (ii) 4   (iii) 3   (iv) 6

2. (i) $\frac{4}{3}$ (ii) $\frac{3}{2}$ (iii) $\frac{5}{4}$ (iv) -3

     (v) -4

3. (i) -3 (ii) 4   (iii) 64   (iv) 8

4. (i) $\frac{1}{2}$ (ii) $\frac{3}{2}$ (iii) $\sqrt{2}$ (iv) -1

5. (i) 3   (ii) 2   (iii) 2

6. (i) 0   (ii) 2

7. (i) $a + 1$ (ii) $a - 1$ (iii) $2a - 1$

     (iv) $2a - 3$ (v) $2a + 1$

8. (i) 7.64   (ii) 3.86   (iii) 1.93

     (iv) -0.279

9. (i) $x = 1 + \dfrac{\log(y - 3)}{\log 2}$

     (ii) $x = 3.3219$

10. Proof

11. Proof

12. (i) 13   (ii) 10   (iii) -3

13. Proof

14. (i) 0.602   (ii) 1.43   (iii) 2.55

     (iv) 3.75   (v) 4.46   (vi) 5.54

     (vii) 6.59

15. Minimum $= 10^3 = 1000$

     Maximum $= 10^4 = 10\,000$

16. 0.143

17. (i) $\frac{4}{3}$ (ii) $\frac{3}{5}$

18. Proof   **19.** Proof

20. $p = 2q^3$ **21.** $a = \sqrt{3}$

22. 5.66   **23.** $x = 4$

24. $x = \pm \frac{4}{3}$ **25.** $x = 21$

26. $x = 3$ **27.** $x = \frac{2}{3}, 5$

28. $x = -2, 6$ **29.** $x = \frac{1}{8}$

30. $x = 3, y = 2$, or $x = \frac{2}{5}, y = 15$

31. (i) $x = \frac{1}{16}, 2$ (ii) $x = \frac{1}{4}, 2$

Exercise 7.10

3. (i)

x	$\frac{1}{9}$	$\frac{1}{3}$	1	3	9
$y = \log_3 x$	-2	-1	0	1	2

     (iii) 0.8   (iv) 0.834

4. One graph is the inverse of the other

5. Graph

6. Graph

7. (i) $x = \dfrac{\log(y + 5)}{\log 3} - 2$ or $\log_3(y + 5) - 2$

     (ii) 1.236

8. Graph

9. Graph

10. Graph

Exercise 7.11

1. (i) (a) €5030   (b) €5060.18   (c) €5090.54

     (ii) $5000 (1.006)^t$

     (iii) 116 months

2. 0.25

3. (ii) 8.8 minutes   (iii) 15°

4. (i) $0.1\ \text{Wm}^{-2}$ and $0.01\ \text{Wm}^{-2}$
   (ii) 130 dB
5. Proof $[E = A^{1.5}.10^{4.8}]$
6. (i) $€100\,(1.045)^t$ (ii) €155.30
   (iii) €80.25
7. (i) 0.6 kg   (ii) 15%   (iii) 5 months
8. (i) $M_0 = 10\,\text{g}, k = 0.00495$
   (ii) 7 g
   (iii) 325 days

Revision Exercise 7 (Core)

1. $-3.5 \leqslant x \leqslant 1$
2. (a) (i) 3162   (ii) 0.65
      (iii) 1.32   (iv) 2.7
   (b) (i) 30   (ii) 6.38
      (iii) 0.00823   (iv) 0.99
3. (i) $a = \frac{1}{2}$ (ii) $b = \frac{3}{2}$
4. $x = 5, x = 11$
5. (i) $n = 1$ (ii) $n = -\frac{10}{3}$
6. (i) $a + b = 2.5, 4a + b = 4$
   (ii) $a = 0.5, b = 2$
7. $C = \ln x, A = \ln x + 1, B = \ln(x + 1)$
8. $x = 2, 3$
9. $A = \frac{9}{2}, b = \ln\frac{4}{3}$
10. $k = \dfrac{4}{\ln 3}$
11. $a = 2, b = 3$
12. $x = 1.96$

Revision Exercise 7 (Advanced)

1. $-5 < x < -2$
2. (i) 30 g   (ii) 1585 years   (iii) 6644 years
3. (i) 1000   (ii) 20
4. $125, \frac{1}{25}$
5. $x \leqslant 3.38$
6. (ii) $x = -1$ (iii) $-3, \leqslant x < 0$
7. $x = e^y + 3$

8. $-24 \geqslant x \geqslant 0$
9. $x + 1$
10. Proof
12. (i) $-3 \leqslant k \leqslant 4\frac{1}{2}$
   (ii) $-\frac{1}{2} < k < \frac{1}{2}$
14. $u_{n+1} = (n - 19)2^{n+1}, u_{n+2} = (n - 18)2^{n+2}$
15. $x = \frac{1}{2}, y = 1$
16. (i) An exponential function
   (ii) 57 030
   (iii) 40 000
   (iv) 23.5 years
17. (i) $P = Ae^{kt}$, where $k = 0.078576$ and
      t = number of years and $A = 8000$
   (ii) 17 553
   (iii) 2016

Revision Exercise 7 (Extended Response Questions)

1. (i) $t = 0, N = 5000; t = 5, N = 2362$; claim is valid
   (ii) 1115.65
   (iii) 5000
   (iv) 26.1 days
2. (i) $0.02\,(0.92)^{\frac{x}{10}}$
   (ii) $0.0197\ \text{mm}^2$
   (iii) $0.02\,(0.92)^{(10 - 2.9x)}$
   (iv) $x > 2.59$
3. (i) $A = (0.83)^n I; B = (0.66)\,(0.89)^n I$
   (ii) 6 stations
4. (i) $A(1.11)^t$ (ii) $10A(0.95)^t$
   (iii) 14.8 years   (iv) 29.6 years
   (v) Graphs
5. (i) Growth   (ii) Proof
   (iii) Proof   (iv) $a = 1, \frac{1}{2}$
   (v) $a = 1, b = 0; a = \frac{1}{2}, b = \frac{1}{2}\ln 2$
   (vi) $A = 20\,000$
   (vii) 6.64 hours